CHRONO·CODE

1994   2010   2274

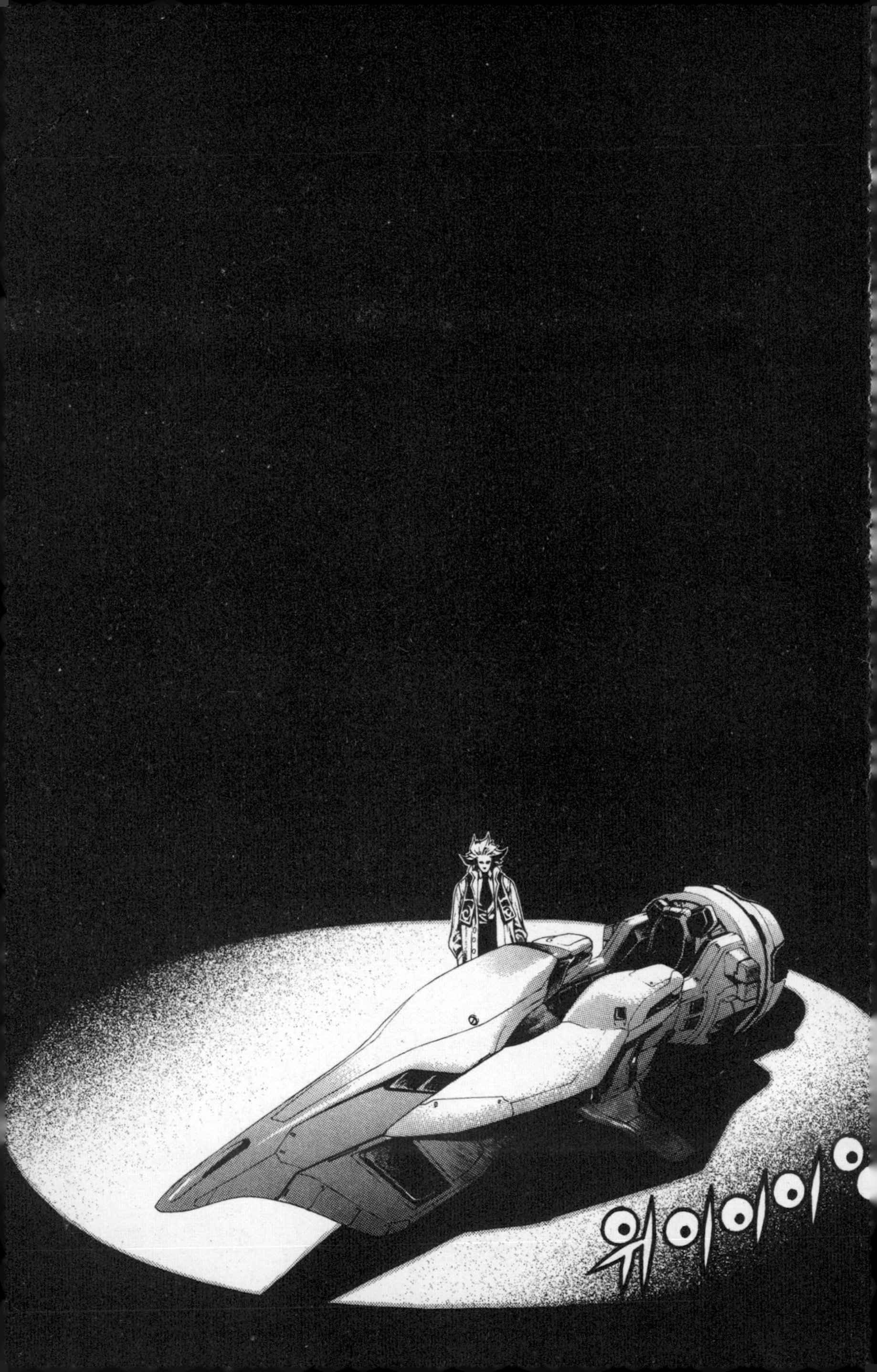
위이이이

Volume 1

Story by
Eui-Cheol Shin

Art by
Il-Ho Choi

TOKYOPOP

HAMBURG // LONDON // LOS ANGELES // TOKYO

Chrono Code vol. 1
Written by Eui-Cheol Shin
Illustrated by Il-Ho Choi

Translation - Sarah Kim
English Adaptation - Steve Bunche
Copy Editor - Suzanne Waldman
Retouch and Lettering - Lucas Rivera
Production Artist - James Dashiell and Jason Milligan
Cover Design - Gary Shum

Editor - Rob Tokar
Digital Imaging Manager - Chris Buford
Production Managers - Jennifer Miller and Mutsumi Miyazaki
Managing Editor - Jill Freshney
VP of Production - Ron Klamert
Publisher and E.I.C. - Mike Kiley
President and C.O.O. - John Parker
C.E.O. - Stuart Levy

A  Manga

TOKYOPOP Inc.
5900 Wilshire Blvd. Suite 2000
Los Angeles, CA 90036

E-mail: info@TOKYOPOP.com
Come visit us online at www.TOKYOPOP.com

ISBN: 1-59532-550-6

First TOKYOPOP printing: July 2005
10 9 8 7 6 5 4 3 2 1
Printed in the USA

:CHRONO:CODE:

Record 1 The Strangers

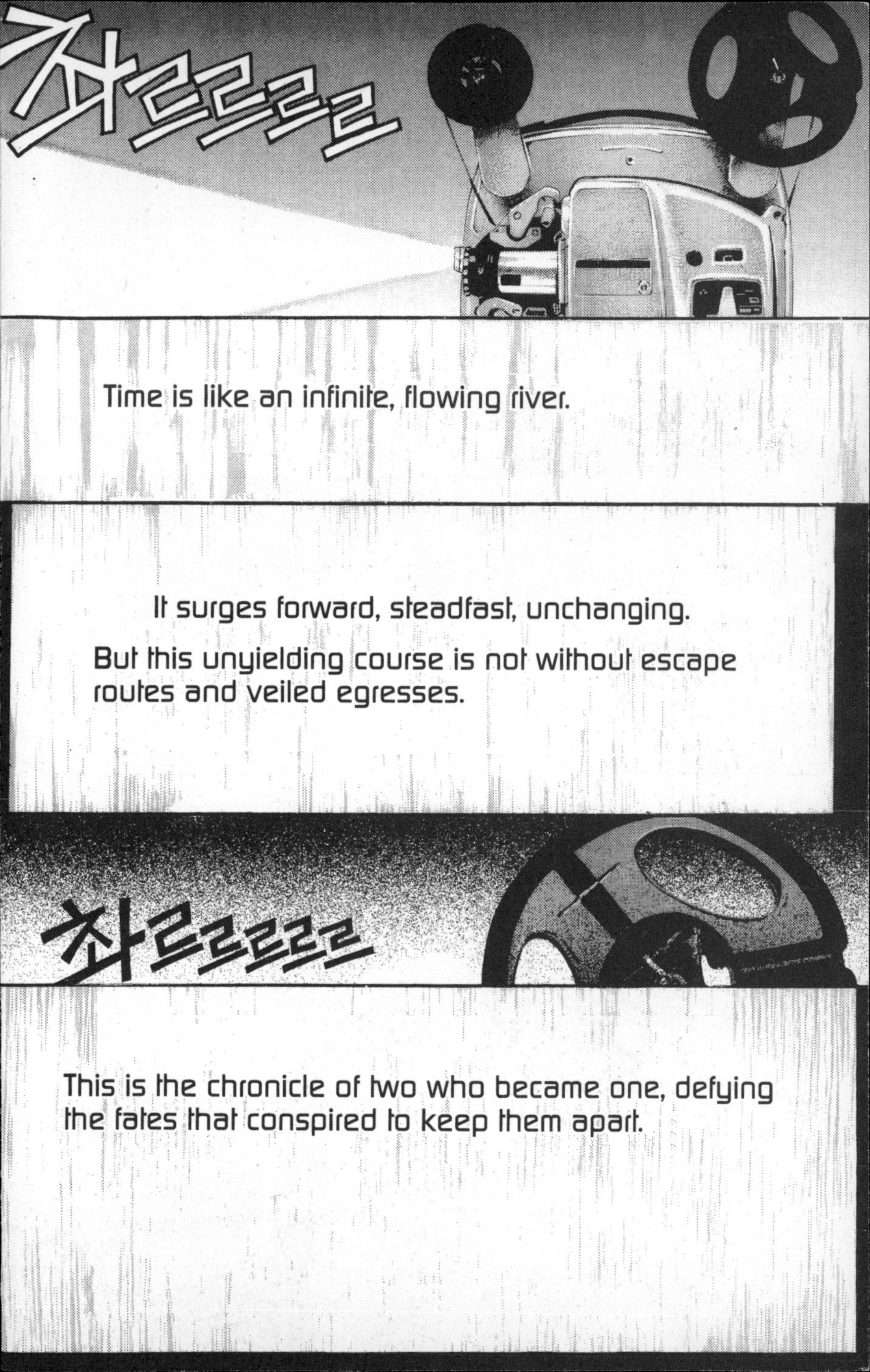
차르르르르
Time is like an infinite, flowing river.
It surges forward, steadfast, unchanging.
But this unyielding course is not without escape routes and veiled egresses.
차르르르르르
This is the chronicle of two who became one, defying the fates that conspired to keep them apart.

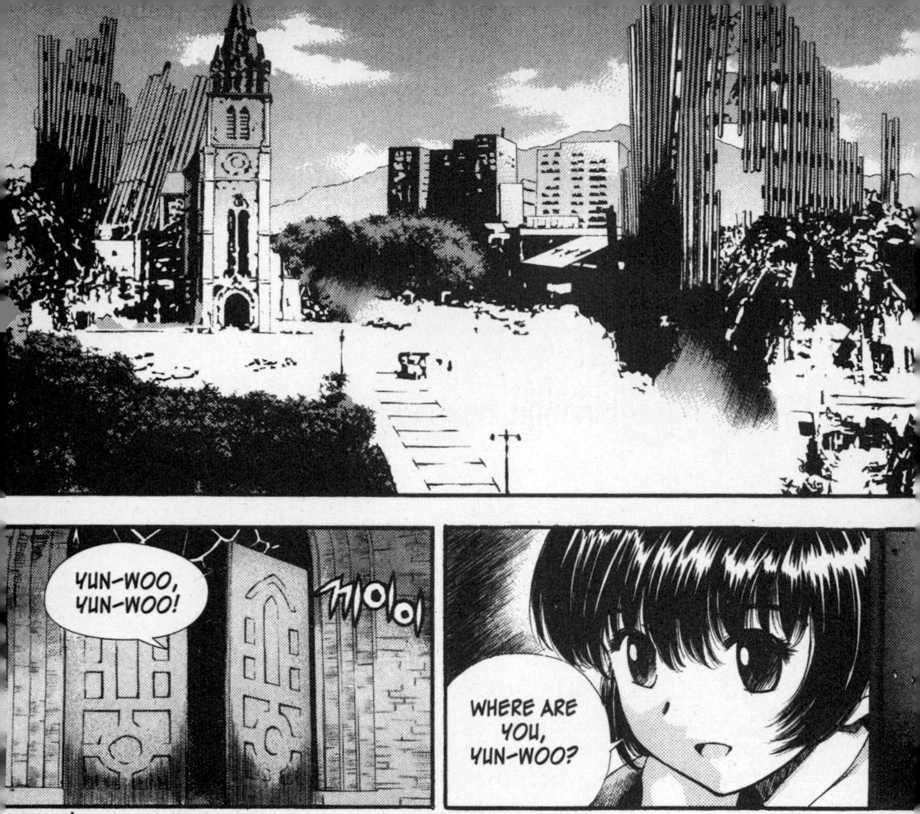
YUN-WOO, YUN-WOO!
WHERE ARE YOU, YUN-WOO?

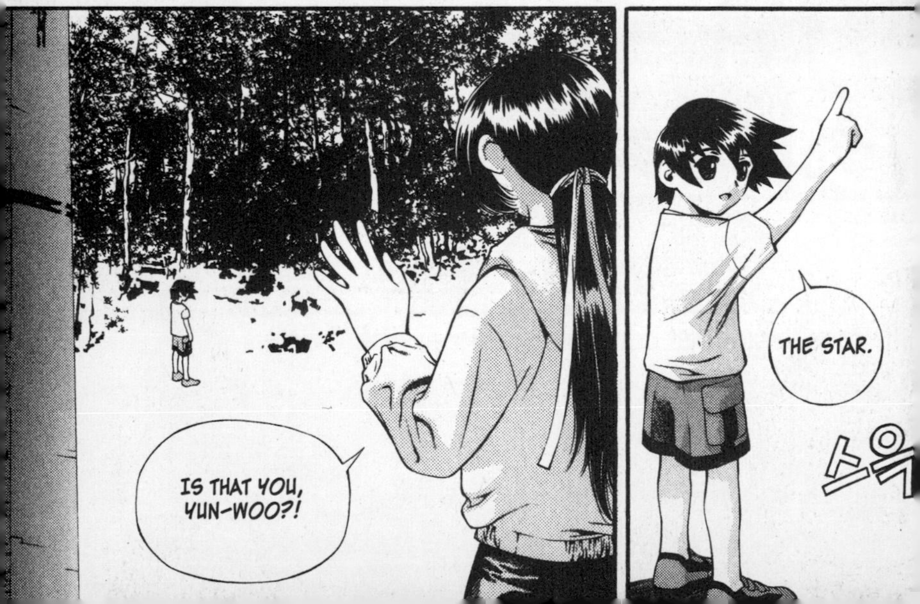
IS THAT YOU, YUN-WOO?!
THE STAR.

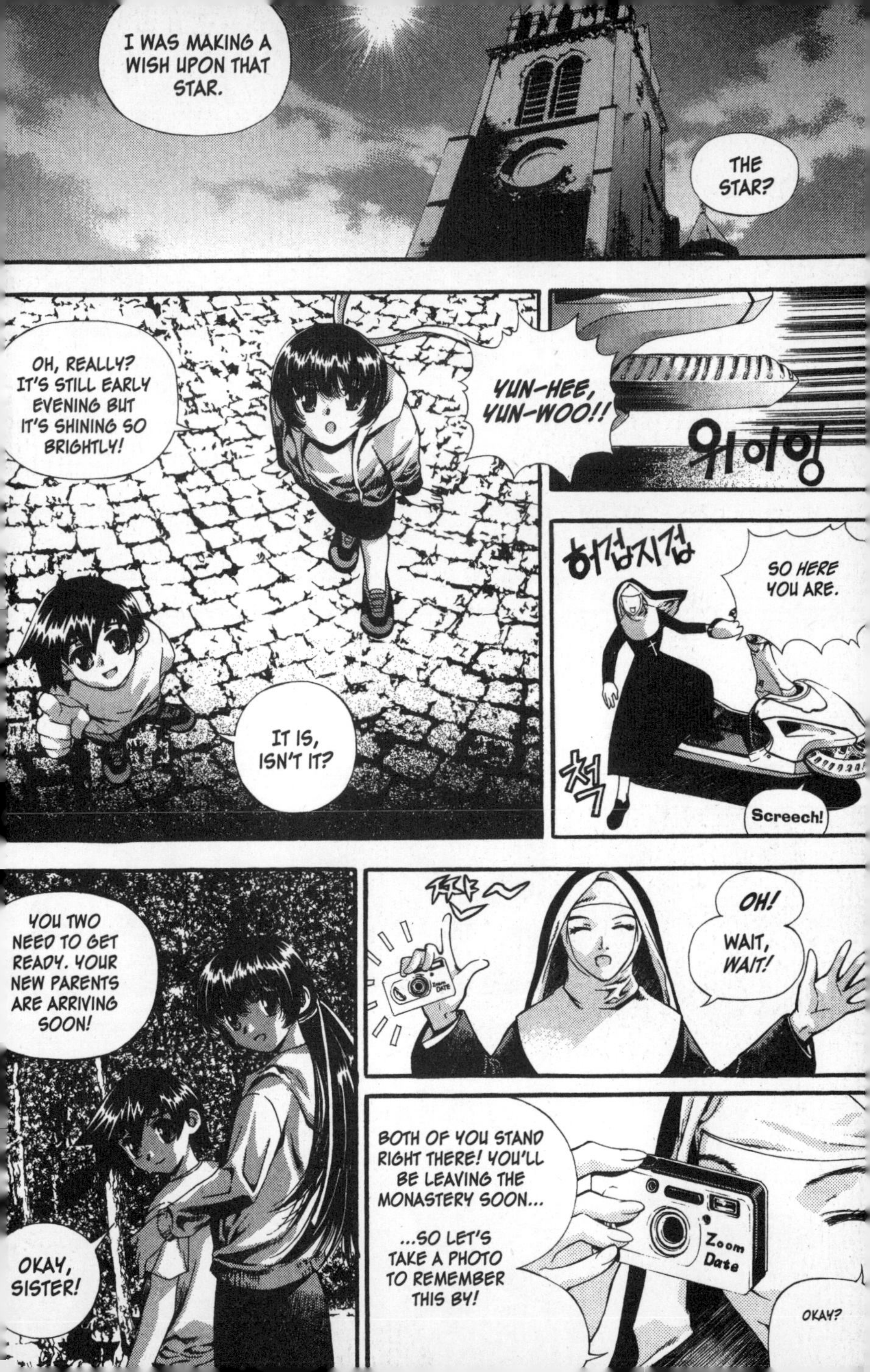
I WAS MAKING A WISH UPON THAT STAR.
THE STAR?
OH, REALLY? IT'S STILL EARLY EVENING BUT IT'S SHINING SO BRIGHTLY!
IT IS, ISN'T IT?
YUN-HEE, YUN-WOO!!
워이잉
허겁지겁
SO HERE YOU ARE.
척
Screech!
YOU TWO NEED TO GET READY. YOUR NEW PARENTS ARE ARRIVING SOON!
OKAY, SISTER!
OH!
WAIT, WAIT!
Zoom Date
BOTH OF YOU STAND RIGHT THERE! YOU'LL BE LEAVING THE MONASTERY SOON...
...SO LET'S TAKE A PHOTO TO REMEMBER THIS BY!
Zoom Date
OKAY?

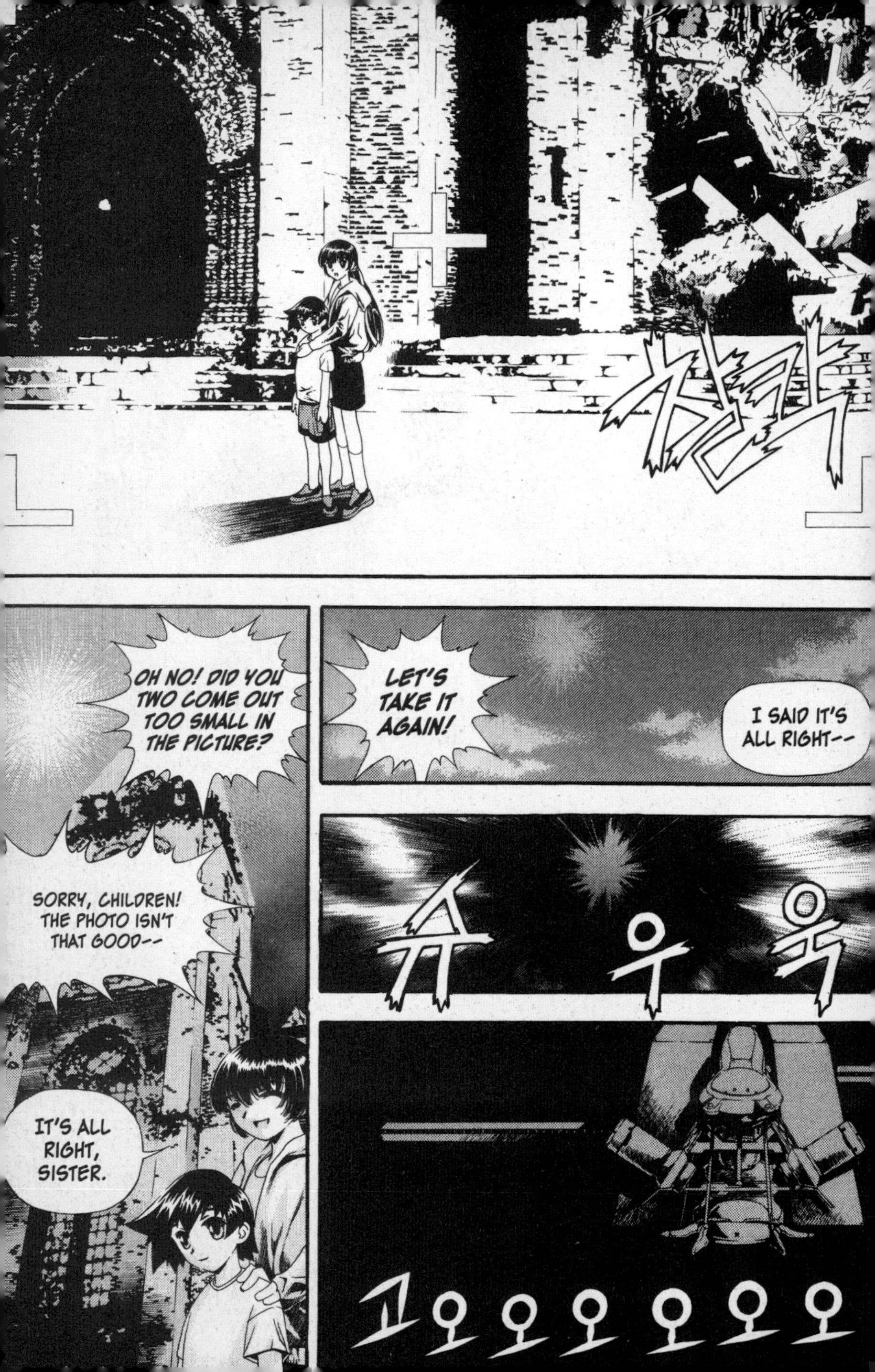
OH NO! DID YOU TWO COME OUT TOO SMALL IN THE PICTURE?
SORRY, CHILDREN! THE PHOTO ISN'T THAT GOOD--
IT'S ALL RIGHT, SISTER.
LET'S TAKE IT AGAIN!
I SAID IT'S ALL RIGHT--
슈우욱
고오오오오오오

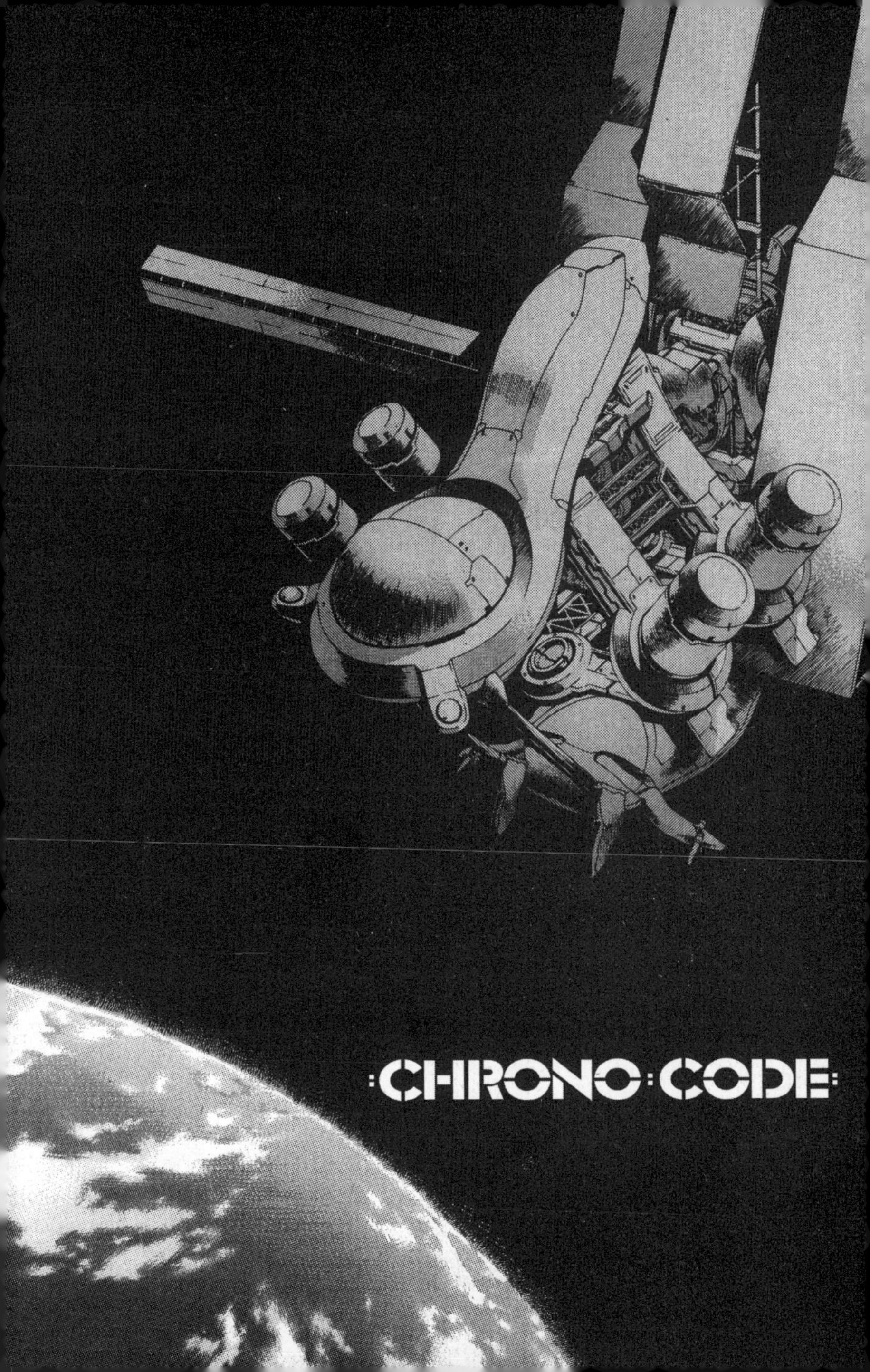
CHRONO CODE

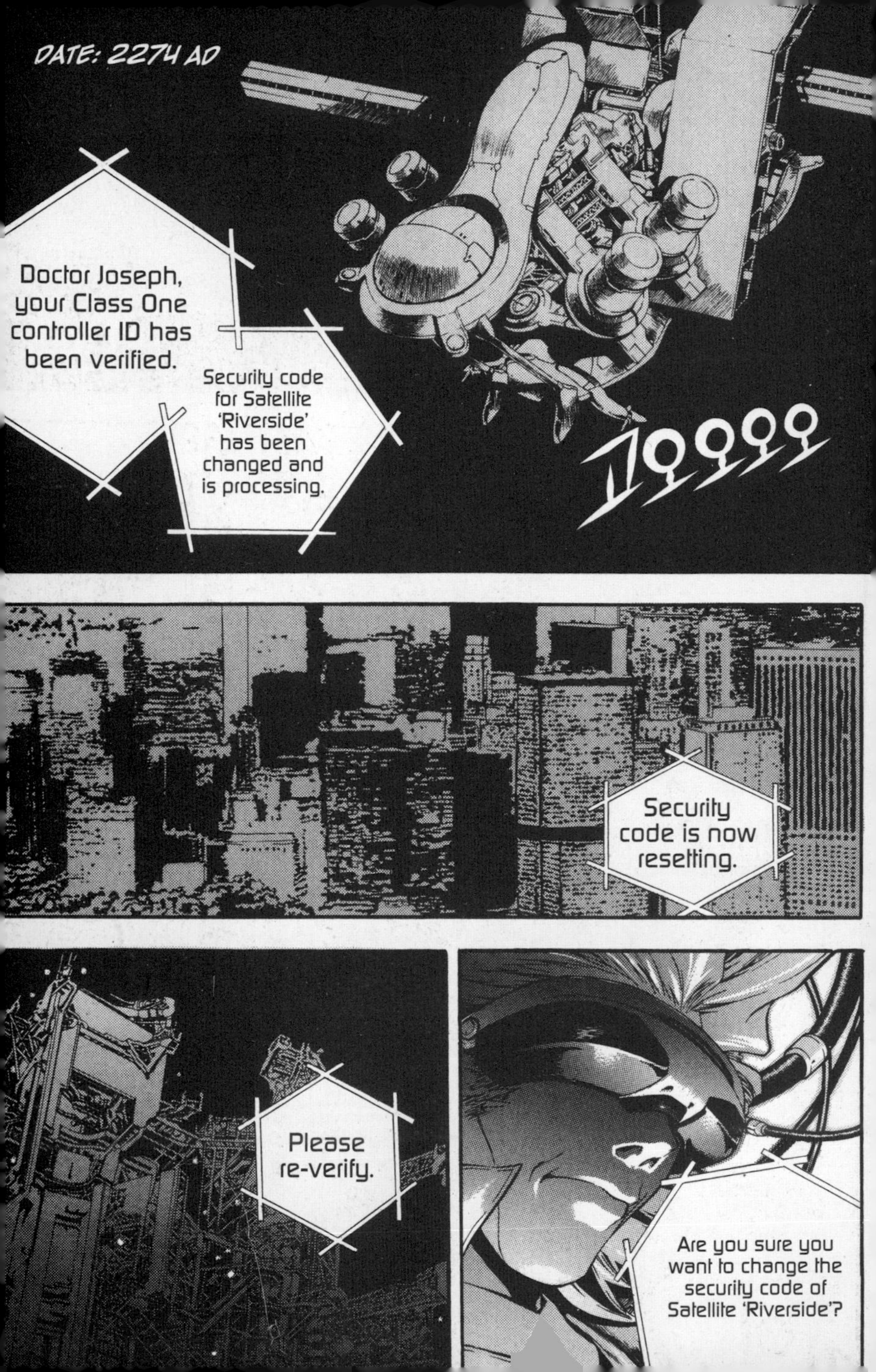
DATE: 2274 AD
Doctor Joseph, your Class One controller ID has been verified.
Security code for Satellite 'Riverside' has been changed and is processing.
ZOOOO
Security code is now resetting.
Please re-verify.
Are you sure you want to change the security code of Satellite 'Riverside'?

탁
Enter
WHEW--
탁
Beep!
Code is resetting.
Code change is confirmed; download is complete. Resetting to Class One safety mode.
WHEW--
--IT'S DONE.

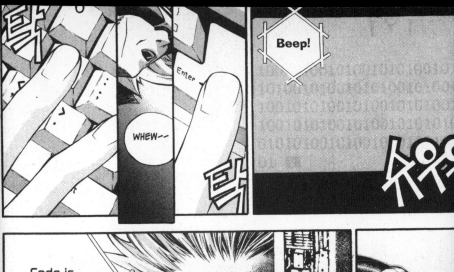

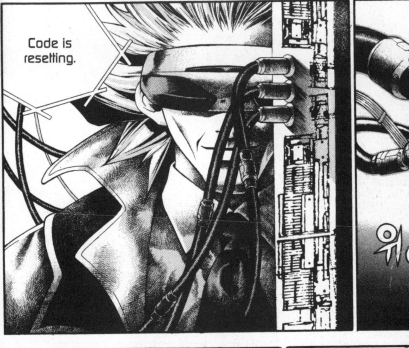

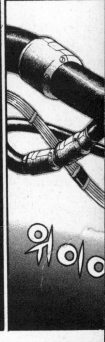

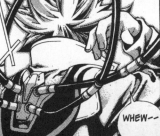

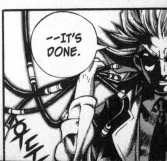

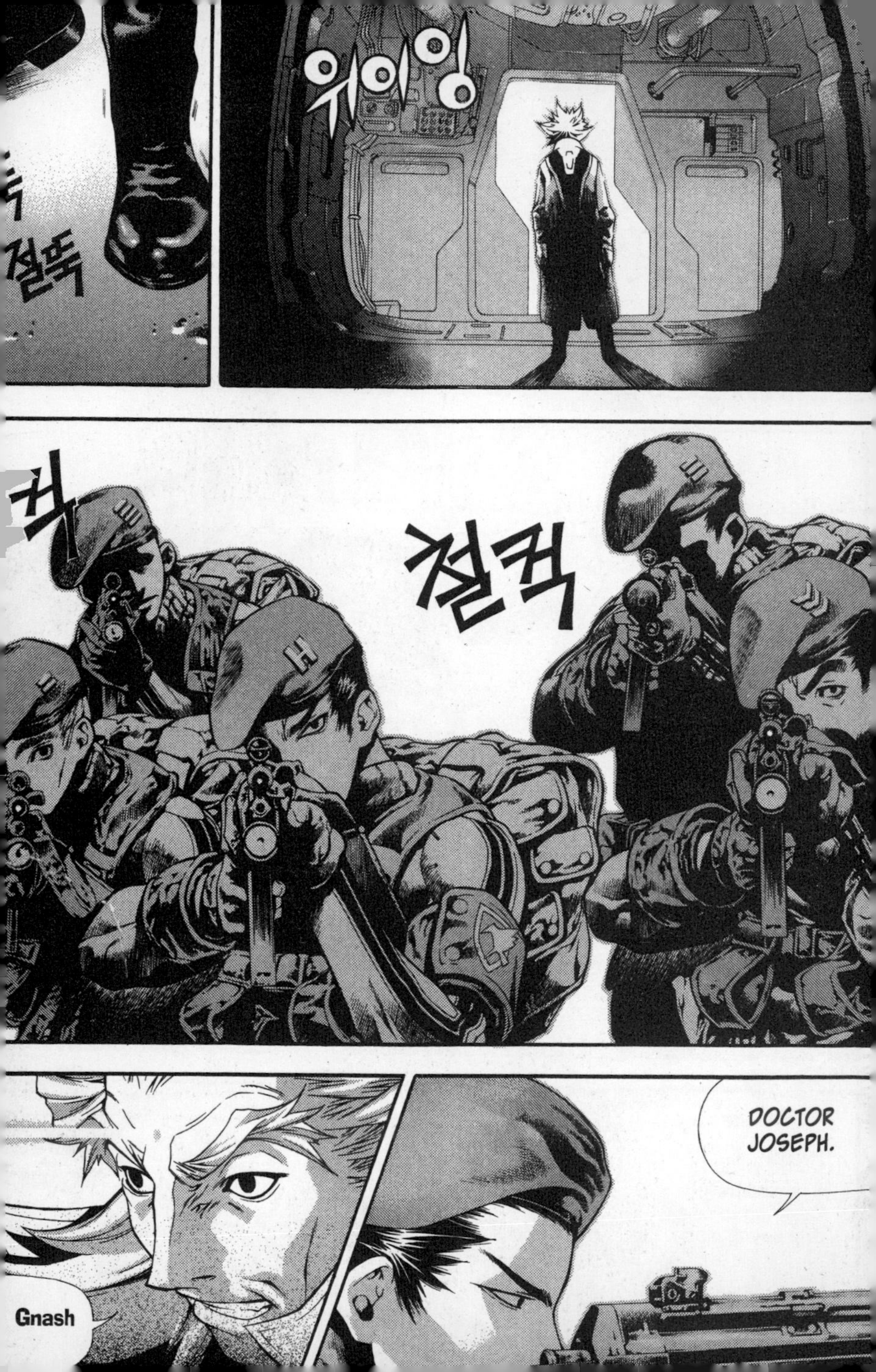

절뚝
위이잉
철컥
Gnash
DOCTOR JOSEPH.

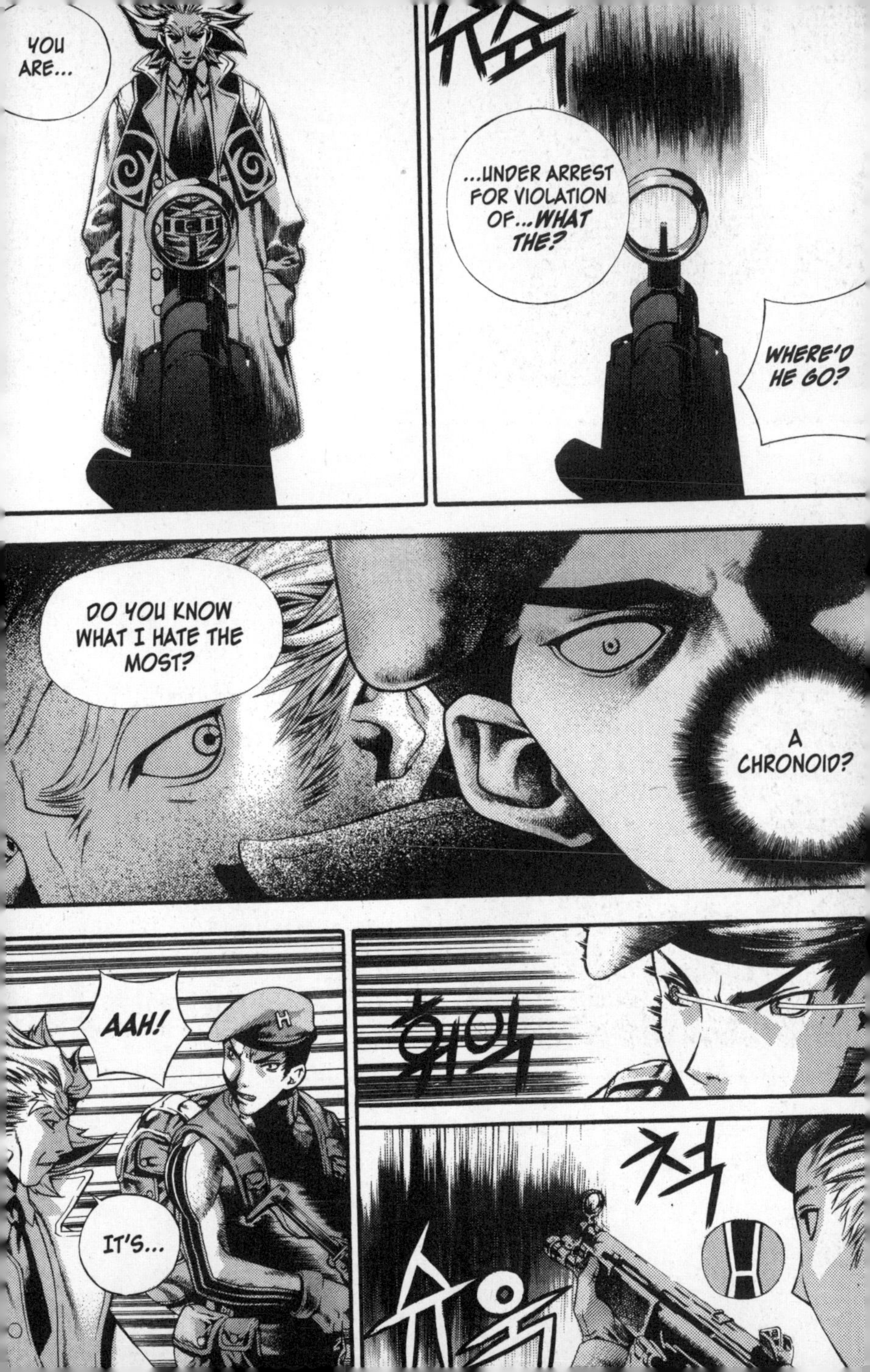
YOU ARE...
...UNDER ARREST FOR VIOLATION OF...WHAT THE?
WHERE'D HE GO?
DO YOU KNOW WHAT I HATE THE MOST?
A CHRONOID?
AAH!
IT'S...

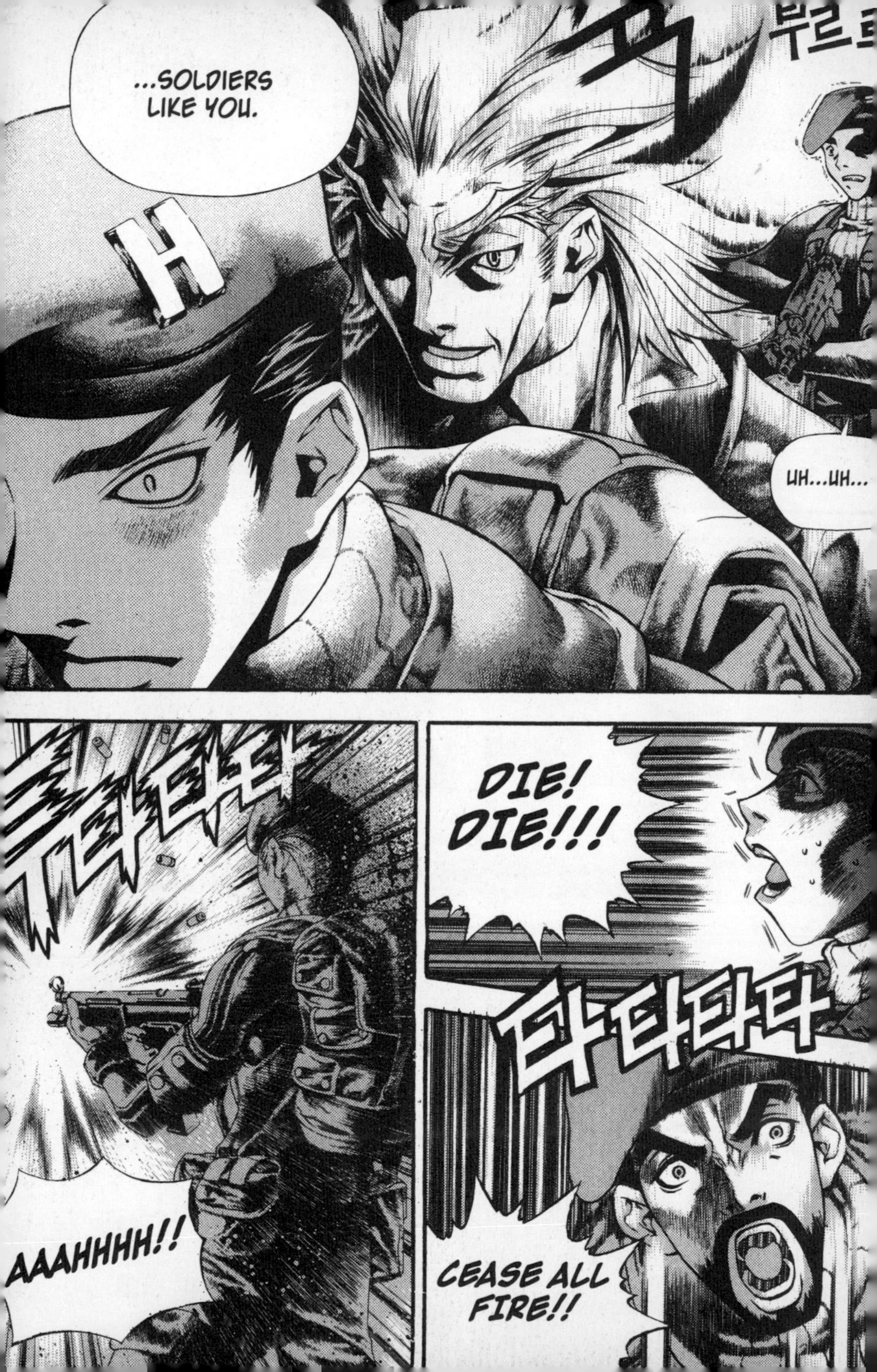
...SOLDIERS LIKE YOU.
UH...UH...
AAAHHHH!!
DIE! DIE!!!
CEASE ALL FIRE!!

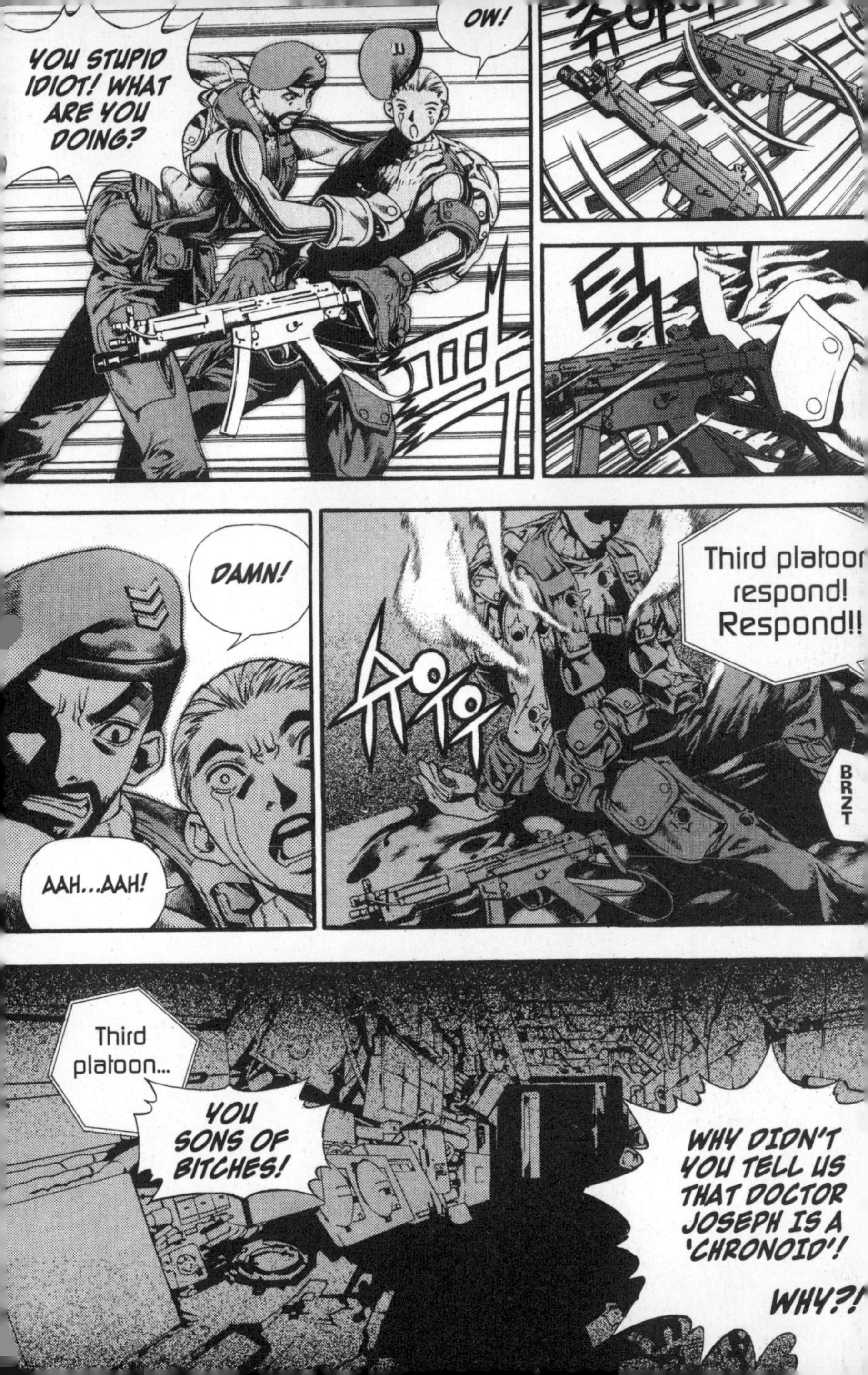
YOU STUPID IDIOT! WHAT ARE YOU DOING?
OW!
DAMN!
AAH...AAH!
Third platoon respond! Respond!!
BRZT
Third platoon...
YOU SONS OF BITCHES!
WHY DIDN'T YOU TELL US THAT DOCTOR JOSEPH IS A 'CHRONOID'!
WHY?!

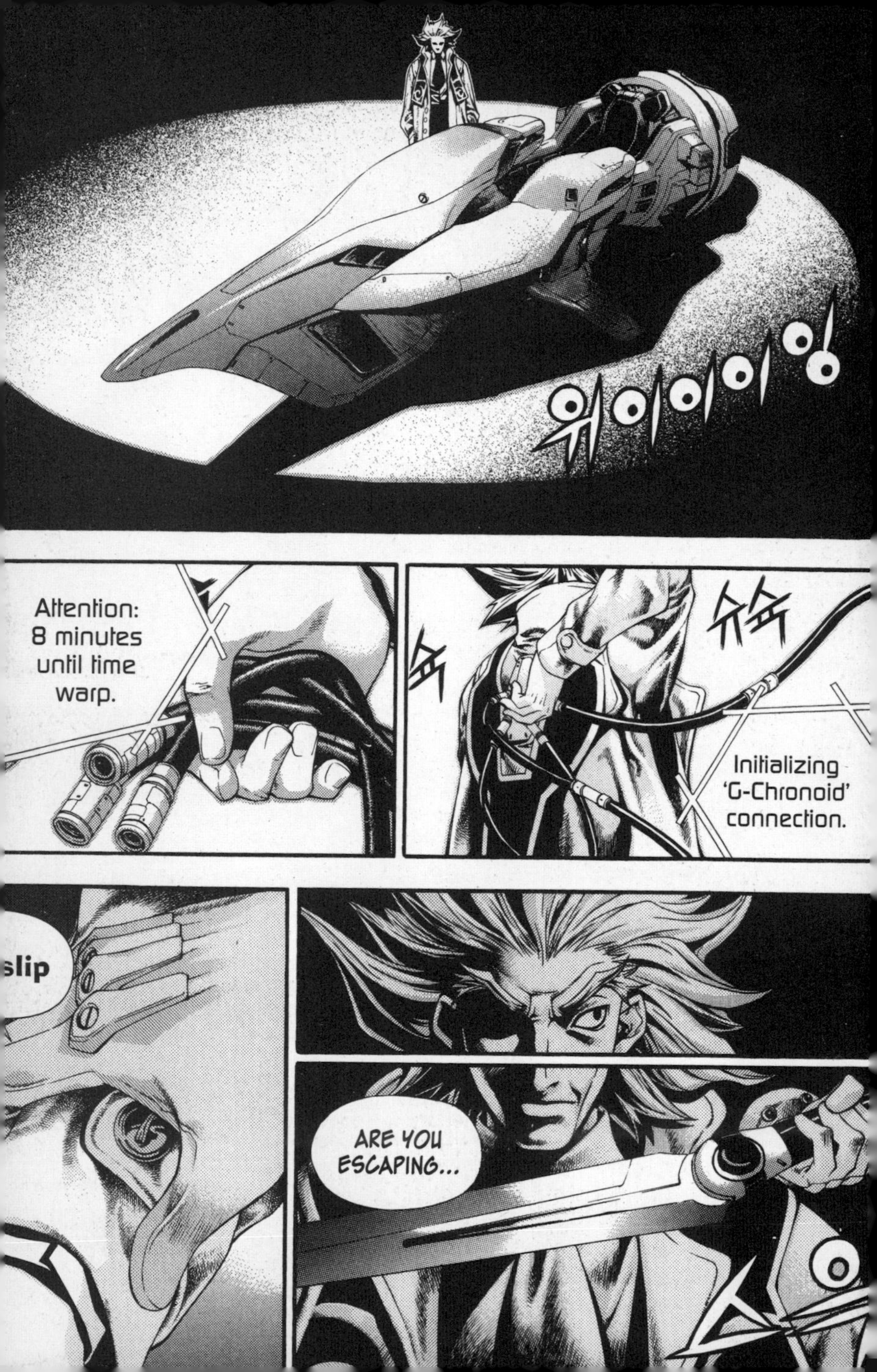

Attention:
8 minutes
until time
warp.
Initializing
'G-Chronoid'
connection.
slip
ARE YOU
ESCAPING...

...INTO THE PAST?

YOU'RE WASTING YOUR TIME. I'LL NEVER DISCLOSE THE SECURITY CODES TO VIOLENT MANIACS LIKE YOU!

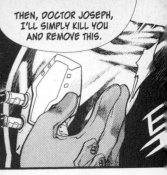

THEN, DOCTOR JOSEPH, I'LL SIMPLY KILL YOU AND REMOVE THIS.

AND YOU ARE...?

BLADE.

FIRST LIEUTENANT BLADE CARRION.

AH, LIEUTENANT CARRION! I'M SORRY, BUT YOU WON'T BE ABLE TO CAPTURE ME.

DOCTOR, OF ALL THE CHRONOIDS IN THE ARMY, I'M THE FASTEST.

REALLY?

SHALL WE PUT THAT TO THE TEST?

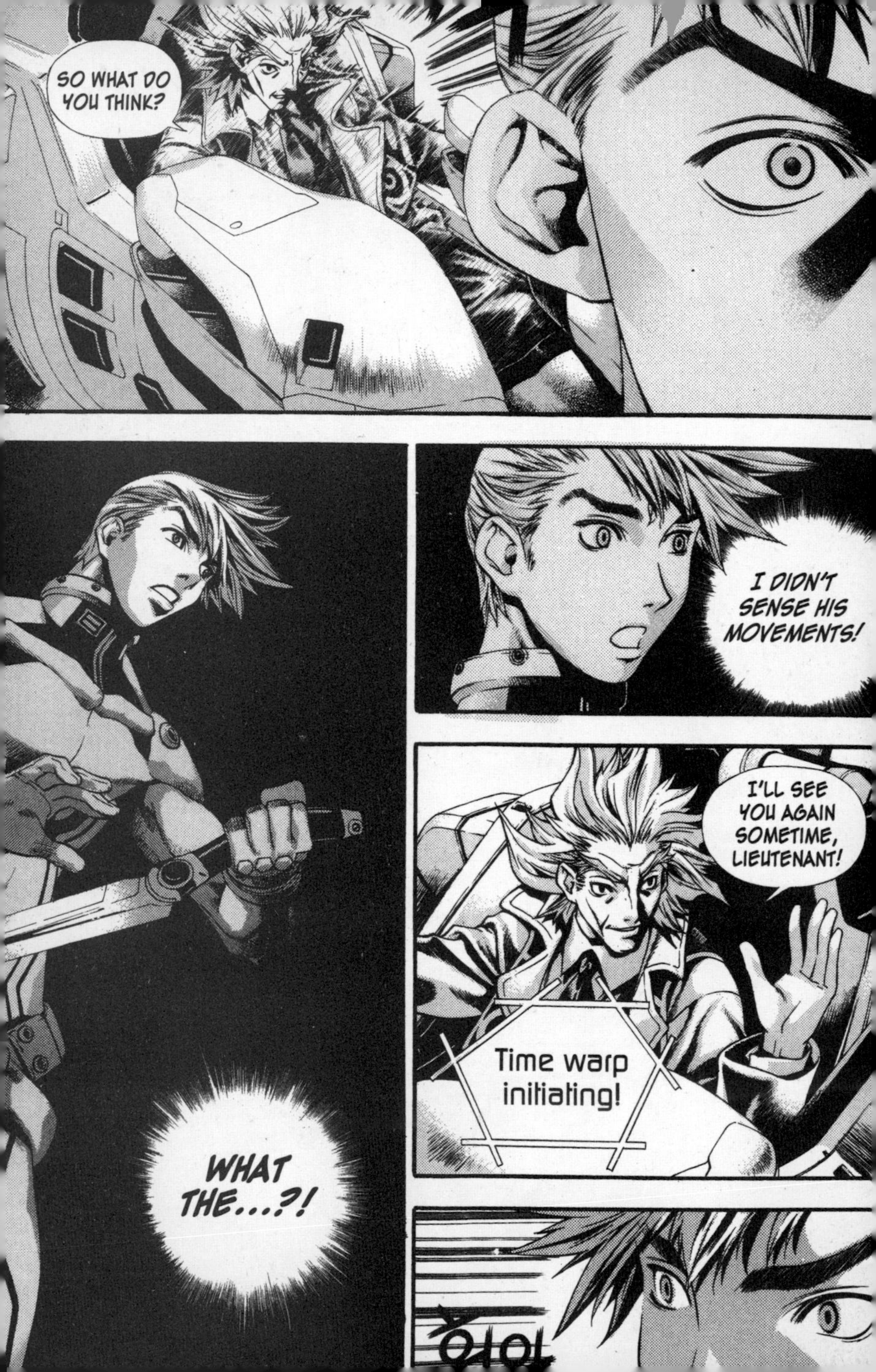
SO WHAT DO YOU THINK?
WHAT THE...?!
I DIDN'T SENSE HIS MOVEMENTS!
I'LL SEE YOU AGAIN SOMETIME, LIEUTENANT!
Time warp initiating!

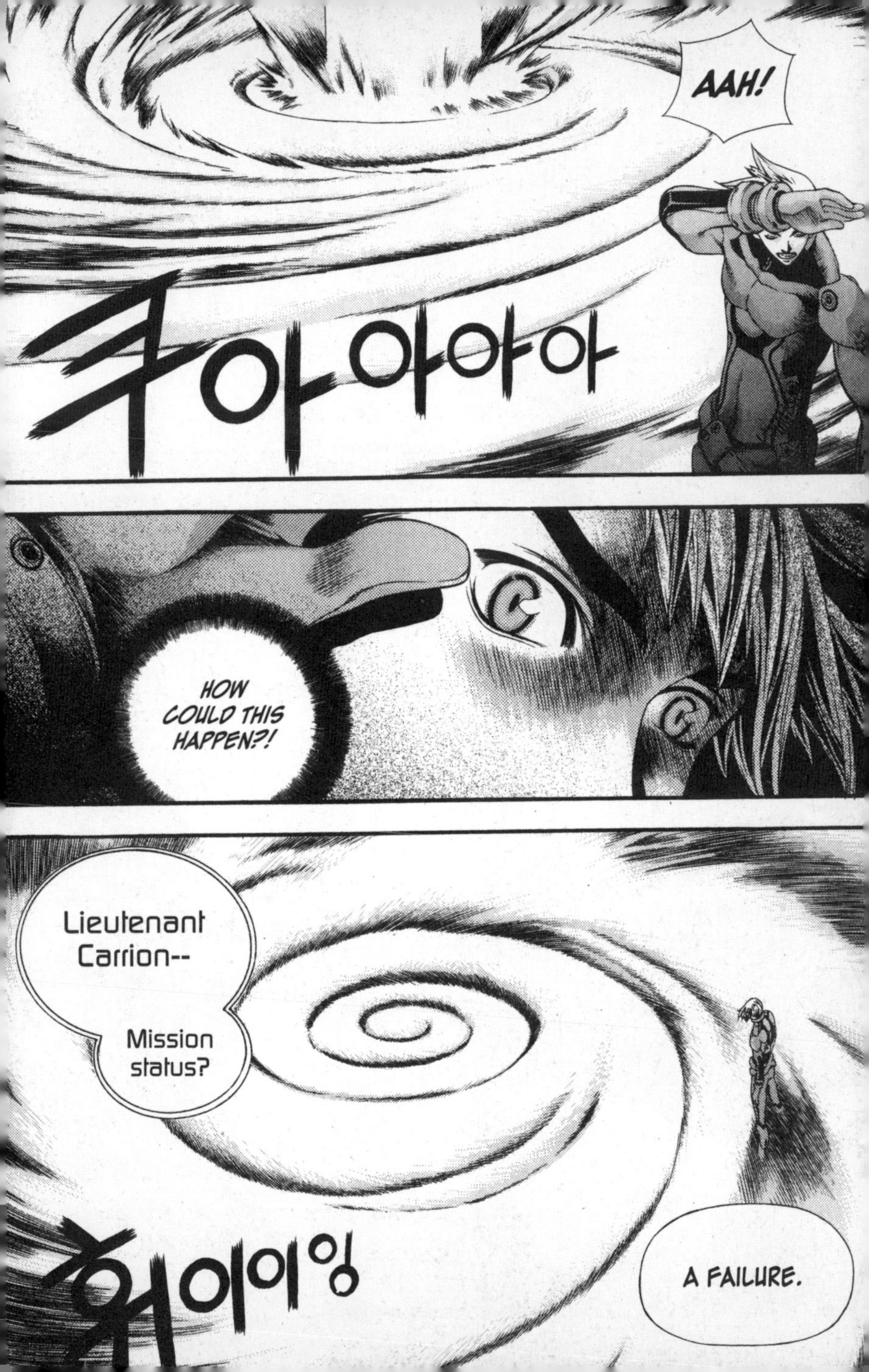
AAH!
쿠아아아아
HOW COULD THIS HAPPEN?!
Lieutenant Carrion--
Mission status?
A FAILURE.

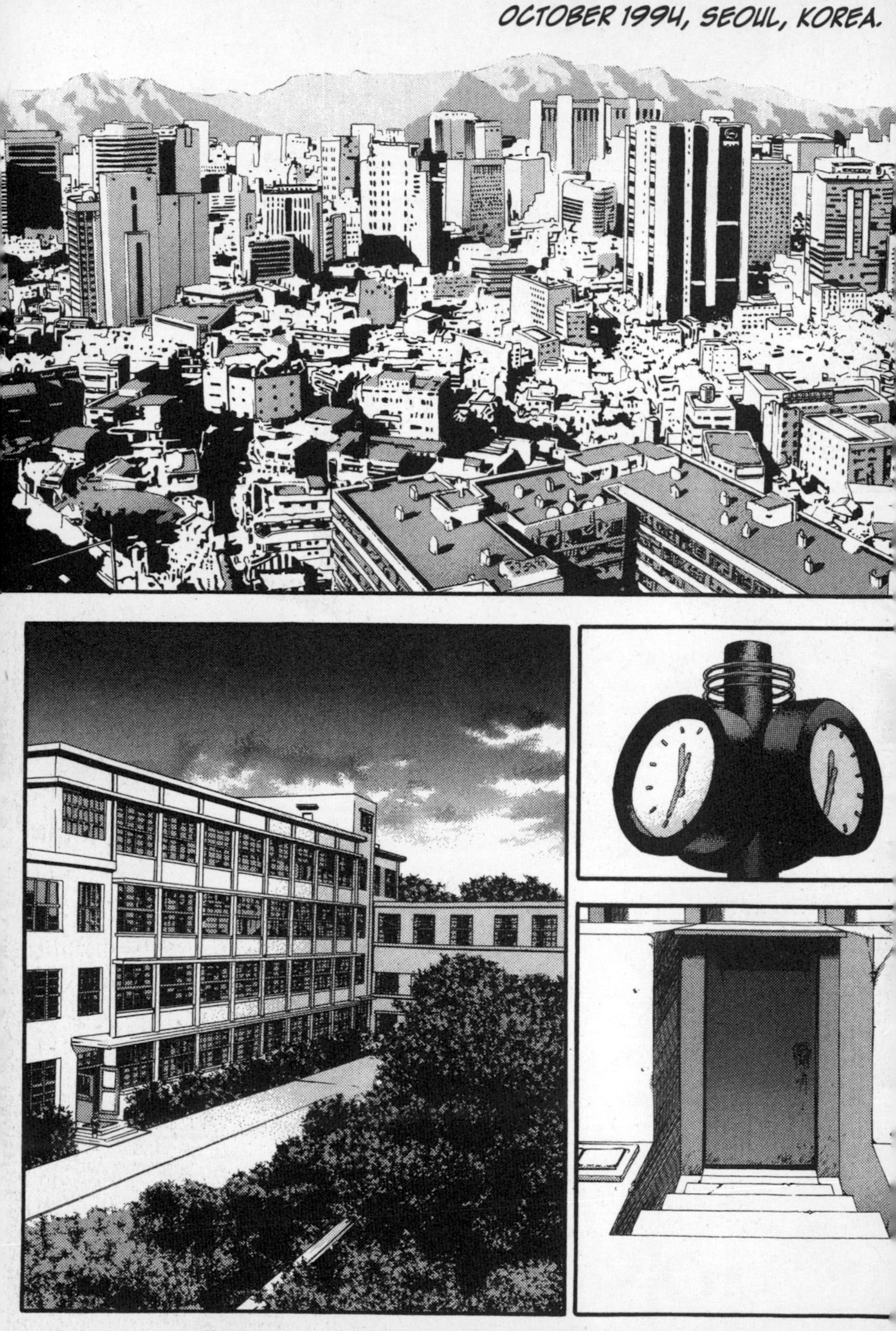
OCTOBER 1994, SEOUL, KOREA.

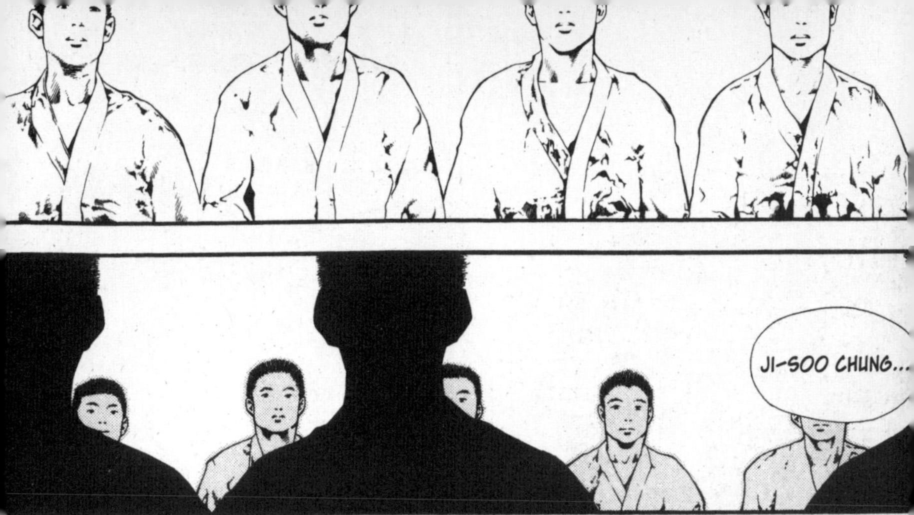
JI-SOO CHUNG...

NOTE: Kum Do is a martial arts fencing sport with long bamboo swords, more commonly known in the USA as kendo.

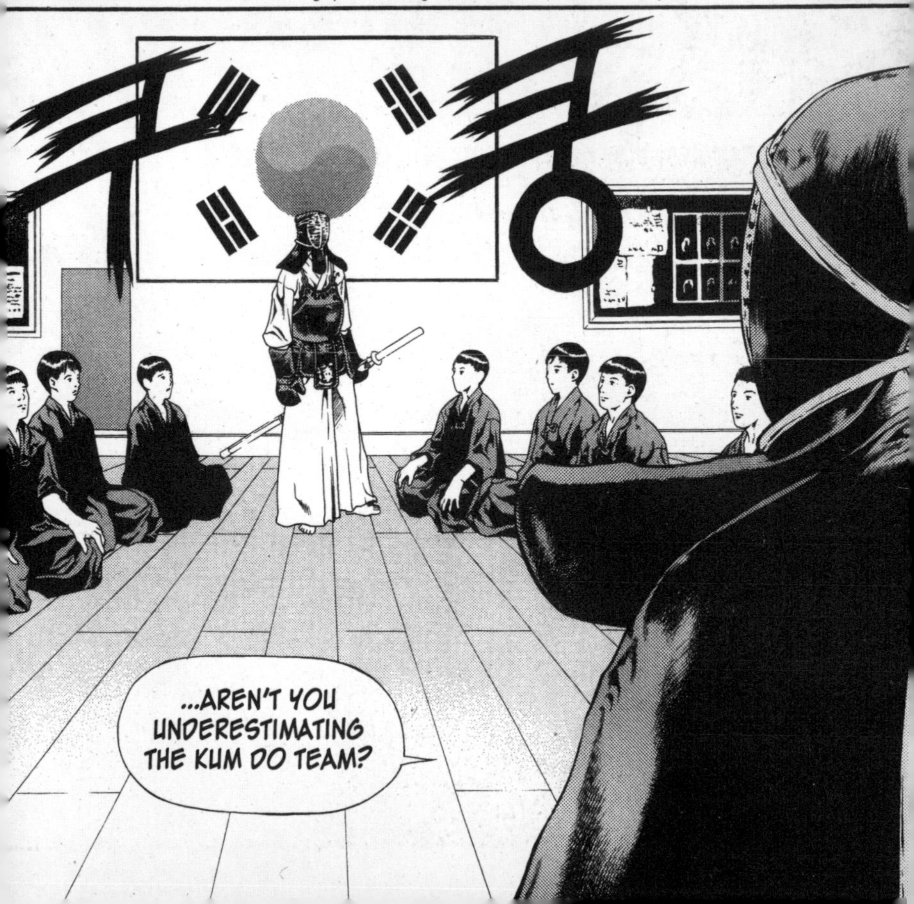
...AREN'T YOU UNDERESTIMATING THE KUM DO TEAM?

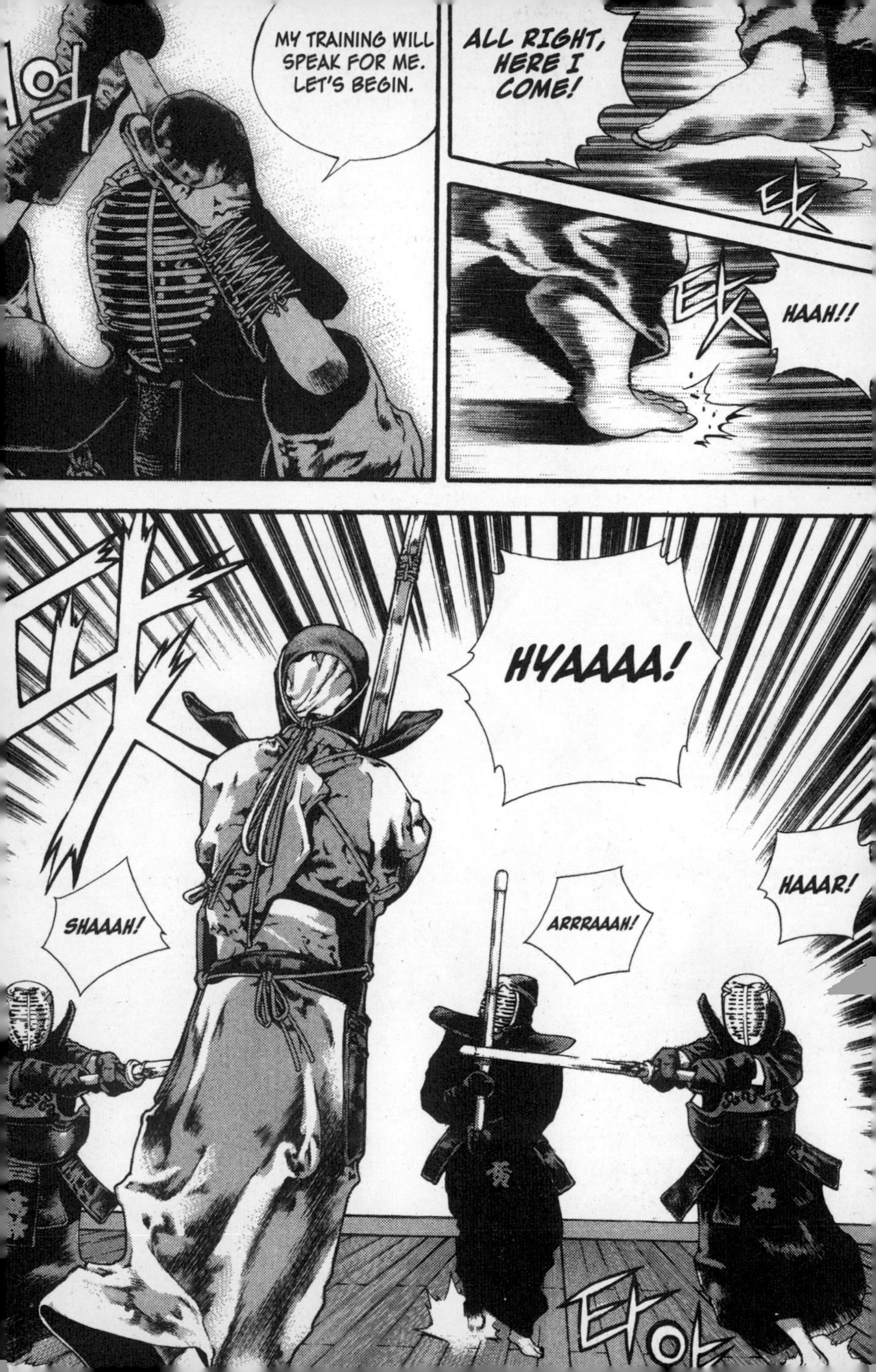
MY TRAINING WILL SPEAK FOR ME. LET'S BEGIN.
ALL RIGHT, HERE I COME!
HAAH!!
HYAAAA!
SHAAAH!
ARRRAAAH!
HAAAR!

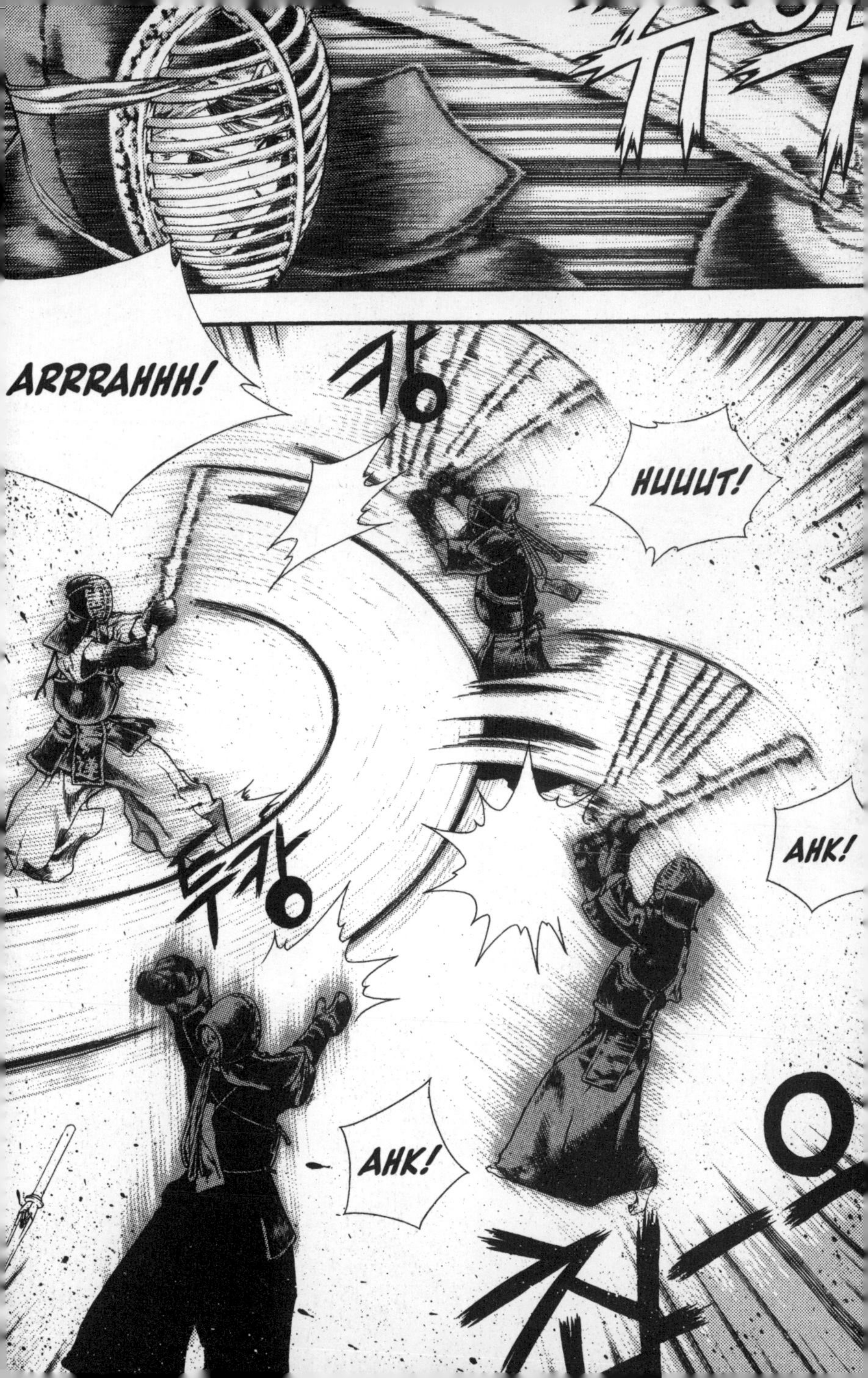
ARRRAHHH!
HUUUT!
AHK!
AHK!

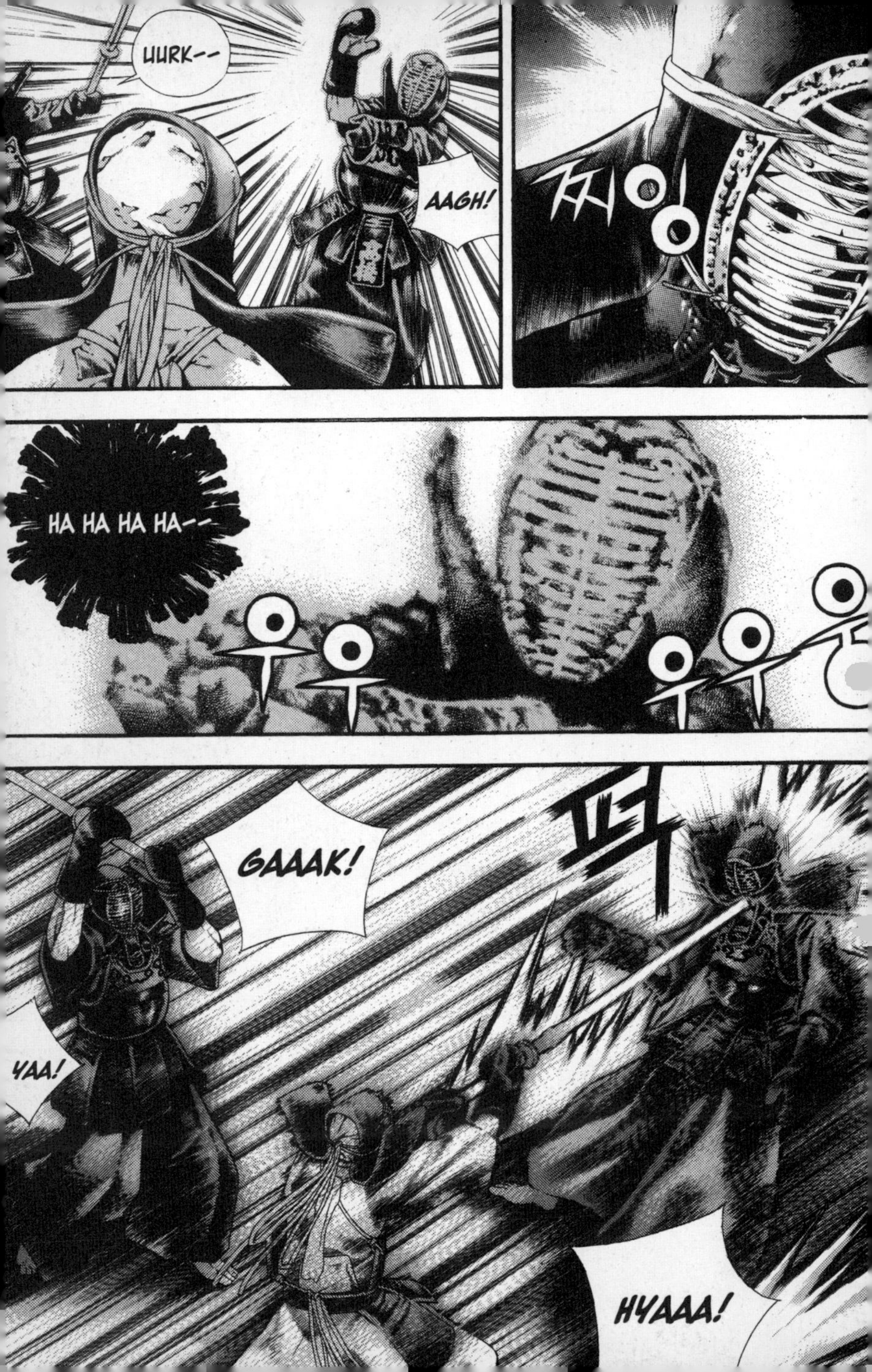
UURK--
AAGH!
HA HA HA HA--
GAAAK!
YAA!
HYAAA!

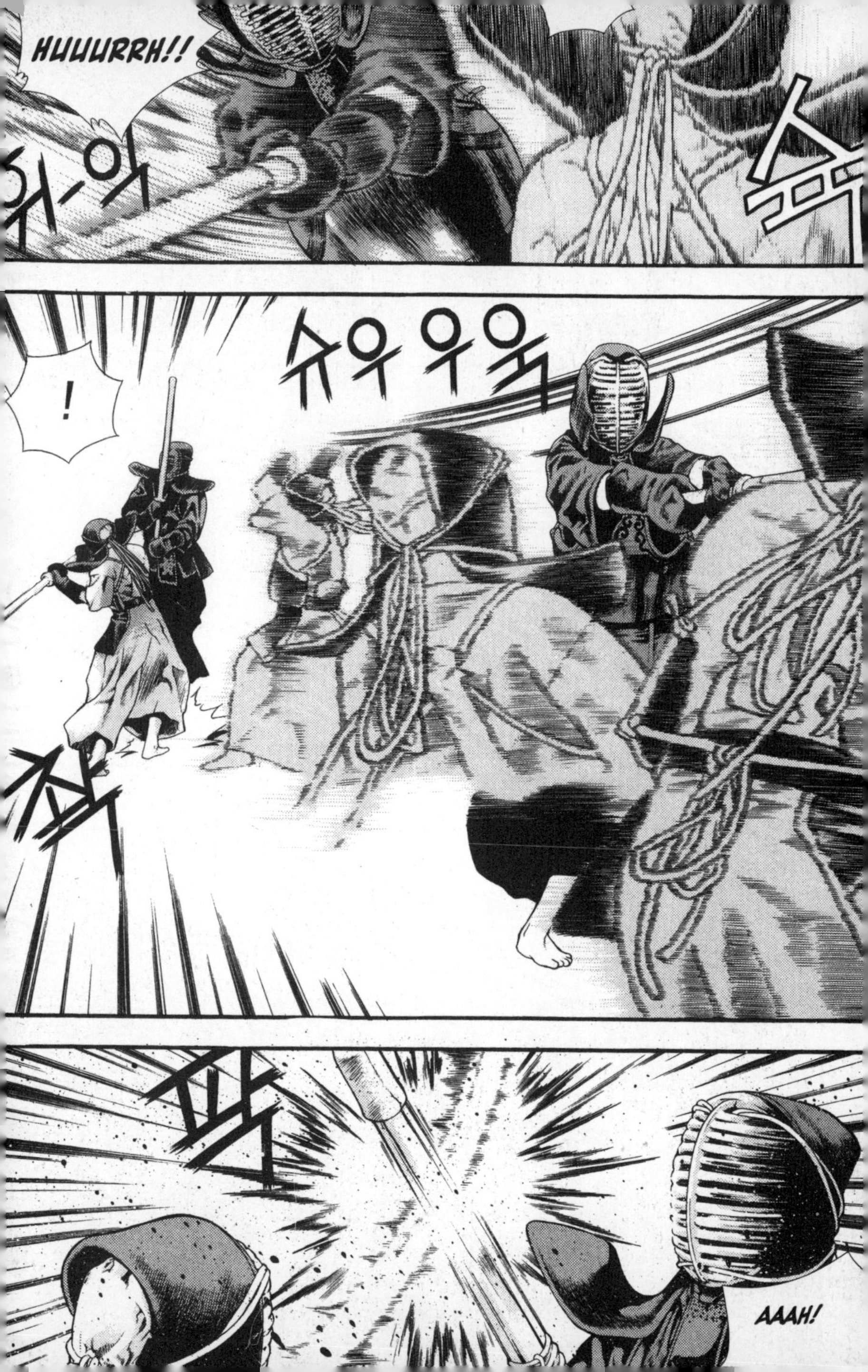

HUUURRH!!
!
슈우우욱
AAAH!

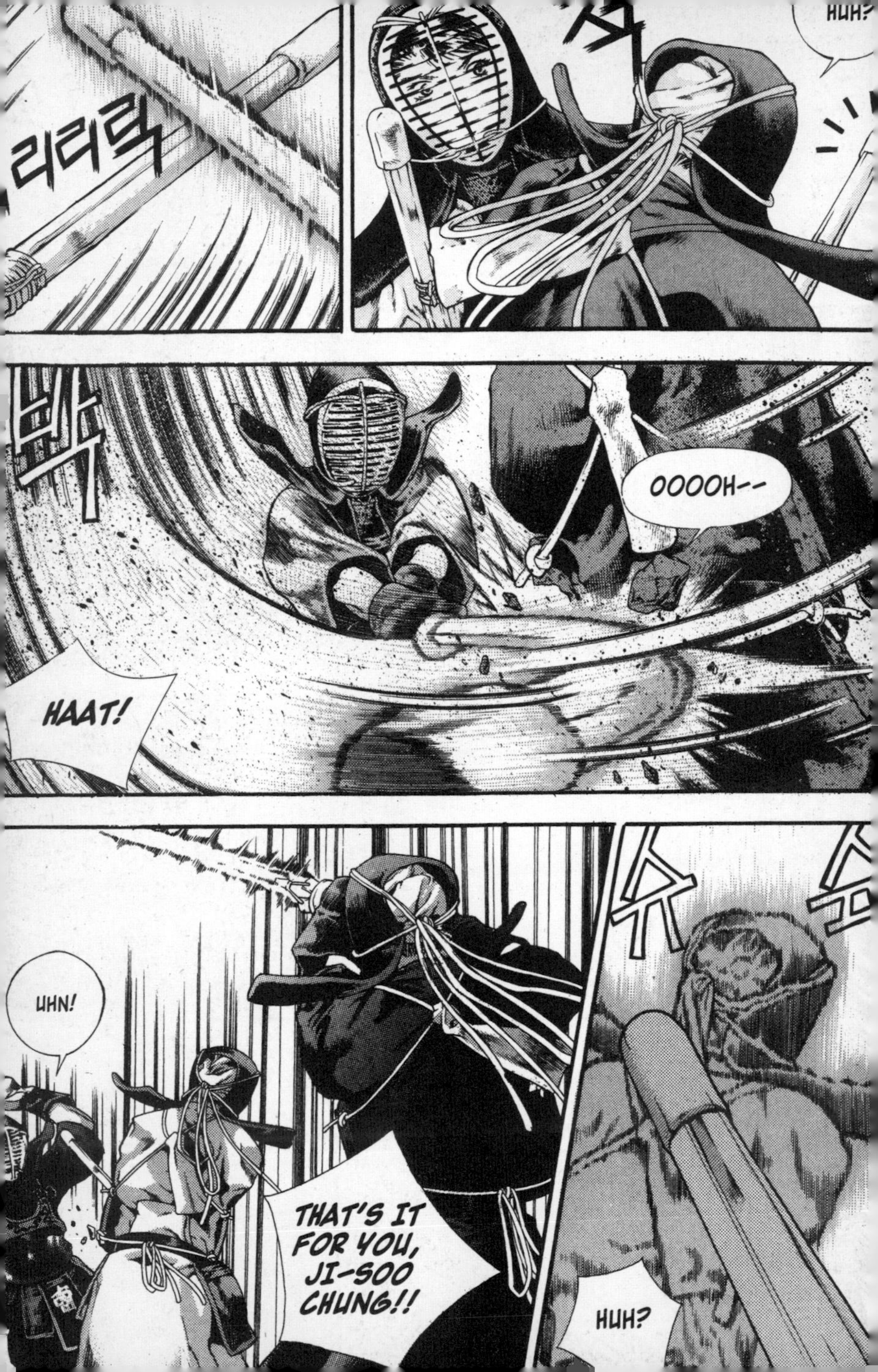

리리럭
HUH?
박
OOOOH--
HAAT!
UHN!
THAT'S IT FOR YOU, JI-SOO CHUNG!!
HUH?

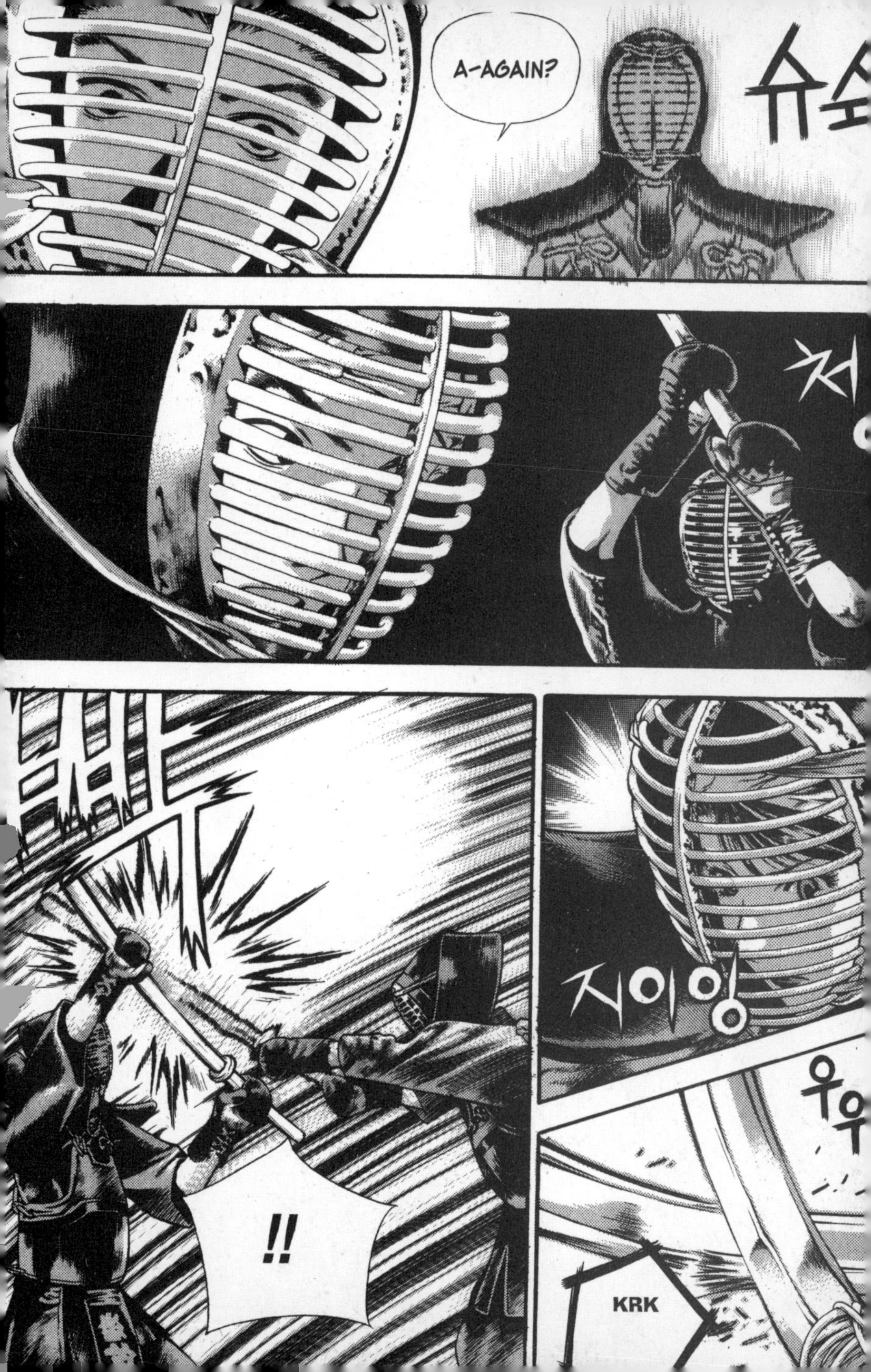
A-AGAIN?
!!
지이잉
우우
KRK

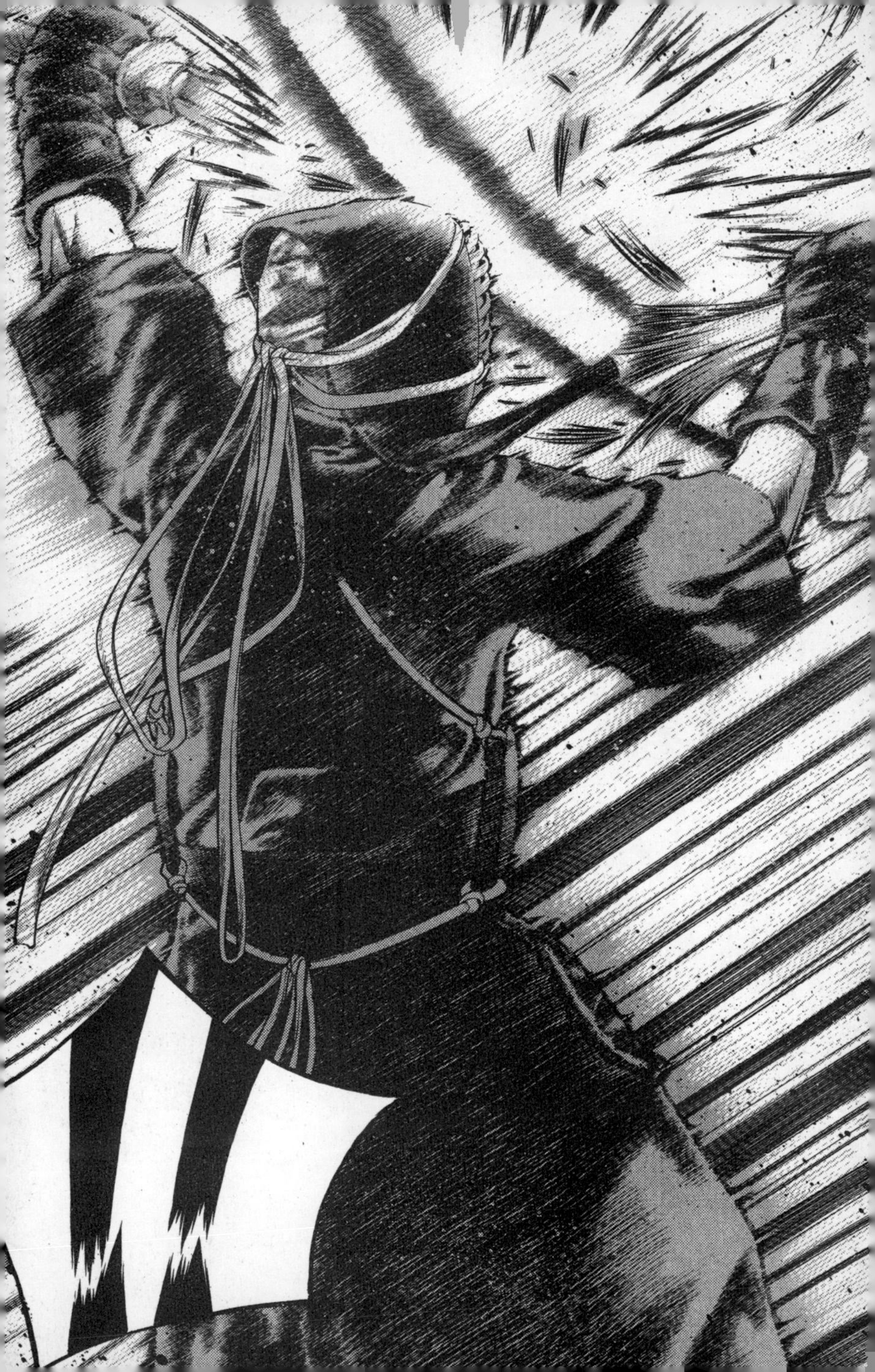

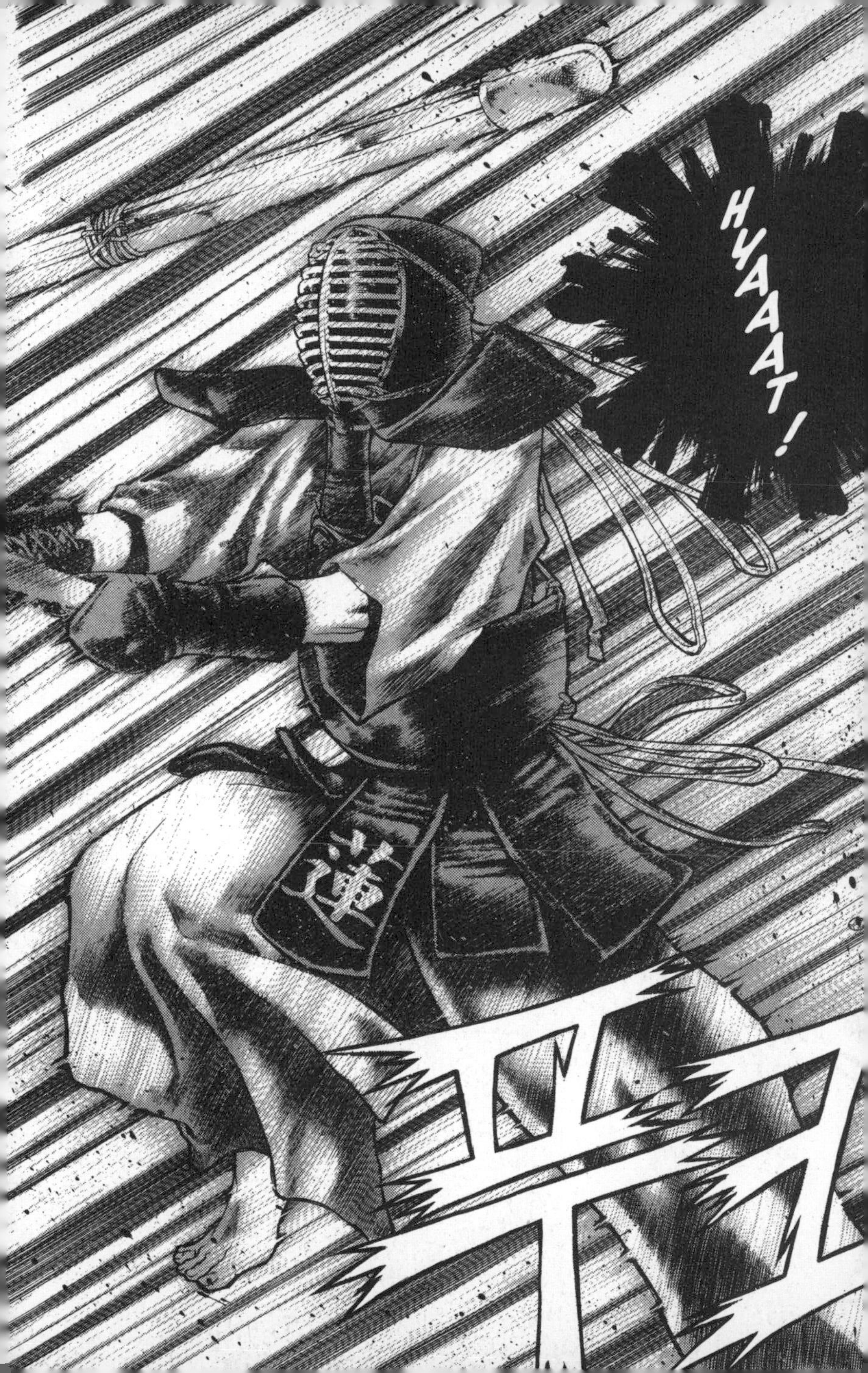
HUAAAT!
蓮

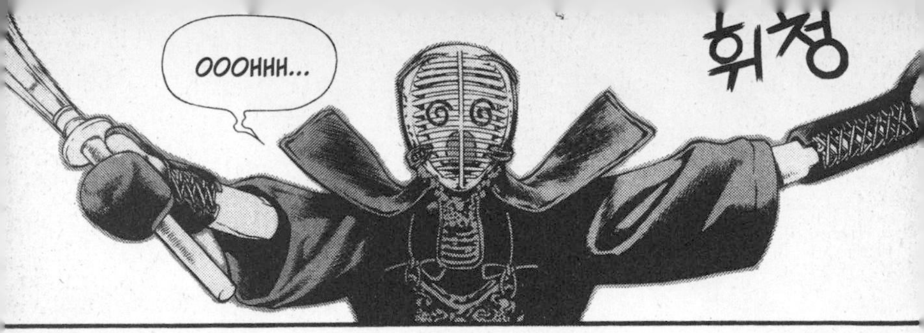
OOOHHH...
휘청
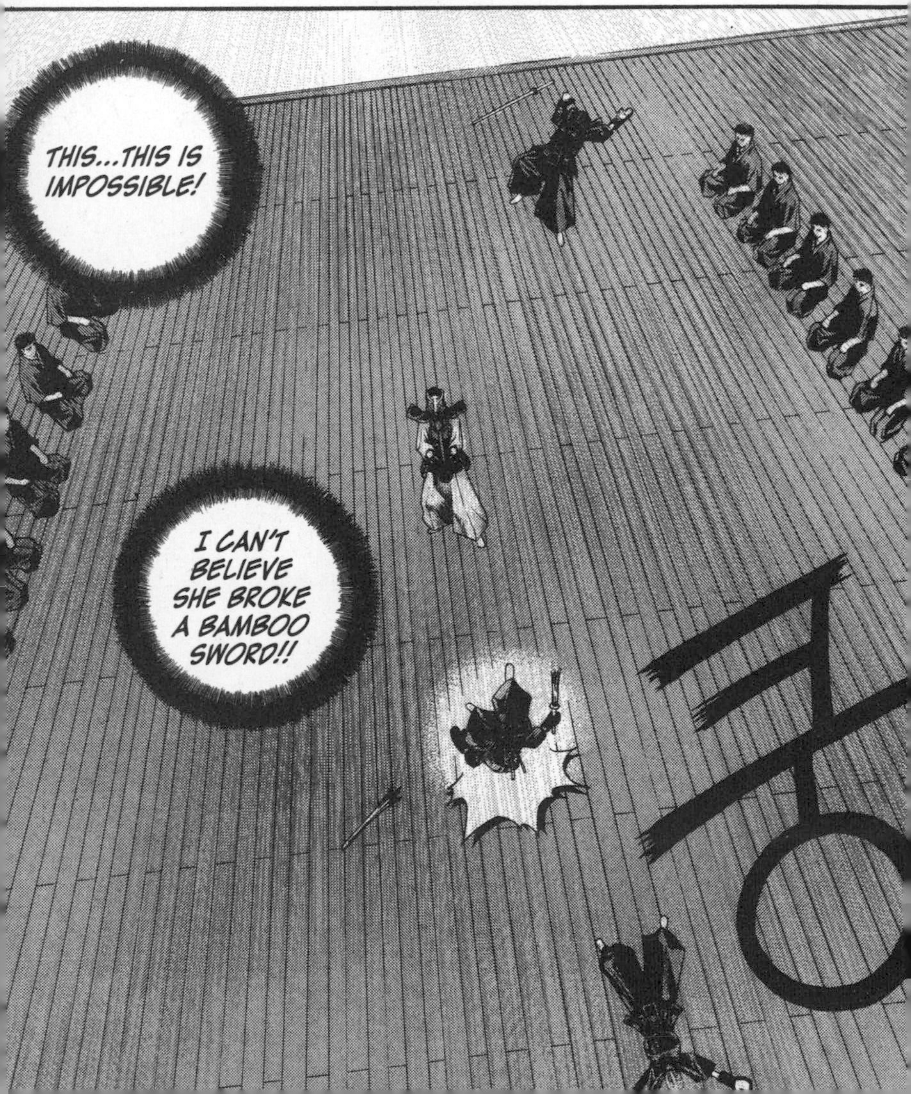
THIS...THIS IS IMPOSSIBLE!
I CAN'T BELIEVE SHE BROKE A BAMBOO SWORD!!
쿵

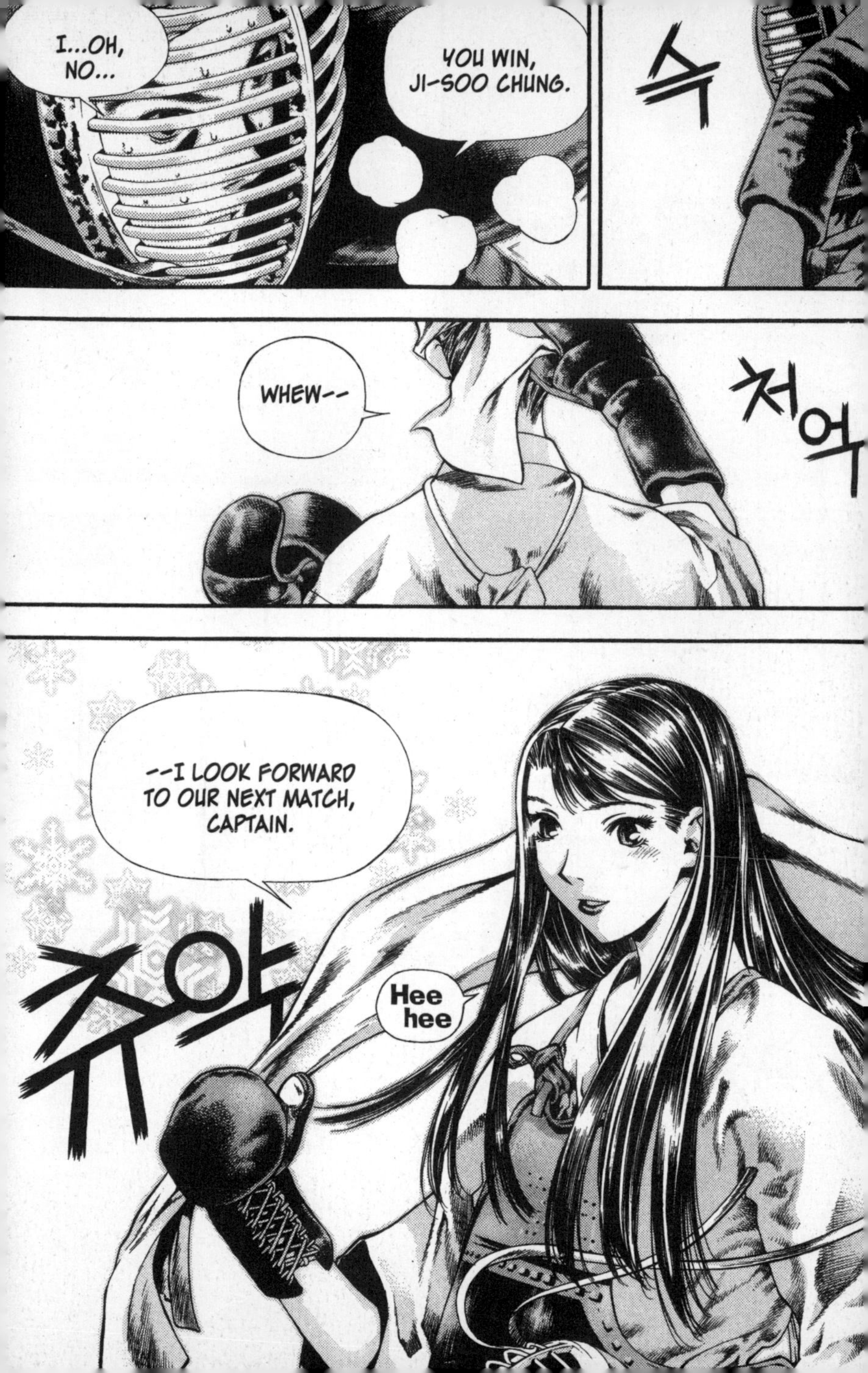
I...OH, NO...
YOU WIN, JI-SOO CHUNG.
슥
WHEW--
처억
--I LOOK FORWARD TO OUR NEXT MATCH, CAPTAIN.
츄악
Hee hee

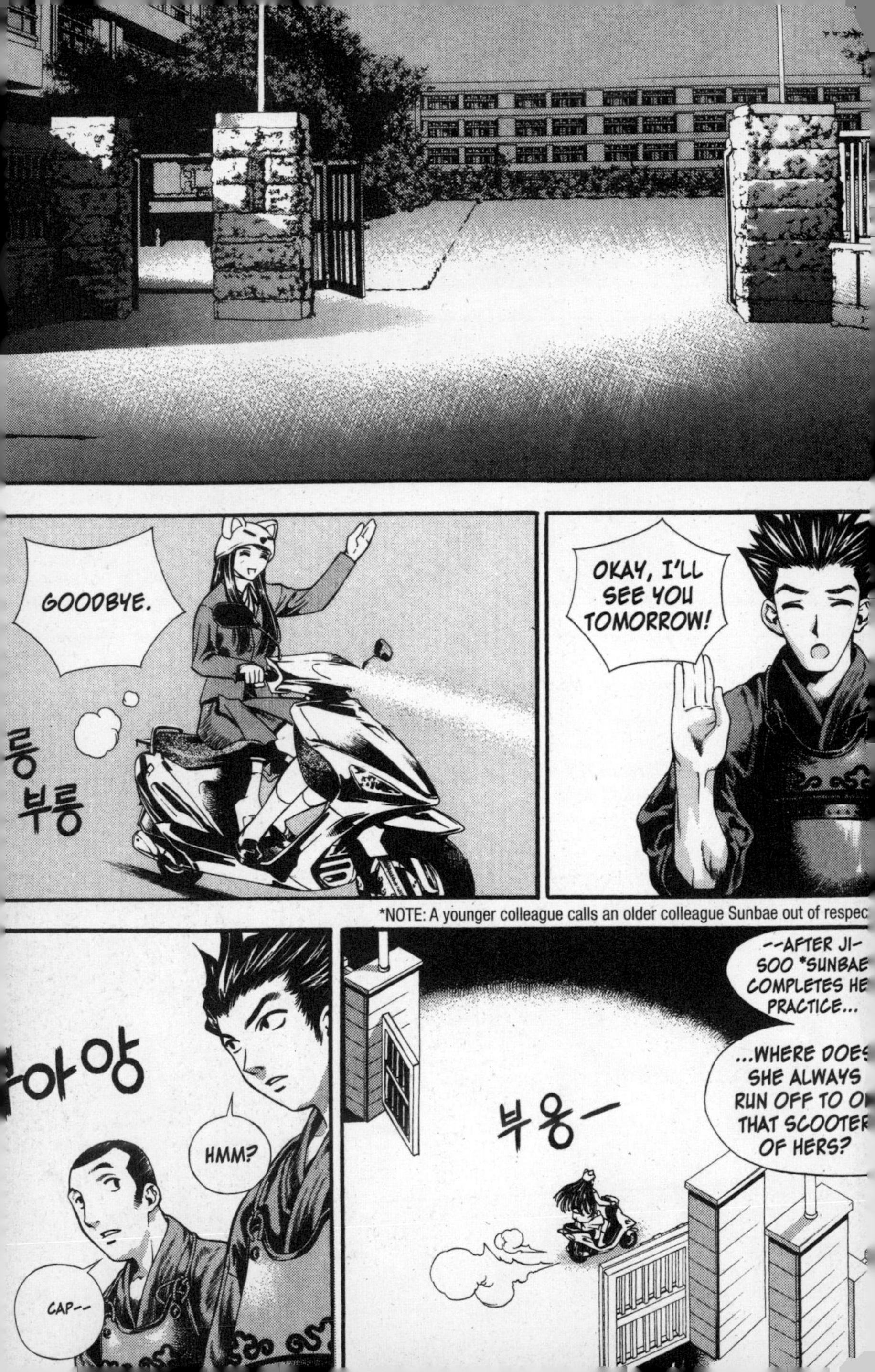
GOODBYE.
릉
부릉
OKAY, I'LL SEE YOU TOMORROW!
아앙
HMM?
CAP--
--AFTER JI-SOO *SUNBAE COMPLETES HE PRACTICE...
...WHERE DOES SHE ALWAYS RUN OFF TO O THAT SCOOTER OF HERS?
부웅—

*NOTE: A younger colleague calls an older colleague Sunbae out of respec

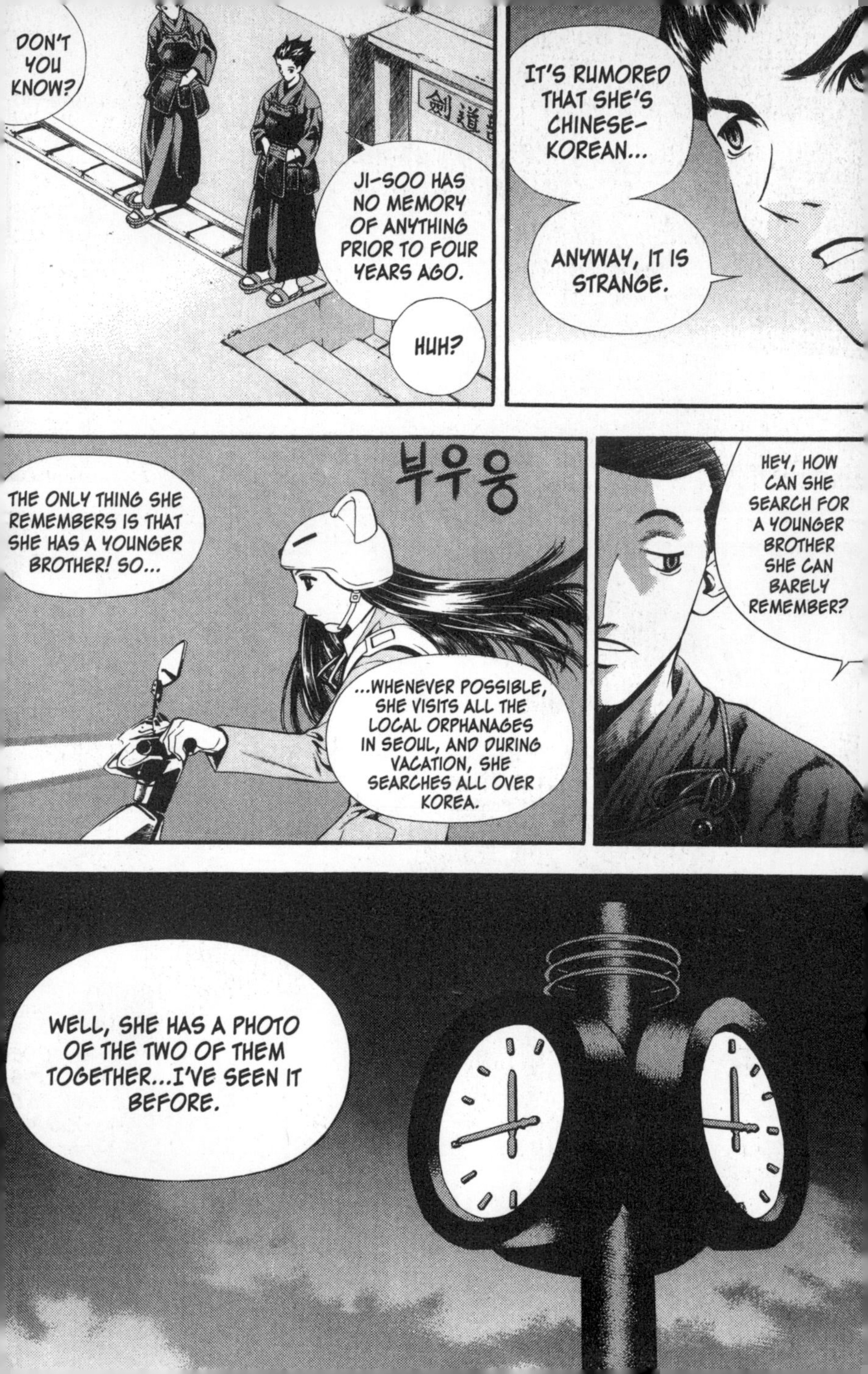
DON'T YOU KNOW?
剣道
JI-SOO HAS NO MEMORY OF ANYTHING PRIOR TO FOUR YEARS AGO.
HUH?
IT'S RUMORED THAT SHE'S CHINESE-KOREAN...
ANYWAY, IT IS STRANGE.
부우웅
THE ONLY THING SHE REMEMBERS IS THAT SHE HAS A YOUNGER BROTHER! SO...
...WHENEVER POSSIBLE, SHE VISITS ALL THE LOCAL ORPHANAGES IN SEOUL, AND DURING VACATION, SHE SEARCHES ALL OVER KOREA.
HEY, HOW CAN SHE SEARCH FOR A YOUNGER BROTHER SHE CAN BARELY REMEMBER?
WELL, SHE HAS A PHOTO OF THE TWO OF THEM TOGETHER...I'VE SEEN IT BEFORE.

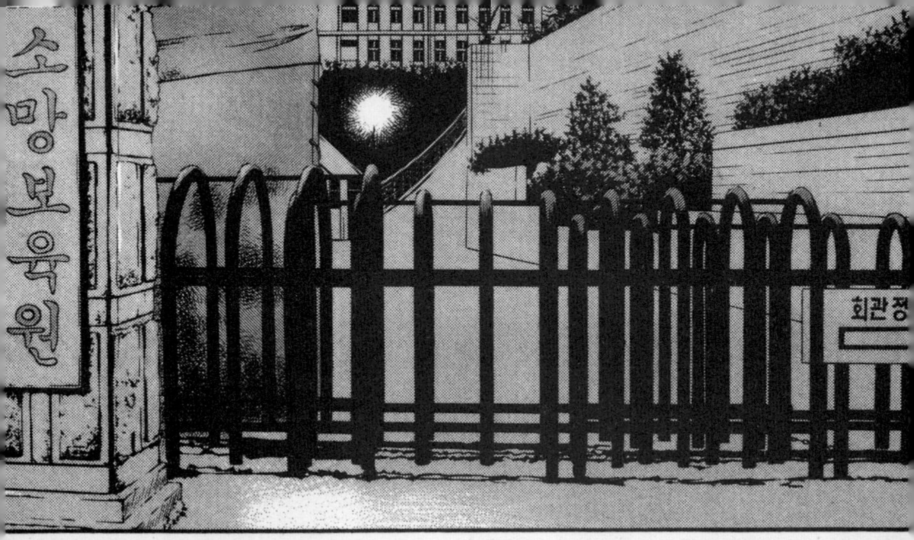
소망보육원
회관정

Hope Orphanage

Please use the front entrance

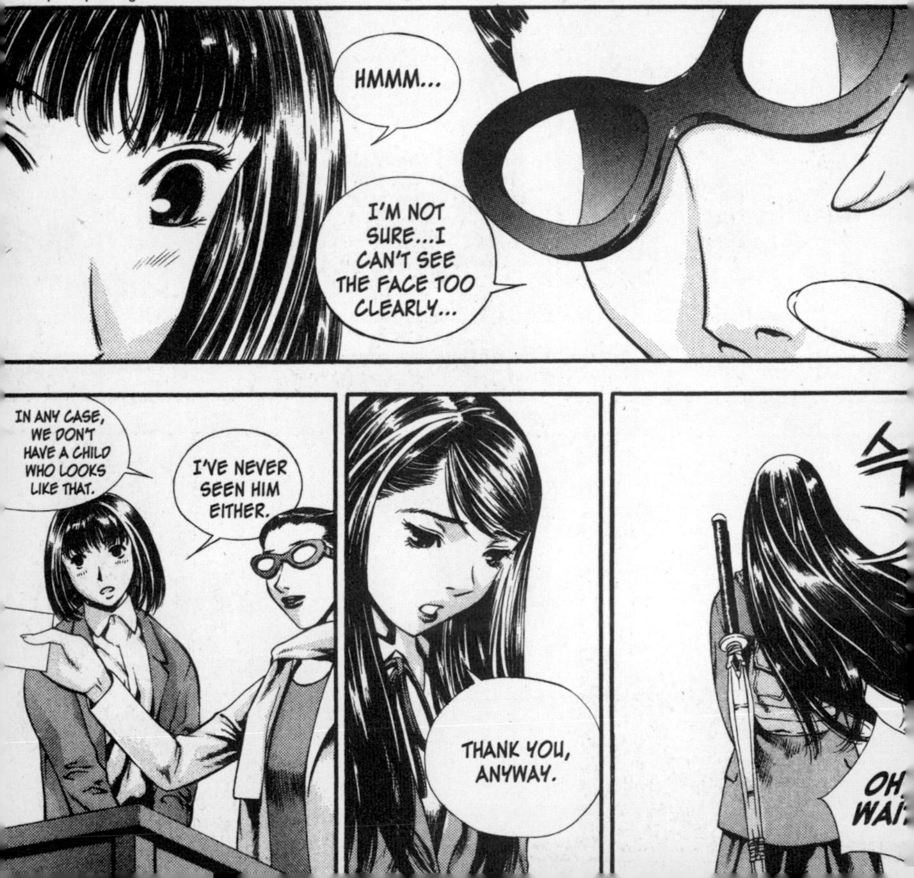
HMMM...
I'M NOT SURE...I CAN'T SEE THE FACE TOO CLEARLY...
IN ANY CASE, WE DON'T HAVE A CHILD WHO LOOKS LIKE THAT.
I'VE NEVER SEEN HIM EITHER.
THANK YOU, ANYWAY.
OH WAI

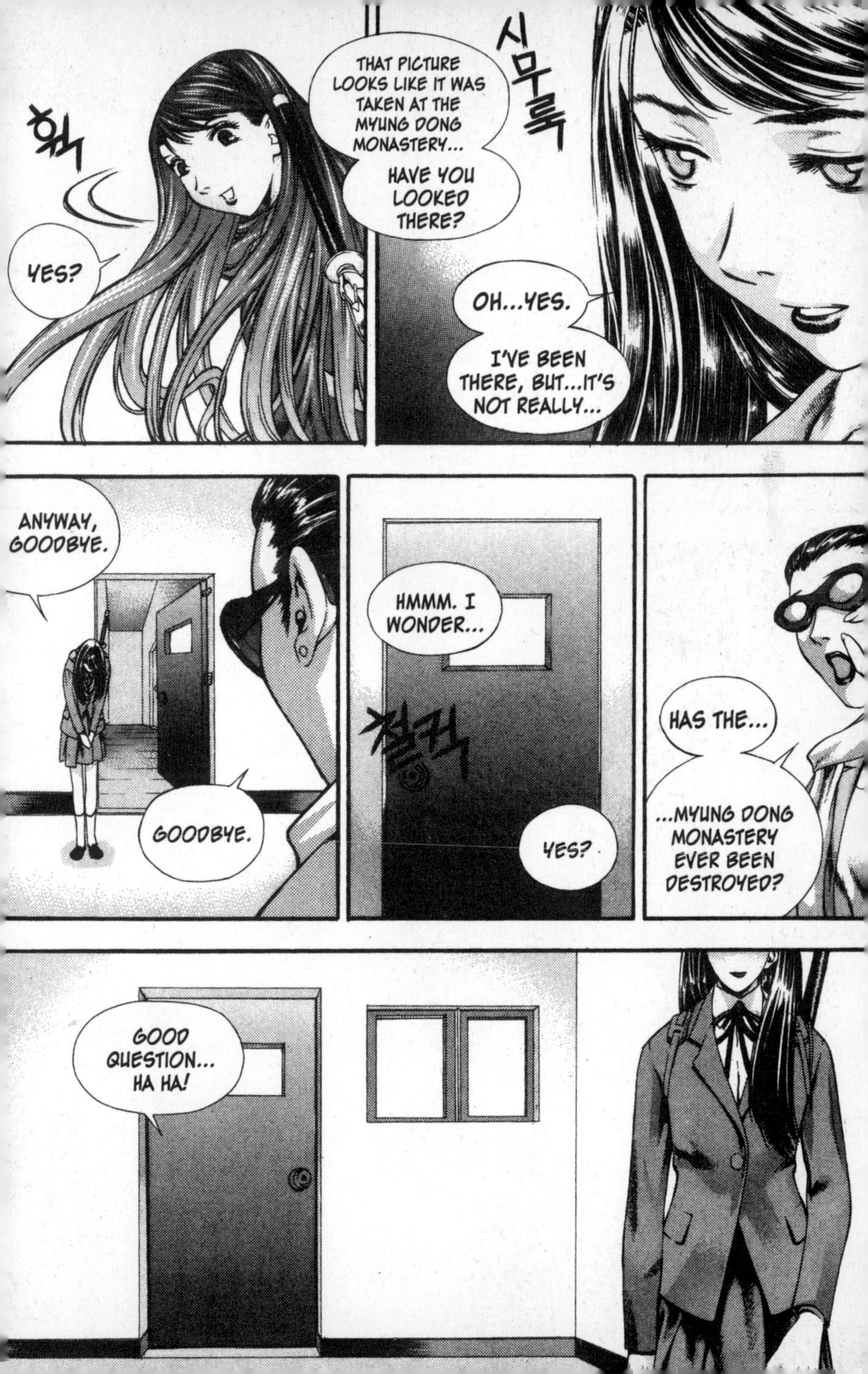
휙
YES?
THAT PICTURE LOOKS LIKE IT WAS TAKEN AT THE MYUNG DONG MONASTERY...
HAVE YOU LOOKED THERE?
시무룩
OH...YES.
I'VE BEEN THERE, BUT...IT'S NOT REALLY...
ANYWAY, GOODBYE.
GOODBYE.
HMMM. I WONDER...
철컥
YES?
HAS THE...
...MYUNG DONG MONASTERY EVER BEEN DESTROYED?
GOOD QUESTION... HA HA!

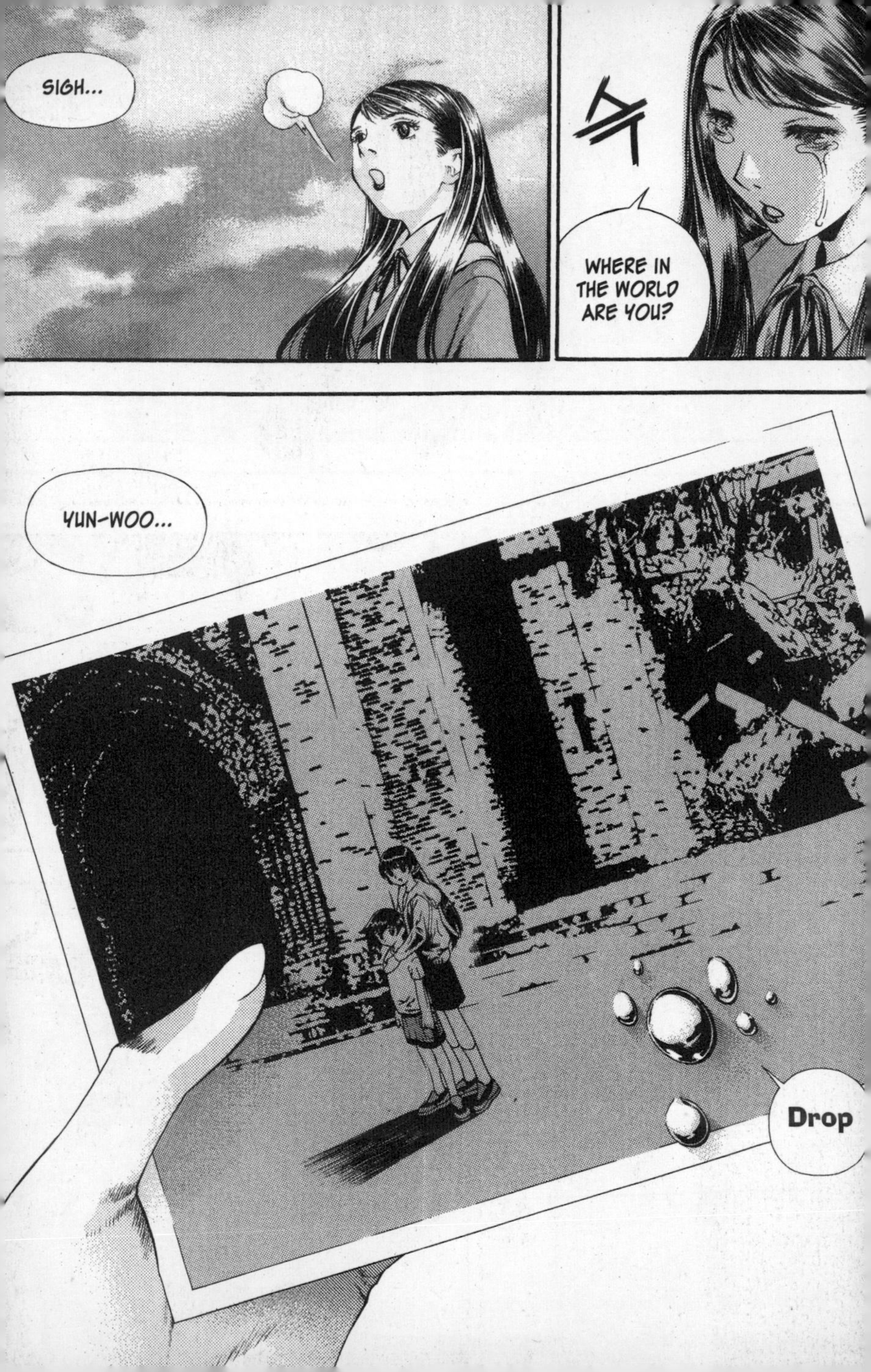
SIGH...
슥
WHERE IN THE WORLD ARE YOU?
YUN-WOO...
Drop

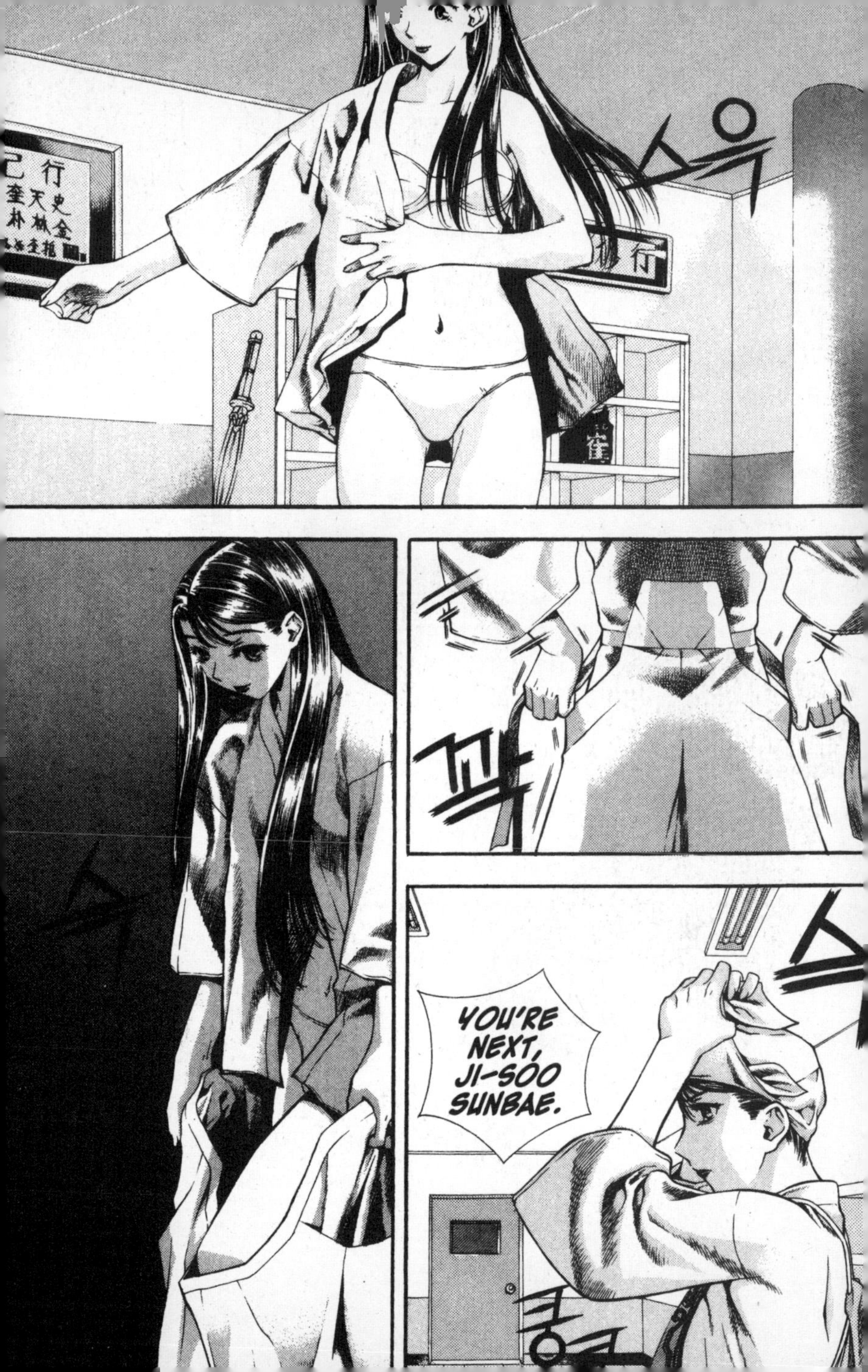
YOU'RE NEXT, JI-SOO SUNBAE.

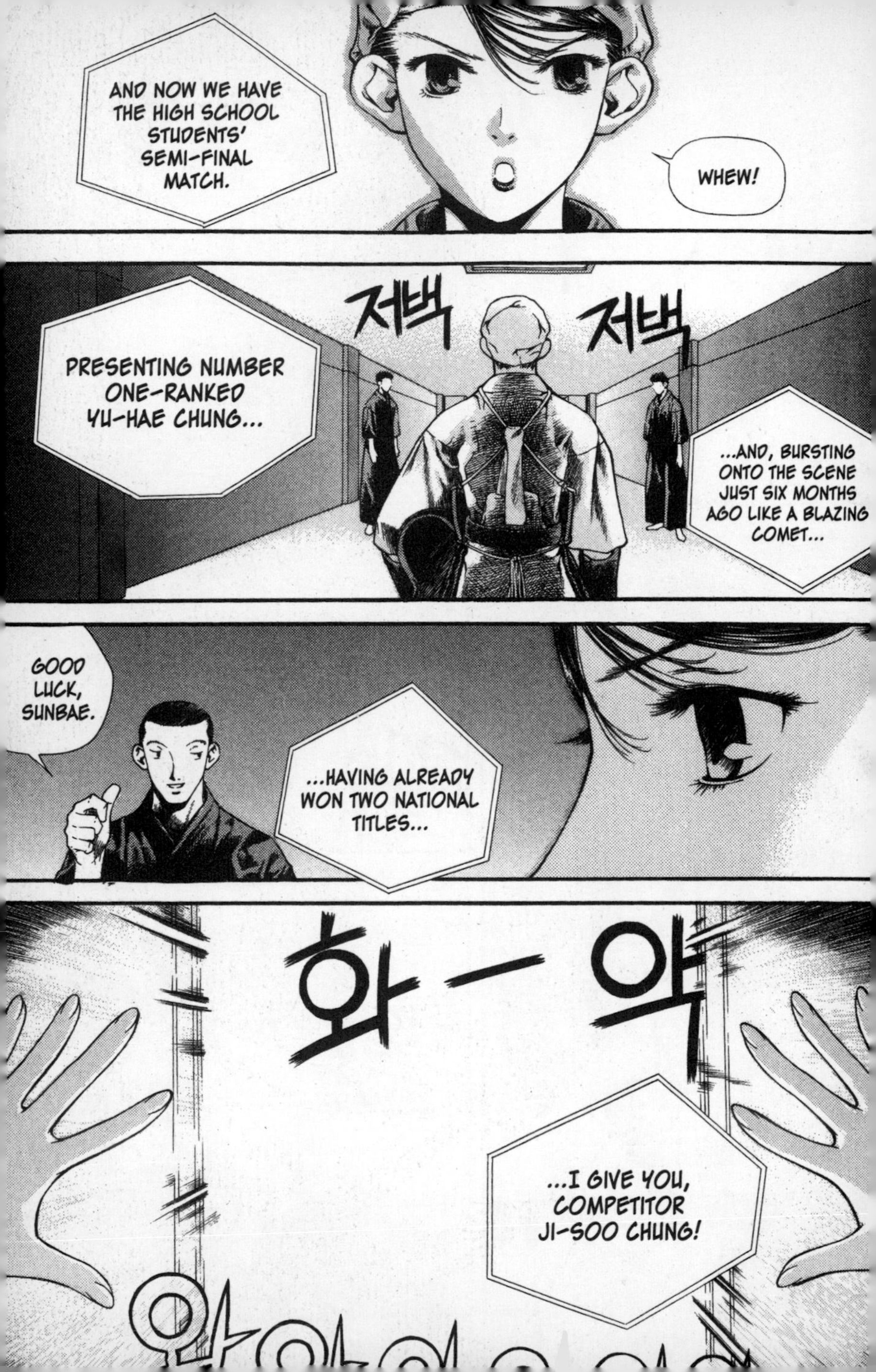
AND NOW WE HAVE THE HIGH SCHOOL STUDENTS' SEMI-FINAL MATCH.
WHEW!
PRESENTING NUMBER ONE-RANKED YU-HAE CHUNG...
저벅
저벅
...AND, BURSTING ONTO THE SCENE JUST SIX MONTHS AGO LIKE A BLAZING COMET...
GOOD LUCK, SUNBAE.
...HAVING ALREADY WON TWO NATIONAL TITLES...
화-악
...I GIVE YOU, COMPETITOR JI-SOO CHUNG!

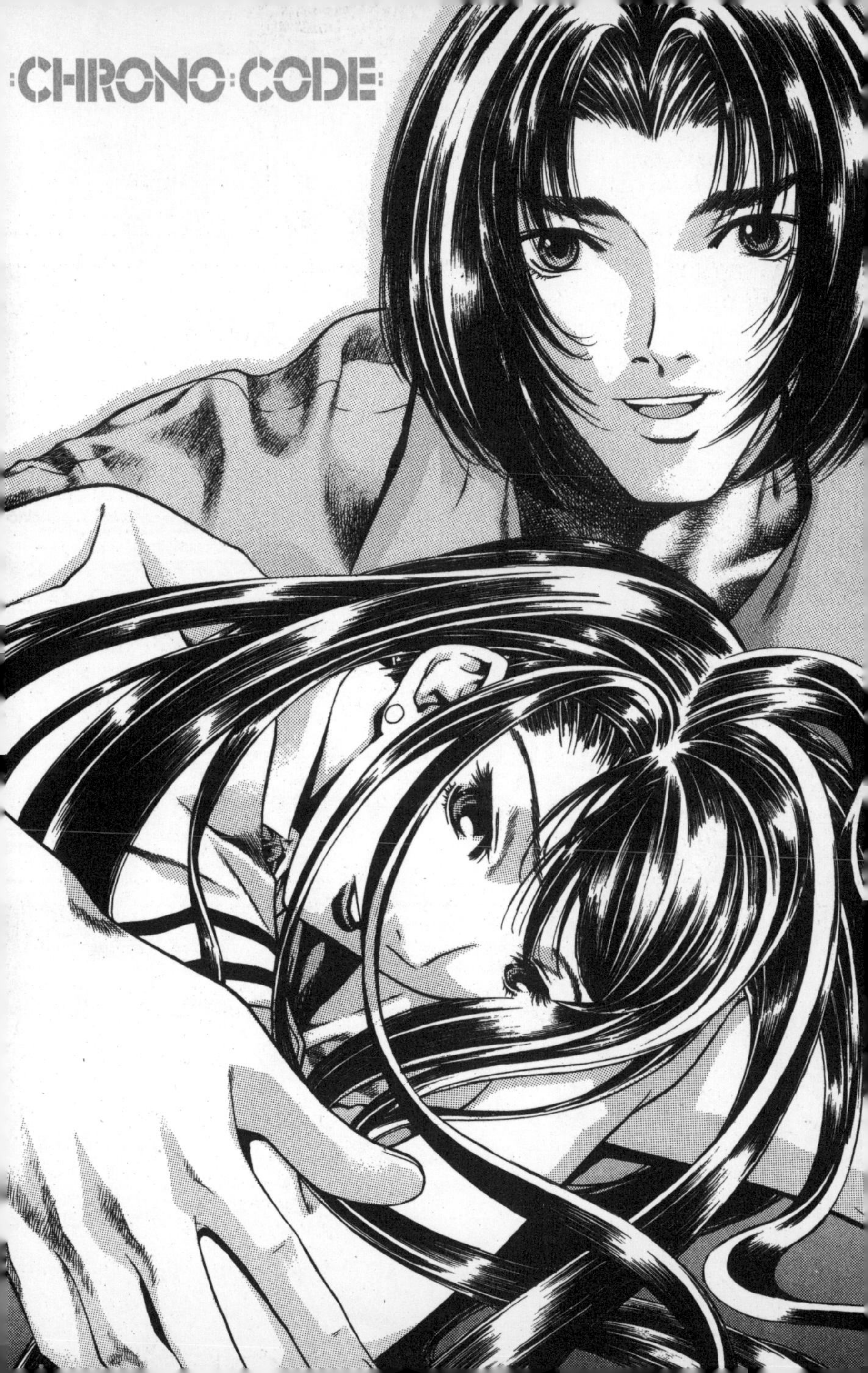
CHRONO CODE

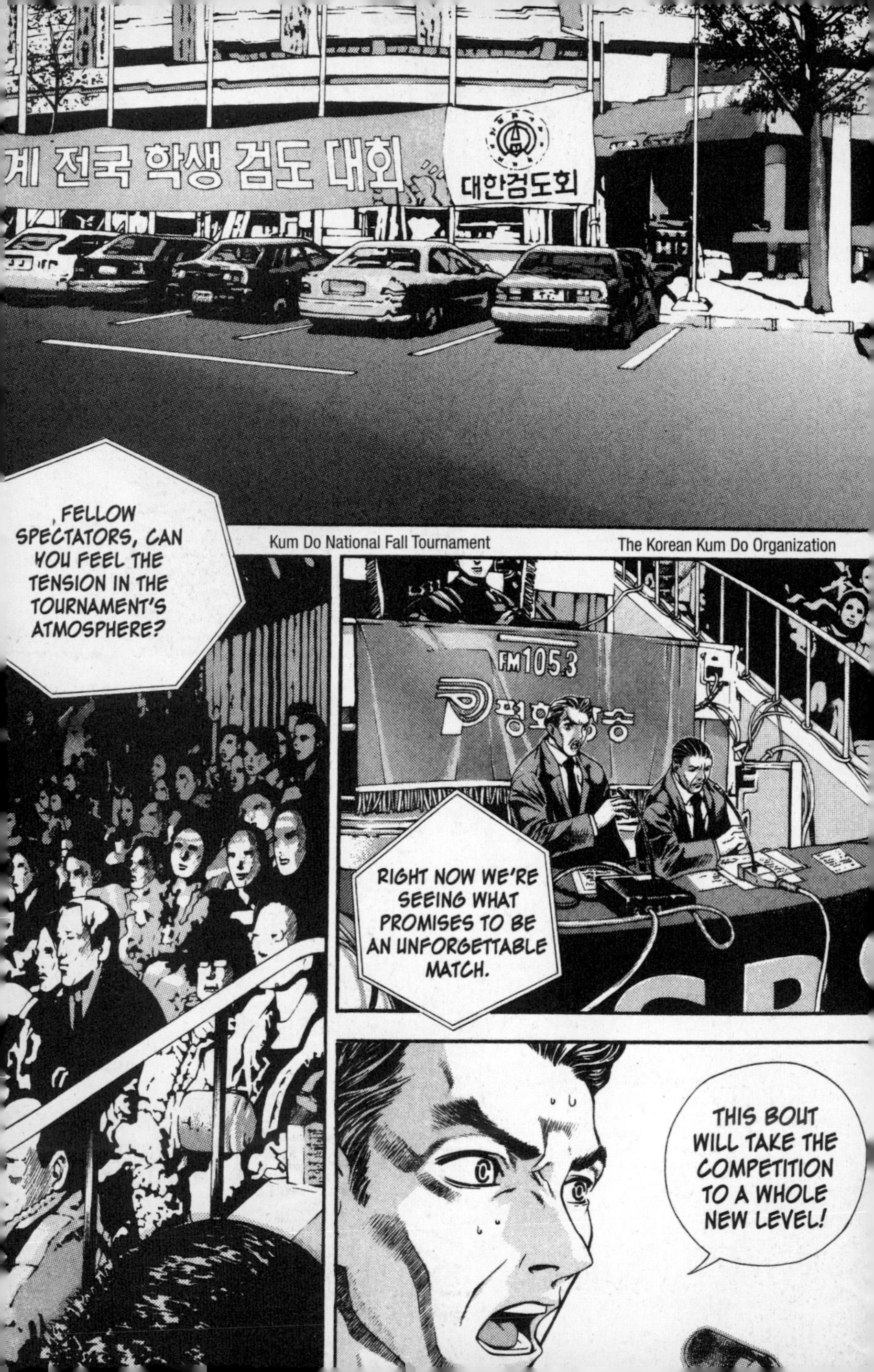
계 전국 학생 검도 대회
대한검도회
Kum Do National Fall Tournament
The Korean Kum Do Organization
FELLOW SPECTATORS, CAN YOU FEEL THE TENSION IN THE TOURNAMENT'S ATMOSPHERE?
FM105.3
RIGHT NOW WE'RE SEEING WHAT PROMISES TO BE AN UNFORGETTABLE MATCH.
THIS BOUT WILL TAKE THE COMPETITION TO A WHOLE NEW LEVEL!

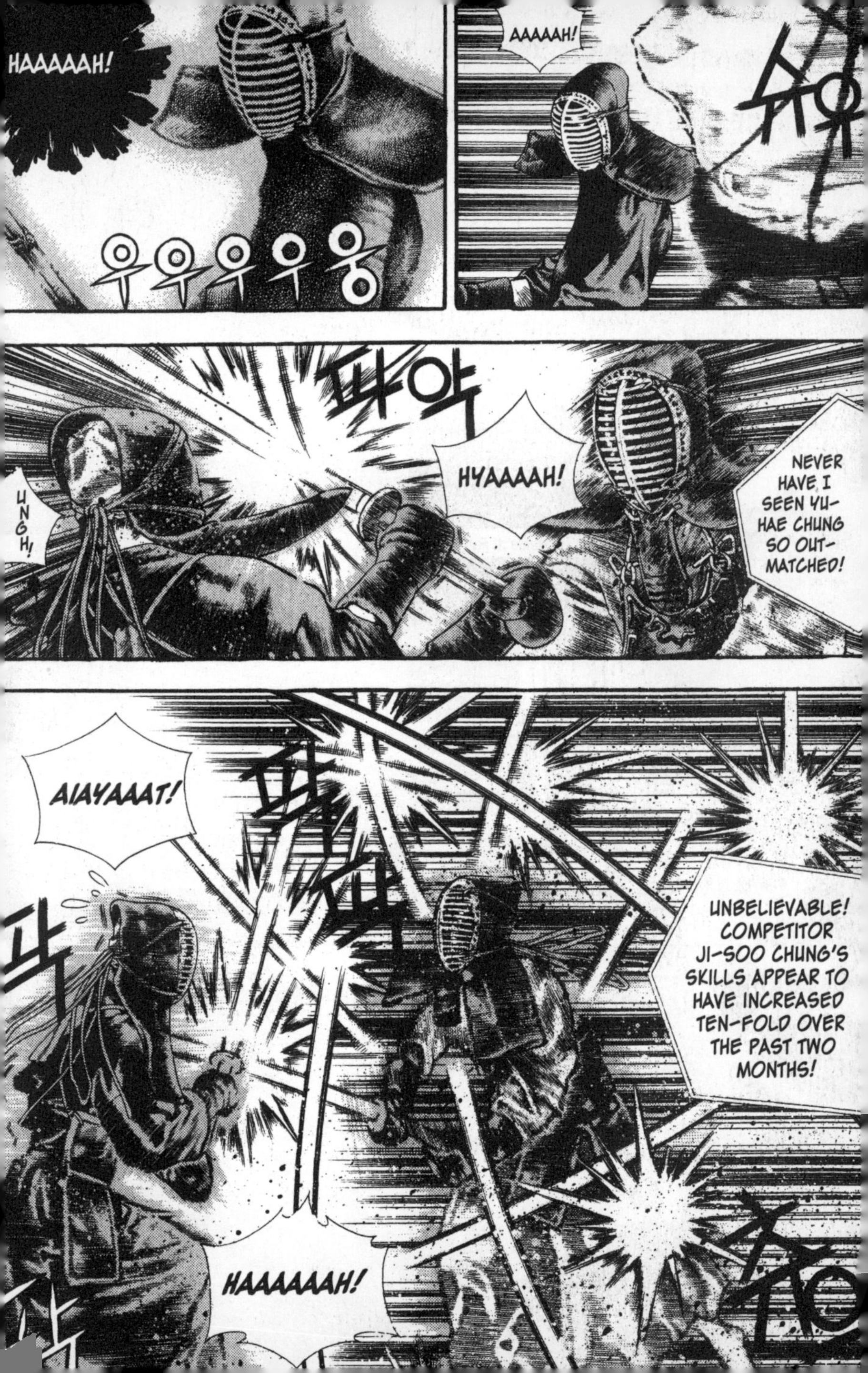
HAAAAAH!
우우우우웅
AAAAAH!
따악
UNGH!
HYAAAAH!
NEVER HAVE I SEEN YU-HAE CHUNG SO OUT-MATCHED!
AIAYAAAT!
UNBELIEVABLE! COMPETITOR JI-SOO CHUNG'S SKILLS APPEAR TO HAVE INCREASED TEN-FOLD OVER THE PAST TWO MONTHS!
HAAAAAAH!

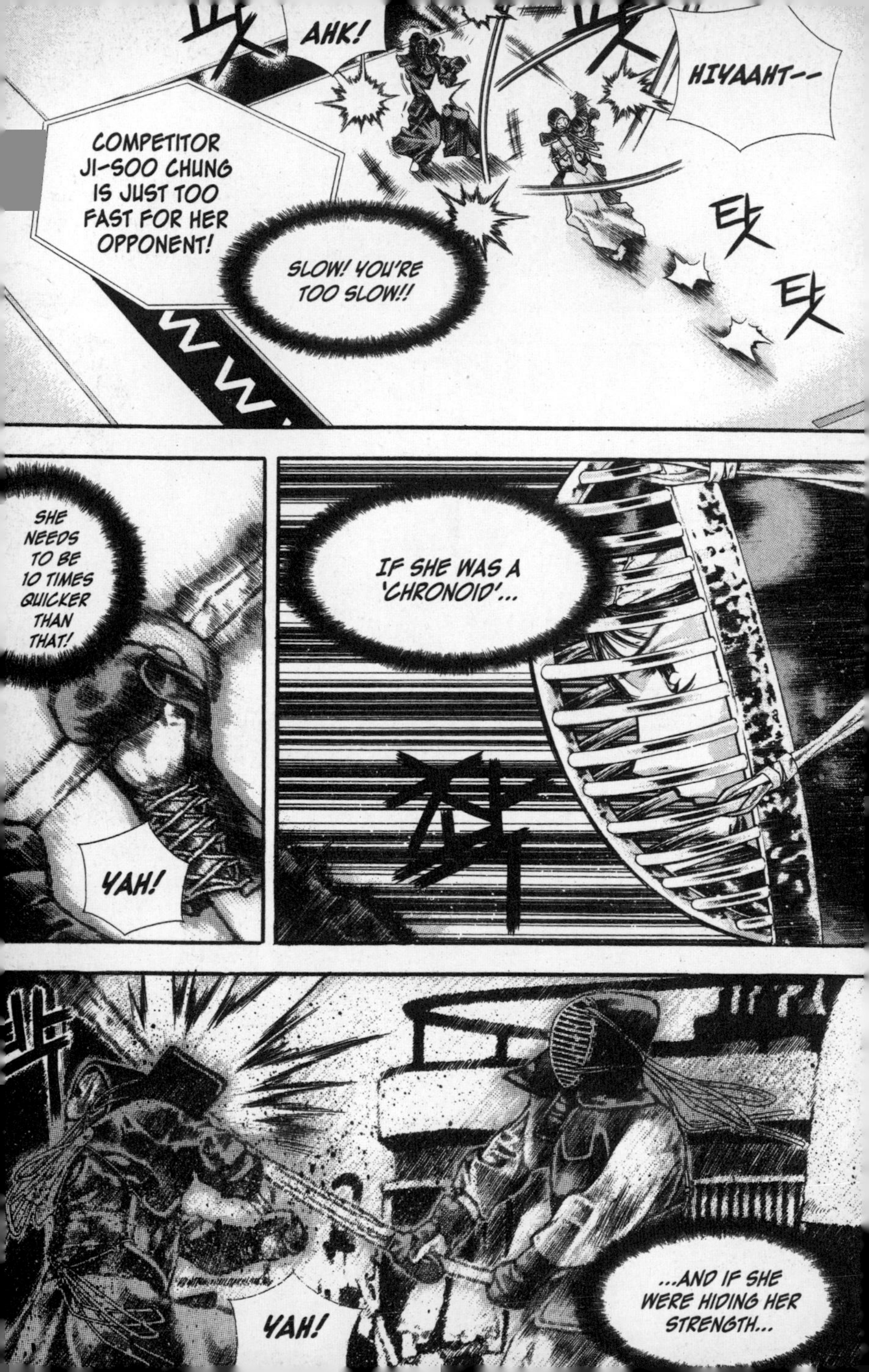
AHK!
HIYAAHT--
COMPETITOR JI-SOO CHUNG IS JUST TOO FAST FOR HER OPPONENT!
SLOW! YOU'RE TOO SLOW!!
탓
탓
SHE NEEDS TO BE 10 TIMES QUICKER THAN THAT!
YAH!
IF SHE WAS A 'CHRONOID'...
YAH!
...AND IF SHE WERE HIDING HER STRENGTH...

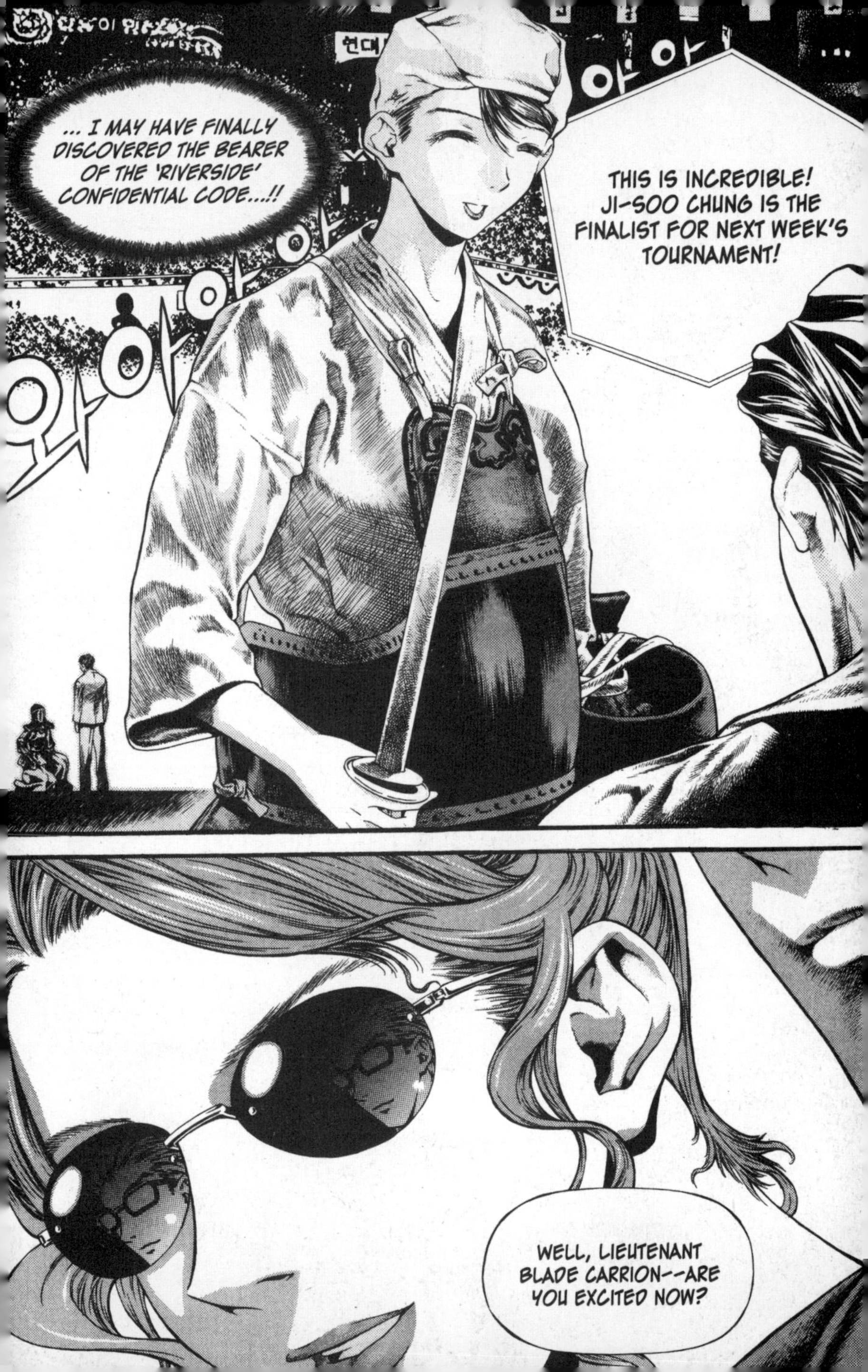
... I MAY HAVE FINALLY DISCOVERED THE BEARER OF THE 'RIVERSIDE' CONFIDENTIAL CODE...!!
THIS IS INCREDIBLE! JI-SOO CHUNG IS THE FINALIST FOR NEXT WEEK'S TOURNAMENT!
WELL, LIEUTENANT BLADE CARRION--ARE YOU EXCITED NOW?

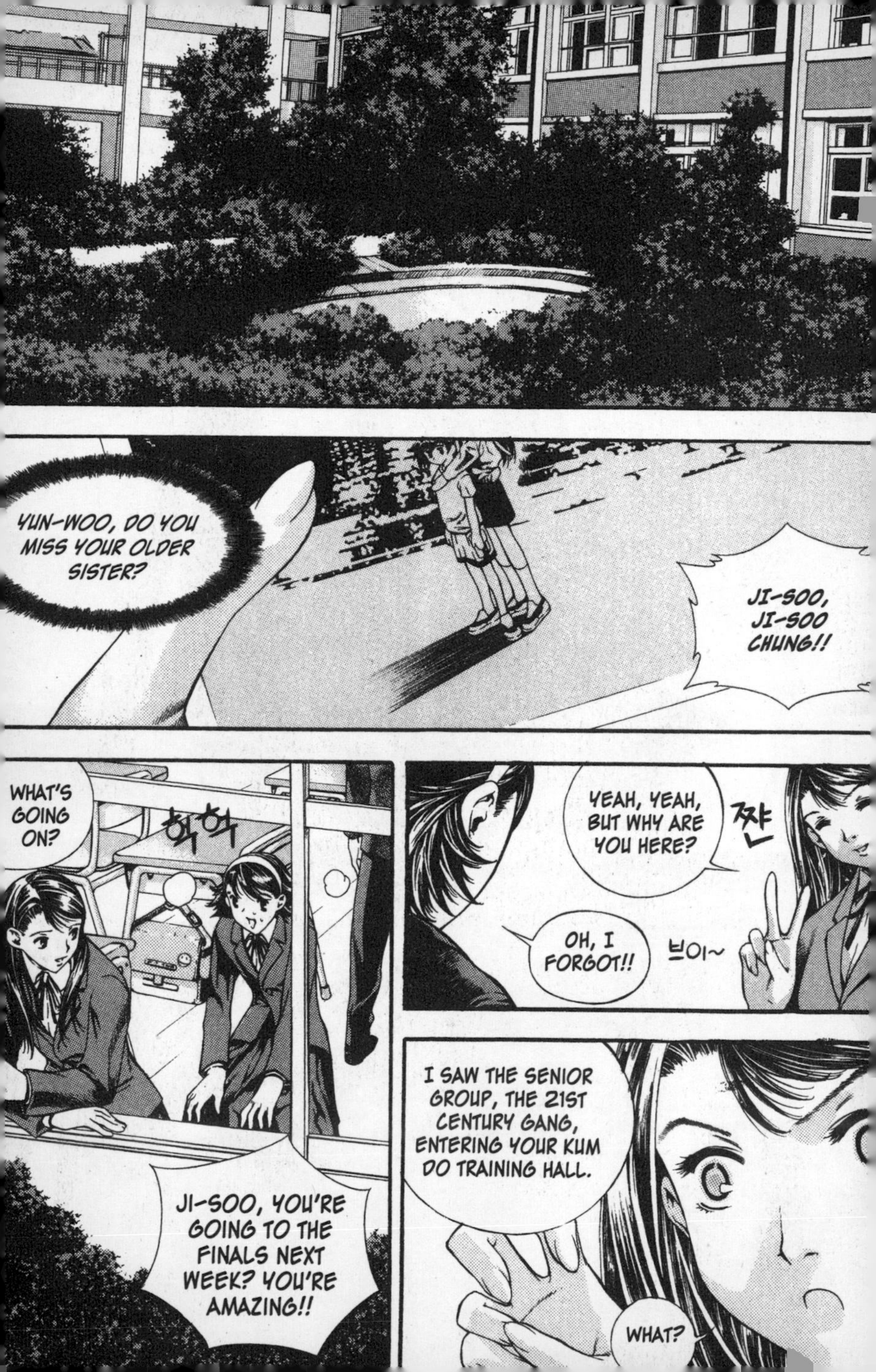
YUN-WOO, DO YOU MISS YOUR OLDER SISTER?
JI-SOO, JI-SOO CHUNG!!
WHAT'S GOING ON?
헉헉
JI-SOO, YOU'RE GOING TO THE FINALS NEXT WEEK? YOU'RE AMAZING!!
YEAH, YEAH, BUT WHY ARE YOU HERE?
짠
OH, I FORGOT!!
브이~
I SAW THE SENIOR GROUP, THE 21ST CENTURY GANG, ENTERING YOUR KUM DO TRAINING HALL.
WHAT?

TEAM CAPTAIN!

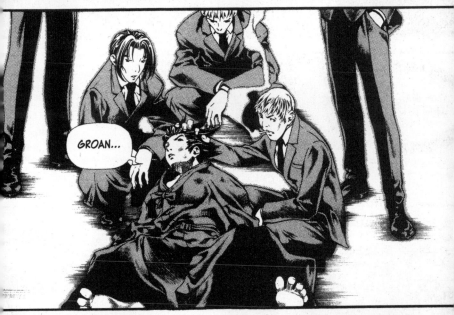

GROAN...

WHO ARE YOU...

HOW DARE YOU COME IN HERE?!

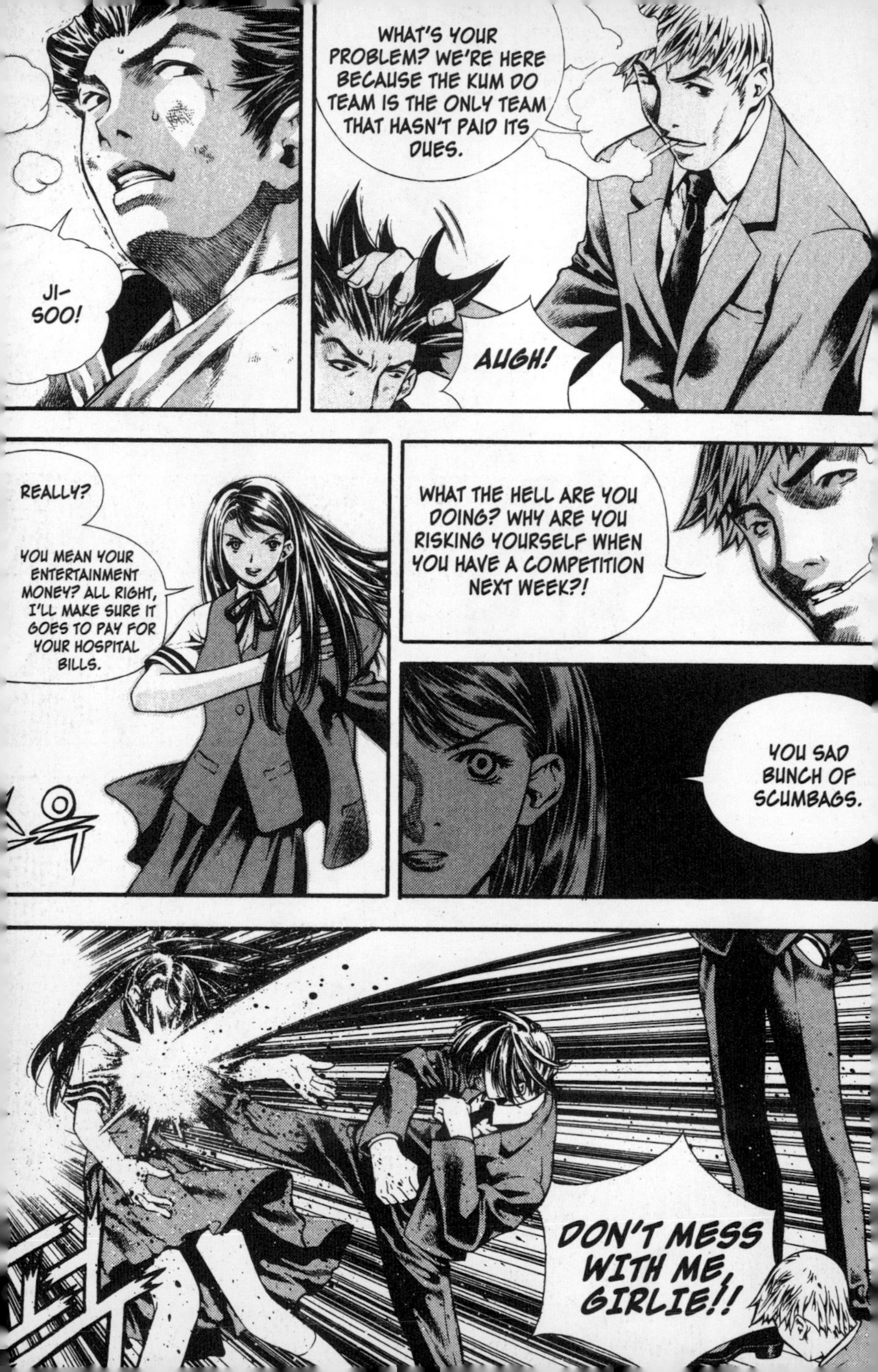
JI-SOO!
WHAT'S YOUR PROBLEM? WE'RE HERE BECAUSE THE KUM DO TEAM IS THE ONLY TEAM THAT HASN'T PAID ITS DUES.
AUGH!
REALLY?
YOU MEAN YOUR ENTERTAINMENT MONEY? ALL RIGHT, I'LL MAKE SURE IT GOES TO PAY FOR YOUR HOSPITAL BILLS.
WHAT THE HELL ARE YOU DOING? WHY ARE YOU RISKING YOURSELF WHEN YOU HAVE A COMPETITION NEXT WEEK?!
YOU SAD BUNCH OF SCUMBAGS.
DON'T MESS WITH ME, GIRLIE!!

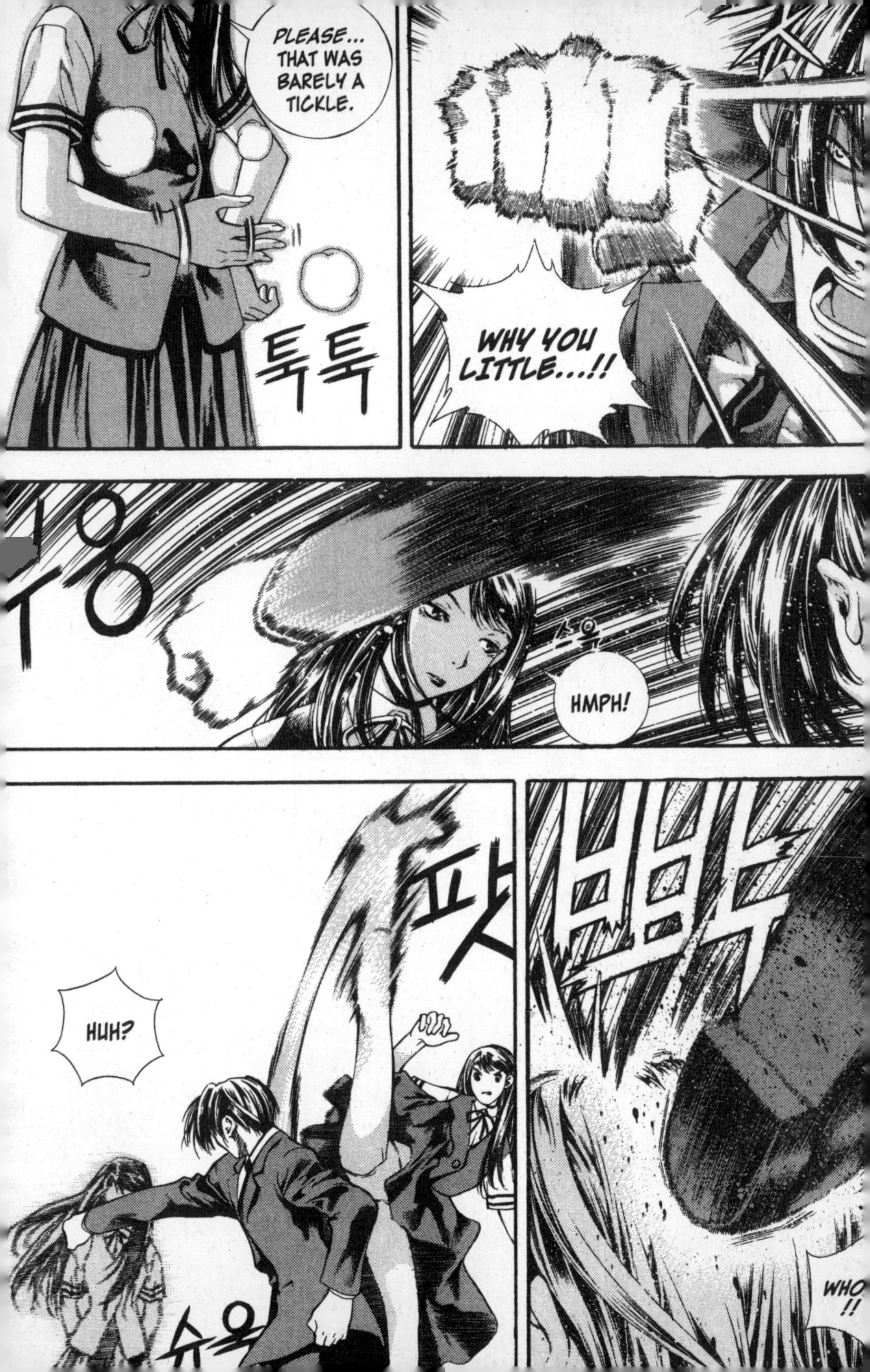
PLEASE... THAT WAS BARELY A TICKLE.
툭툭
WHY YOU LITTLE...!!
휘잉
스윽
HMPH!
HUH?
슈욱
팟
빠악
WHO !!

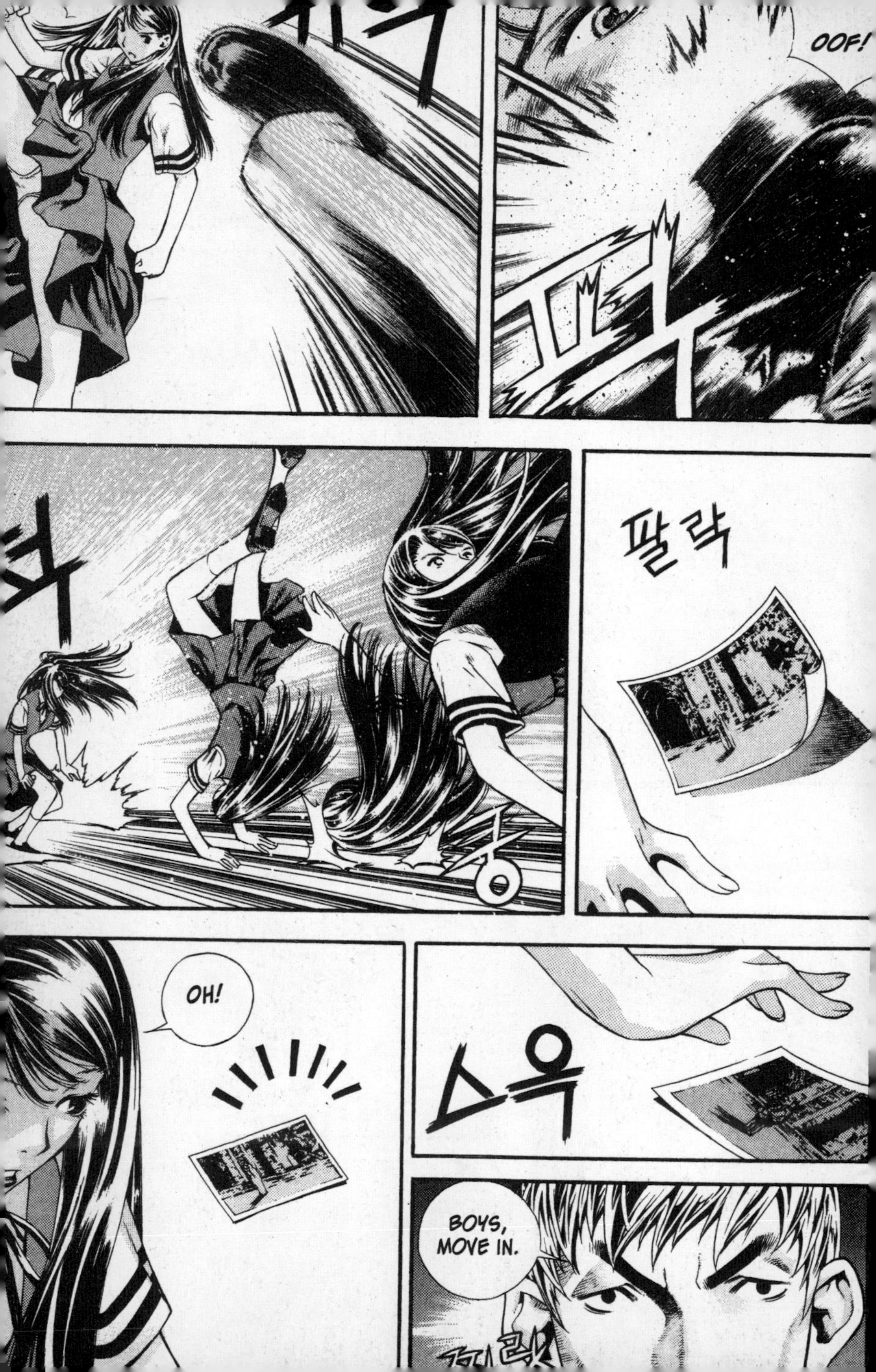
OOF!
퍽
팔락
OH!
스욱
BOYS, MOVE IN.

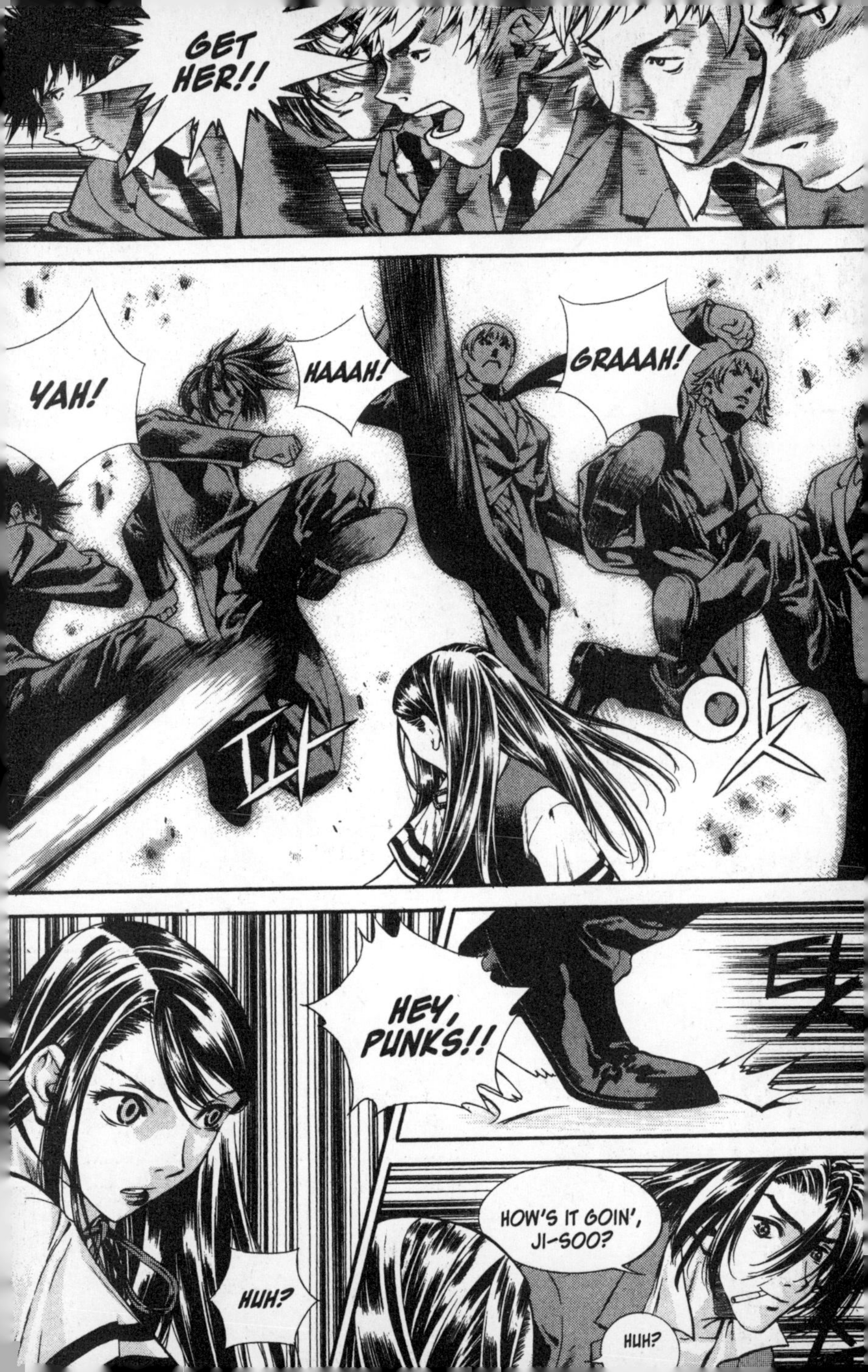
GET HER!!
YAH!
HAAAH!
GRAAAH!
HUH?
HEY, PUNKS!!
HOW'S IT GOIN', JI-SOO?
HUH?

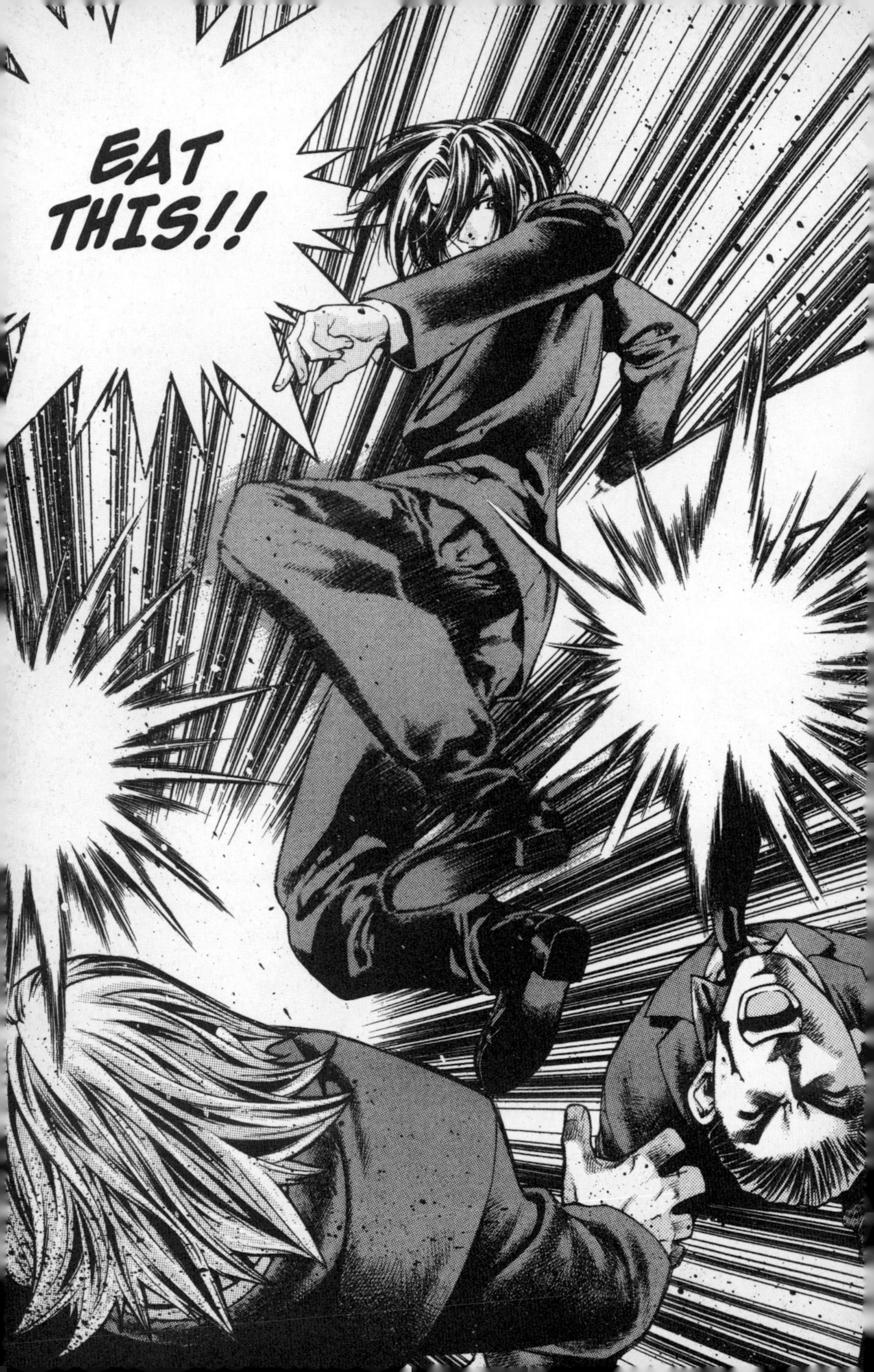
EAT THIS!!

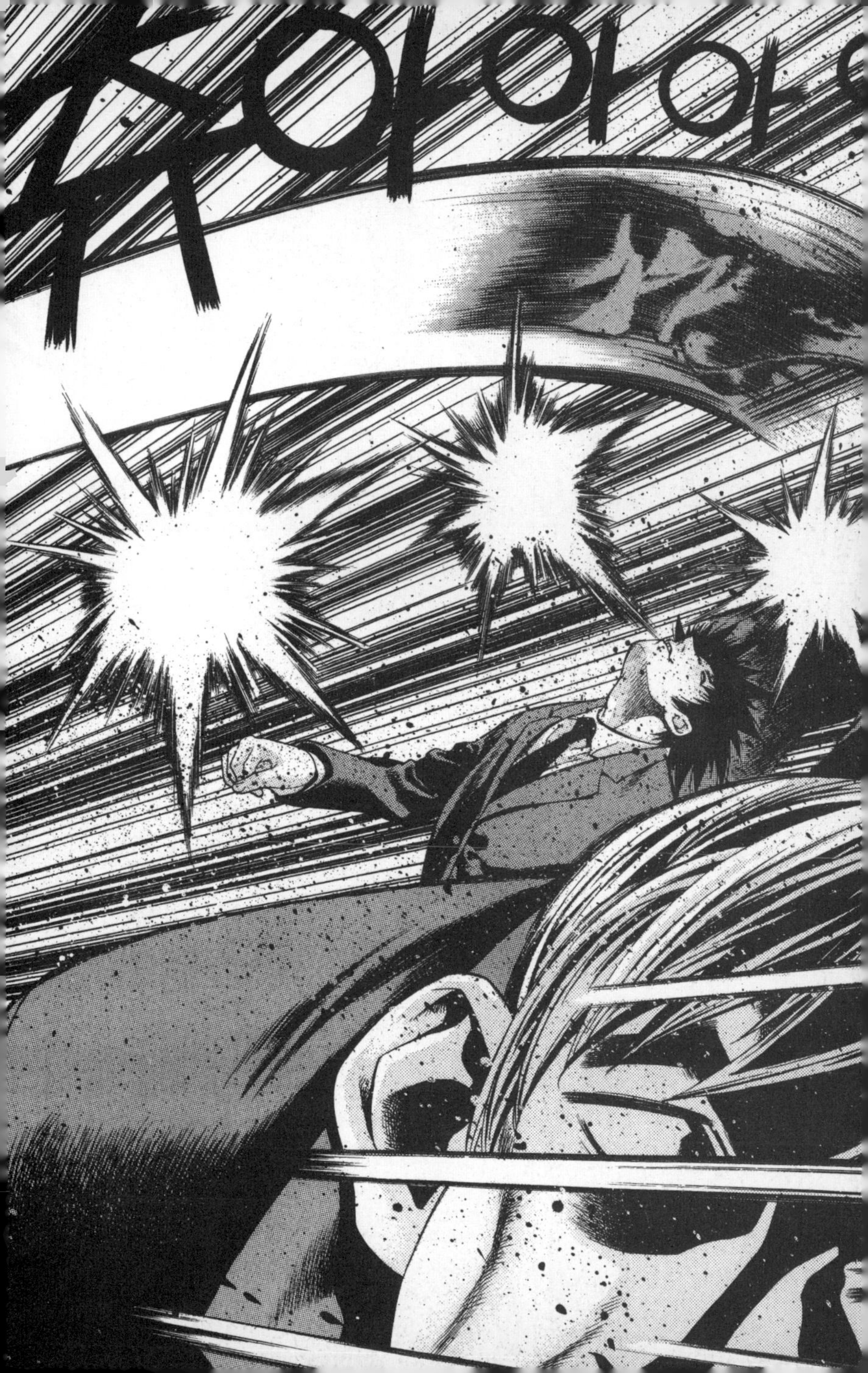
자아아아

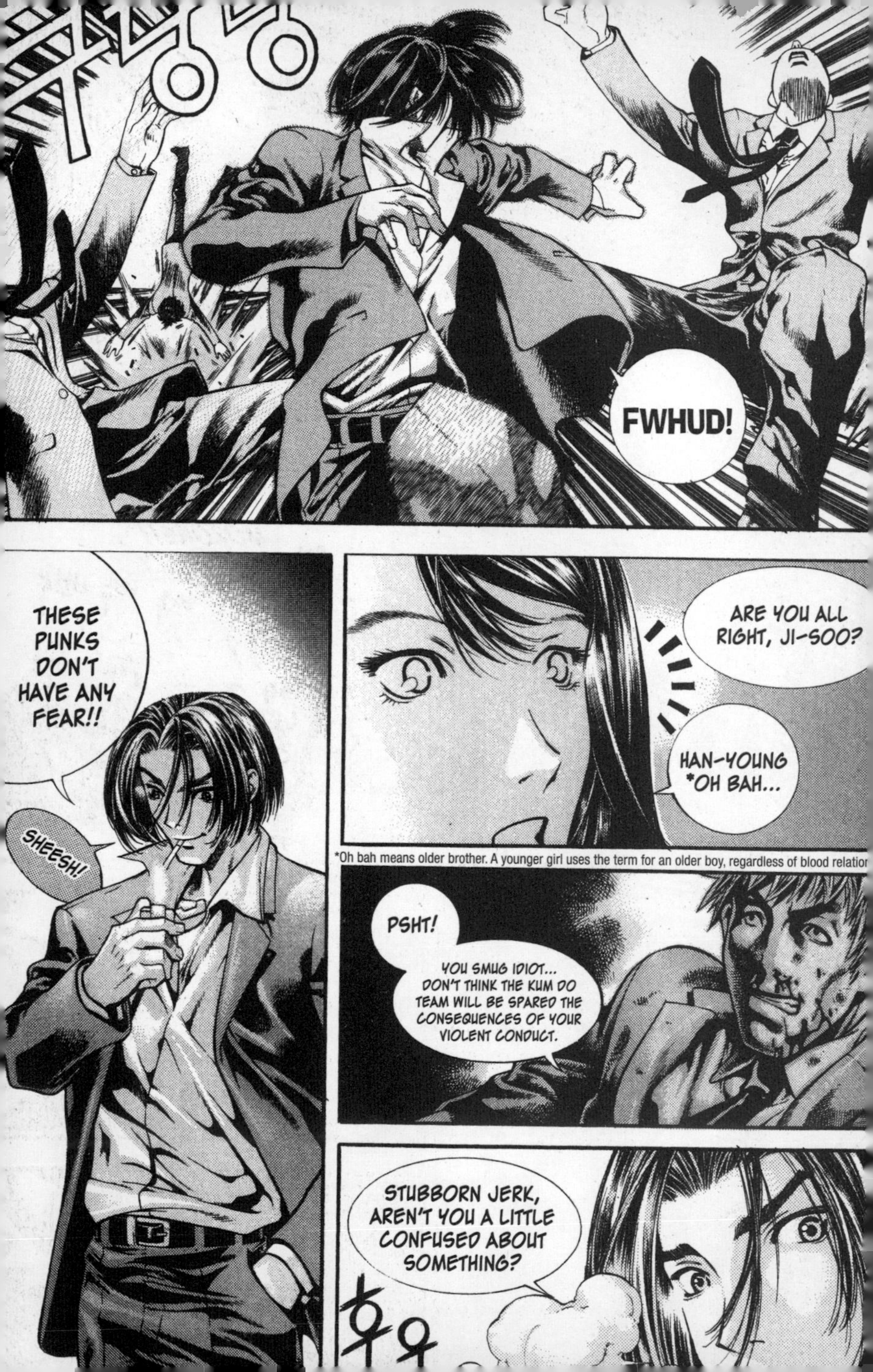
FWHUD!
THESE PUNKS DON'T HAVE ANY FEAR!!
SHEESH!
ARE YOU ALL RIGHT, JI-SOO?
HAN-YOUNG *OH BAH...
*Oh bah means older brother. A younger girl uses the term for an older boy, regardless of blood relation
PSHT!
YOU SMUG IDIOT... DON'T THINK THE KUM DO TEAM WILL BE SPARED THE CONSEQUENCES OF YOUR VIOLENT CONDUCT.
STUBBORN JERK, AREN'T YOU A LITTLE CONFUSED ABOUT SOMETHING?

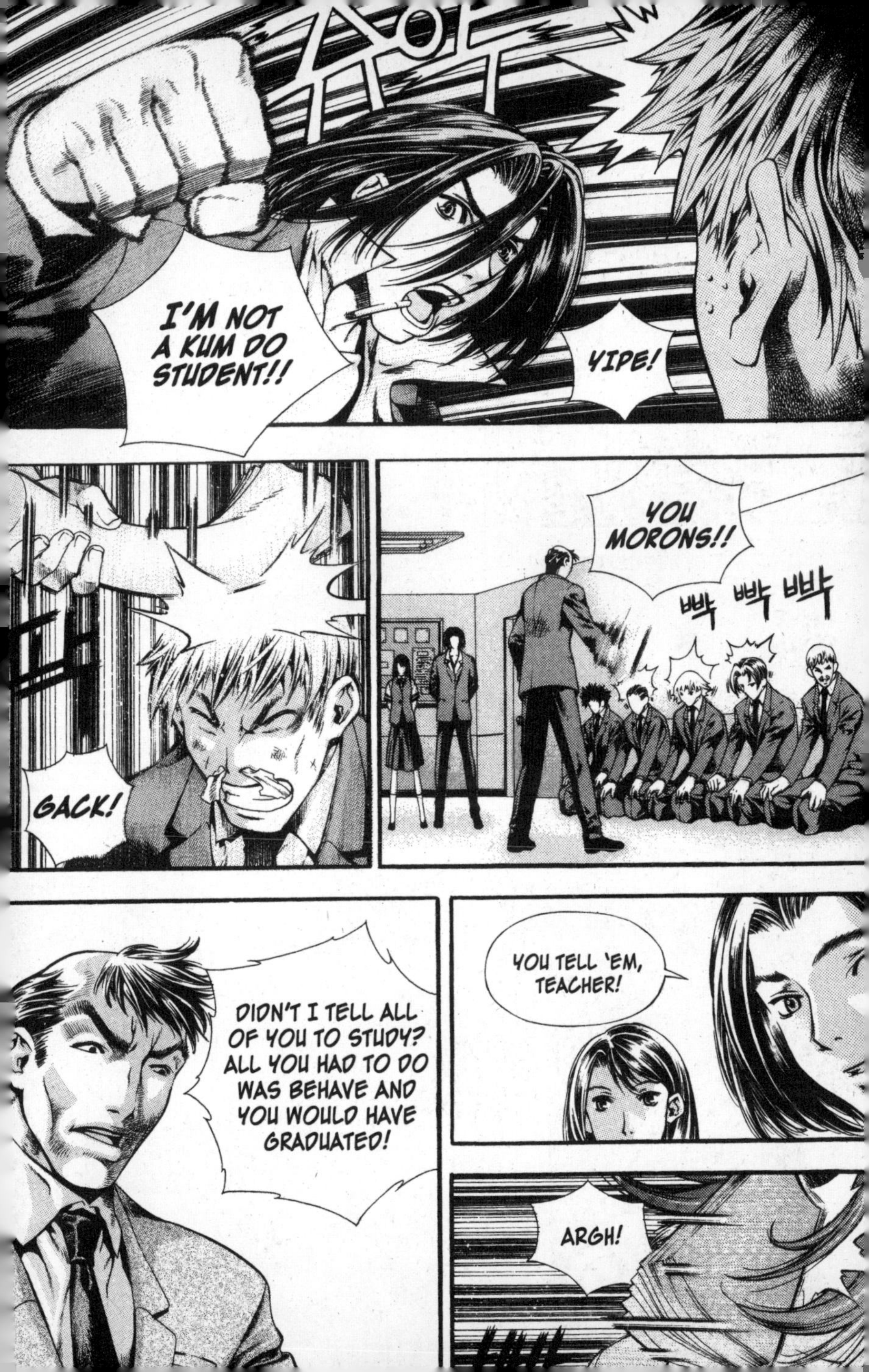
I'M NOT A KUM DO STUDENT!!
YIPE!
GACK!
YOU MORONS!!
빡 빡 빡
DIDN'T I TELL ALL OF YOU TO STUDY? ALL YOU HAD TO DO WAS BEHAVE AND YOU WOULD HAVE GRADUATED!
YOU TELL 'EM, TEACHER!
ARGH!

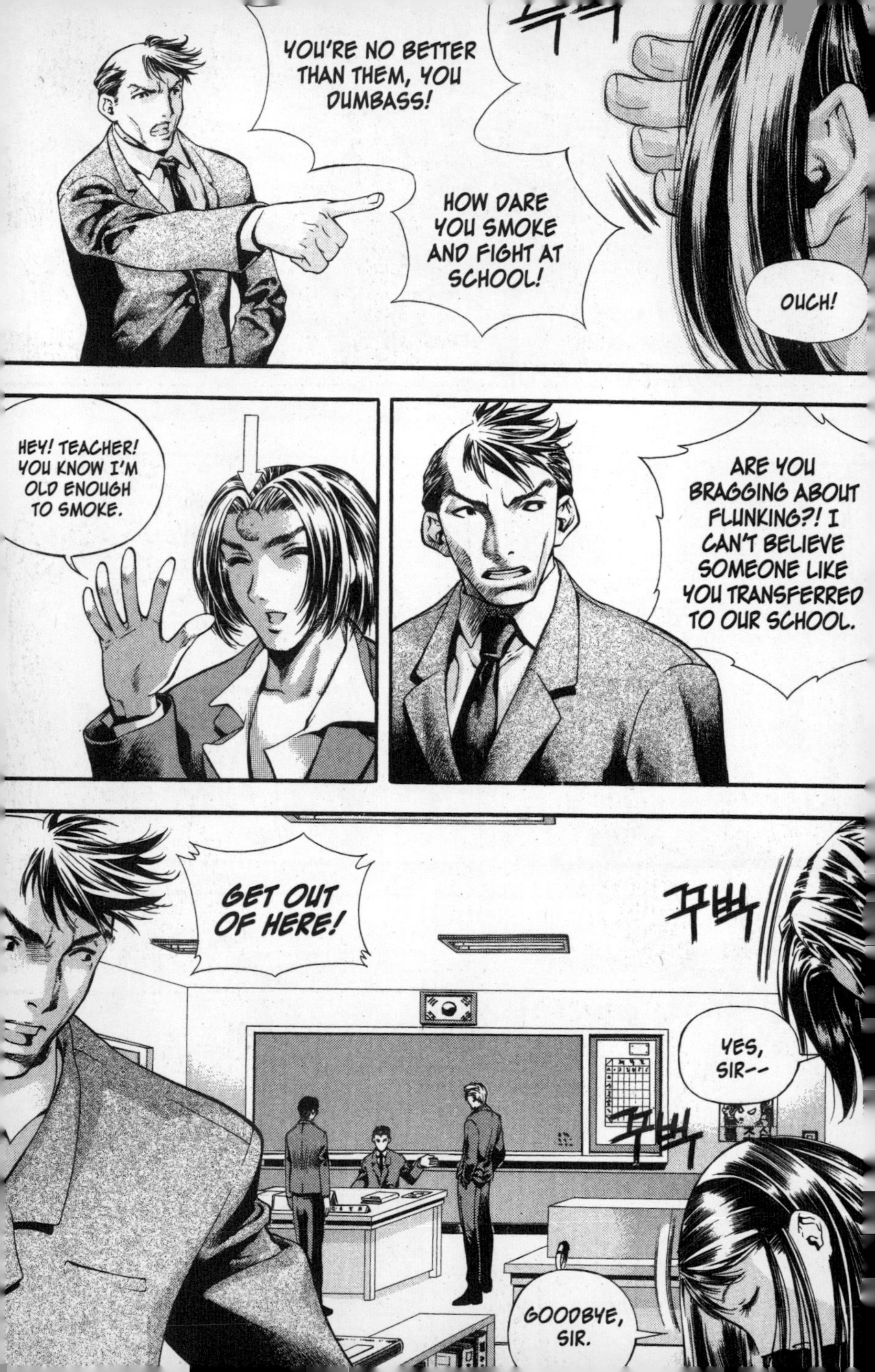
YOU'RE NO BETTER THAN THEM, YOU DUMBASS!
HOW DARE YOU SMOKE AND FIGHT AT SCHOOL!
OUCH!
HEY! TEACHER! YOU KNOW I'M OLD ENOUGH TO SMOKE.
ARE YOU BRAGGING ABOUT FLUNKING?! I CAN'T BELIEVE SOMEONE LIKE YOU TRANSFERRED TO OUR SCHOOL.
GET OUT OF HERE!
꾸벅
YES, SIR--
꾸벅
GOODBYE, SIR.

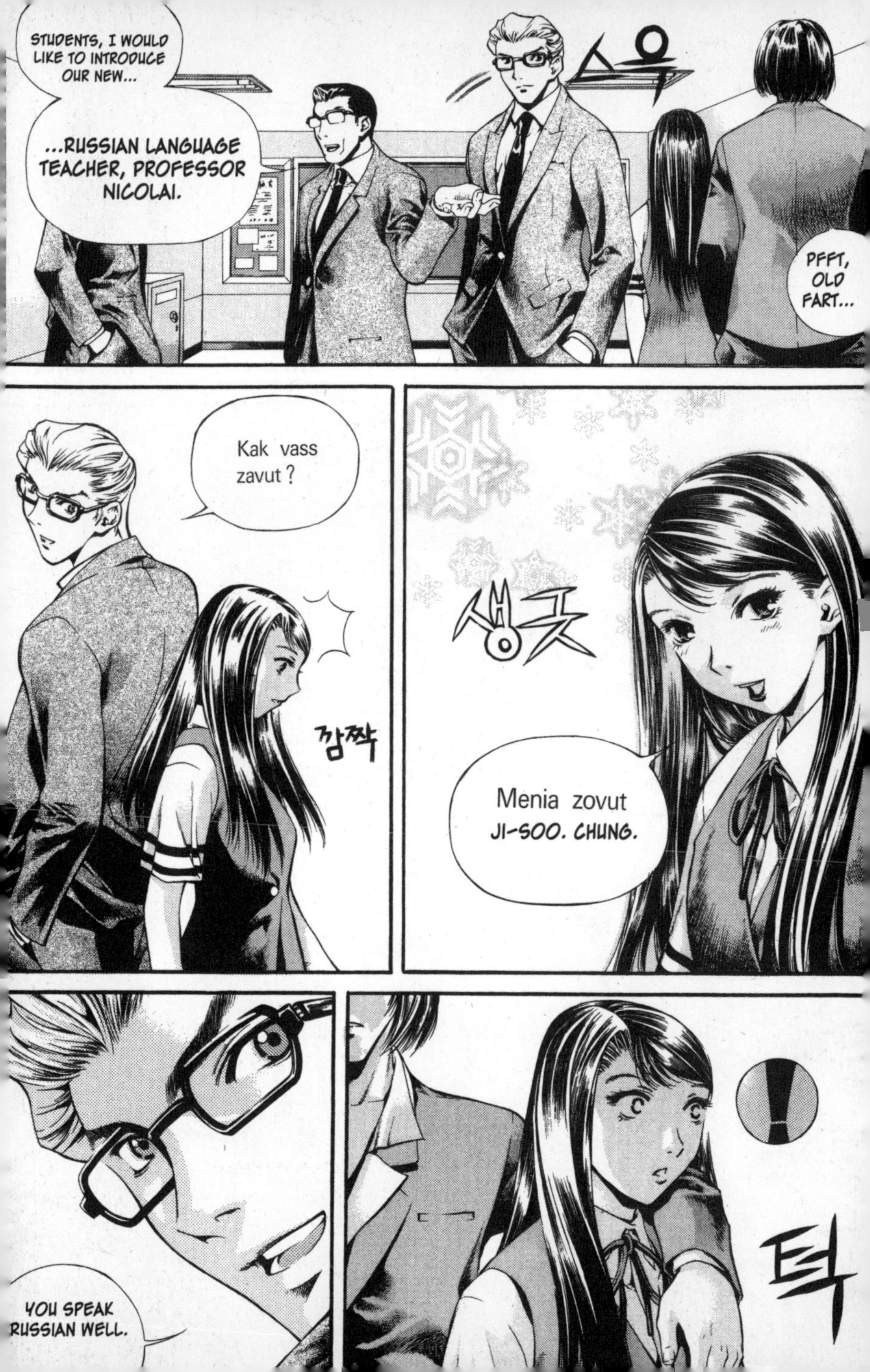
STUDENTS, I WOULD LIKE TO INTRODUCE OUR NEW...
...RUSSIAN LANGUAGE TEACHER, PROFESSOR NICOLAI.
스윽
PFFT, OLD FART...
Kak vass zavut?
깜짝
생긋
Menia zovut JI-SOO. CHUNG.
YOU SPEAK RUSSIAN WELL.
턱

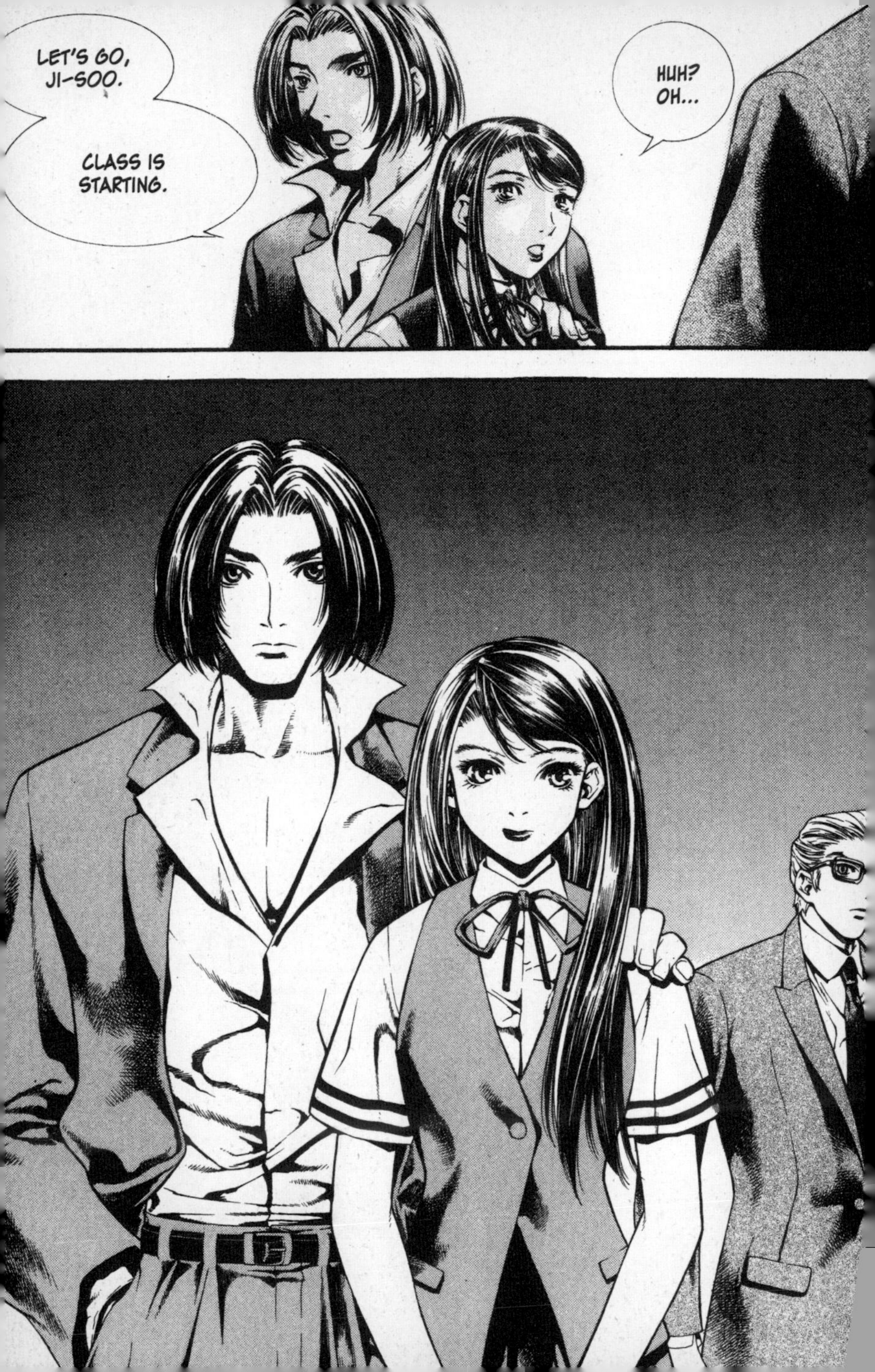
LET'S GO, JI-SOO.
CLASS IS STARTING.
HUH? OH...

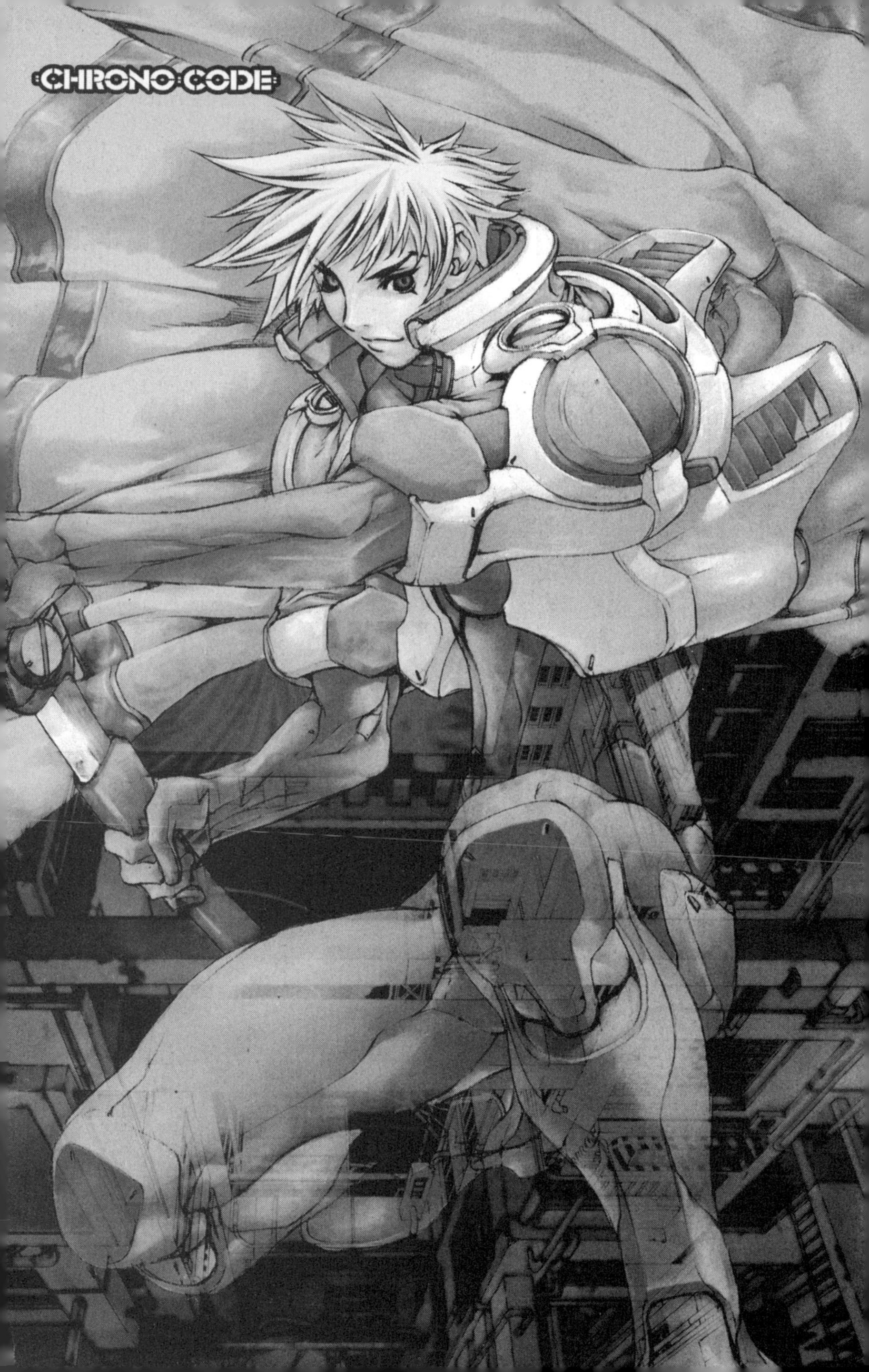
CHRONO CODE

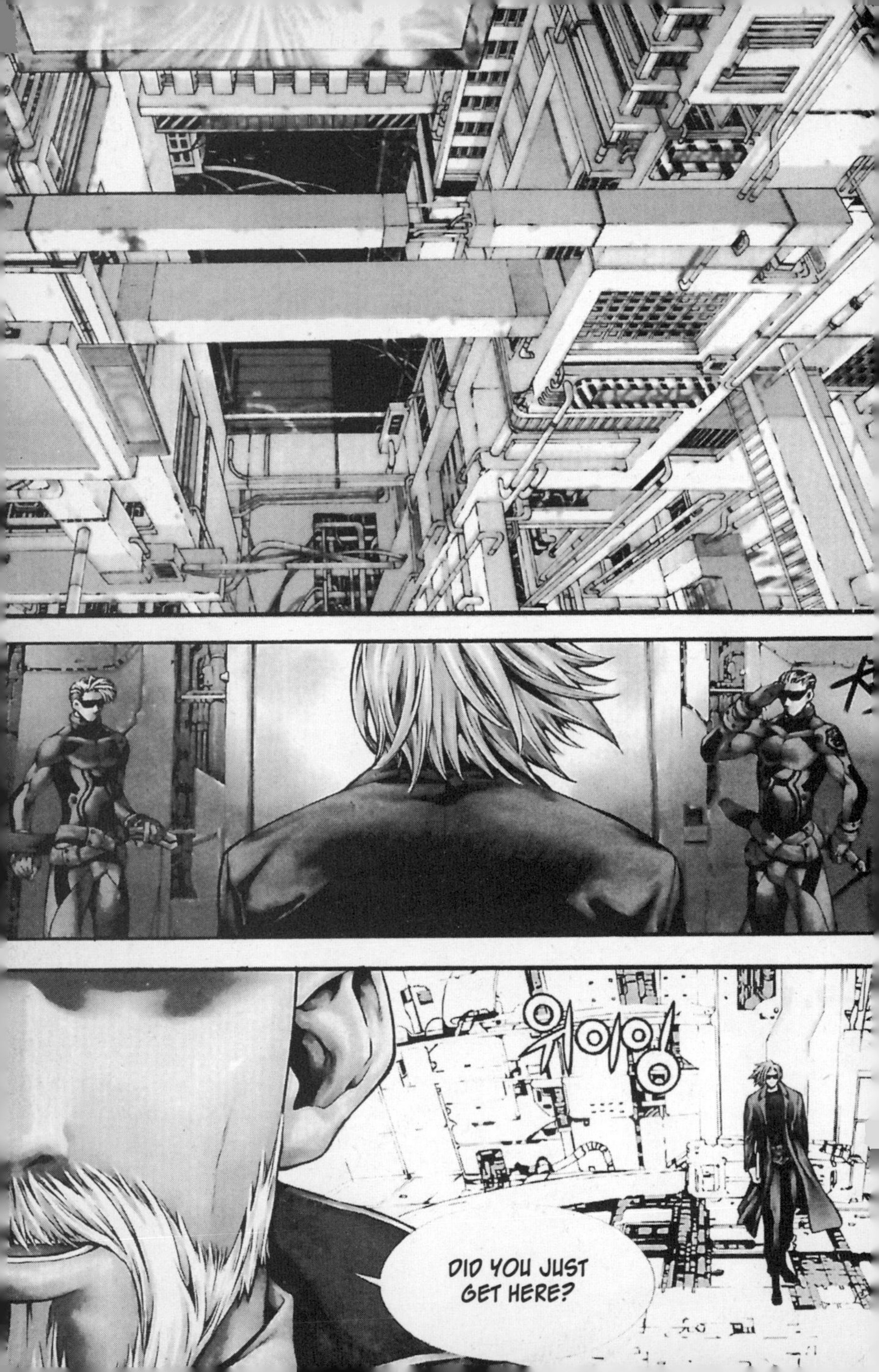
DID YOU JUST
GET HERE?

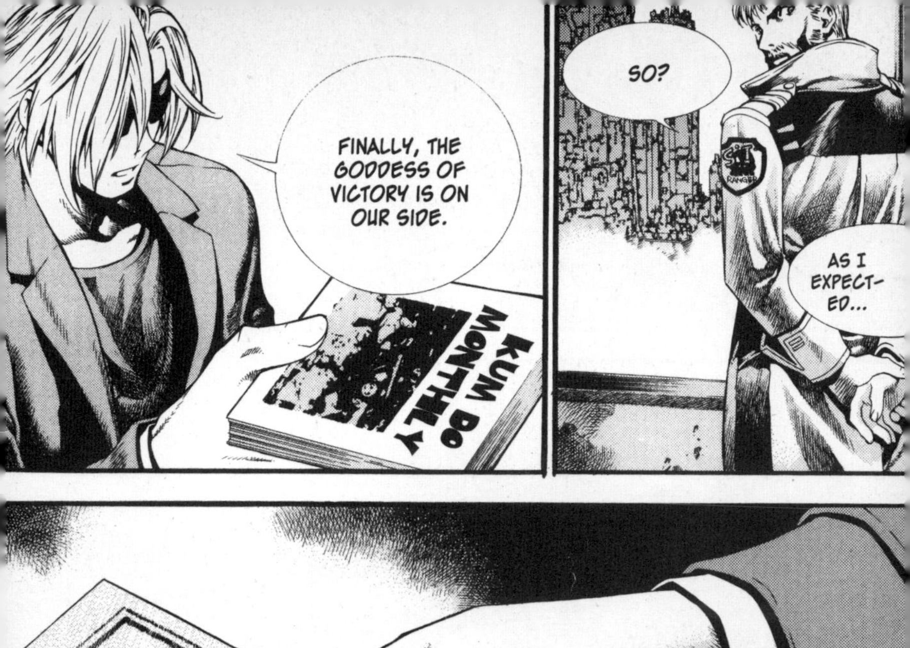
FINALLY, THE GODDESS OF VICTORY IS ON OUR SIDE.
KUM DO MONTHLY
SO?
AS I EXPECTED...
...THE NEWSPAPER STORY HAS CHANGED.

Newspaper below: Ji-Soo Chung Missing

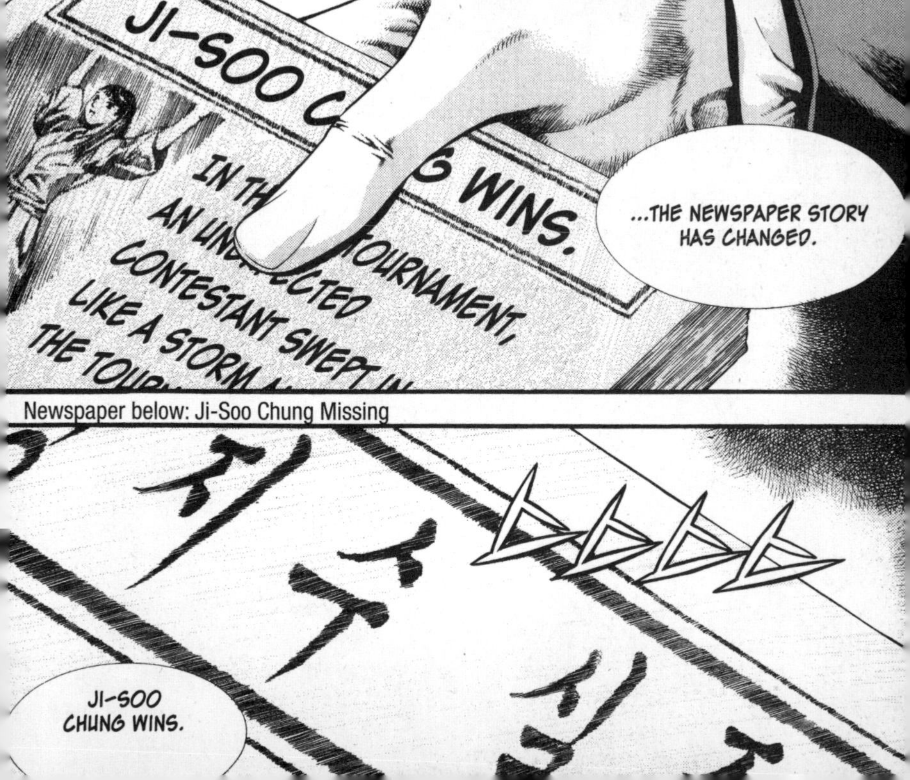
JI-SOO CHUNG WINS.

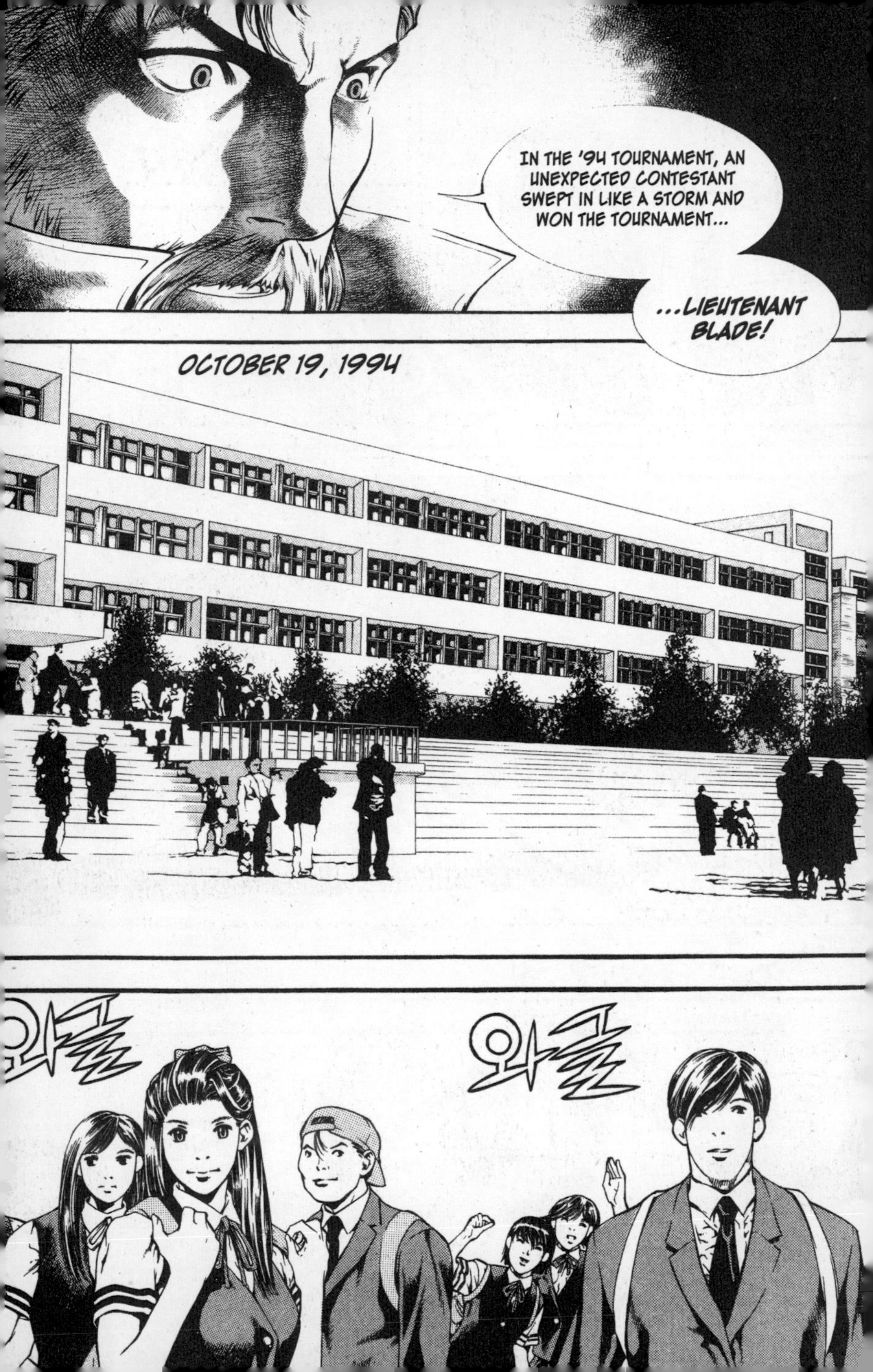
IN THE '94 TOURNAMENT, AN UNEXPECTED CONTESTANT SWEPT IN LIKE A STORM AND WON THE TOURNAMENT...
...LIEUTENANT BLADE!
OCTOBER 19, 1994
와글
와글

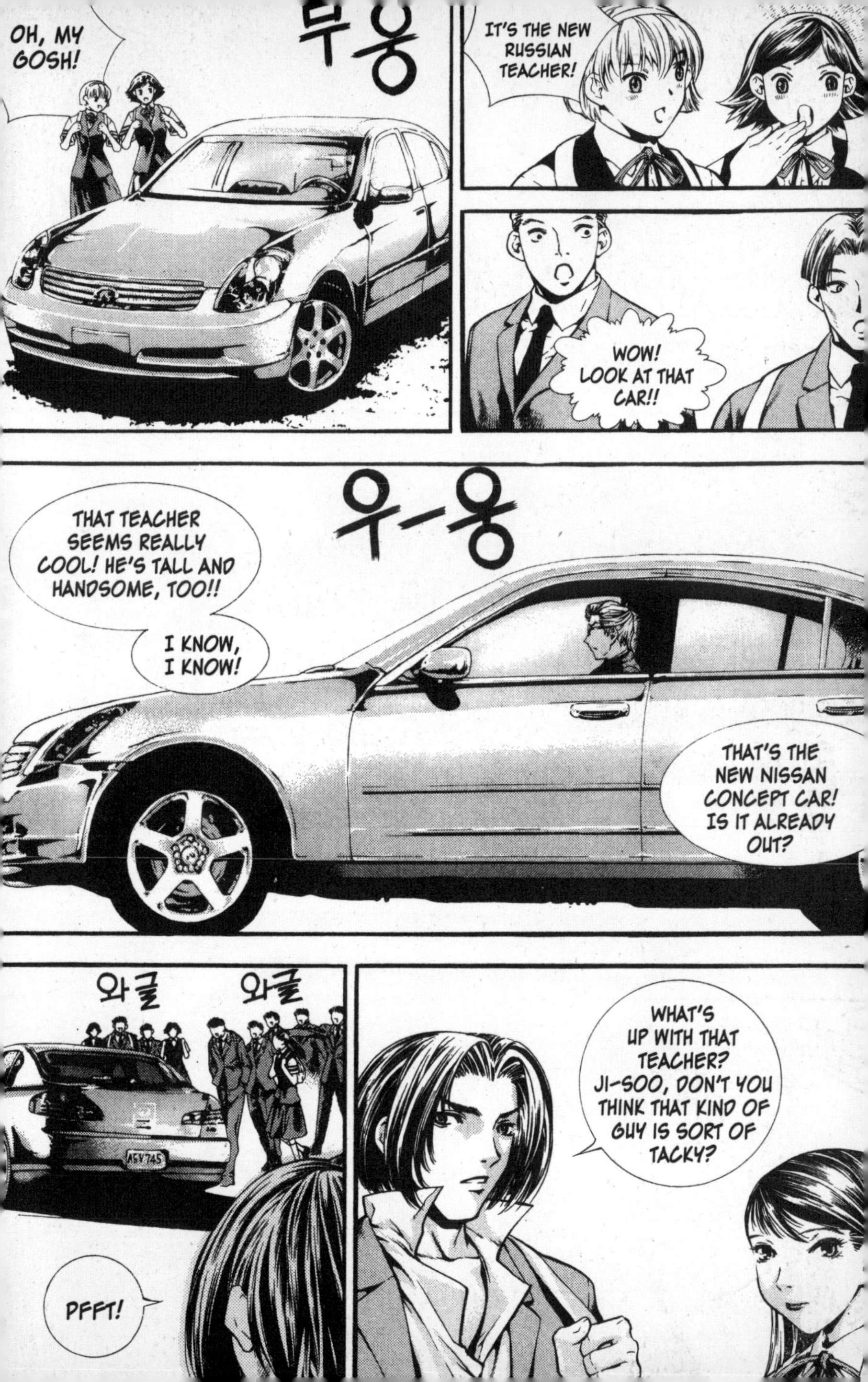
OH, MY GOSH!
무웅
IT'S THE NEW RUSSIAN TEACHER!
WOW! LOOK AT THAT CAR!!
우-웅
THAT TEACHER SEEMS REALLY COOL! HE'S TALL AND HANDSOME, TOO!!
I KNOW, I KNOW!
THAT'S THE NEW NISSAN CONCEPT CAR! IS IT ALREADY OUT?
와글 와글
WHAT'S UP WITH THAT TEACHER? JI-SOO, DON'T YOU THINK THAT KIND OF GUY IS SORT OF TACKY?
PFFT!

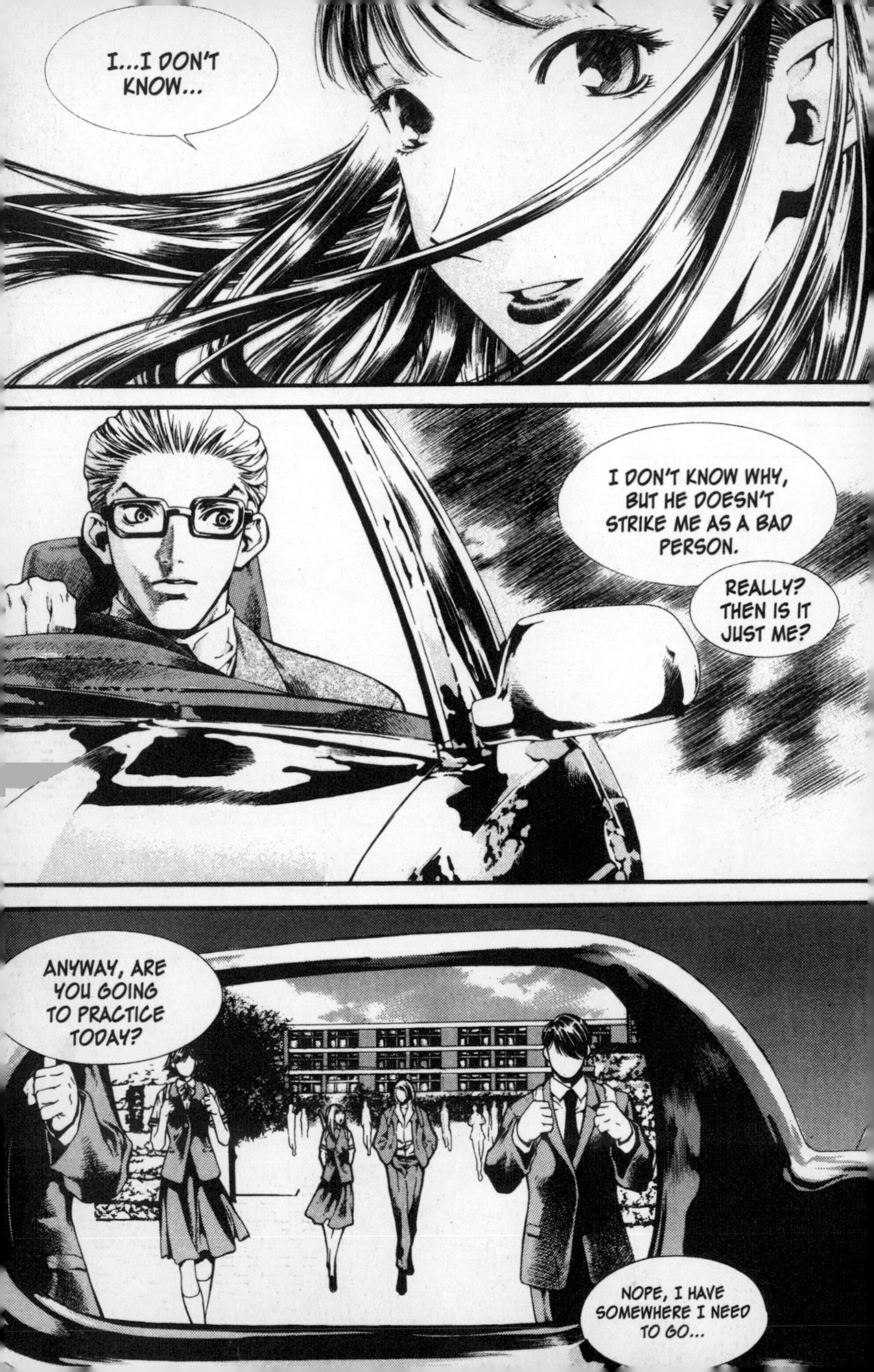
I...I DON'T KNOW...
I DON'T KNOW WHY, BUT HE DOESN'T STRIKE ME AS A BAD PERSON.
REALLY? THEN IS IT JUST ME?
ANYWAY, ARE YOU GOING TO PRACTICE TODAY?
NOPE, I HAVE SOMEWHERE I NEED TO GO...

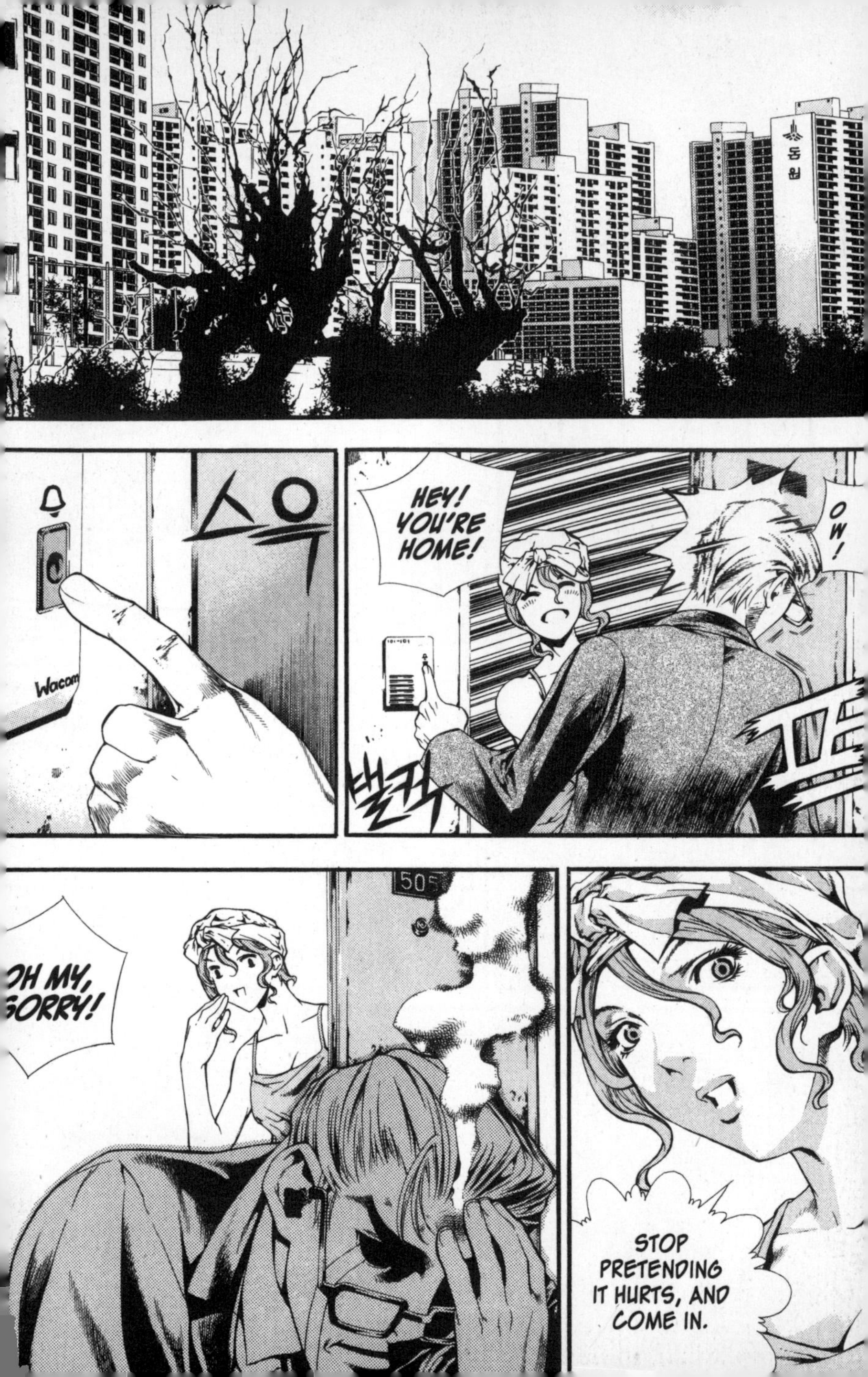
스윽
Wacom
HEY! YOU'RE HOME!
OW!
OH MY, SORRY!
505
STOP PRETENDING IT HURTS, AND COME IN.

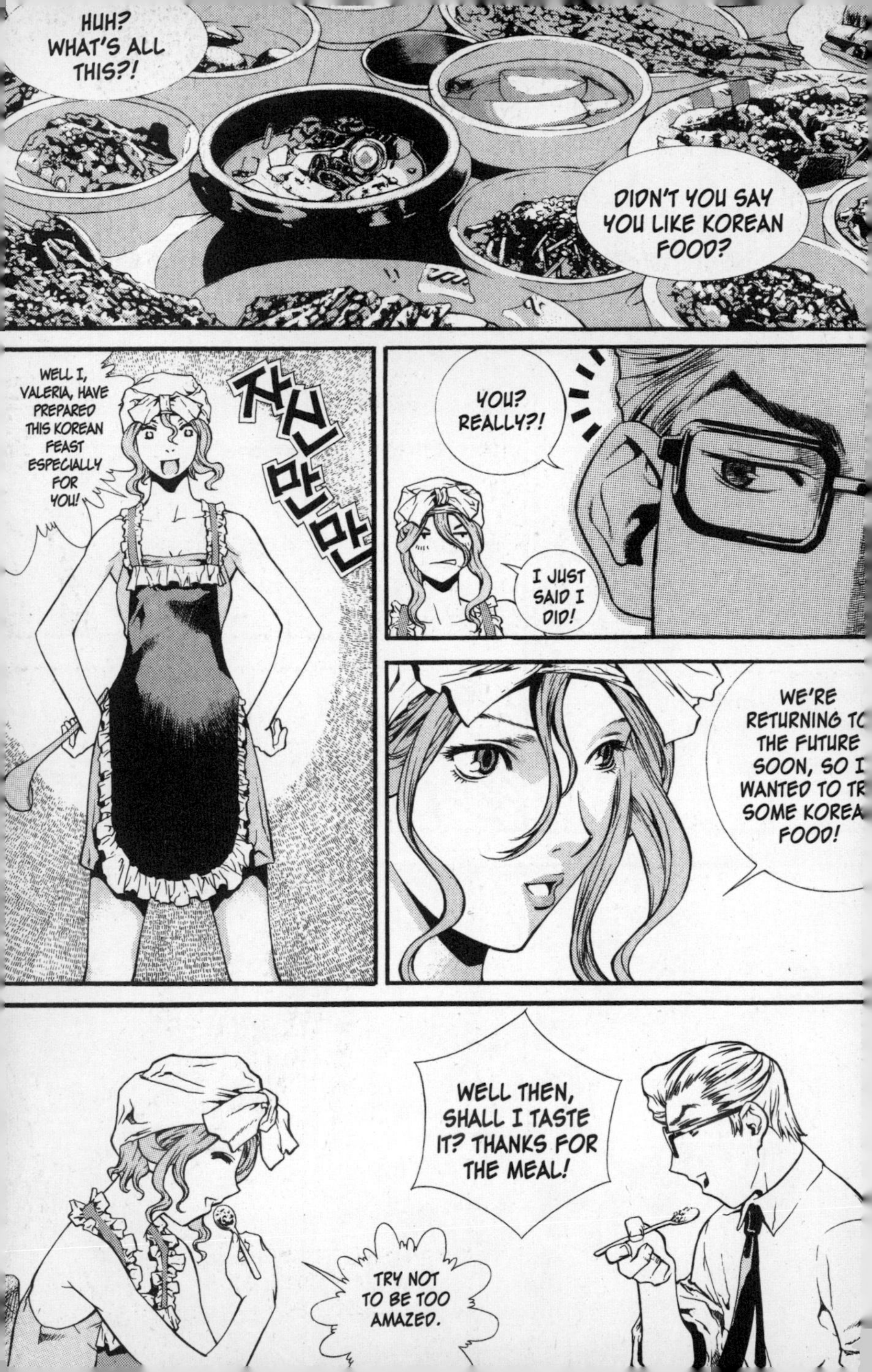
HUH? WHAT'S ALL THIS?!
DIDN'T YOU SAY YOU LIKE KOREAN FOOD?
WELL I, VALERIA, HAVE PREPARED THIS KOREAN FEAST ESPECIALLY FOR YOU!
자신만만
YOU? REALLY?!
I JUST SAID I DID!
WE'RE RETURNING TO THE FUTURE SOON, SO I WANTED TO TRY SOME KOREAN FOOD!
WELL THEN, SHALL I TASTE IT? THANKS FOR THE MEAL!
TRY NOT TO BE TOO AMAZED.

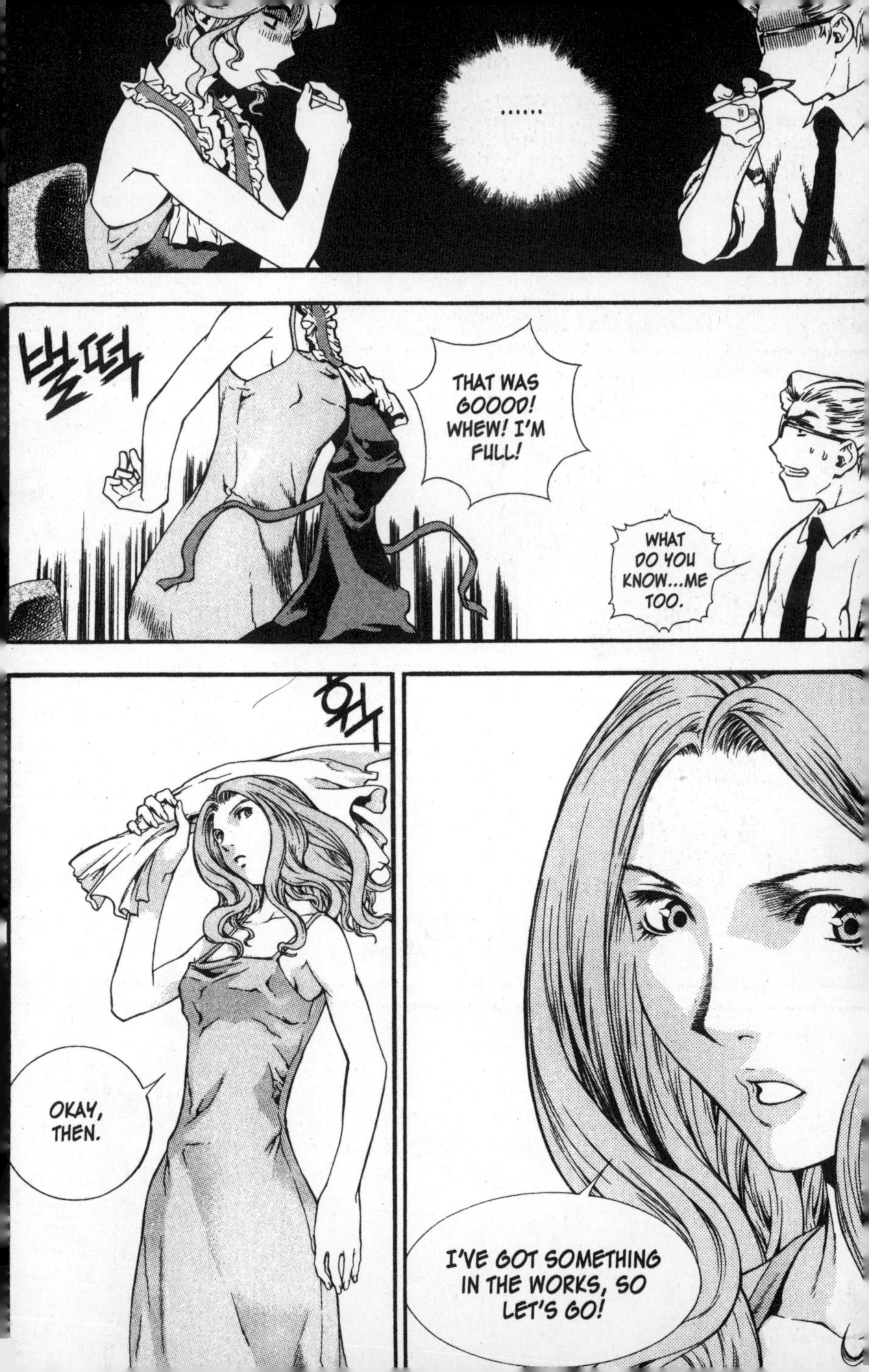
......
발딱
THAT WAS GOOOD! WHEW! I'M FULL!
WHAT DO YOU KNOW...ME TOO.
OKAY, THEN.
I'VE GOT SOMETHING IN THE WORKS, SO LET'S GO!

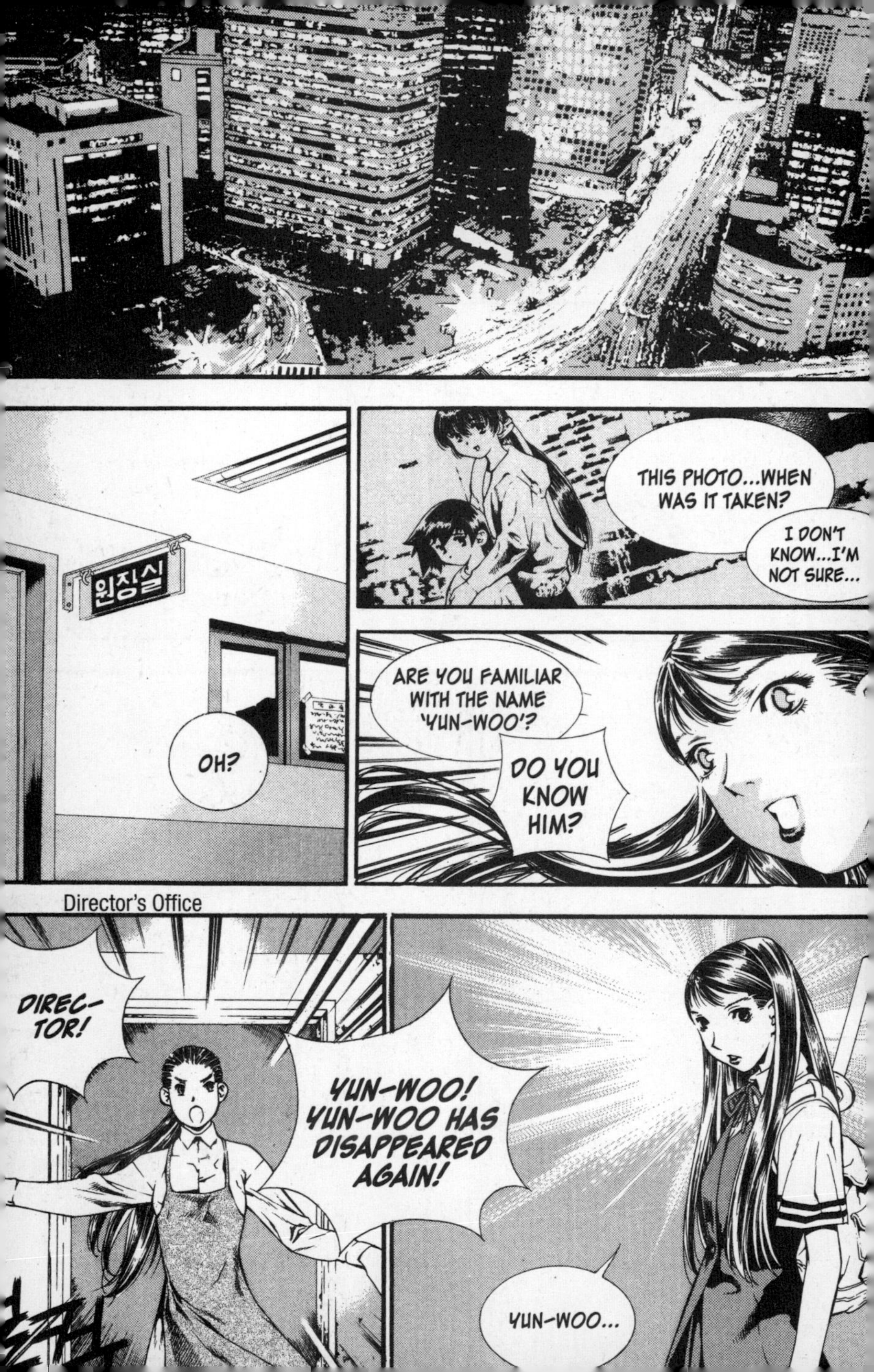
원장실
OH?
THIS PHOTO...WHEN WAS IT TAKEN?
I DON'T KNOW...I'M NOT SURE...
ARE YOU FAMILIAR WITH THE NAME 'YUN-WOO'?
DO YOU KNOW HIM?
Director's Office
DIREC-TOR!
YUN-WOO! YUN-WOO HAS DISAPPEARED AGAIN!
YUN-WOO...

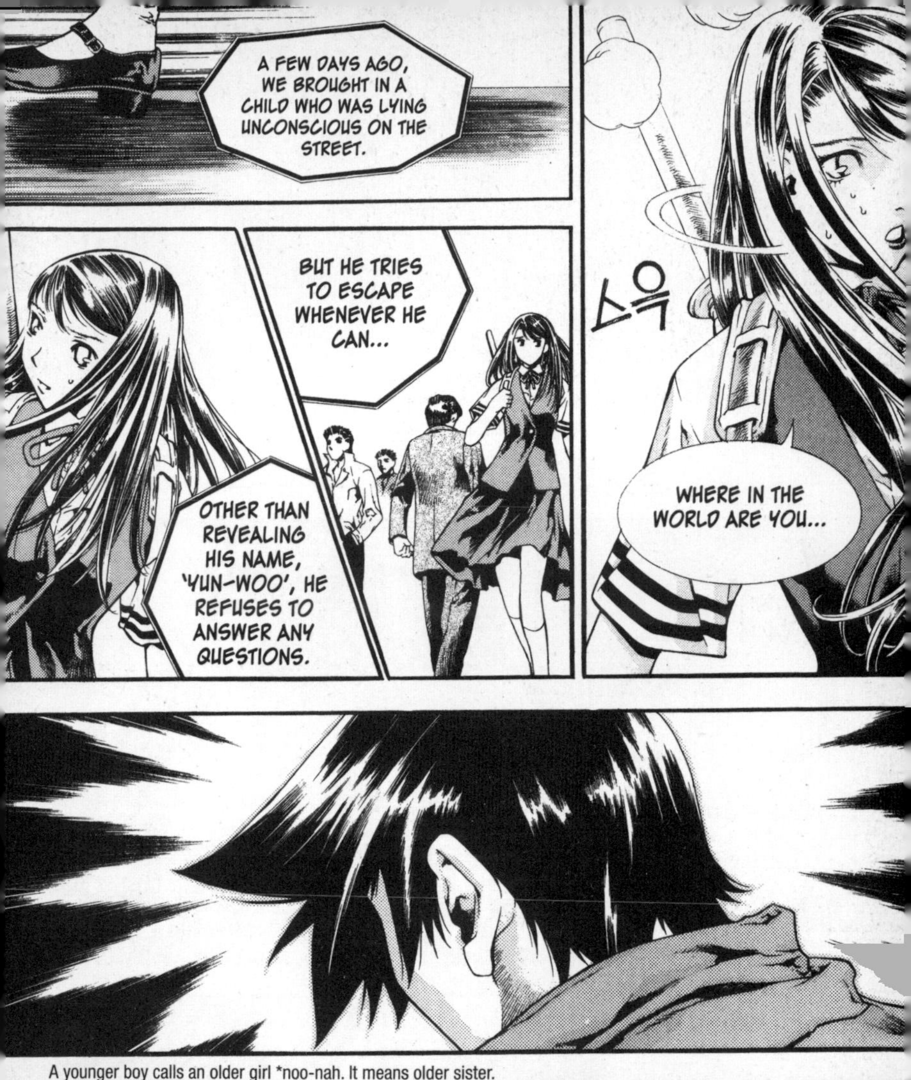
A FEW DAYS AGO, WE BROUGHT IN A CHILD WHO WAS LYING UNCONSCIOUS ON THE STREET.
BUT HE TRIES TO ESCAPE WHENEVER HE CAN...
OTHER THAN REVEALING HIS NAME, 'YUN-WOO', HE REFUSES TO ANSWER ANY QUESTIONS.
스윽
WHERE IN THE WORLD ARE YOU...

A younger boy calls an older girl *noo-nah. It means older sister.

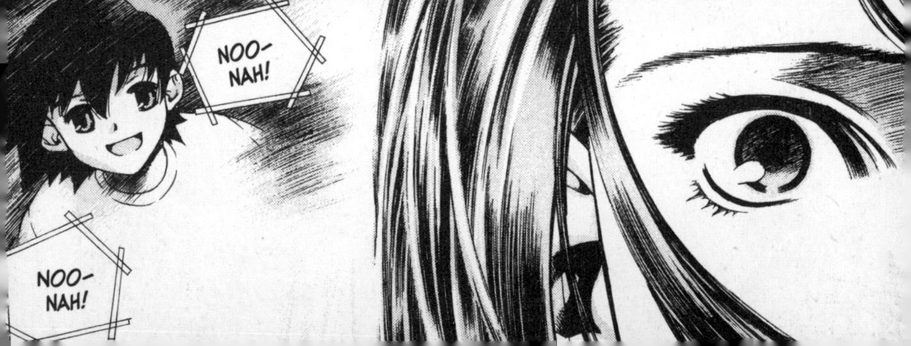
NOO-NAH!
NOO-NAH!

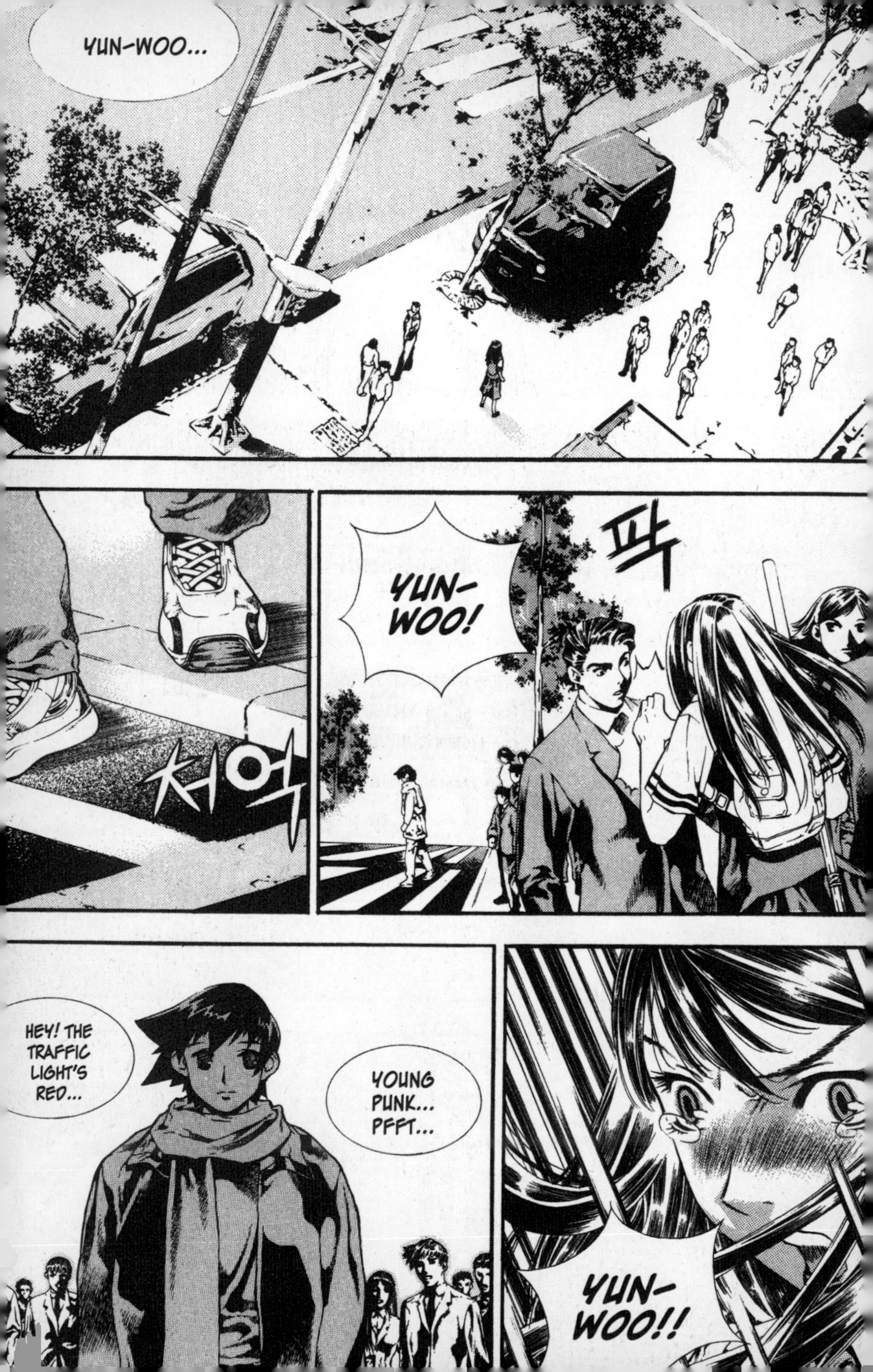
YUN-WOO...
처억
YUN-WOO!
팍
HEY! THE TRAFFIC LIGHT'S RED...
YOUNG PUNK... PFFT...
YUN-WOO!!

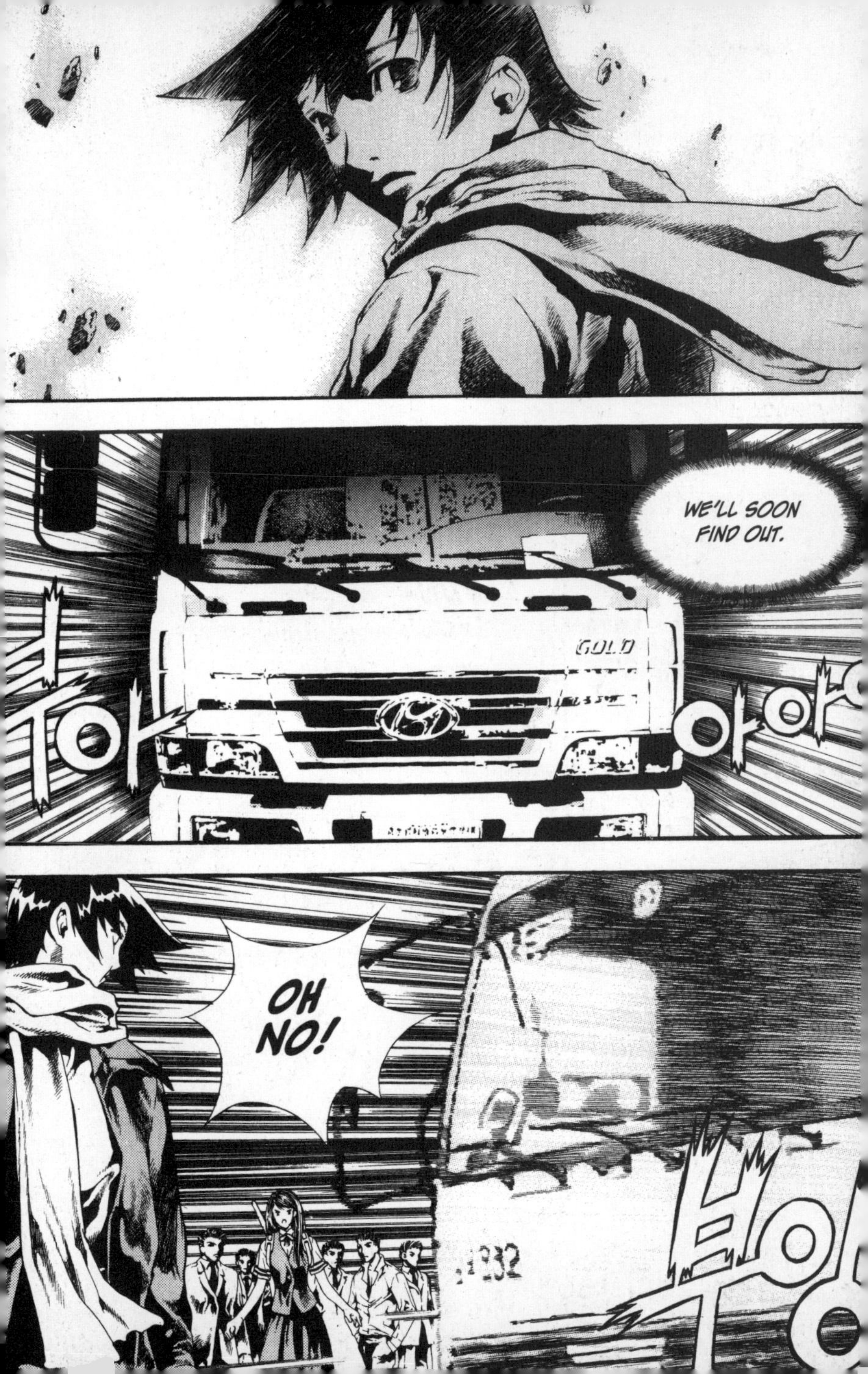
WE'LL SOON FIND OUT.
GOLD
OH NO!

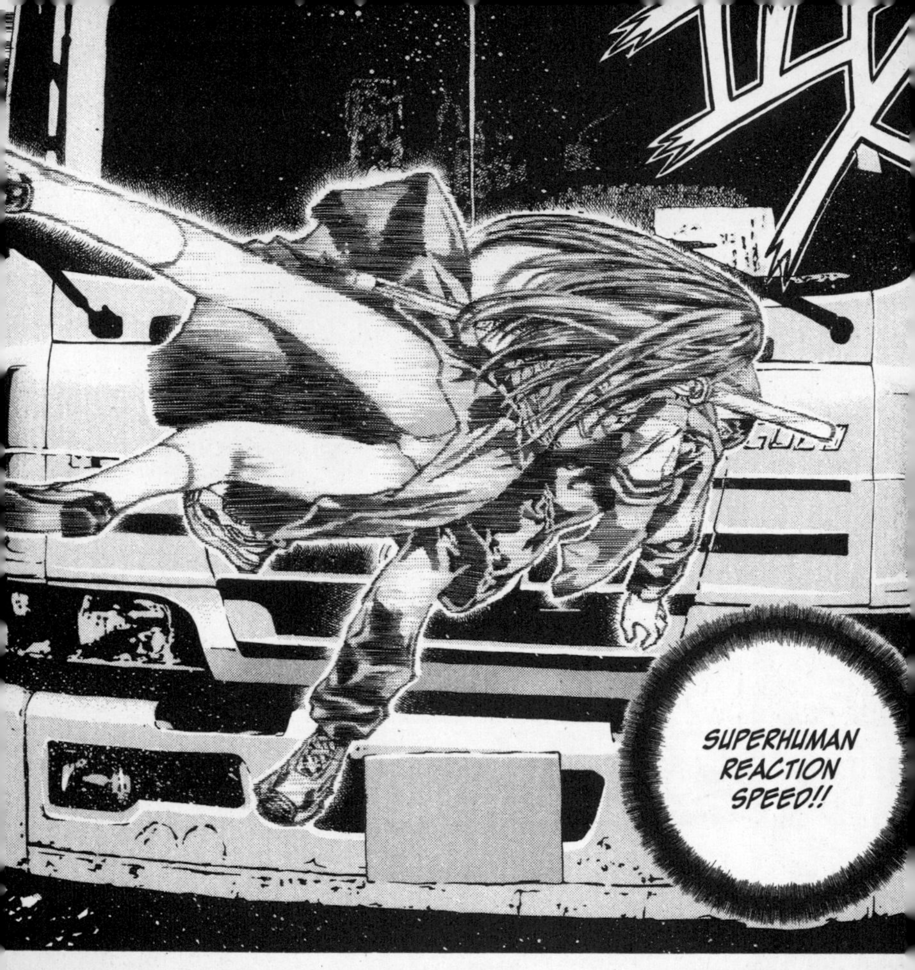
SUPERHUMAN REACTION SPEED!!

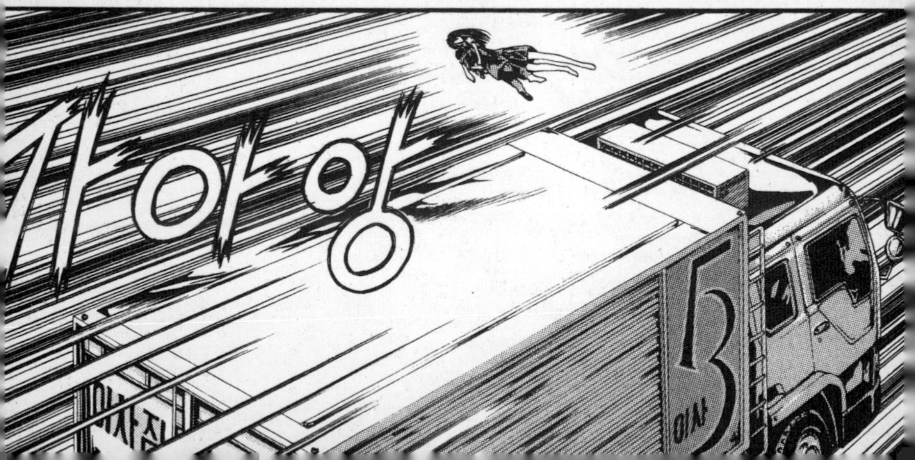
가아앙

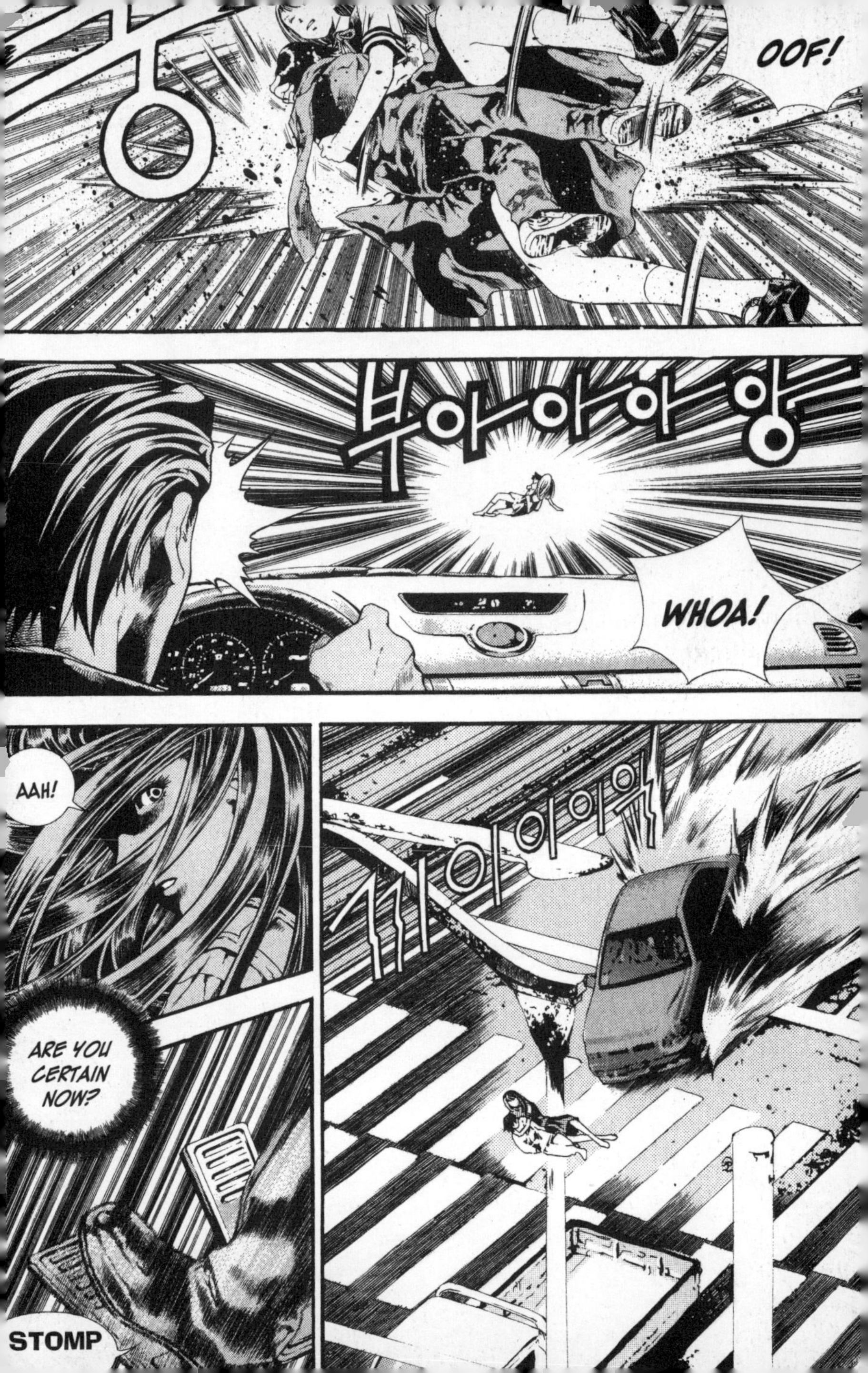
OOF!
부아아아 앙
WHOA!
AAH!
ARE YOU CERTAIN NOW?
STOMP
끼이이이이익

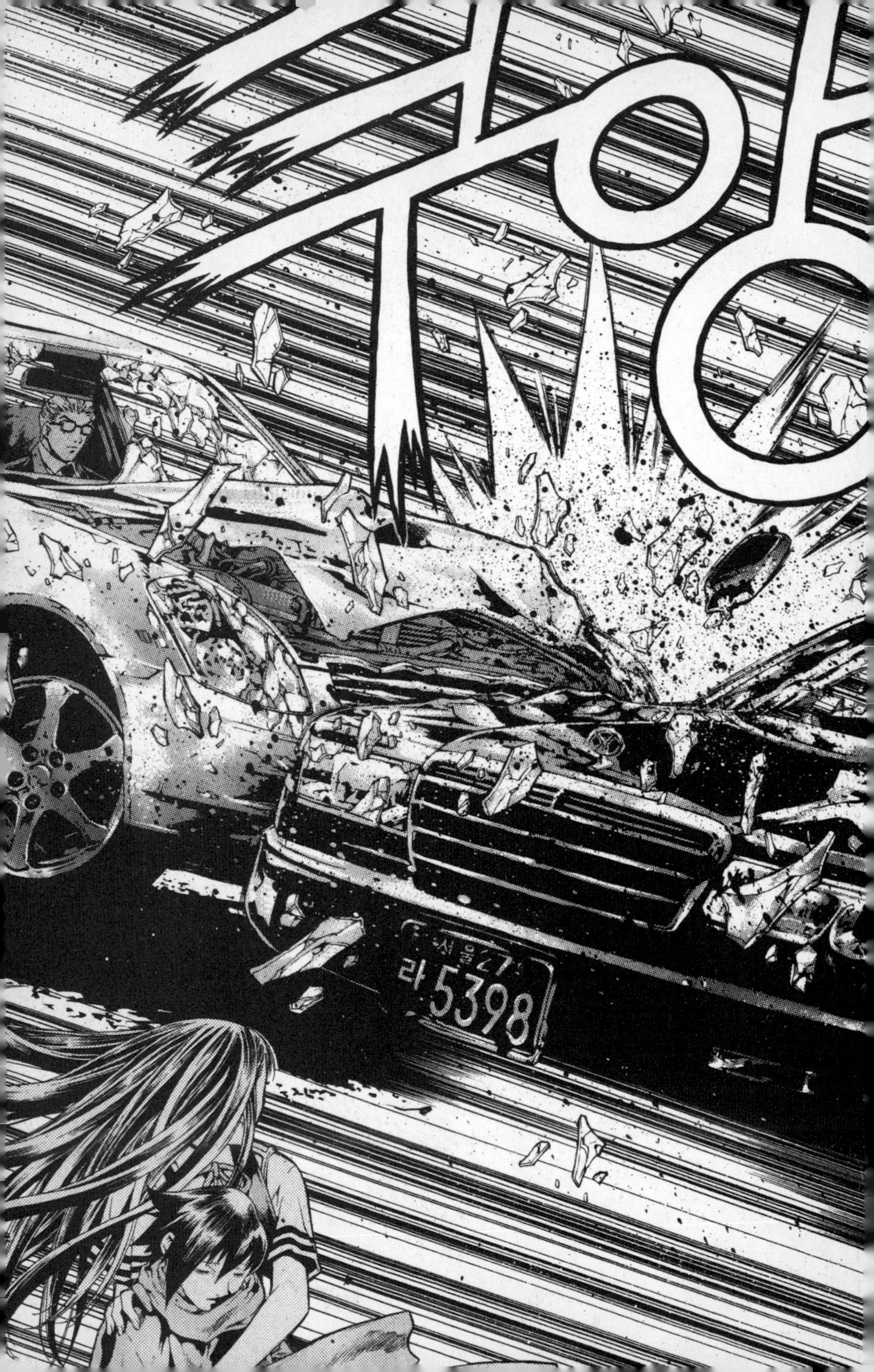
라 5398

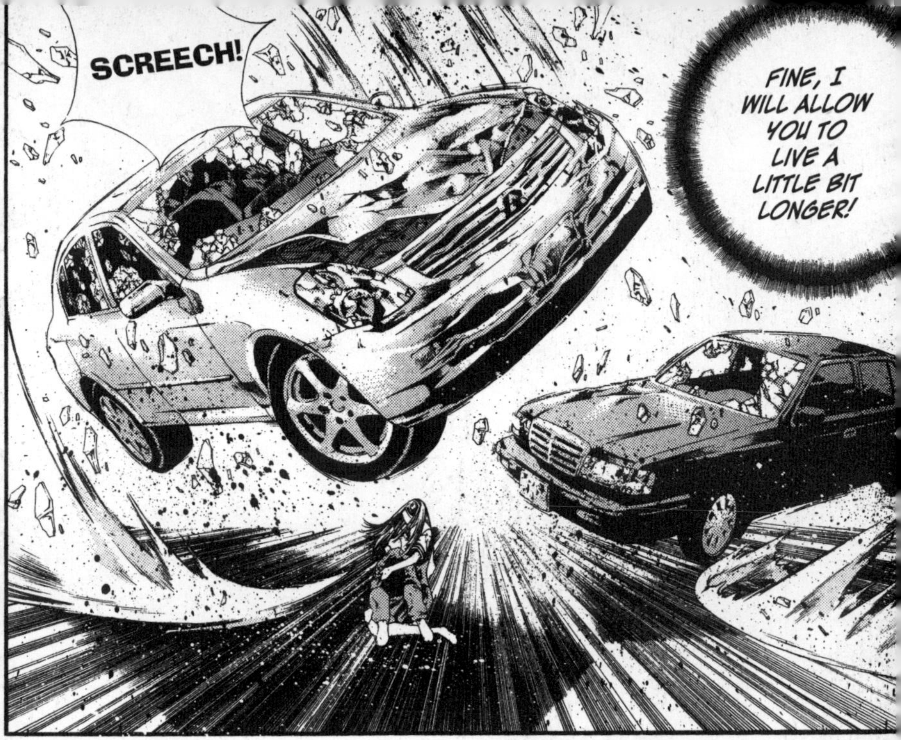
SCREECH!
FINE, I WILL ALLOW YOU TO LIVE A LITTLE BIT LONGER!

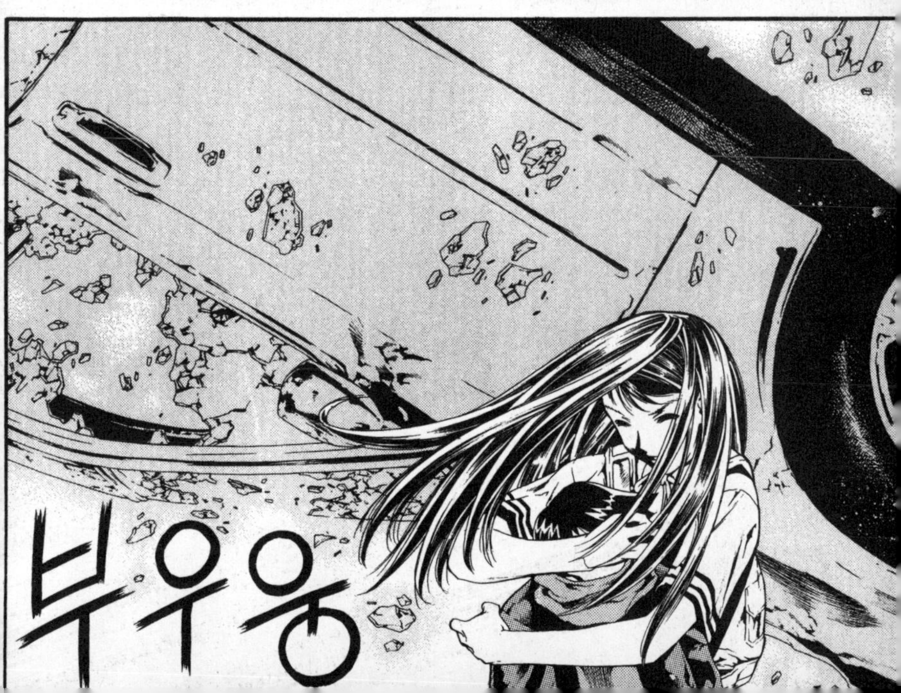
부우웅

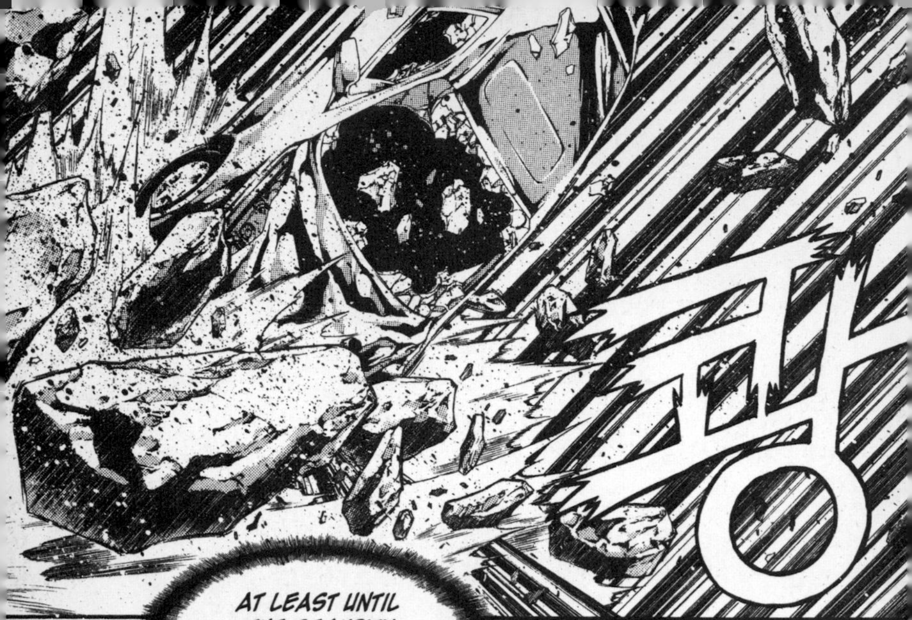

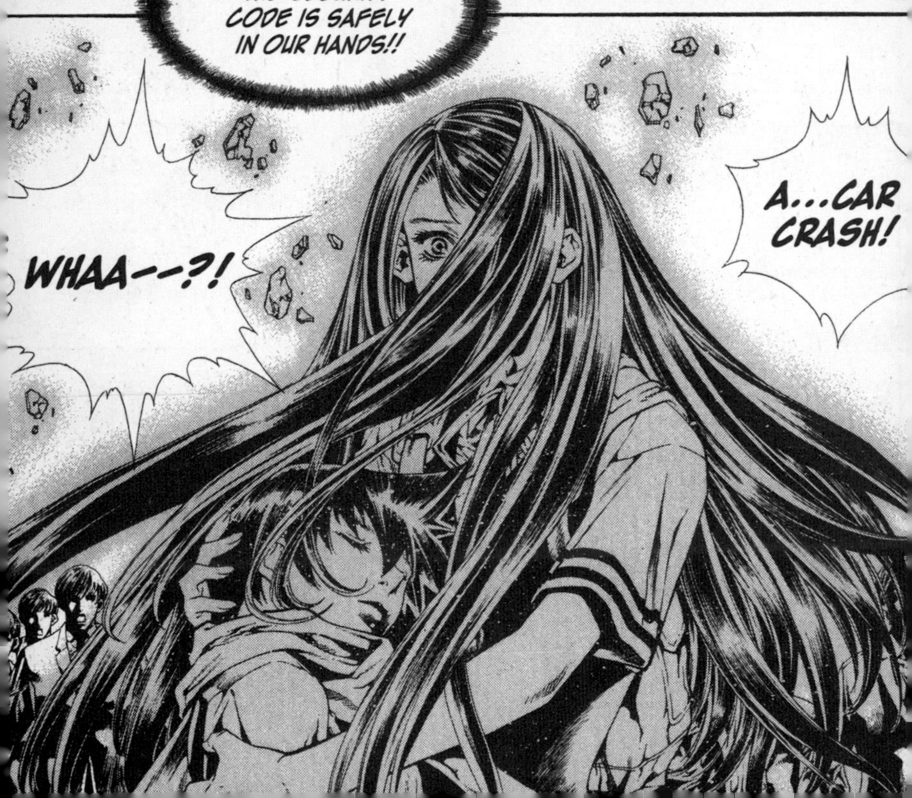
AT LEAST UNTIL THE SECURITY CODE IS SAFELY IN OUR HANDS!!
WHAA--?!
A...CAR CRASH!

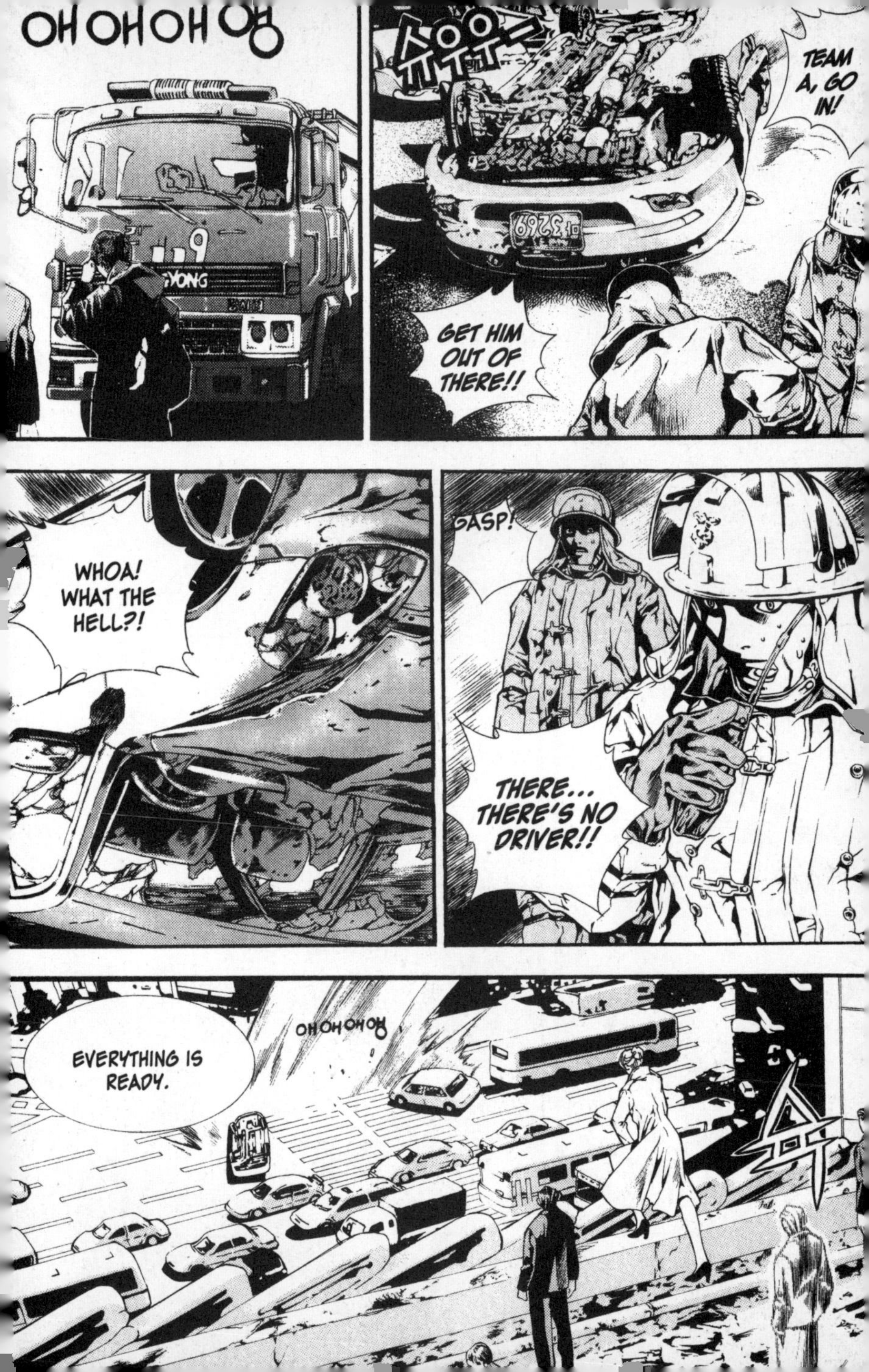
OH OH OH OH 앵
TEAM A, GO IN!
GET HIM OUT OF THERE!!
WHOA! WHAT THE HELL?!
GASP!
THERE... THERE'S NO DRIVER!!
EVERYTHING IS READY.
OH OH OH OH 앵

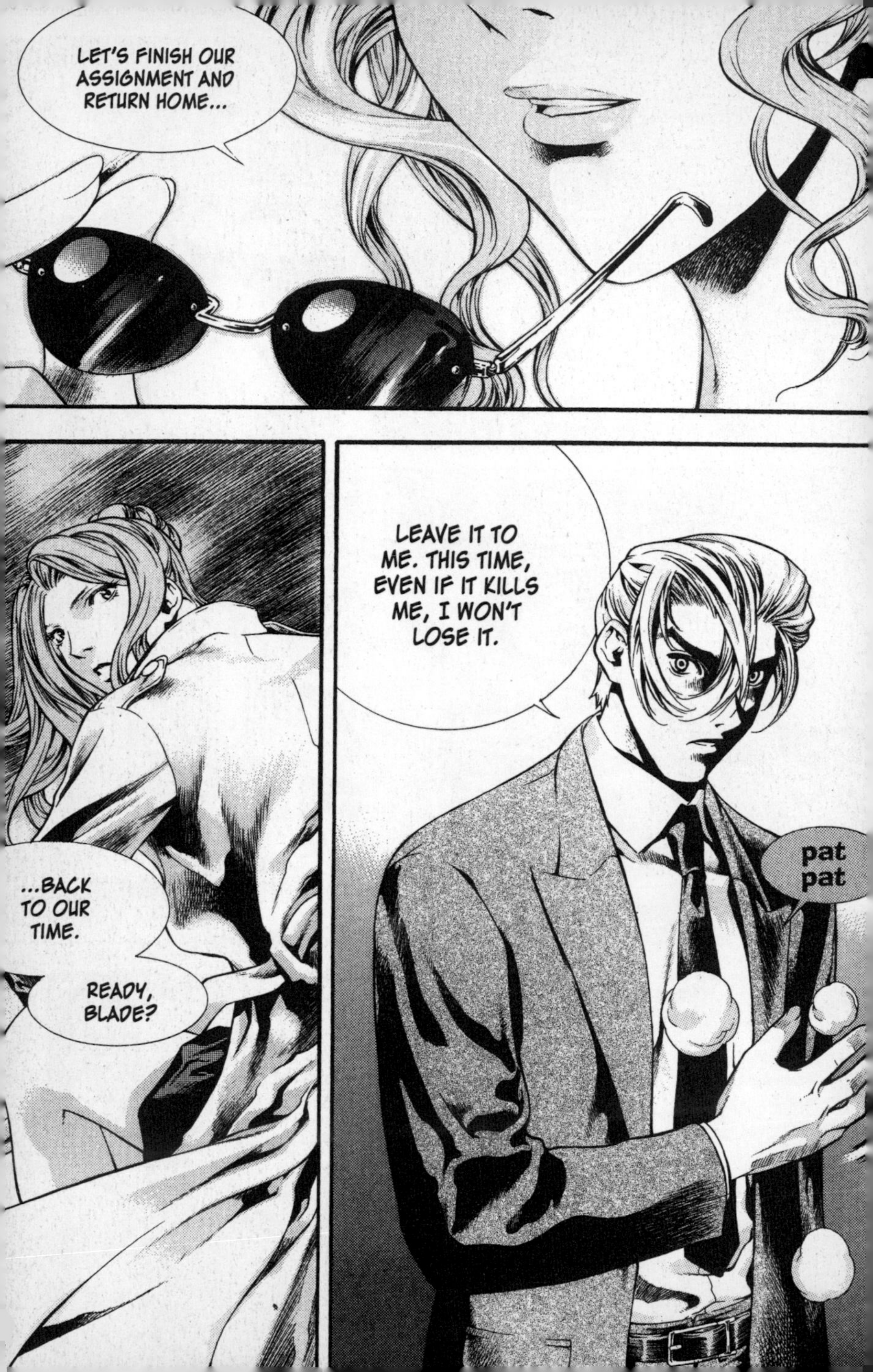
LET'S FINISH OUR ASSIGNMENT AND RETURN HOME...
...BACK TO OUR TIME.
READY, BLADE?
LEAVE IT TO ME. THIS TIME, EVEN IF IT KILLS ME, I WON'T LOSE IT.
pat pat

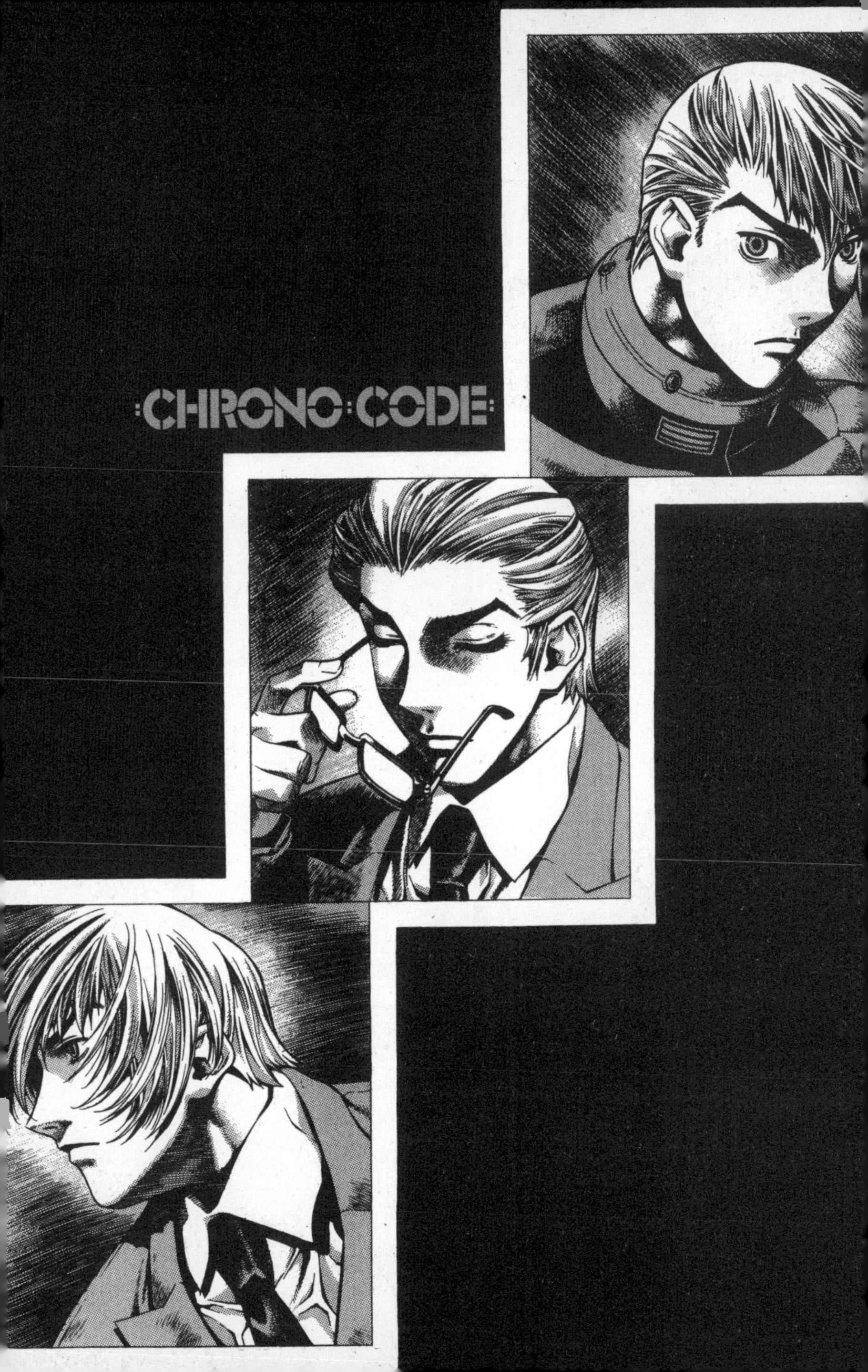
CHRONO CODE

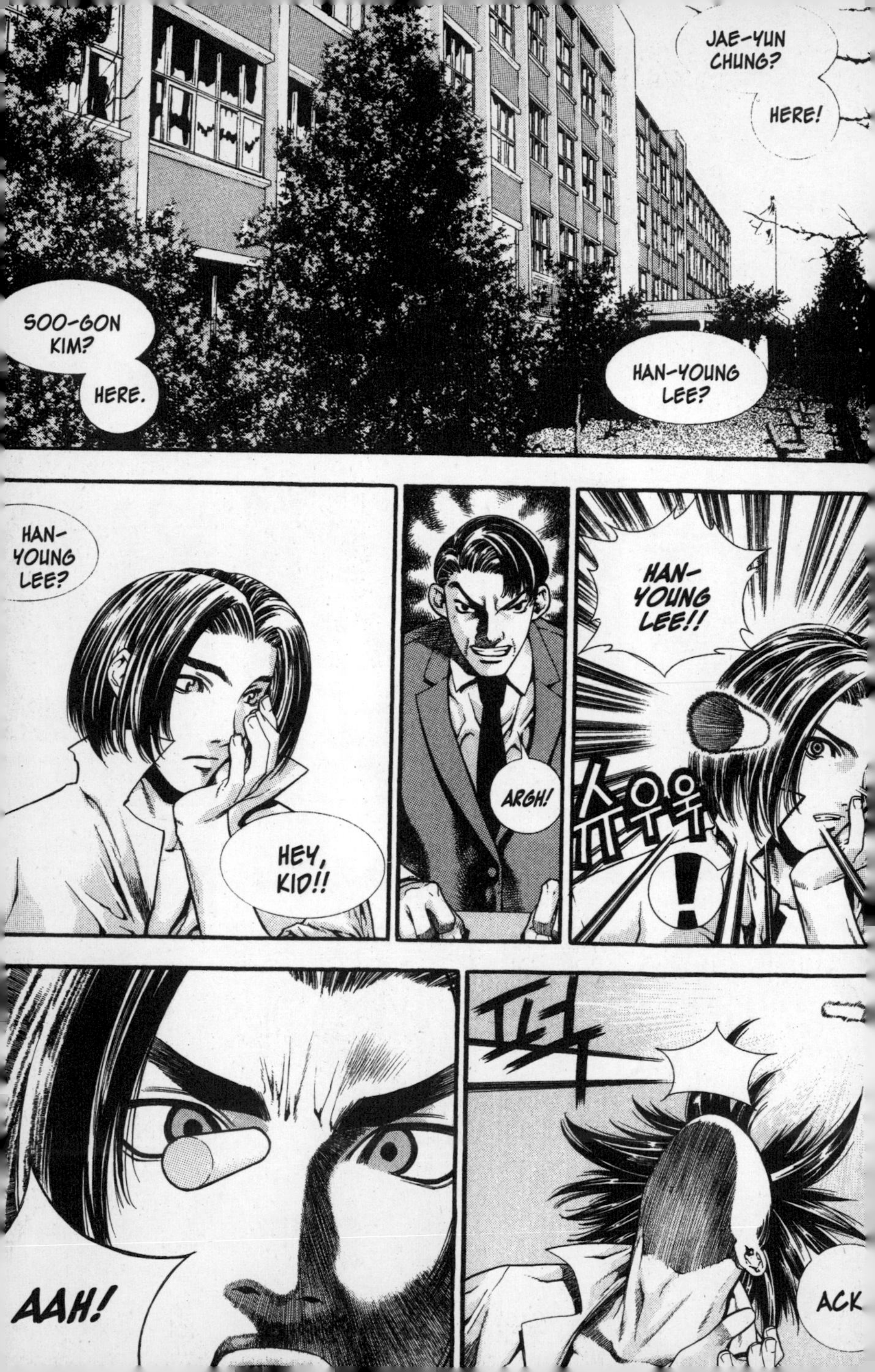
JAE-YUN CHUNG?
HERE!
SOO-GON KIM?
HERE.
HAN-YOUNG LEE?
HAN-YOUNG LEE?
HEY, KID!!
ARGH!
HAN-YOUNG LEE!!
!
AAH!
퍽
ACK

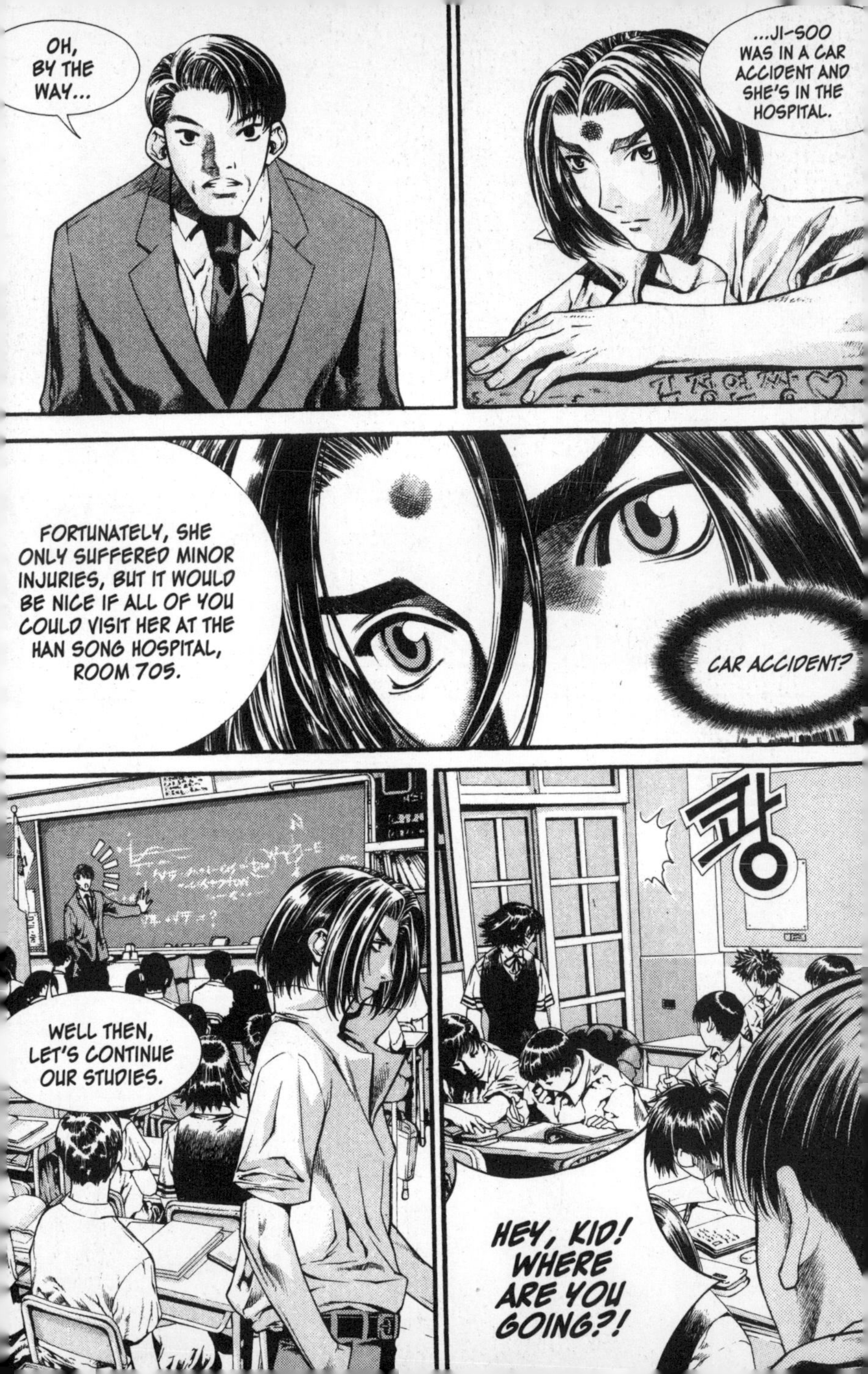
OH, BY THE WAY...
...JI-SOO WAS IN A CAR ACCIDENT AND SHE'S IN THE HOSPITAL.
FORTUNATELY, SHE ONLY SUFFERED MINOR INJURIES, BUT IT WOULD BE NICE IF ALL OF YOU COULD VISIT HER AT THE HAN SONG HOSPITAL, ROOM 705.
CAR ACCIDENT?
WELL THEN, LET'S CONTINUE OUR STUDIES.
쾅
HEY, KID! WHERE ARE YOU GOING?!

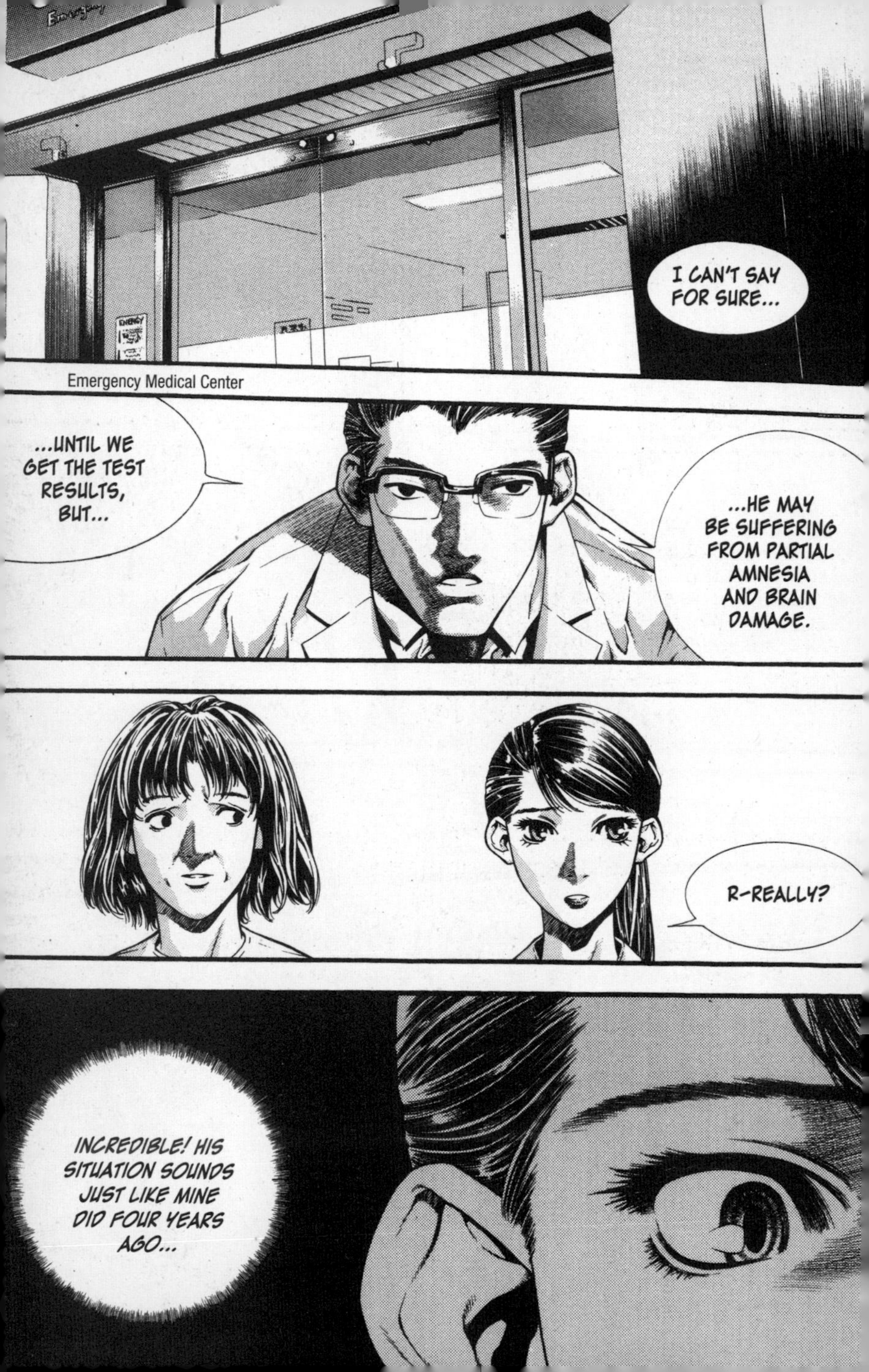
I CAN'T SAY FOR SURE...
Emergency Medical Center
...UNTIL WE GET THE TEST RESULTS, BUT...
...HE MAY BE SUFFERING FROM PARTIAL AMNESIA AND BRAIN DAMAGE.
R-REALLY?
INCREDIBLE! HIS SITUATION SOUNDS JUST LIKE MINE DID FOUR YEARS AGO...

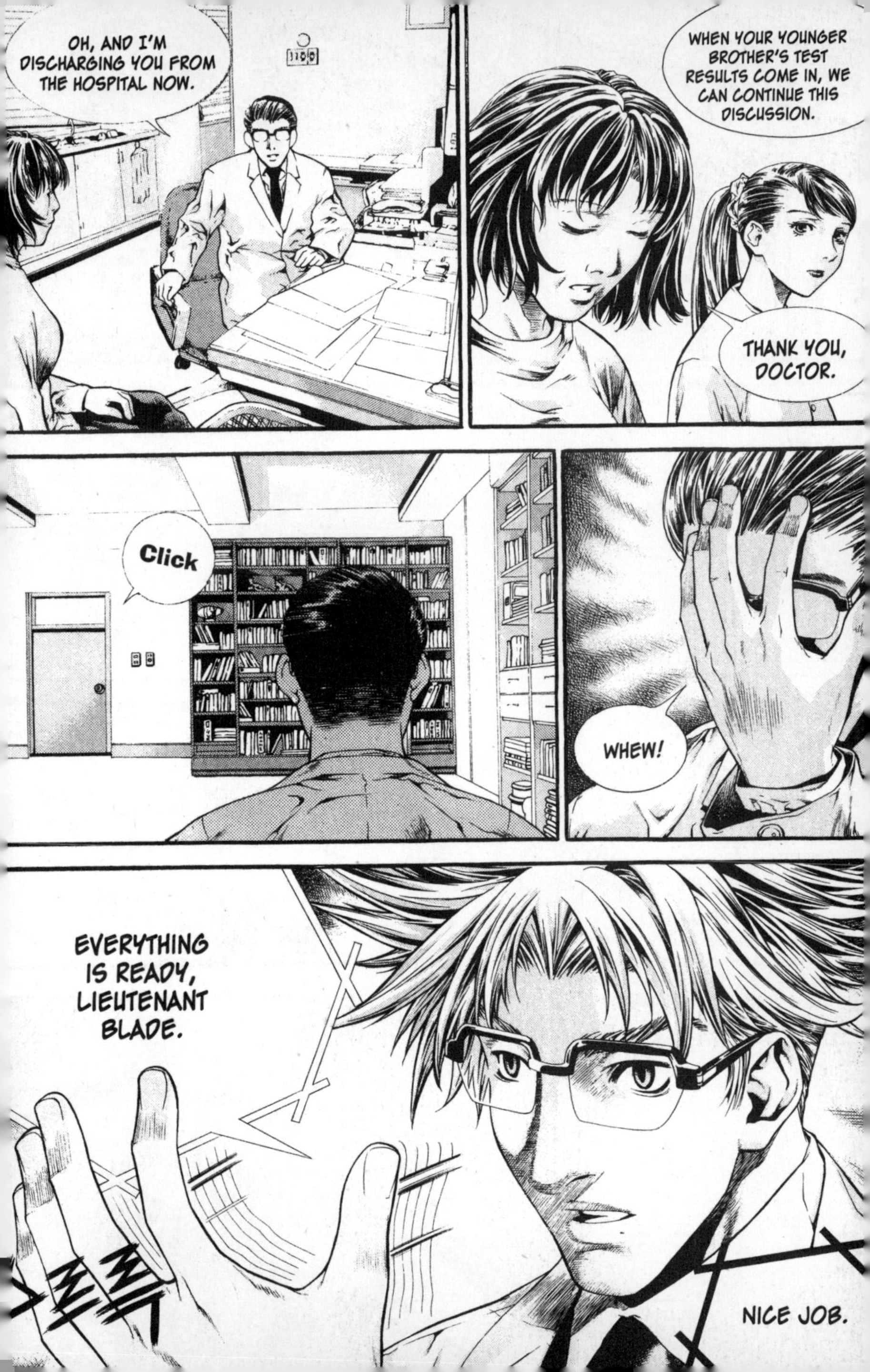
OH, AND I'M DISCHARGING YOU FROM THE HOSPITAL NOW.
WHEN YOUR YOUNGER BROTHER'S TEST RESULTS COME IN, WE CAN CONTINUE THIS DISCUSSION.
THANK YOU, DOCTOR.
Click
WHEW!
EVERYTHING IS READY, LIEUTENANT BLADE.
NICE JOB.

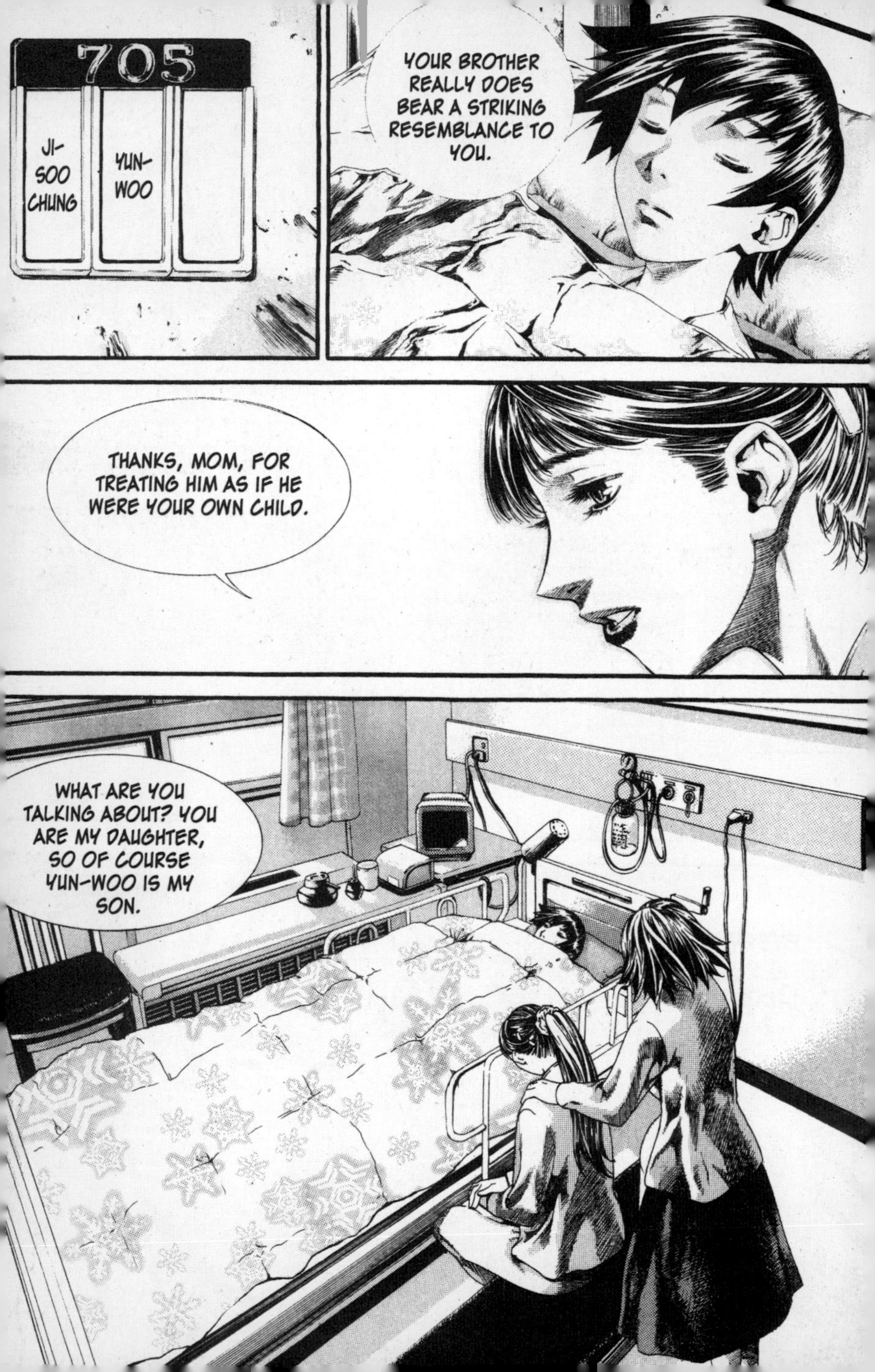
705
JI-SOO CHUNG
YUN-WOO
YOUR BROTHER REALLY DOES BEAR A STRIKING RESEMBLANCE TO YOU.
THANKS, MOM, FOR TREATING HIM AS IF HE WERE YOUR OWN CHILD.
WHAT ARE YOU TALKING ABOUT? YOU ARE MY DAUGHTER, SO OF COURSE YUN-WOO IS MY SON.

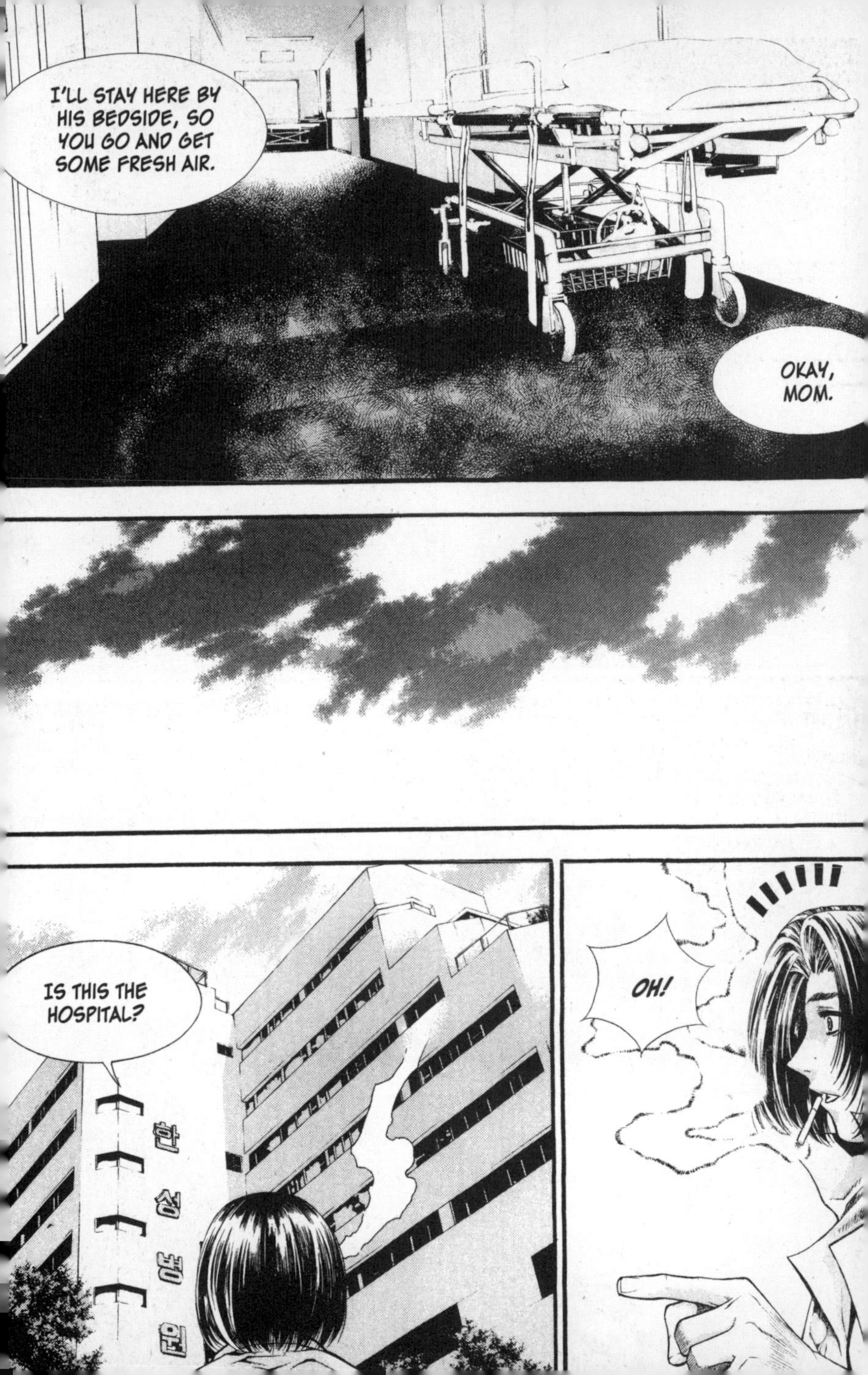
I'LL STAY HERE BY HIS BEDSIDE, SO YOU GO AND GET SOME FRESH AIR.
OKAY, MOM.
IS THIS THE HOSPITAL?
한성병원
OH!

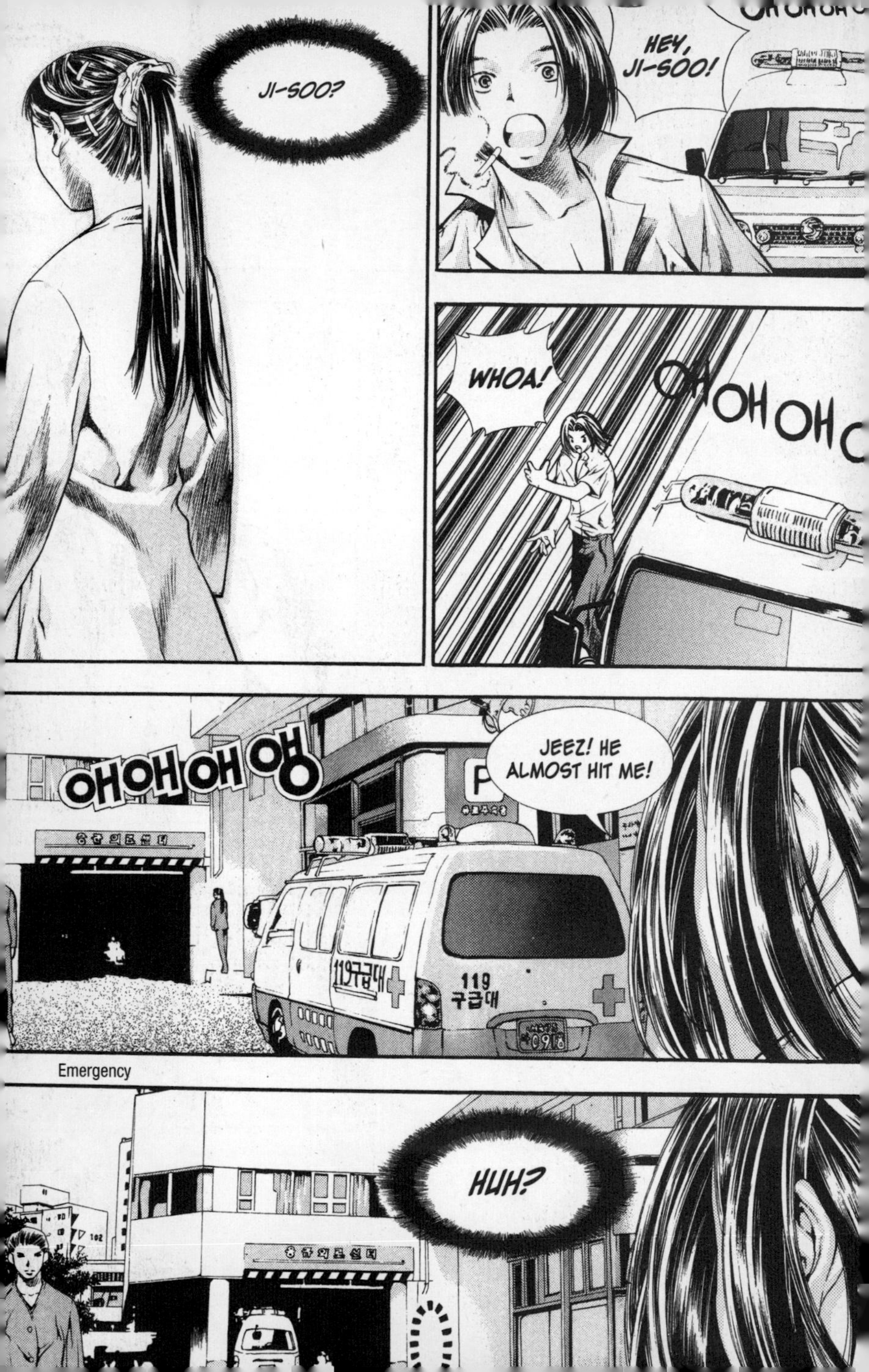
JI-SOO?
OH OH OH
HEY, JI-SOO!
WHOA!
OH OH OH O
OHOH OH OH
JEEZ! HE ALMOST HIT ME!
119구급대
119 구급대
Emergency
HUH?

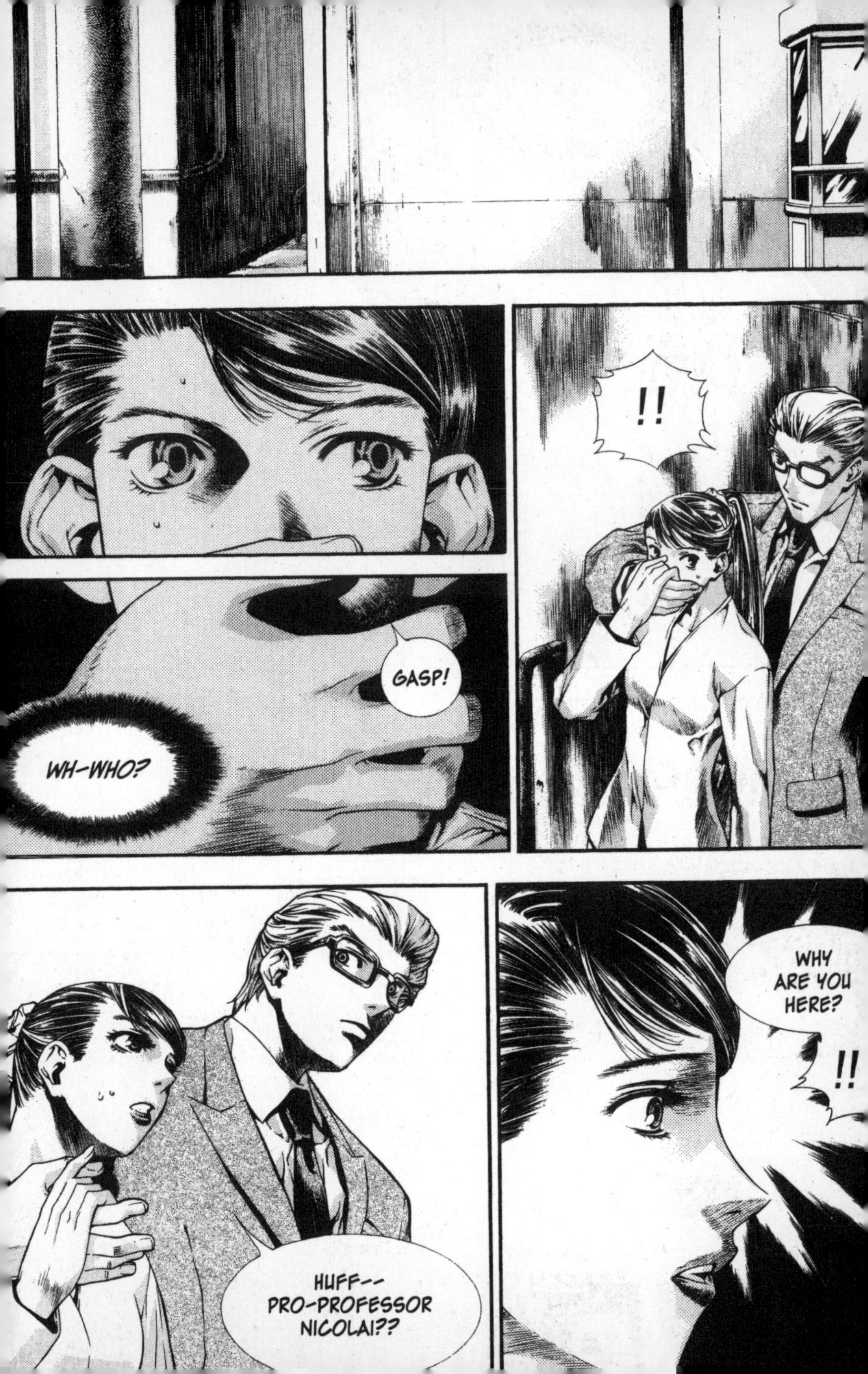
GASP!
WH-WHO?
!!
HUFF--
PRO-PROFESSOR
NICOLAI??
WHY
ARE YOU
HERE?
!!

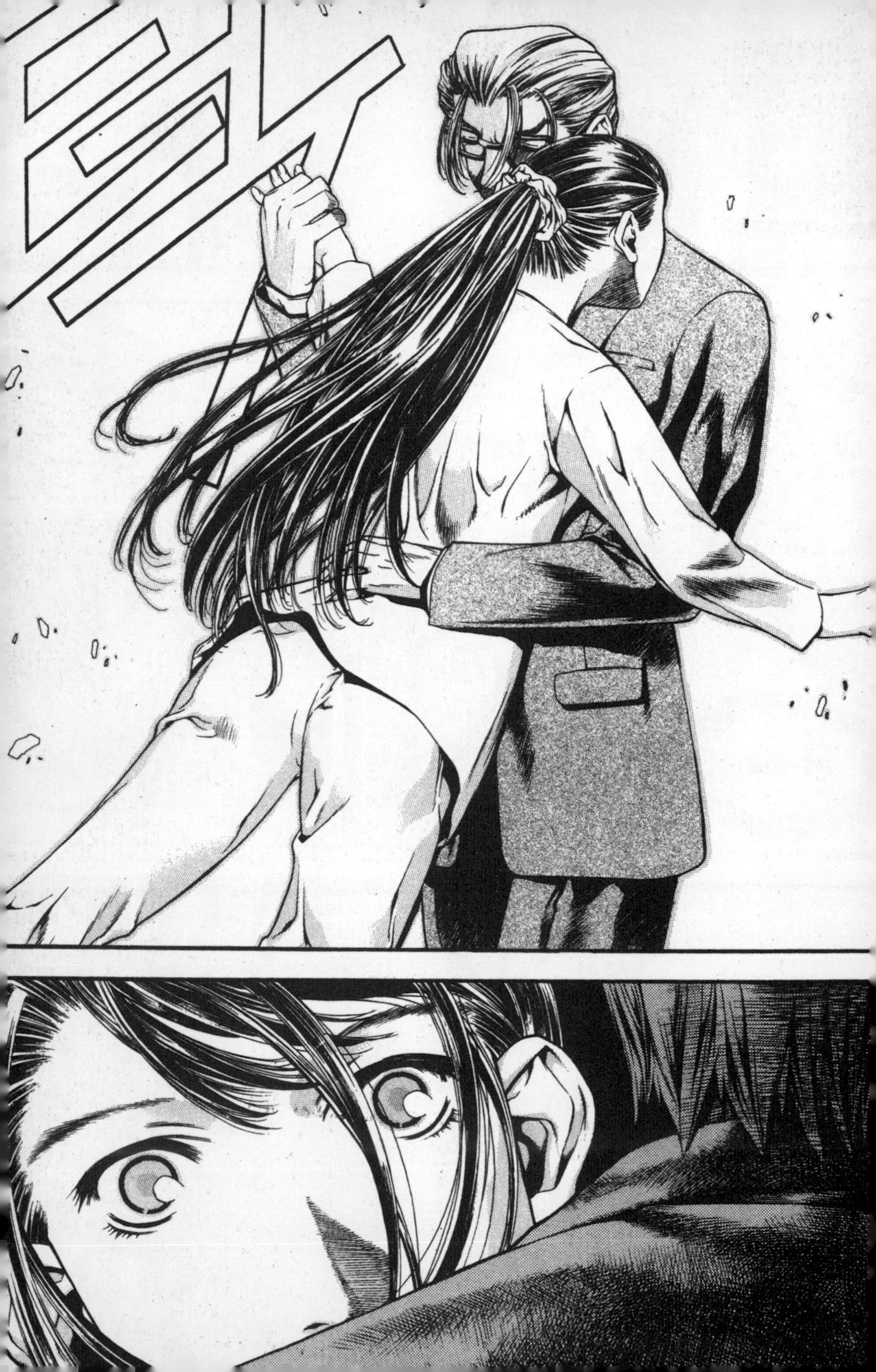

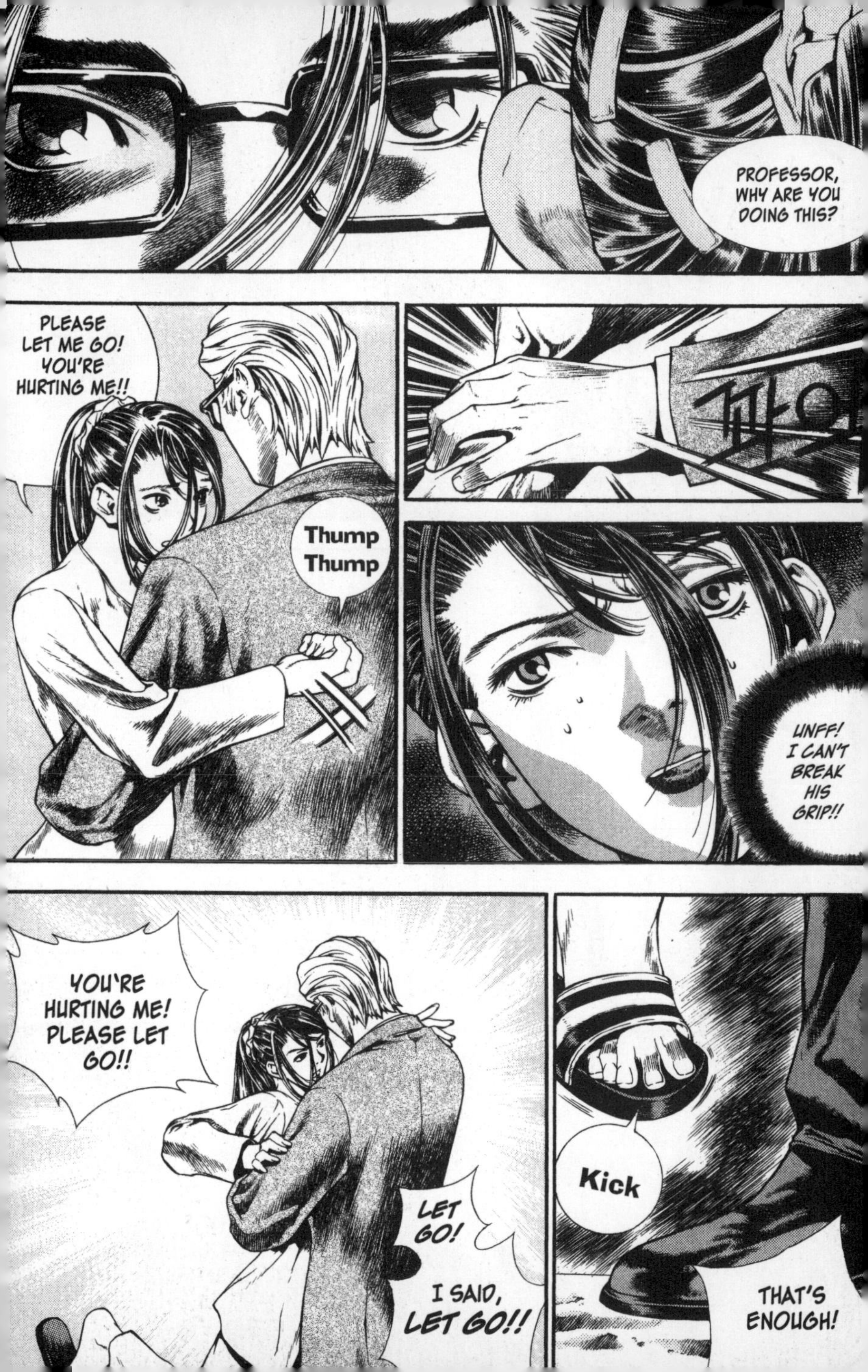
PROFESSOR, WHY ARE YOU DOING THIS?
PLEASE LET ME GO! YOU'RE HURTING ME!!
Thump Thump
UNFF! I CAN'T BREAK HIS GRIP!!
YOU'RE HURTING ME! PLEASE LET GO!!
LET GO!
I SAID, LET GO!!
Kick
THAT'S ENOUGH!

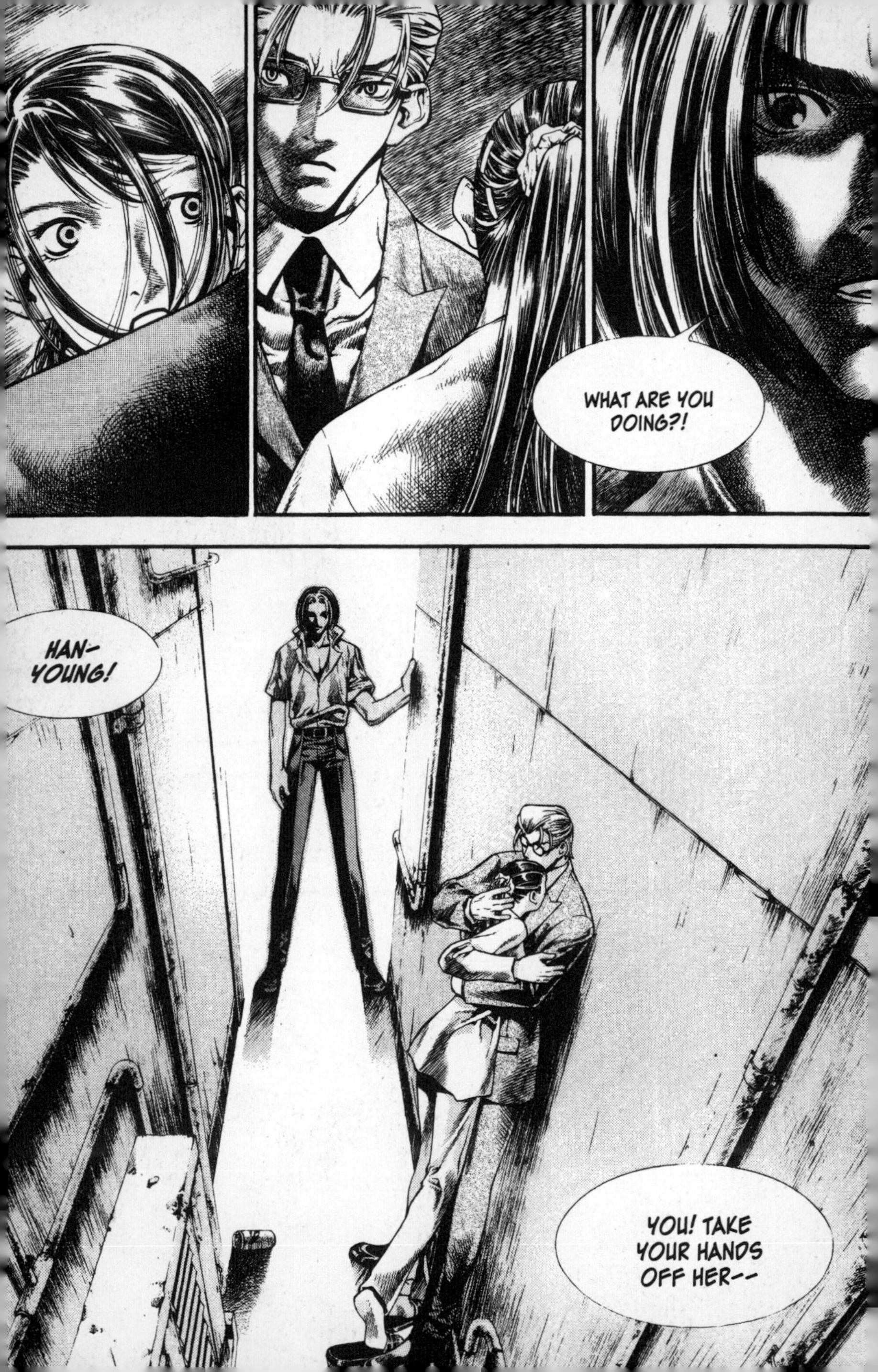
WHAT ARE YOU DOING?!
HAN-YOUNG!
YOU! TAKE YOUR HANDS OFF HER--

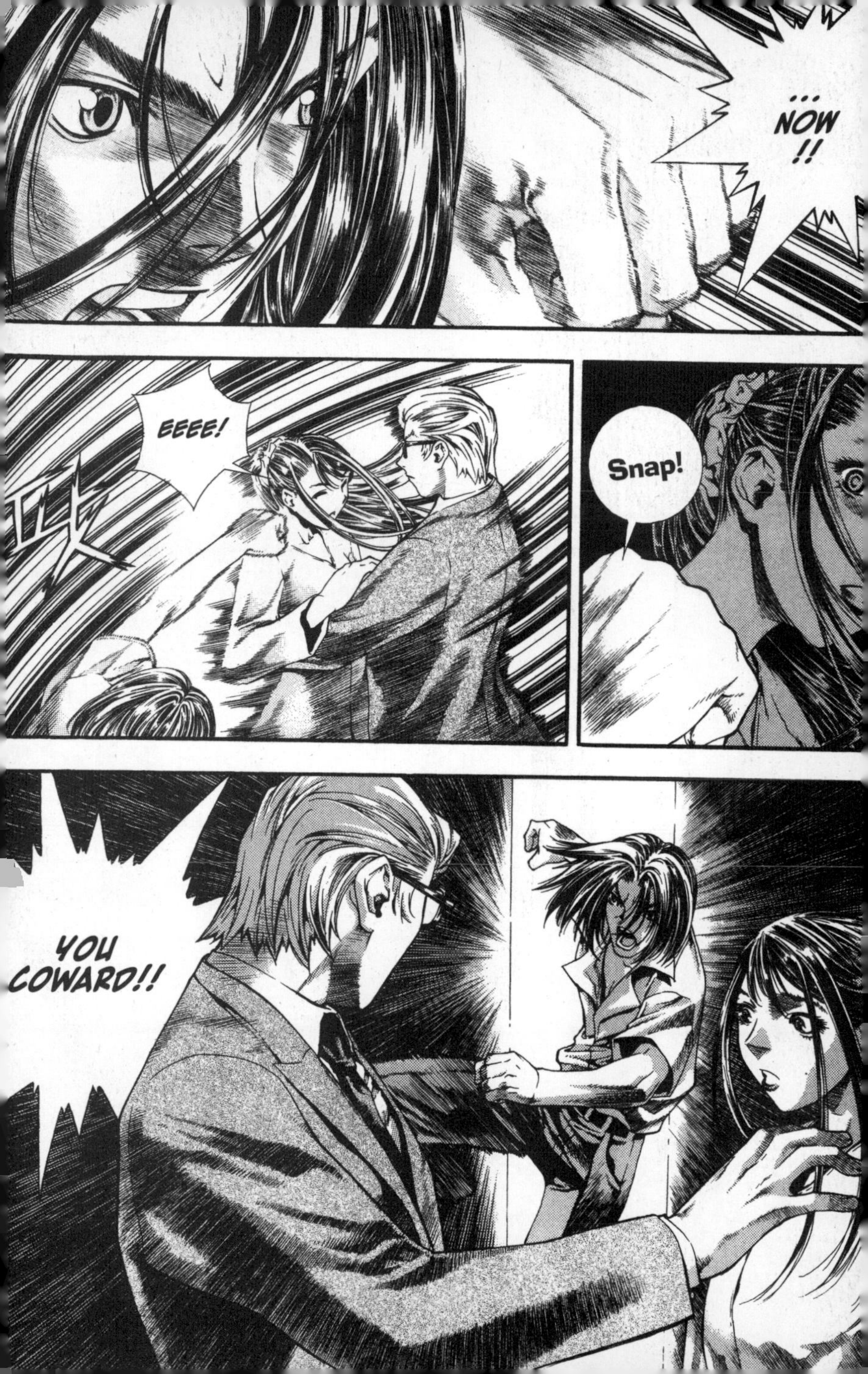
...NOW !!
EEEE!
Snap!
YOU COWARD!!

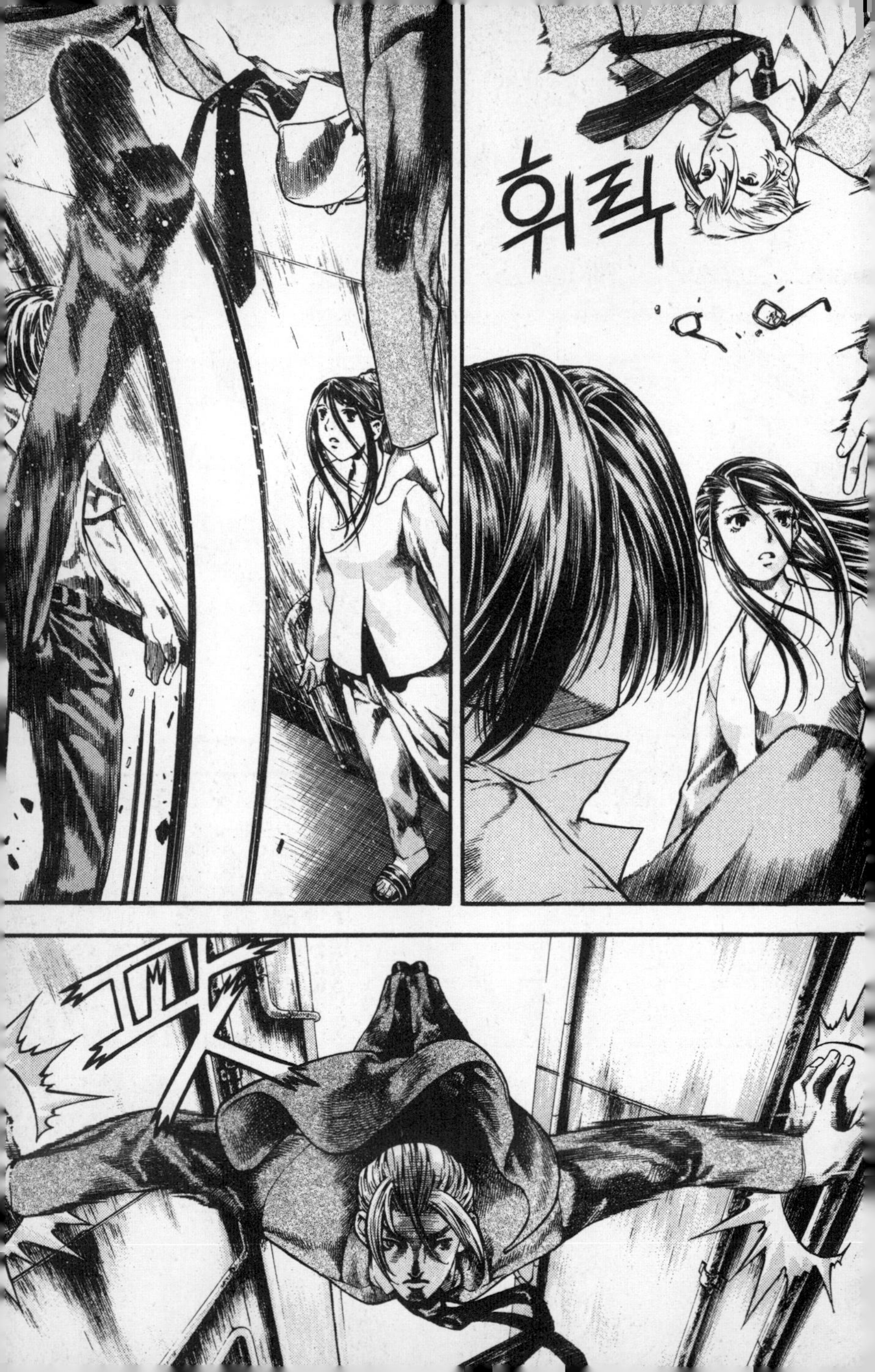
휘락

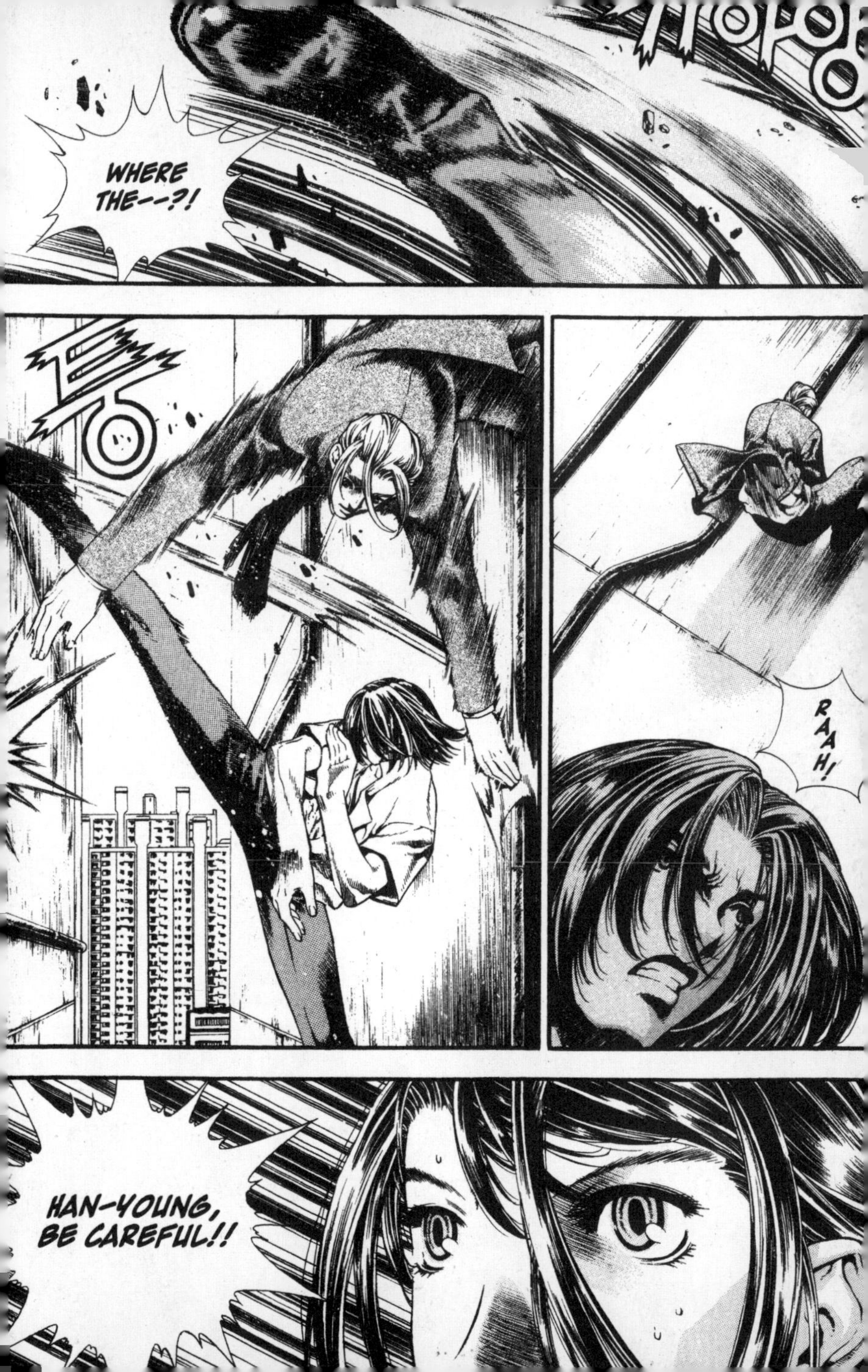
WHERE THE--?!
RAAH!
HAN-YOUNG, BE CAREFUL!!

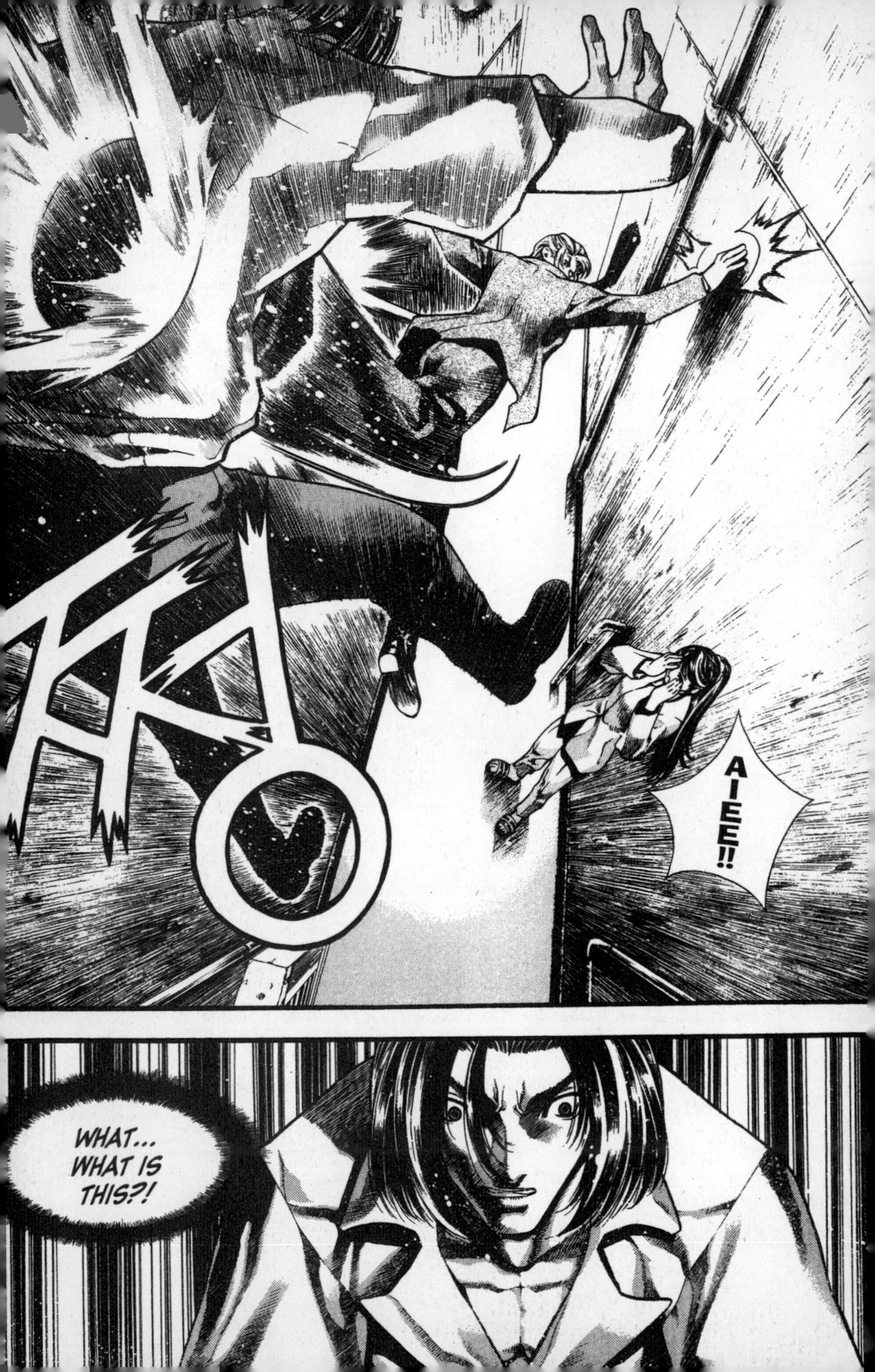
AIEE!!
WHAT... WHAT IS THIS?!

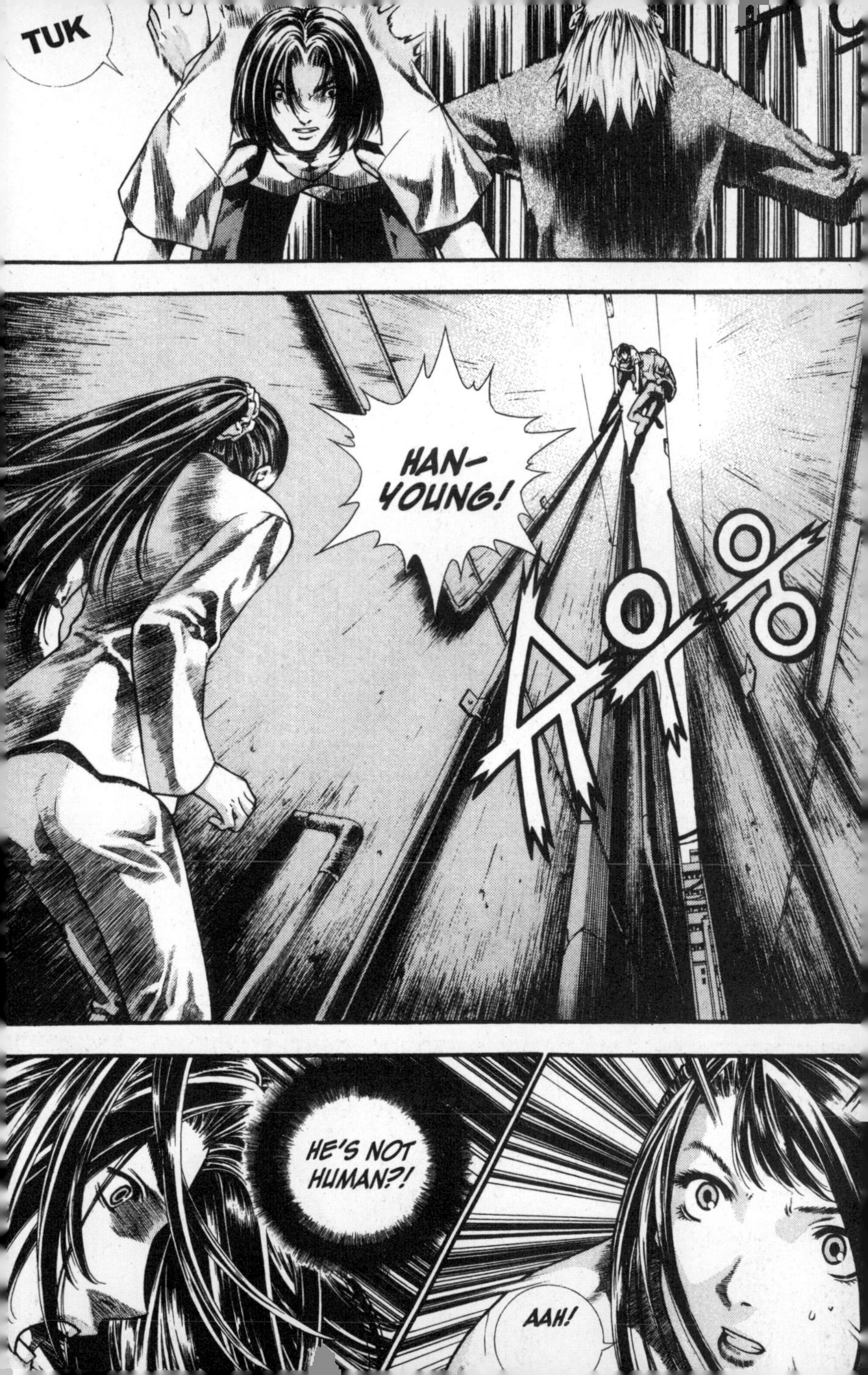
TUK
HAN-YOUNG!
HE'S NOT HUMAN?!
AAH!

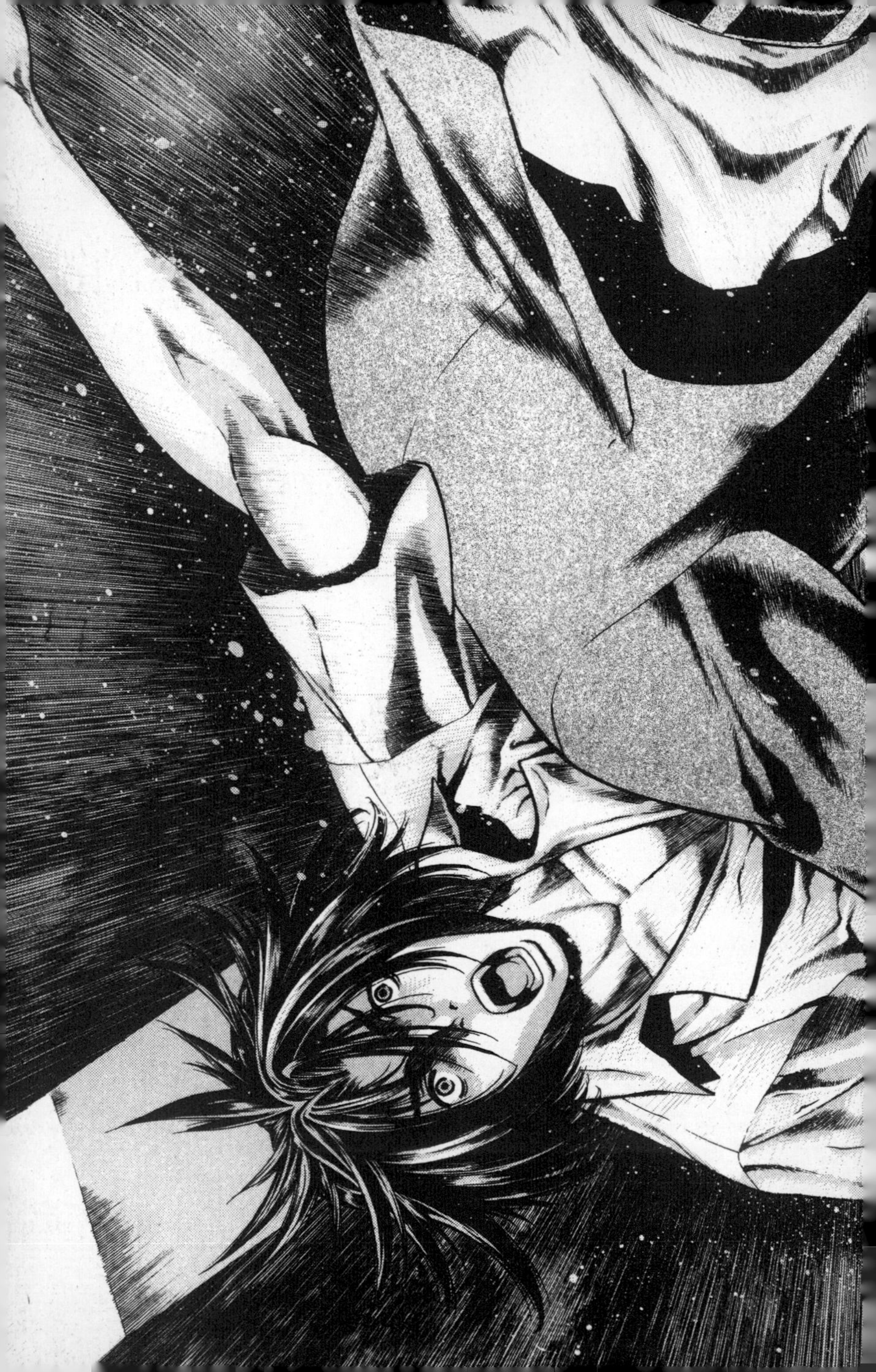

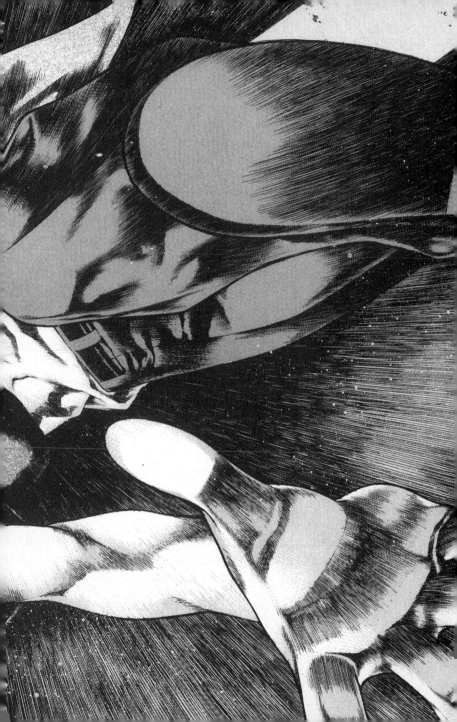

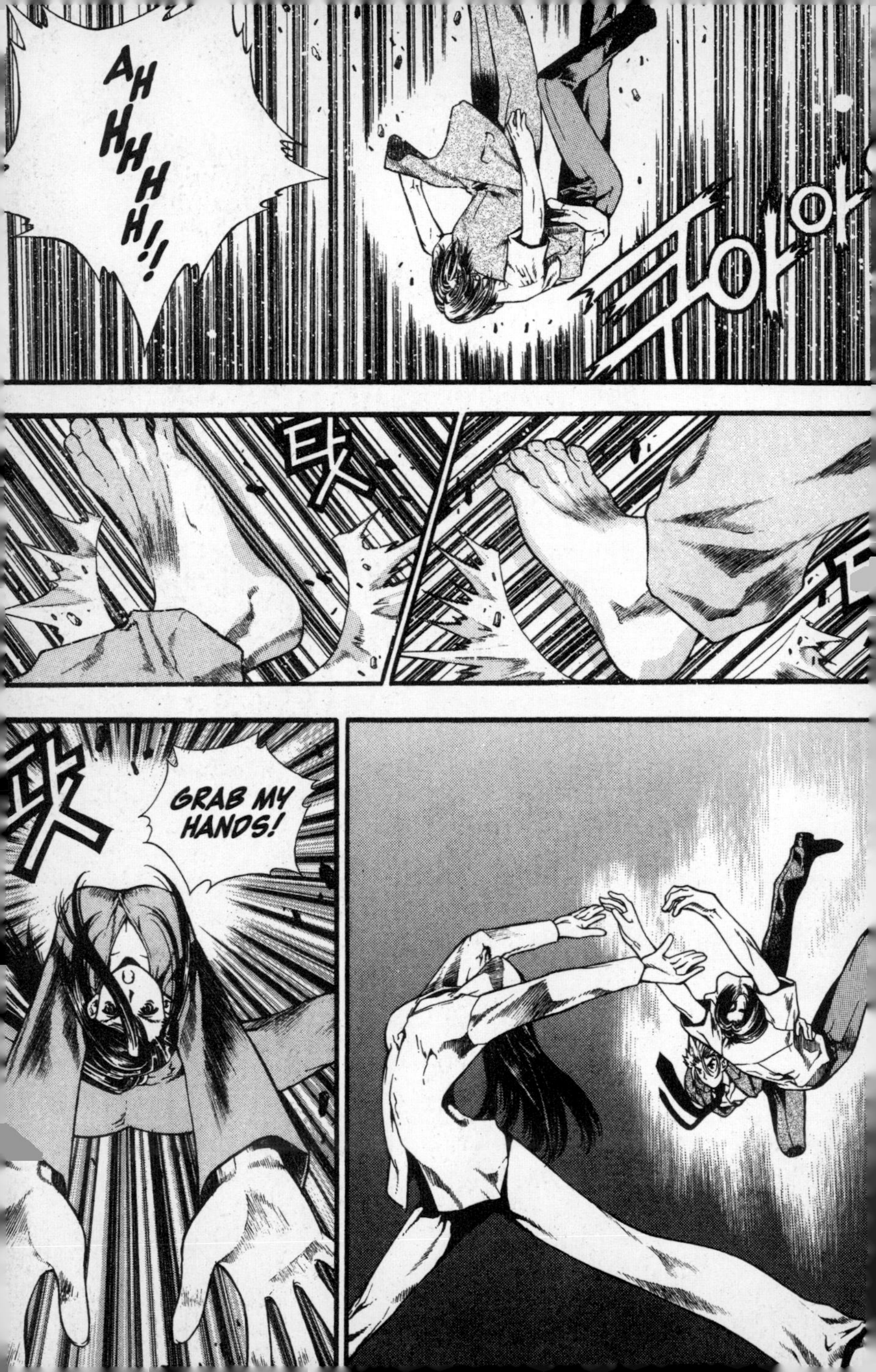
AHHHHHH!!
GRAB MY HANDS!

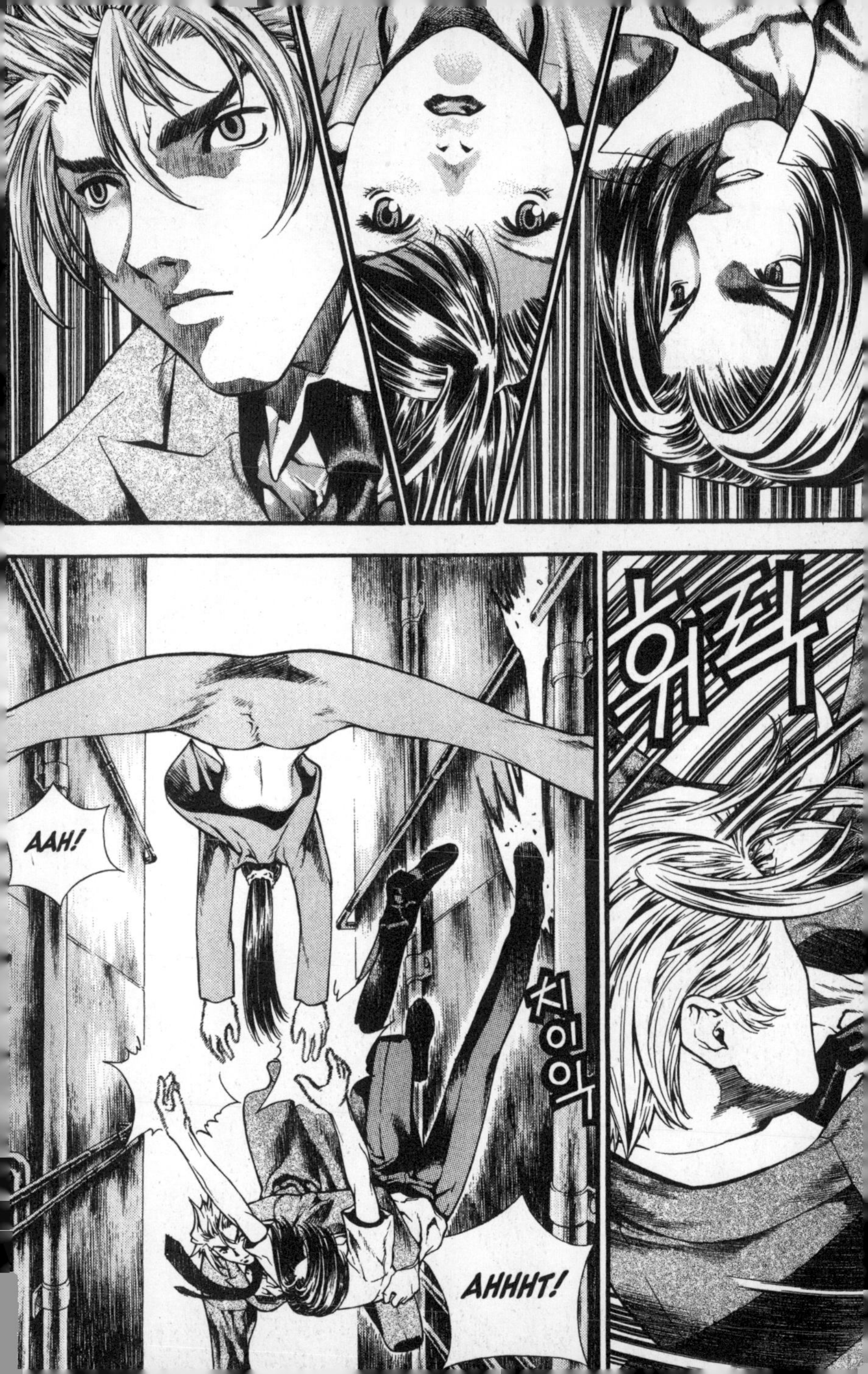
휘릭
AAH!
AHHHT!

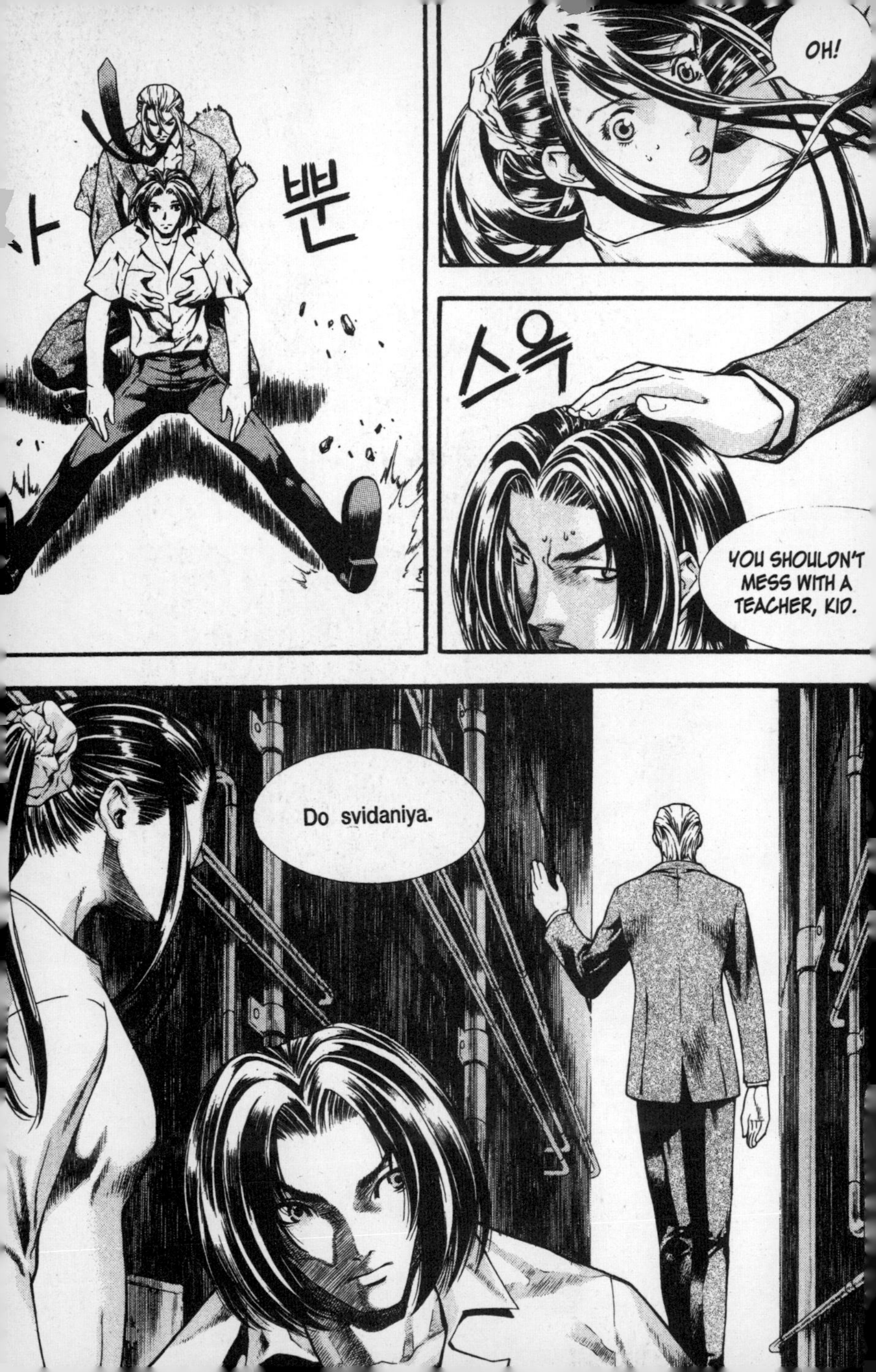
뿐
OH!
스욱
YOU SHOULDN'T MESS WITH A TEACHER, KID.
Do svidaniya.

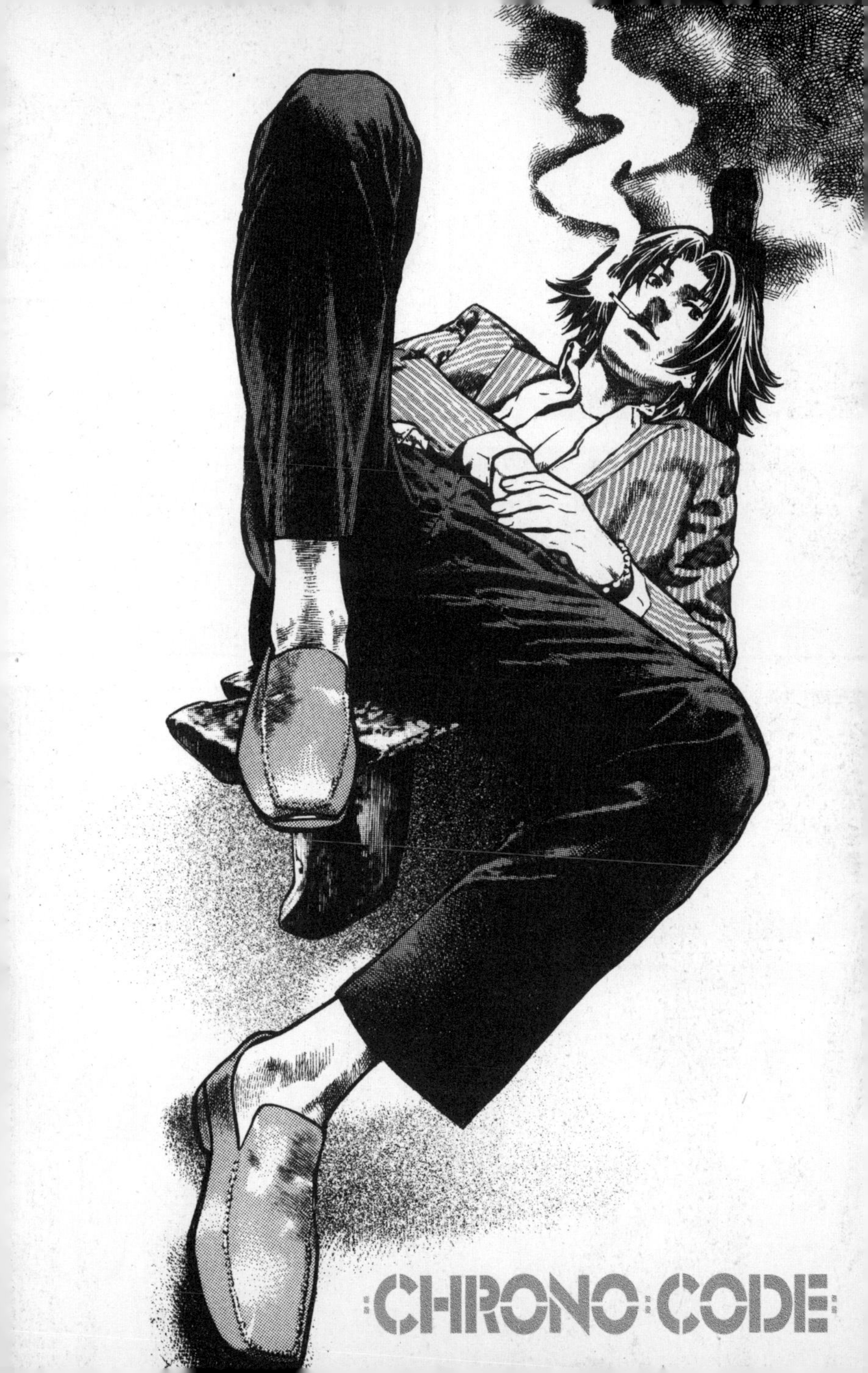
CHRONO CODE

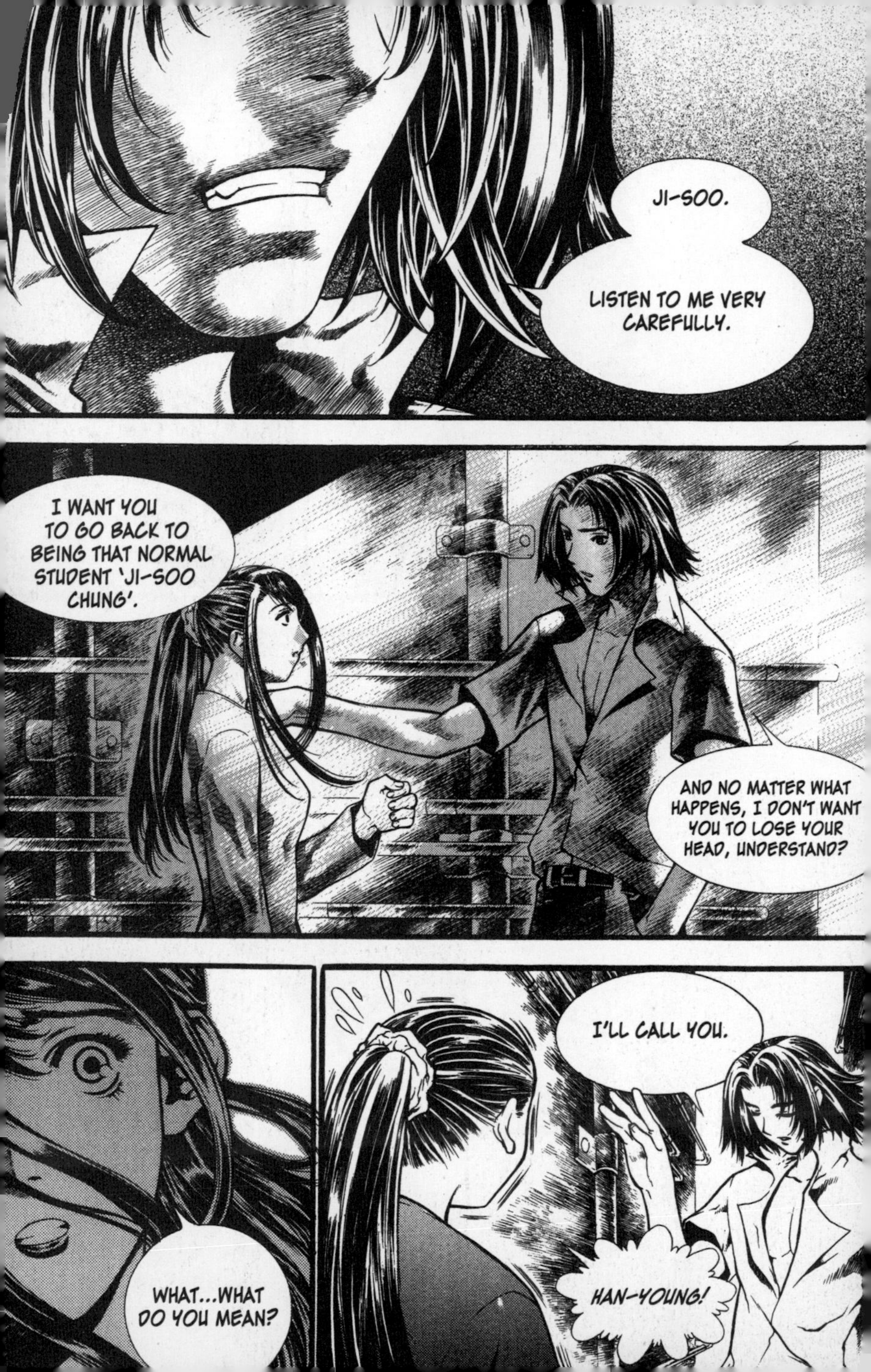
JI-SOO.
LISTEN TO ME VERY CAREFULLY.
I WANT YOU TO GO BACK TO BEING THAT NORMAL STUDENT 'JI-SOO CHUNG'.
AND NO MATTER WHAT HAPPENS, I DON'T WANT YOU TO LOSE YOUR HEAD, UNDERSTAND?
WHAT...WHAT DO YOU MEAN?
I'LL CALL YOU.
HAN-YOUNG!

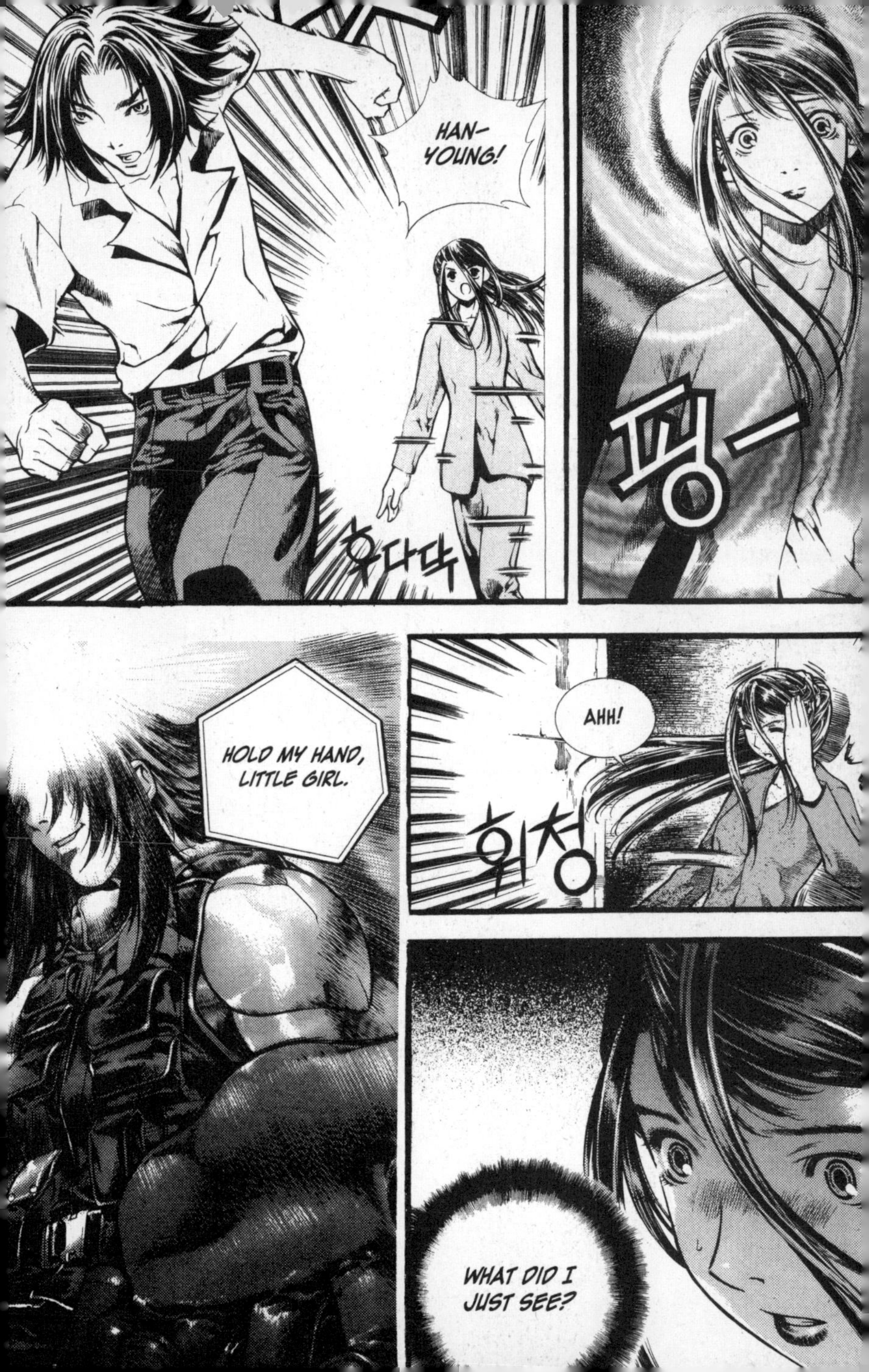
HAN-YOUNG!
후다닥
펑—
HOLD MY HAND, LITTLE GIRL.
AHH!
휘청
WHAT DID I JUST SEE?

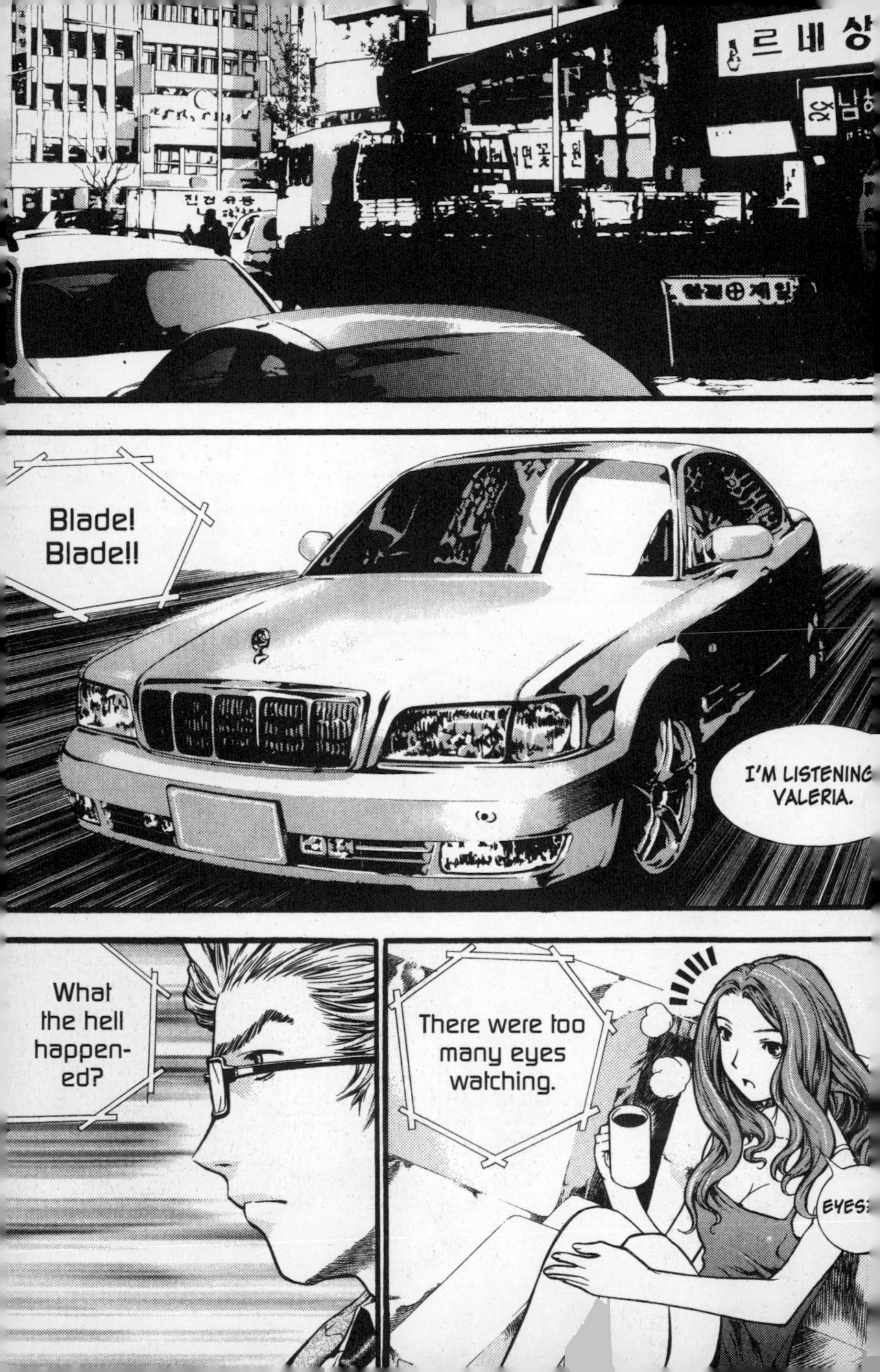
르베상
Blade! Blade!!
I'M LISTENING VALERIA.
What the hell happen-ed?
There were too many eyes watching.
EYES?

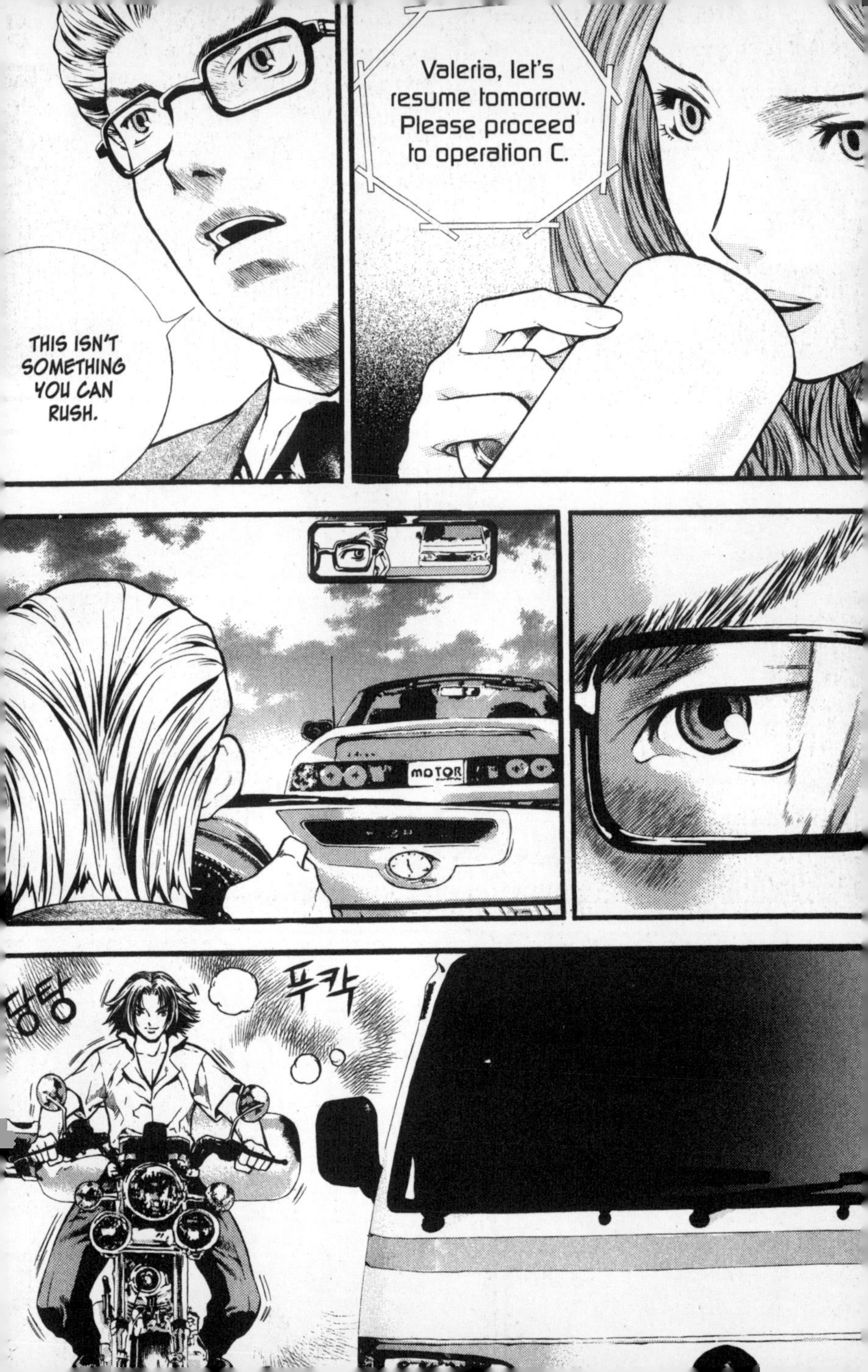
THIS ISN'T SOMETHING YOU CAN RUSH.
Valeria, let's resume tomorrow. Please proceed to operation C.
MOTOR
당당
푸칵

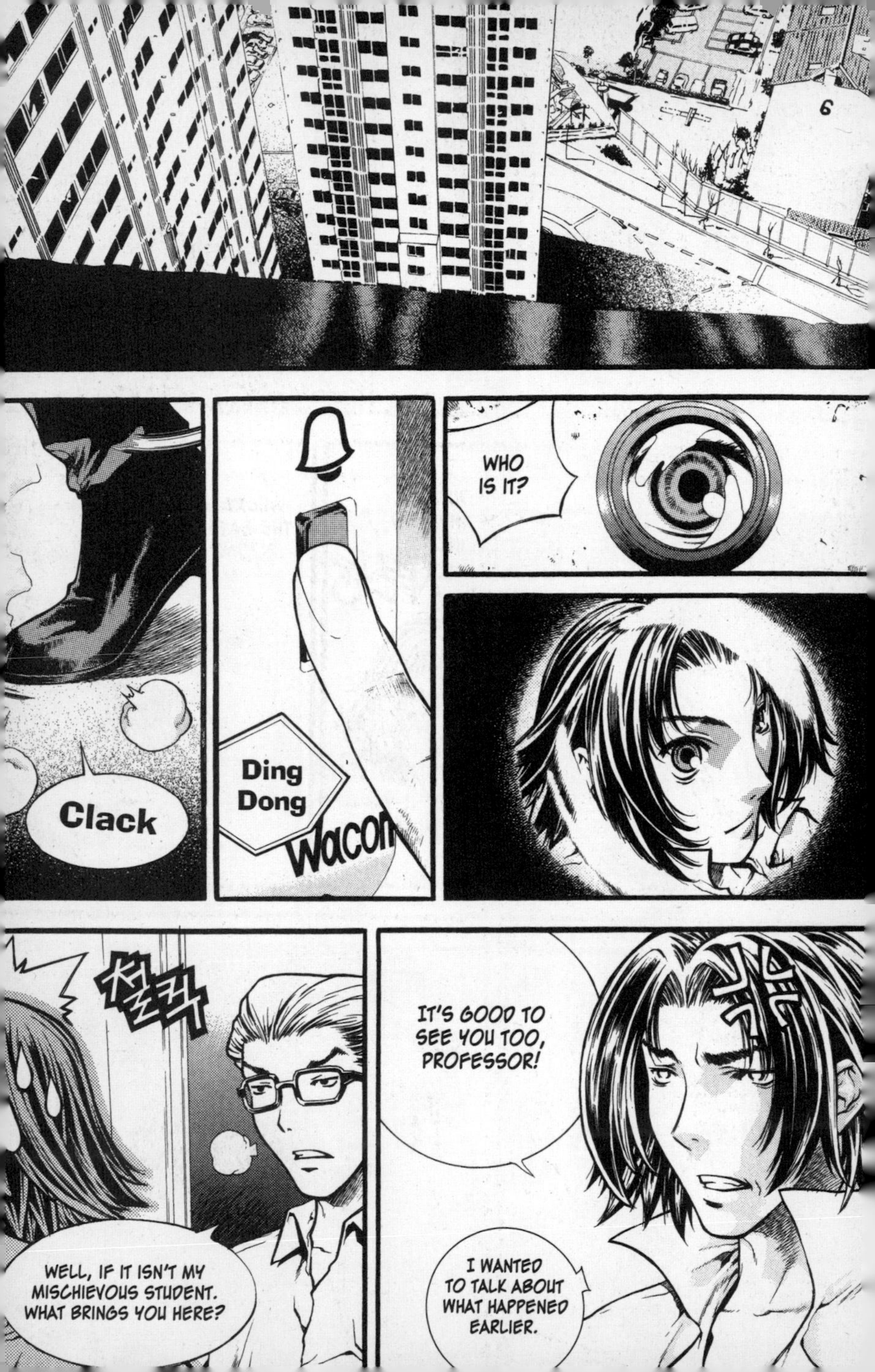
Clack
Ding Dong
Wacom
WHO IS IT?
WELL, IF IT ISN'T MY MISCHIEVOUS STUDENT. WHAT BRINGS YOU HERE?
IT'S GOOD TO SEE YOU TOO, PROFESSOR!
I WANTED TO TALK ABOUT WHAT HAPPENED EARLIER.

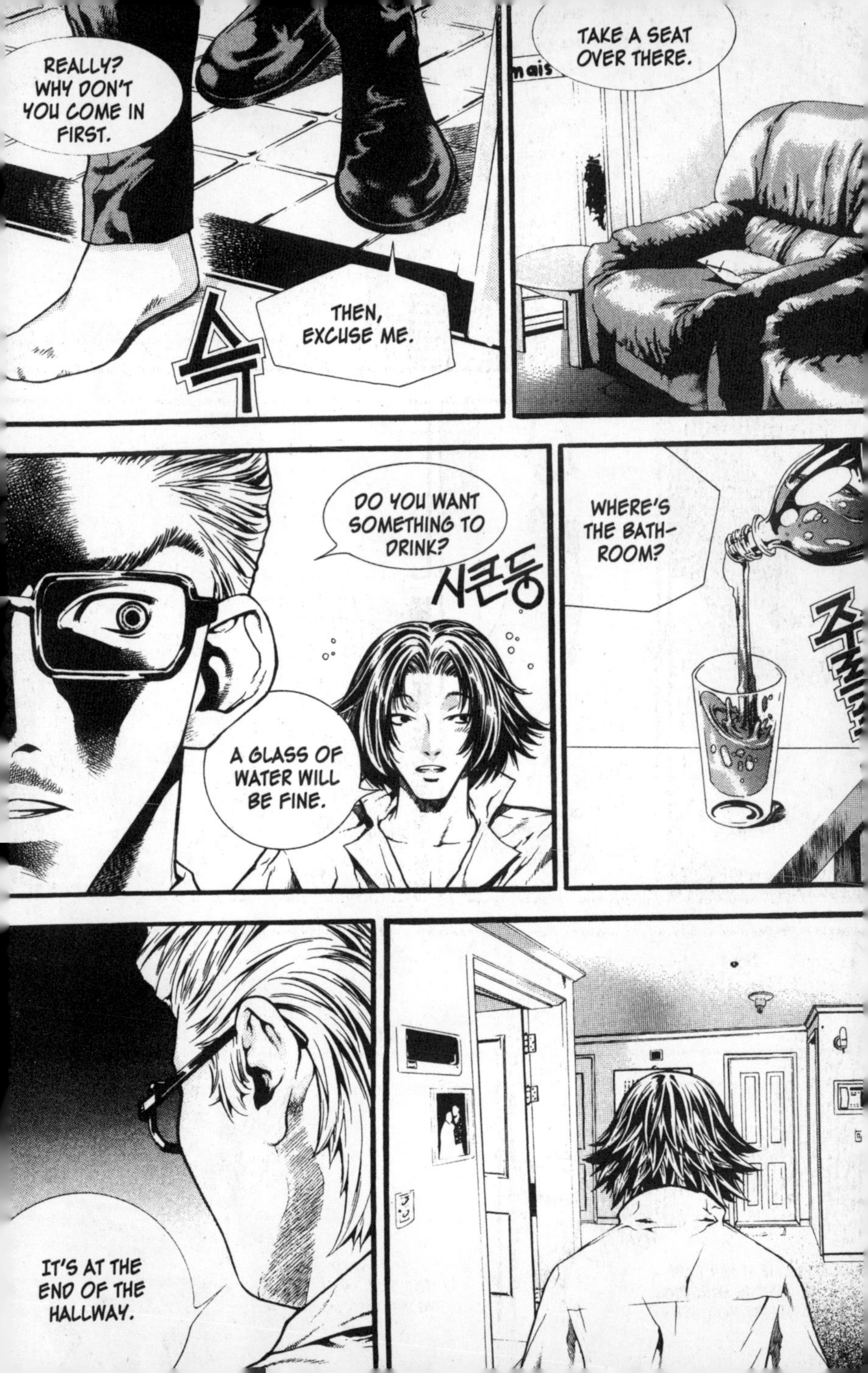
REALLY? WHY DON'T YOU COME IN FIRST.
슥
THEN, EXCUSE ME.
mais
TAKE A SEAT OVER THERE.
DO YOU WANT SOMETHING TO DRINK?
시큰둥
A GLASS OF WATER WILL BE FINE.
WHERE'S THE BATH-ROOM?
IT'S AT THE END OF THE HALLWAY.

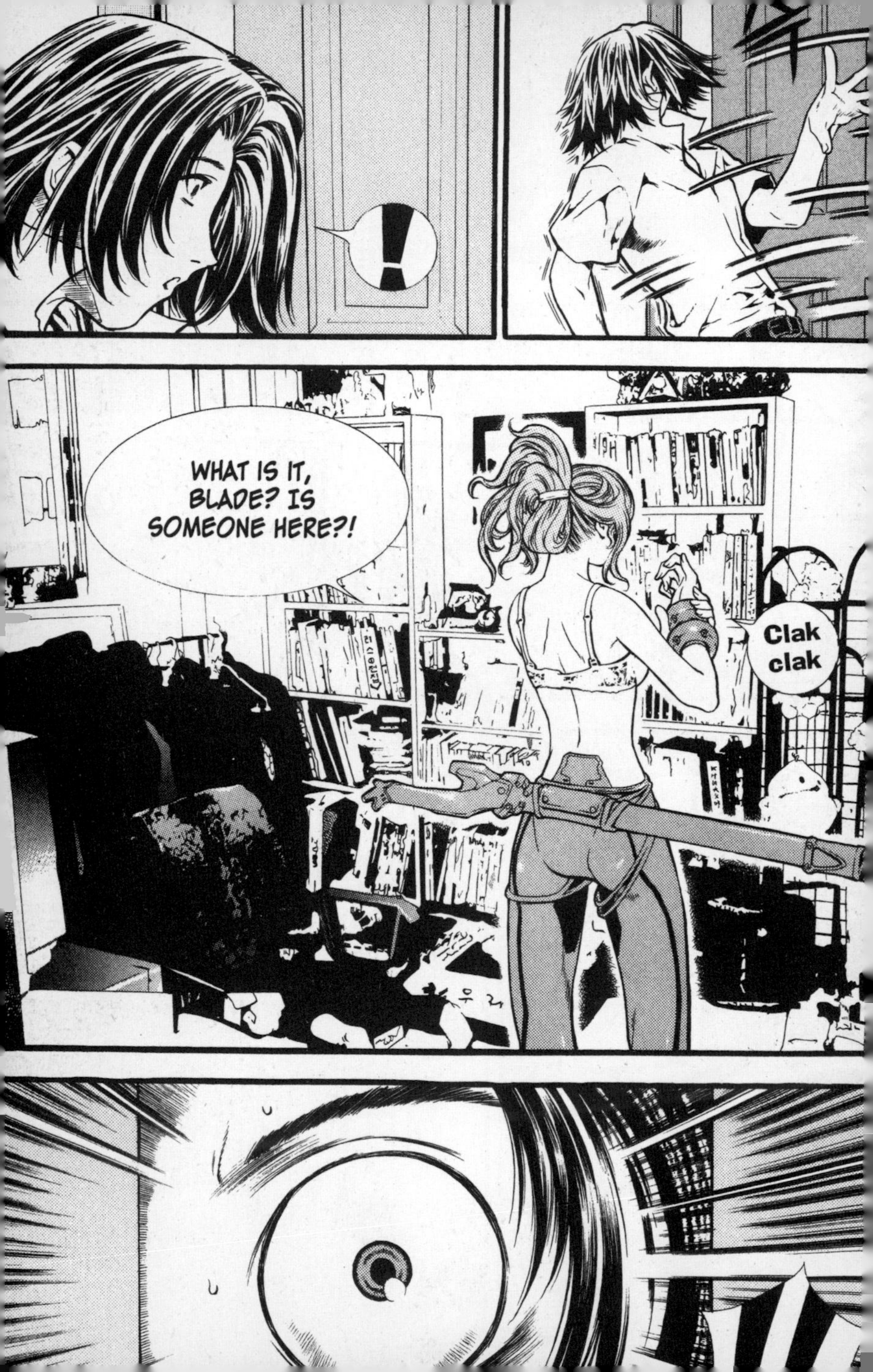
!
WHAT IS IT, BLADE? IS SOMEONE HERE?!
Clak clak

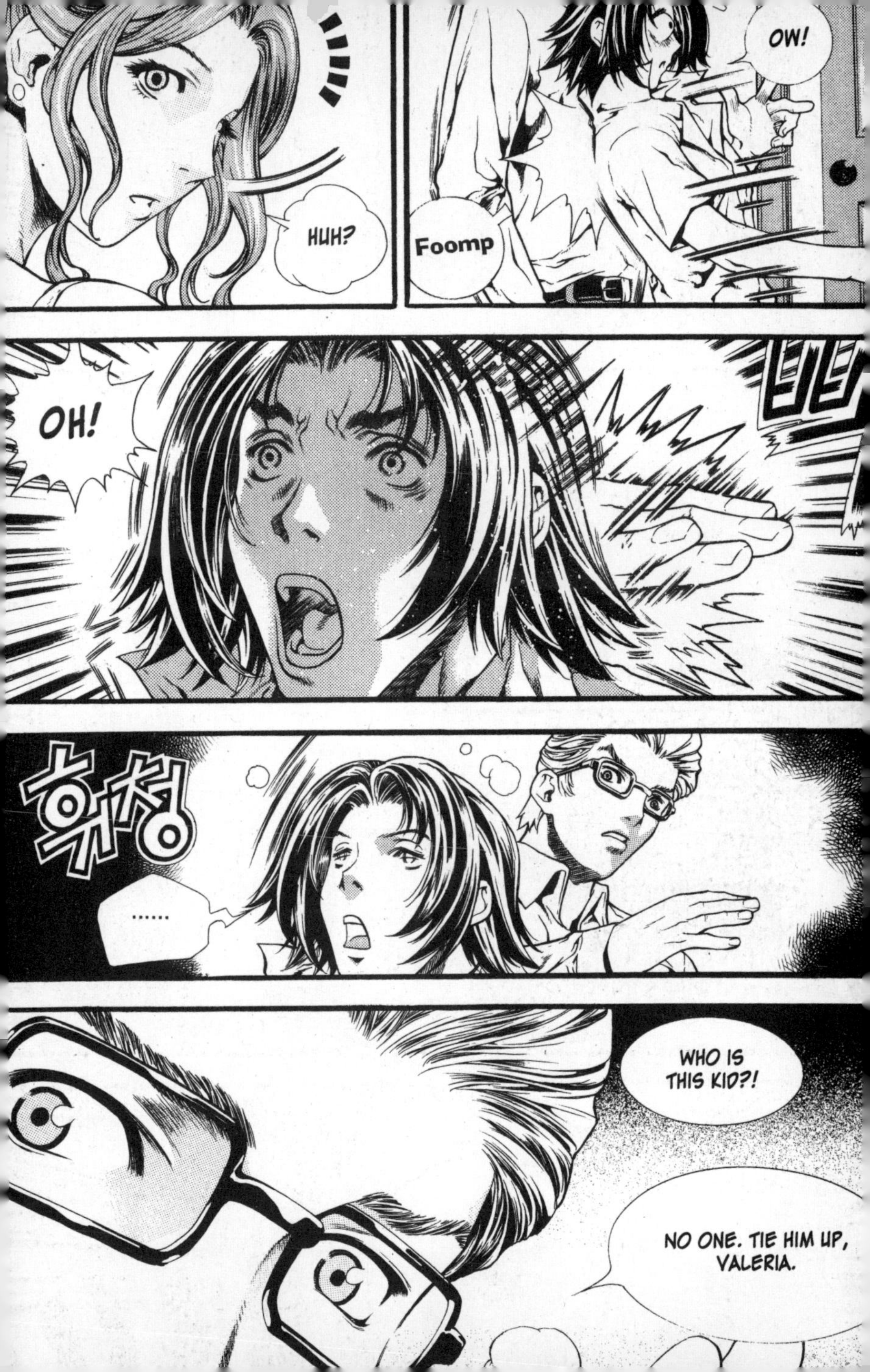
HUH?
OW!
Foomp
OH!
......
WHO IS THIS KID?!
NO ONE. TIE HIM UP, VALERIA.

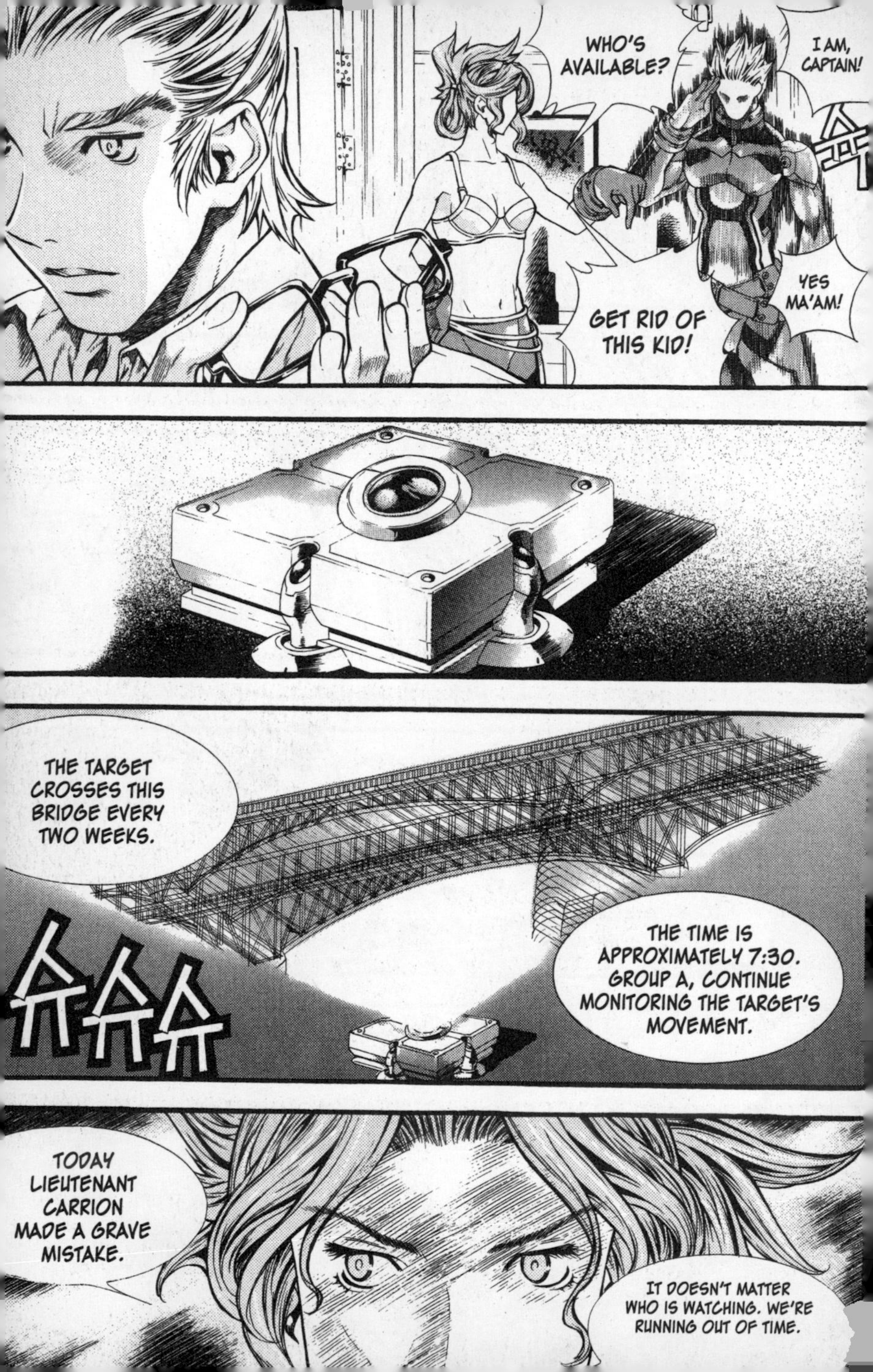
WHO'S AVAILABLE?
I AM, CAPTAIN!
GET RID OF THIS KID!
YES MA'AM!
THE TARGET CROSSES THIS BRIDGE EVERY TWO WEEKS.
THE TIME IS APPROXIMATELY 7:30. GROUP A, CONTINUE MONITORING THE TARGET'S MOVEMENT.
TODAY LIEUTENANT CARRION MADE A GRAVE MISTAKE.
IT DOESN'T MATTER WHO IS WATCHING. WE'RE RUNNING OUT OF TIME.

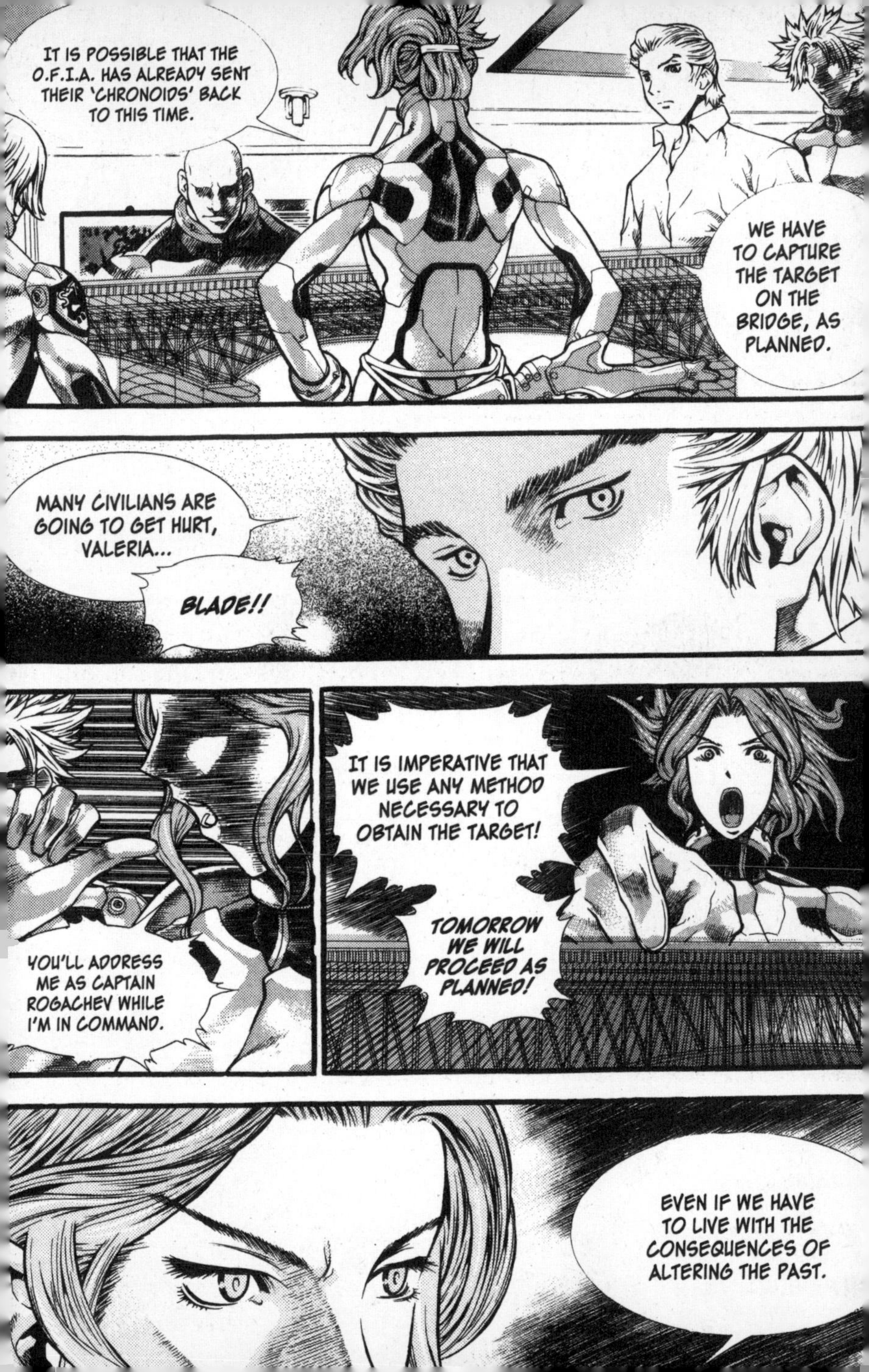
IT IS POSSIBLE THAT THE O.F.I.A. HAS ALREADY SENT THEIR 'CHRONOIDS' BACK TO THIS TIME.
WE HAVE TO CAPTURE THE TARGET ON THE BRIDGE, AS PLANNED.
MANY CIVILIANS ARE GOING TO GET HURT, VALERIA...
BLADE!!
YOU'LL ADDRESS ME AS CAPTAIN ROGACHEV WHILE I'M IN COMMAND.
IT IS IMPERATIVE THAT WE USE ANY METHOD NECESSARY TO OBTAIN THE TARGET!
TOMORROW WE WILL PROCEED AS PLANNED!
EVEN IF WE HAVE TO LIVE WITH THE CONSEQUENCES OF ALTERING THE PAST.

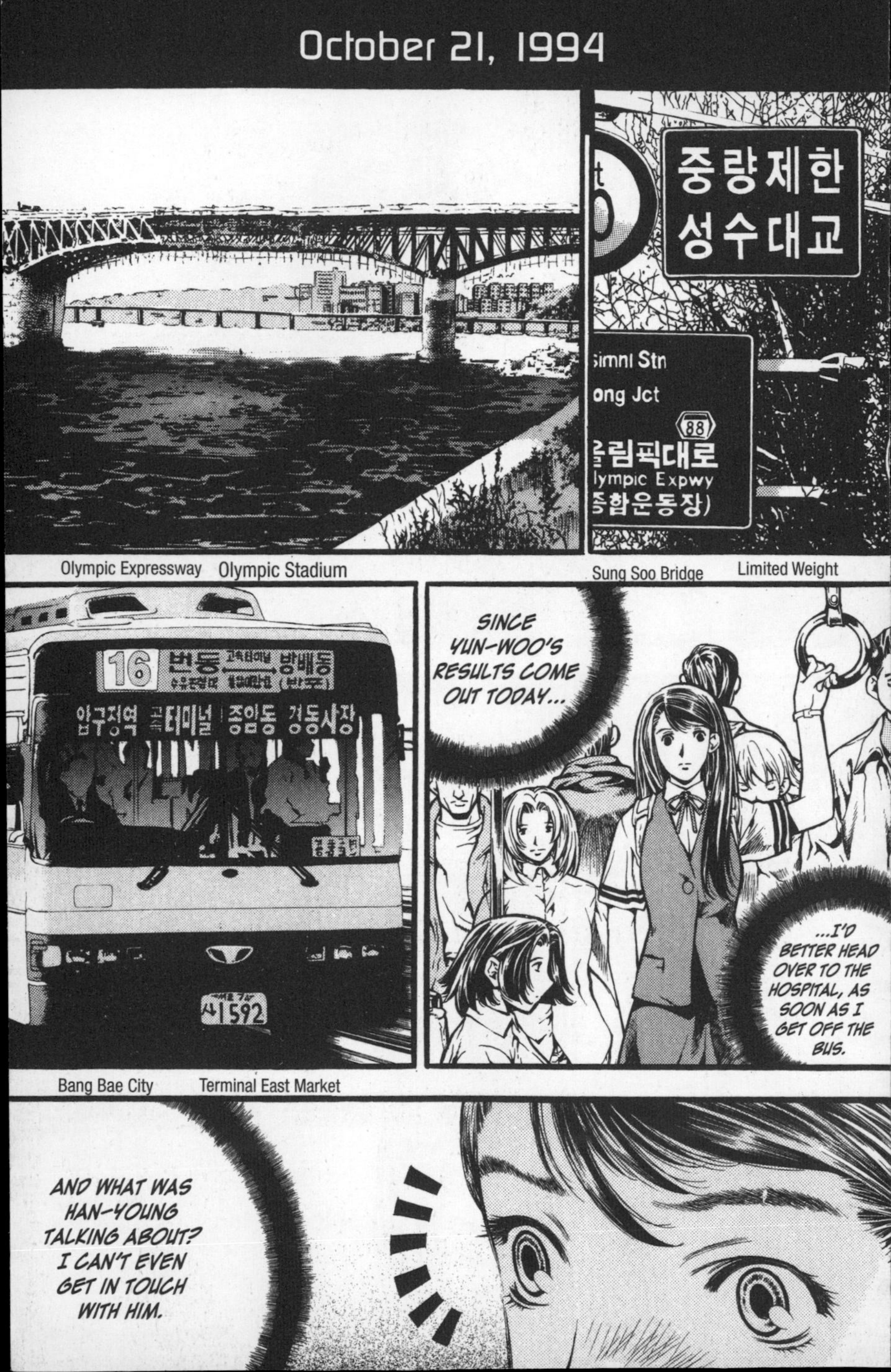
October 21, 1994
중량제한
성수대교
Olympic Expressway
Olympic Stadium
Sung Soo Bridge
Limited Weight
16
SINCE YUN-WOO'S RESULTS COME OUT TODAY...
...I'D BETTER HEAD OVER TO THE HOSPITAL, AS SOON AS I GET OFF THE BUS.
Bang Bae City
Terminal East Market
AND WHAT WAS HAN-YOUNG TALKING ABOUT? I CAN'T EVEN GET IN TOUCH WITH HIM.

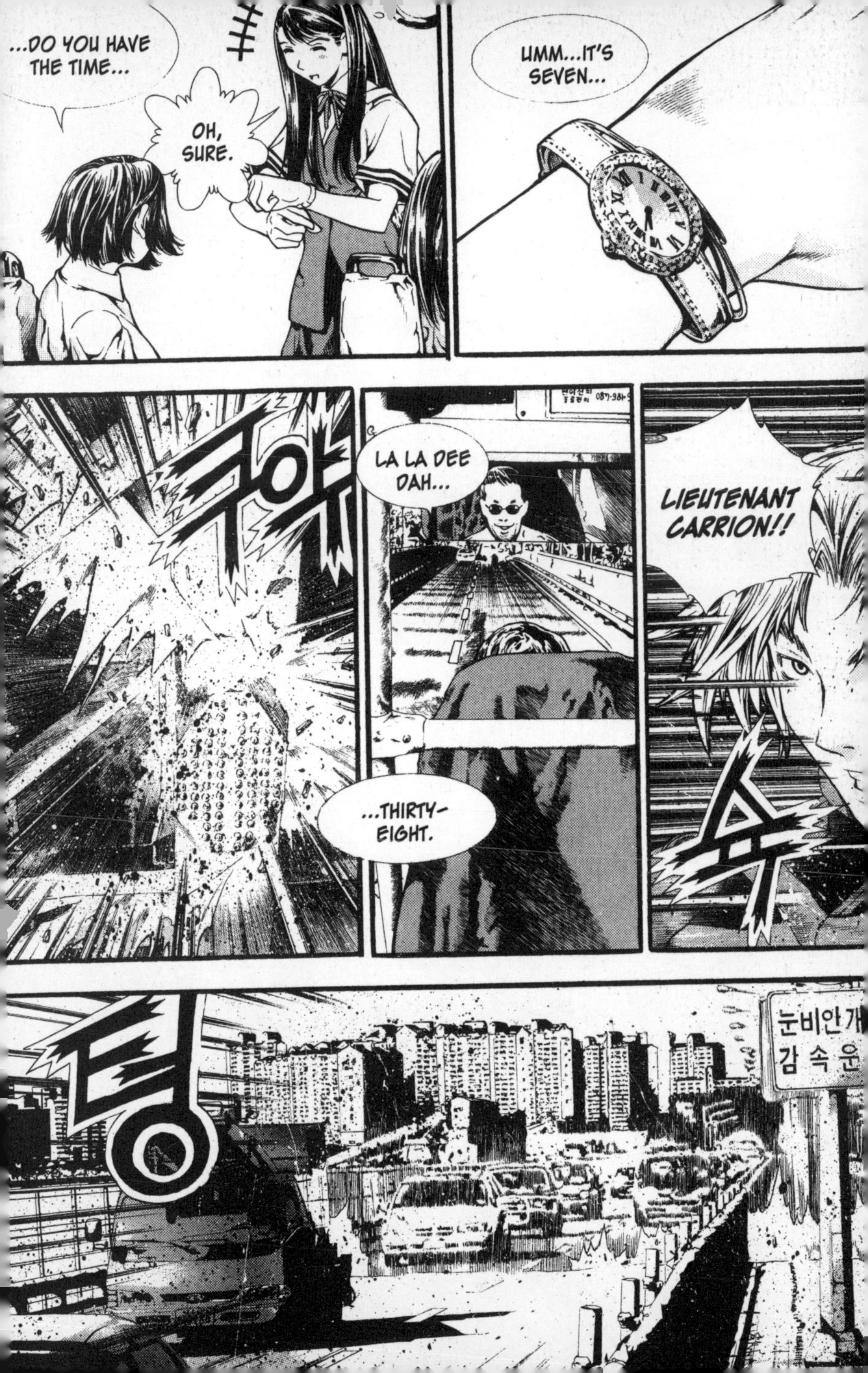
...DO YOU HAVE THE TIME...
OH, SURE.
UMM...IT'S SEVEN...
LA LA DEE DAH...
...THIRTY-EIGHT.
LIEUTENANT CARRION!!
눈비안개
감속운

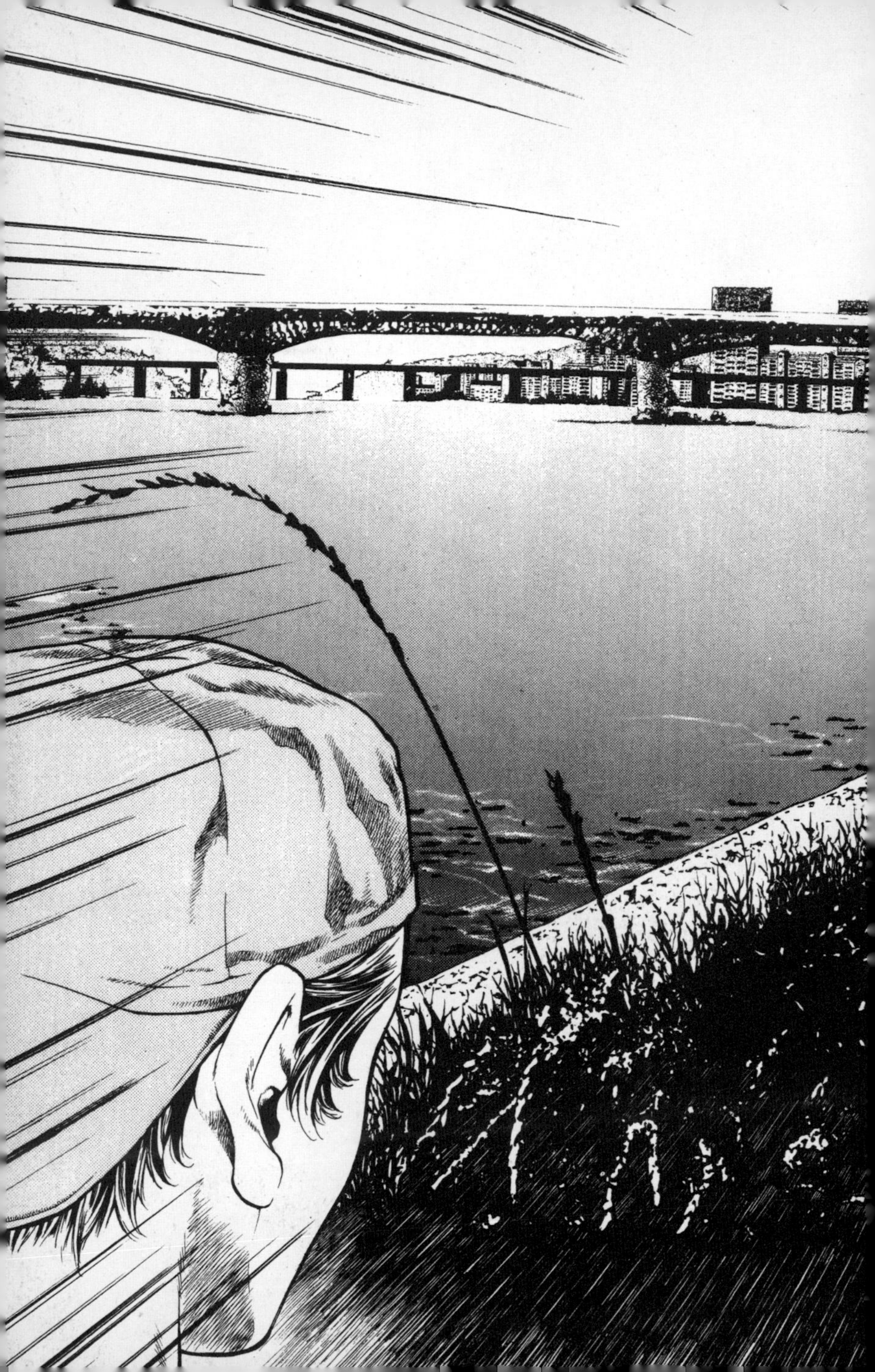

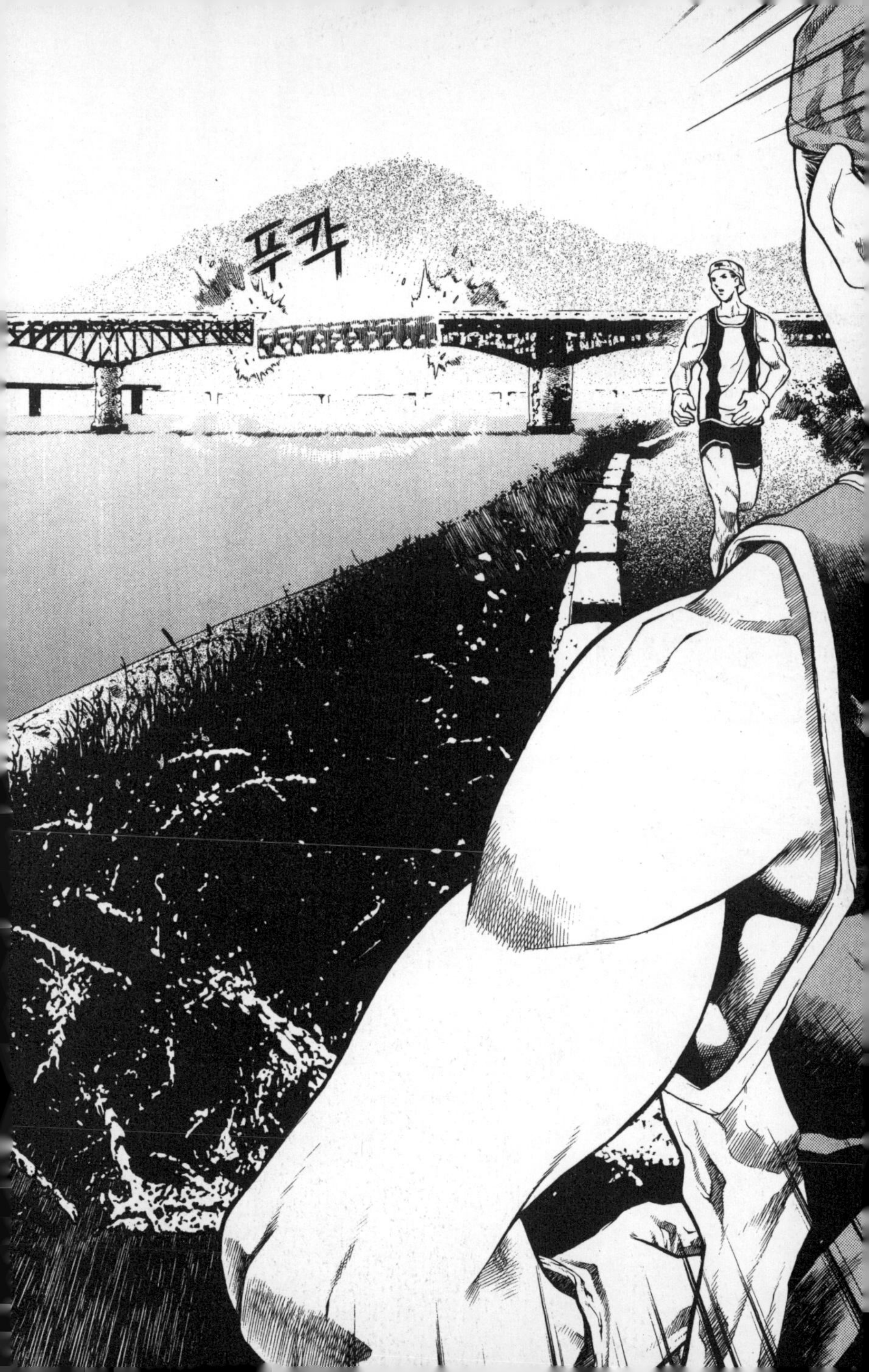
푸콱

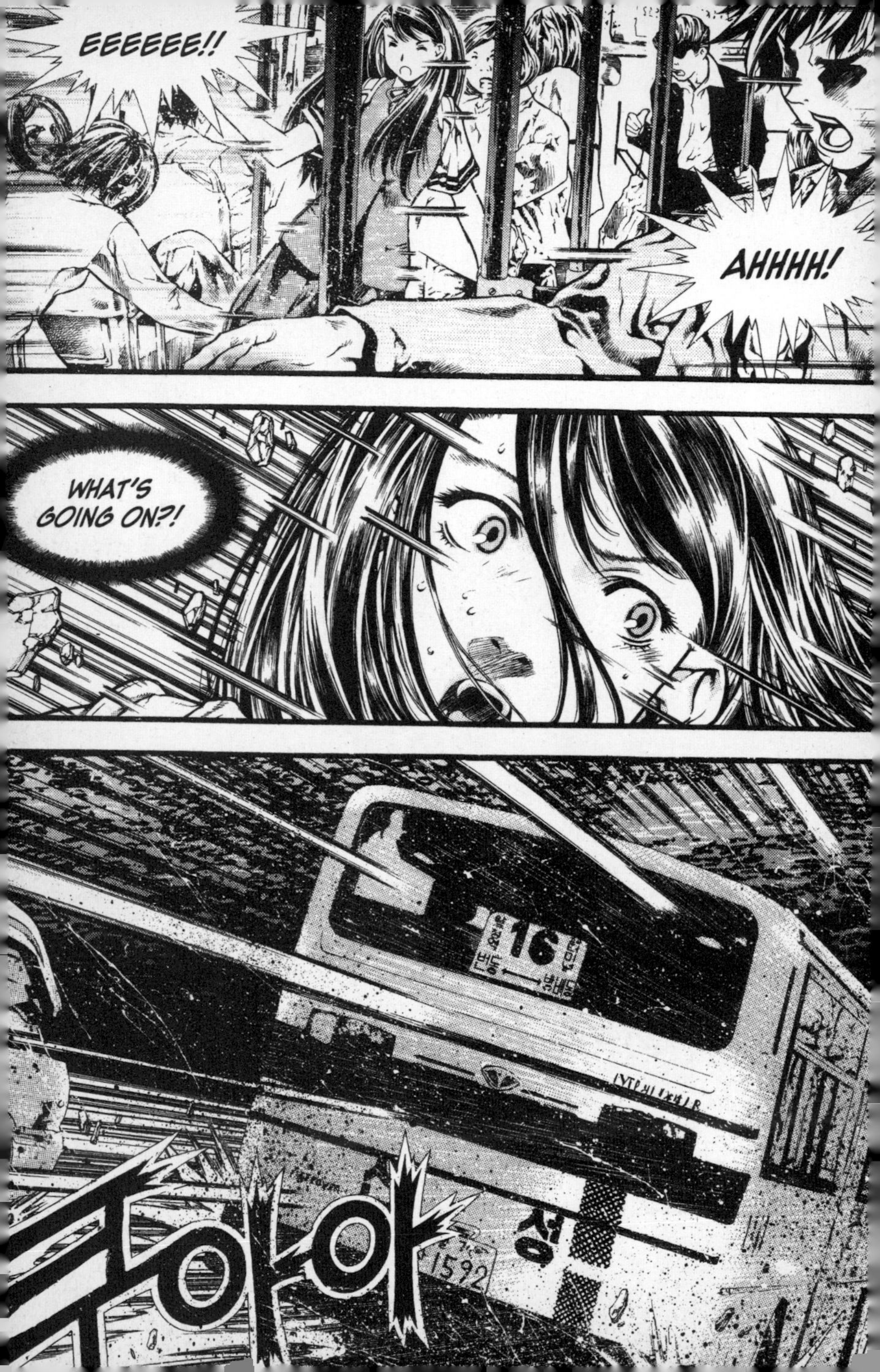
EEEEEE!!
AHHHH!
WHAT'S GOING ON?!
16
1592

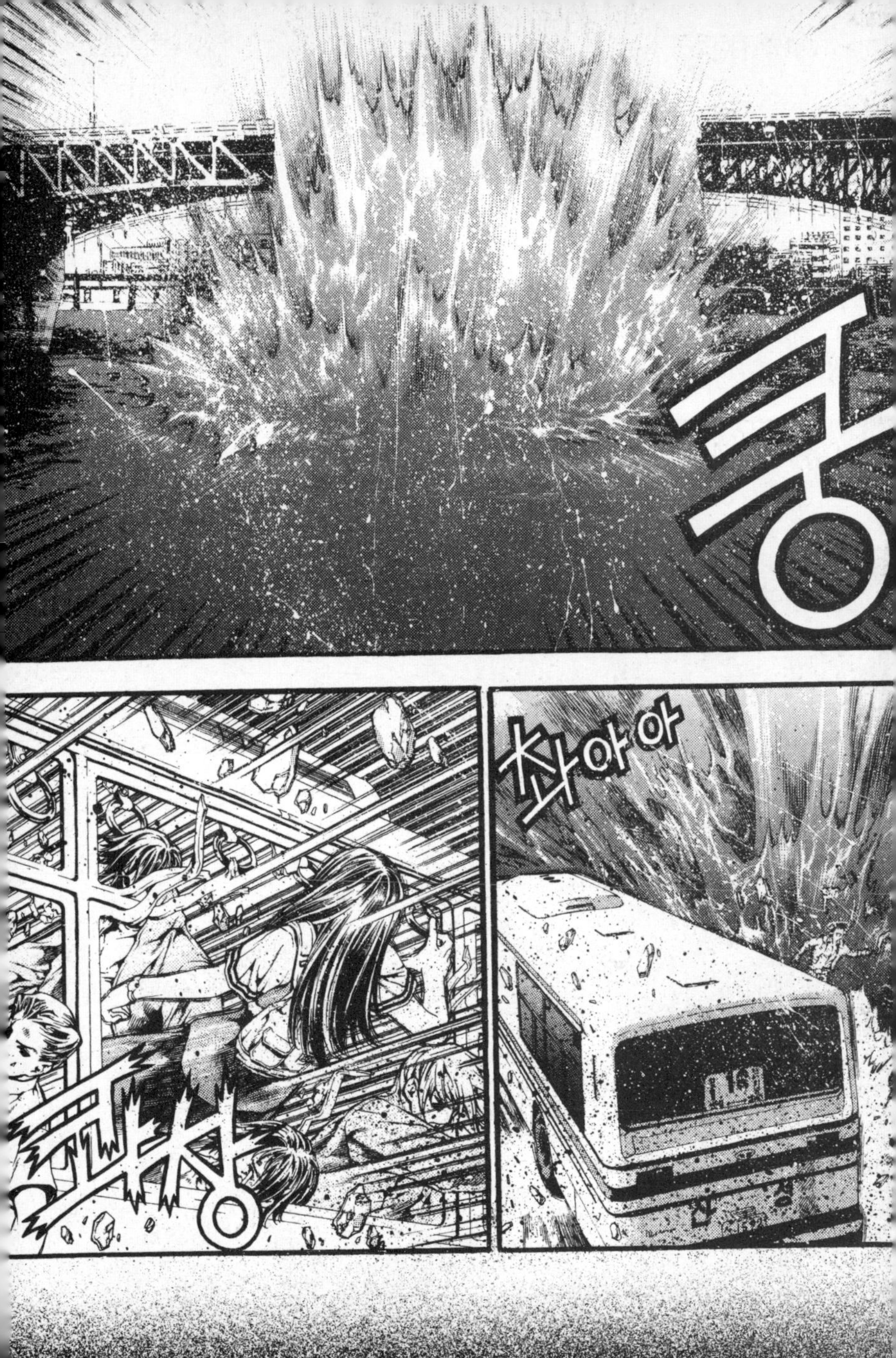
쿵
촤아아

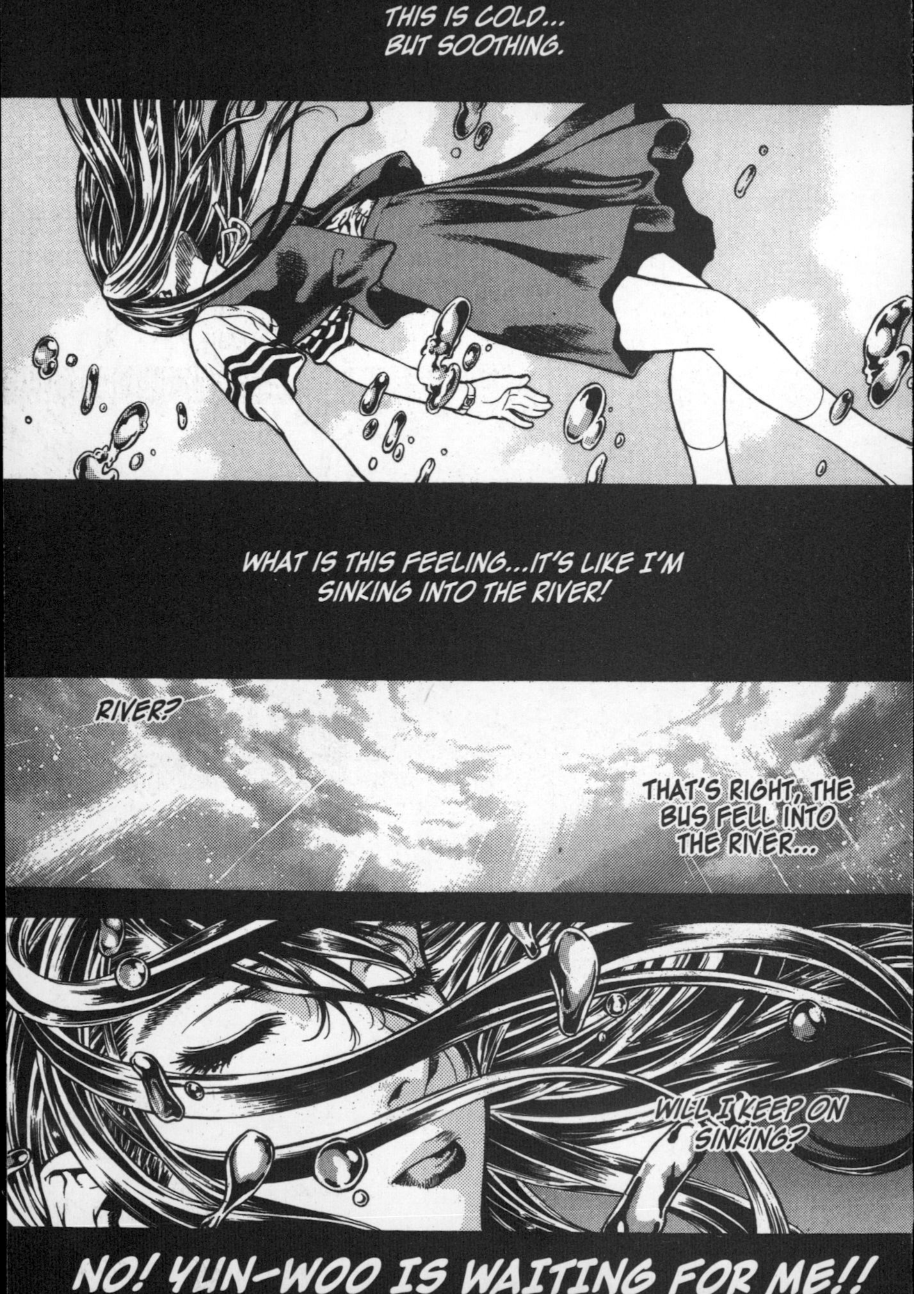
THIS IS COLD... BUT SOOTHING.
WHAT IS THIS FEELING...IT'S LIKE I'M SINKING INTO THE RIVER!
RIVER?
THAT'S RIGHT, THE BUS FELL INTO THE RIVER...
WILL I KEEP ON SINKING?
NO! YUN-WOO IS WAITING FOR ME!!

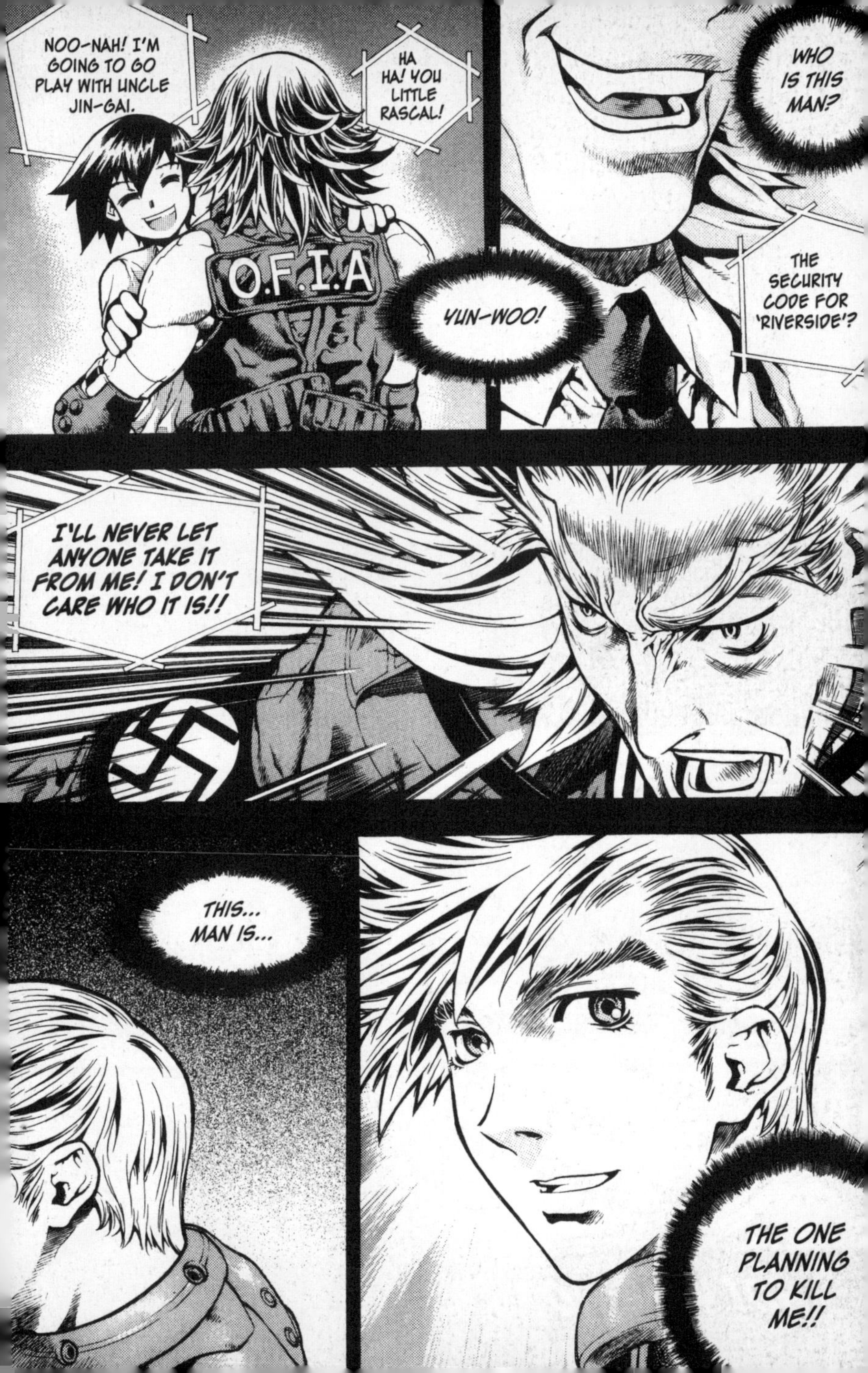
NOO-NAH! I'M GOING TO GO PLAY WITH UNCLE JIN-GAI.
HA HA! YOU LITTLE RASCAL!
O.F.I.A
YUN-WOO!
WHO IS THIS MAN?
THE SECURITY CODE FOR 'RIVERSIDE'?
I'LL NEVER LET ANYONE TAKE IT FROM ME! I DON'T CARE WHO IT IS!!
THIS... MAN IS...
THE ONE PLANNING TO KILL ME!!

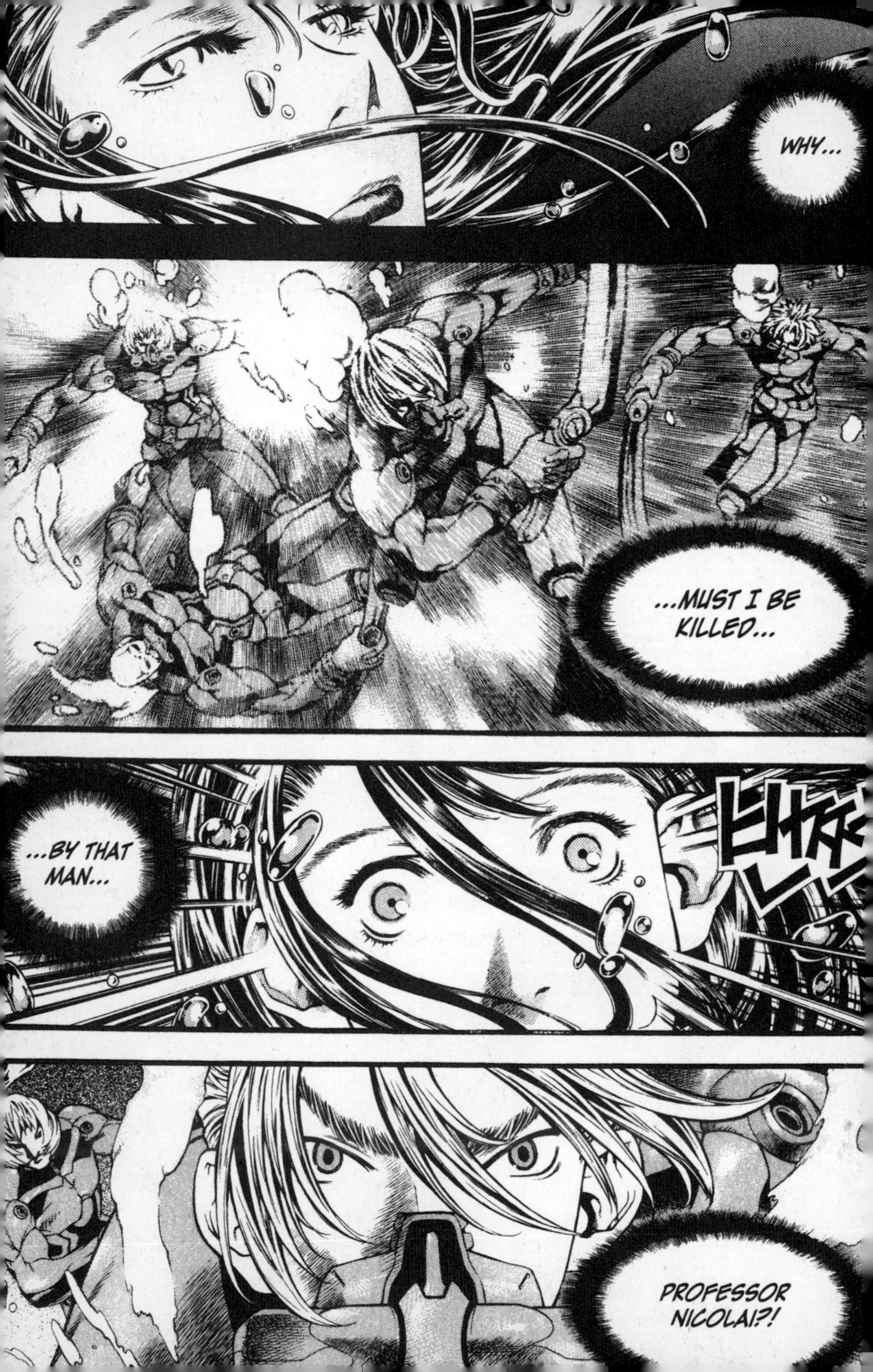
WHY...
...MUST I BE KILLED...
...BY THAT MAN...
PROFESSOR NICOLAI?!

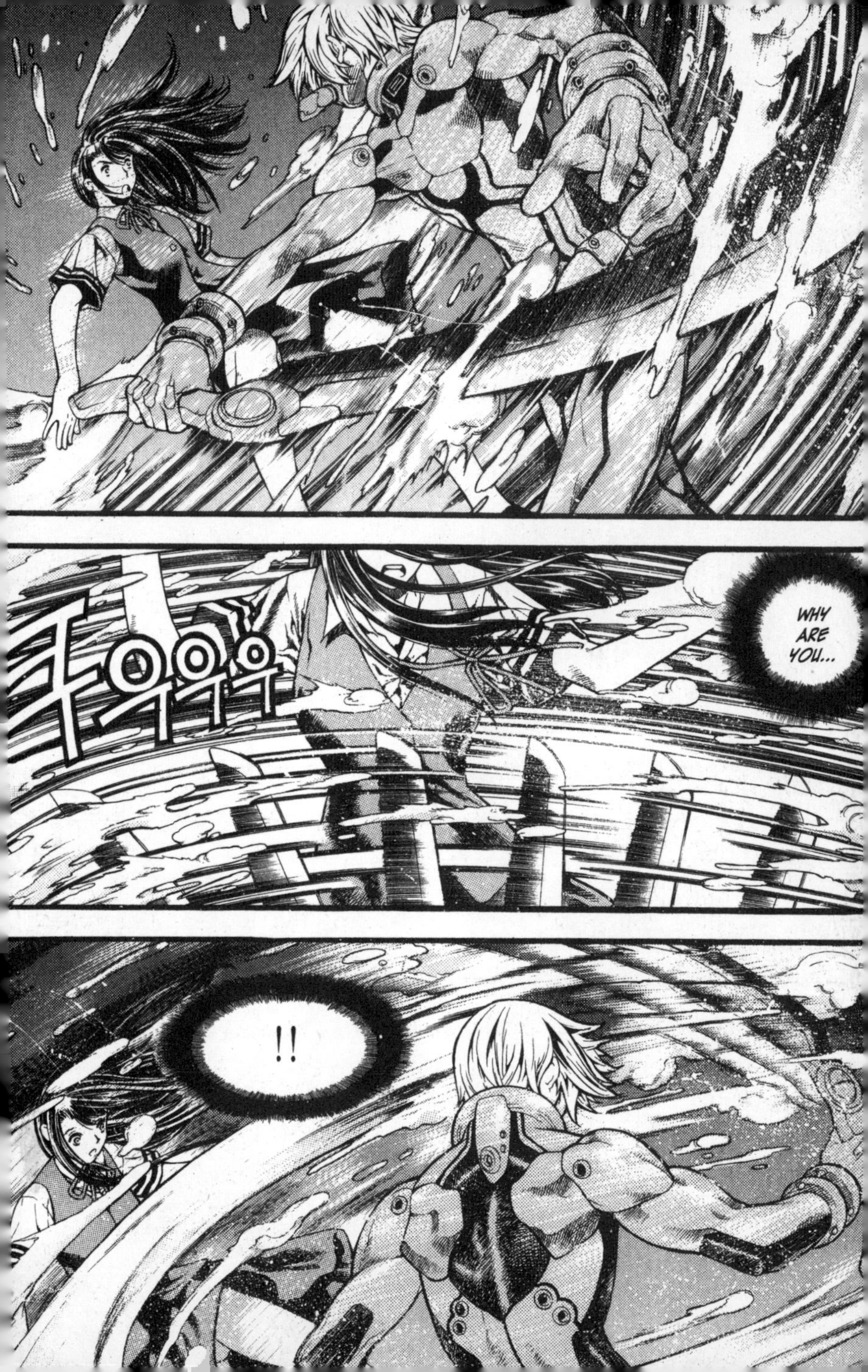
WHY ARE YOU...
!!

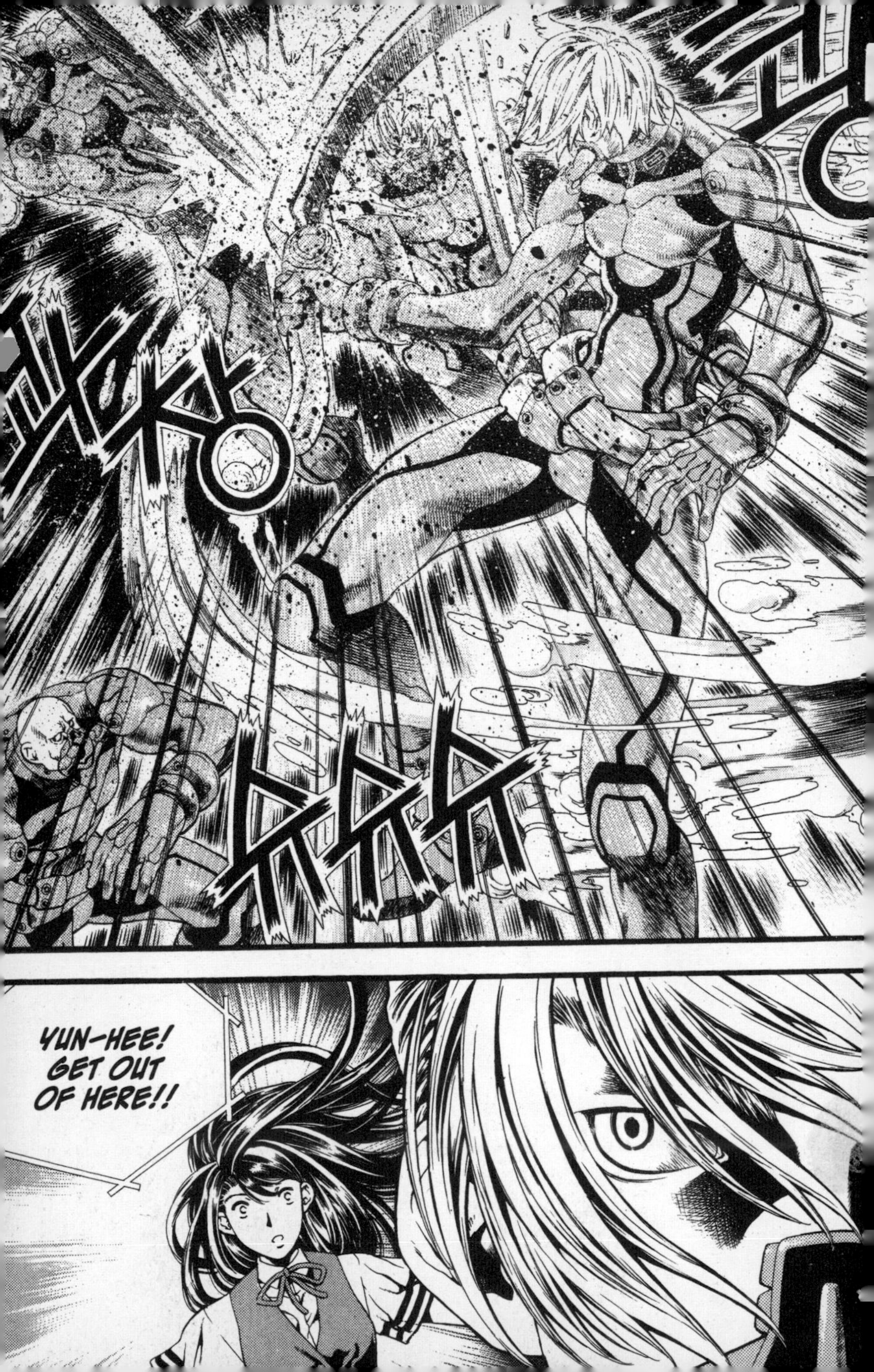
YUN-HEE! GET OUT OF HERE!!

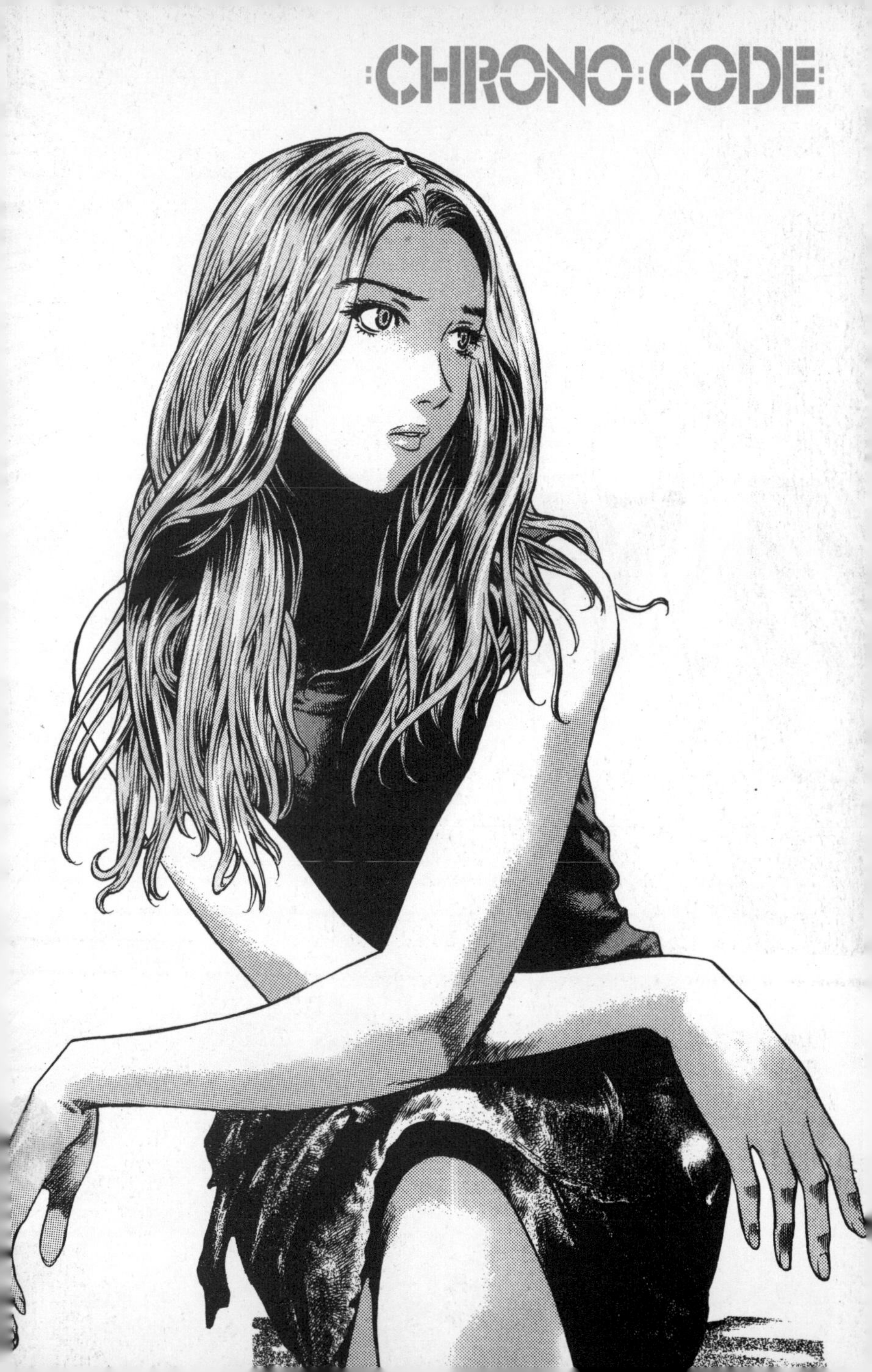
CHRONO CODE

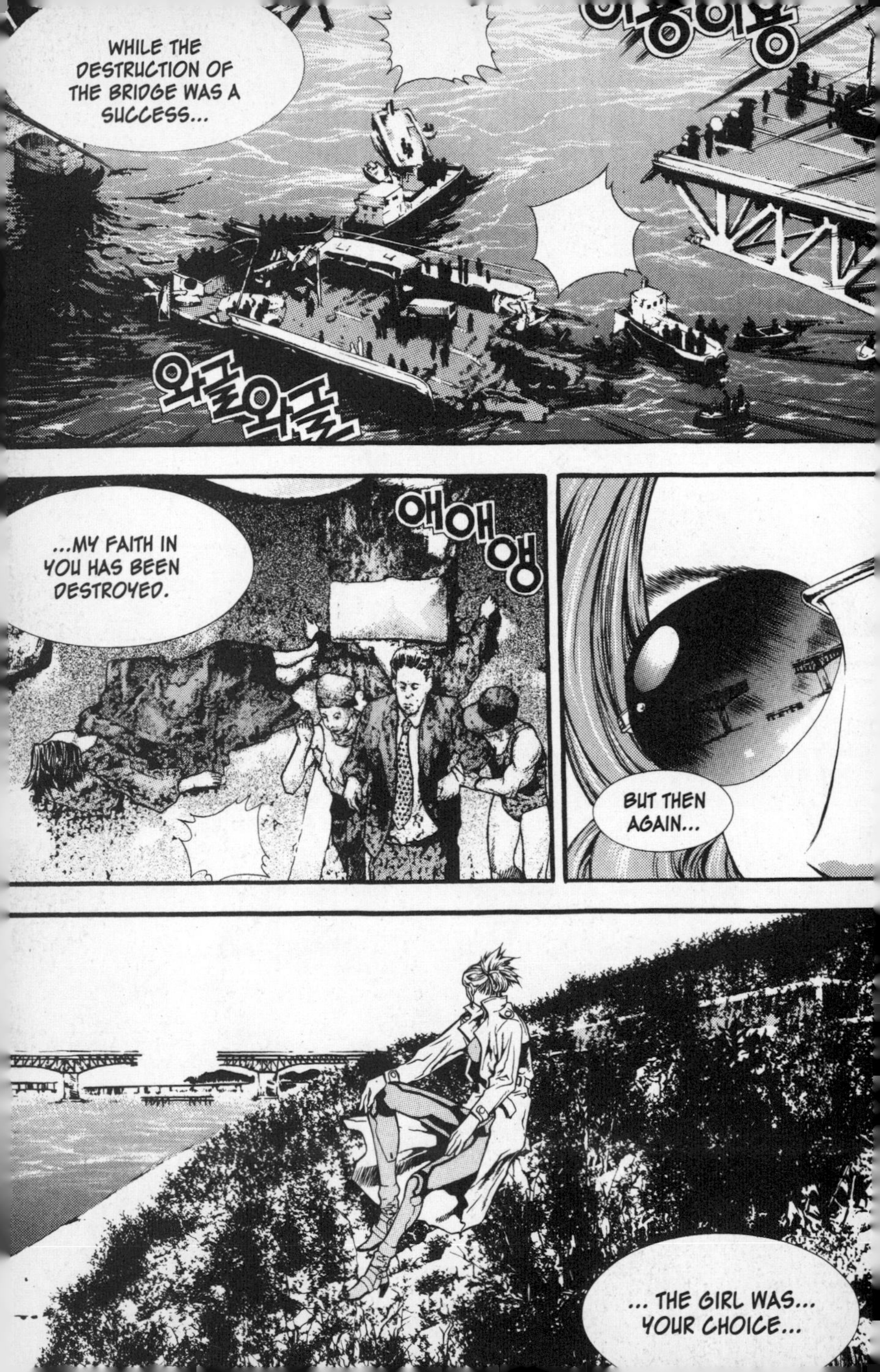
WHILE THE DESTRUCTION OF THE BRIDGE WAS A SUCCESS...
와글와글
...MY FAITH IN YOU HAS BEEN DESTROYED.
애애애앵
BUT THEN AGAIN...
... THE GIRL WAS... YOUR CHOICE...

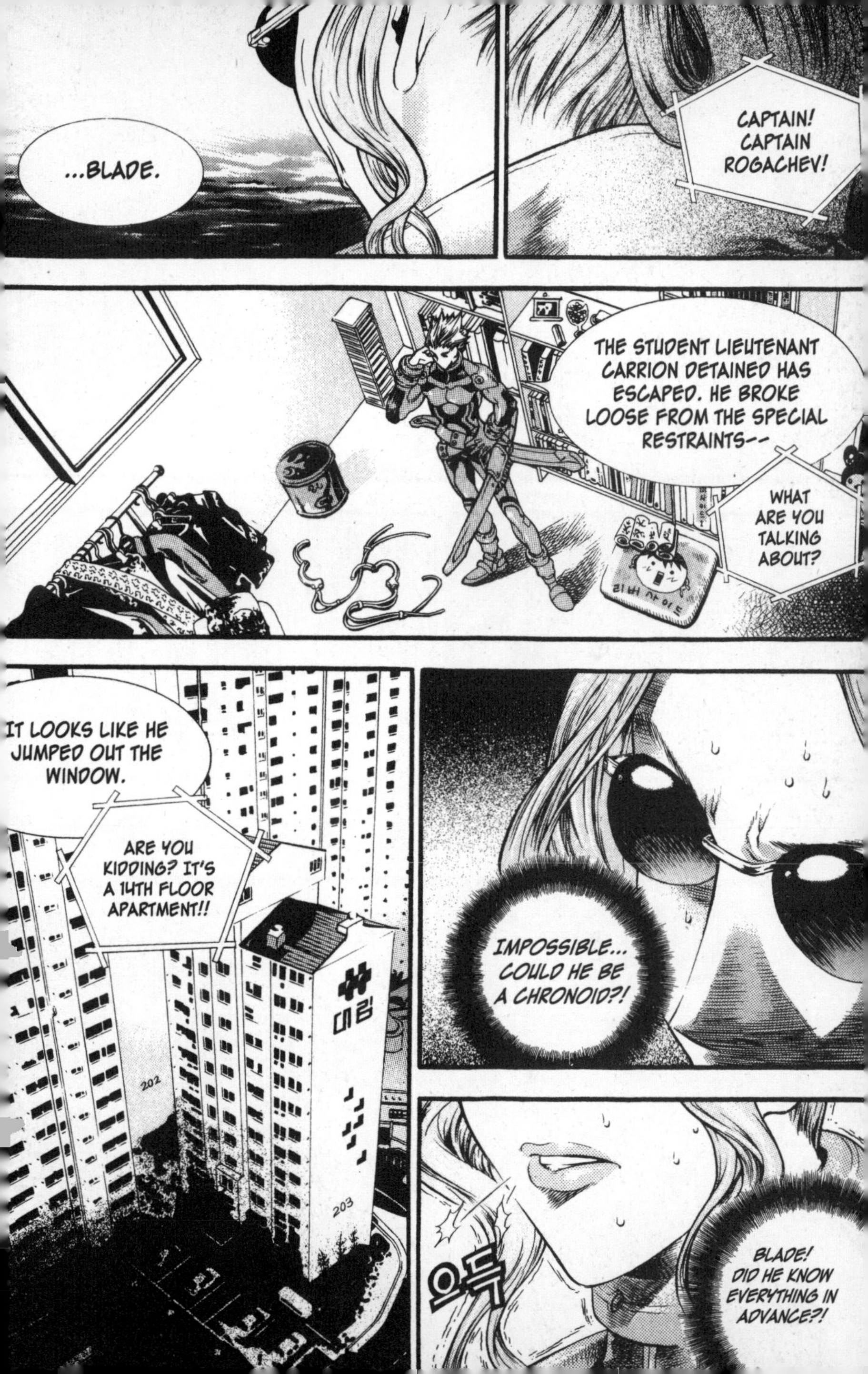
...BLADE.
CAPTAIN! CAPTAIN ROGACHEV!
THE STUDENT LIEUTENANT CARRION DETAINED HAS ESCAPED. HE BROKE LOOSE FROM THE SPECIAL RESTRAINTS--
WHAT ARE YOU TALKING ABOUT?
IT LOOKS LIKE HE JUMPED OUT THE WINDOW.
ARE YOU KIDDING? IT'S A 14TH FLOOR APARTMENT!!
IMPOSSIBLE... COULD HE BE A CHRONOID?!
BLADE! DID HE KNOW EVERYTHING IN ADVANCE?!

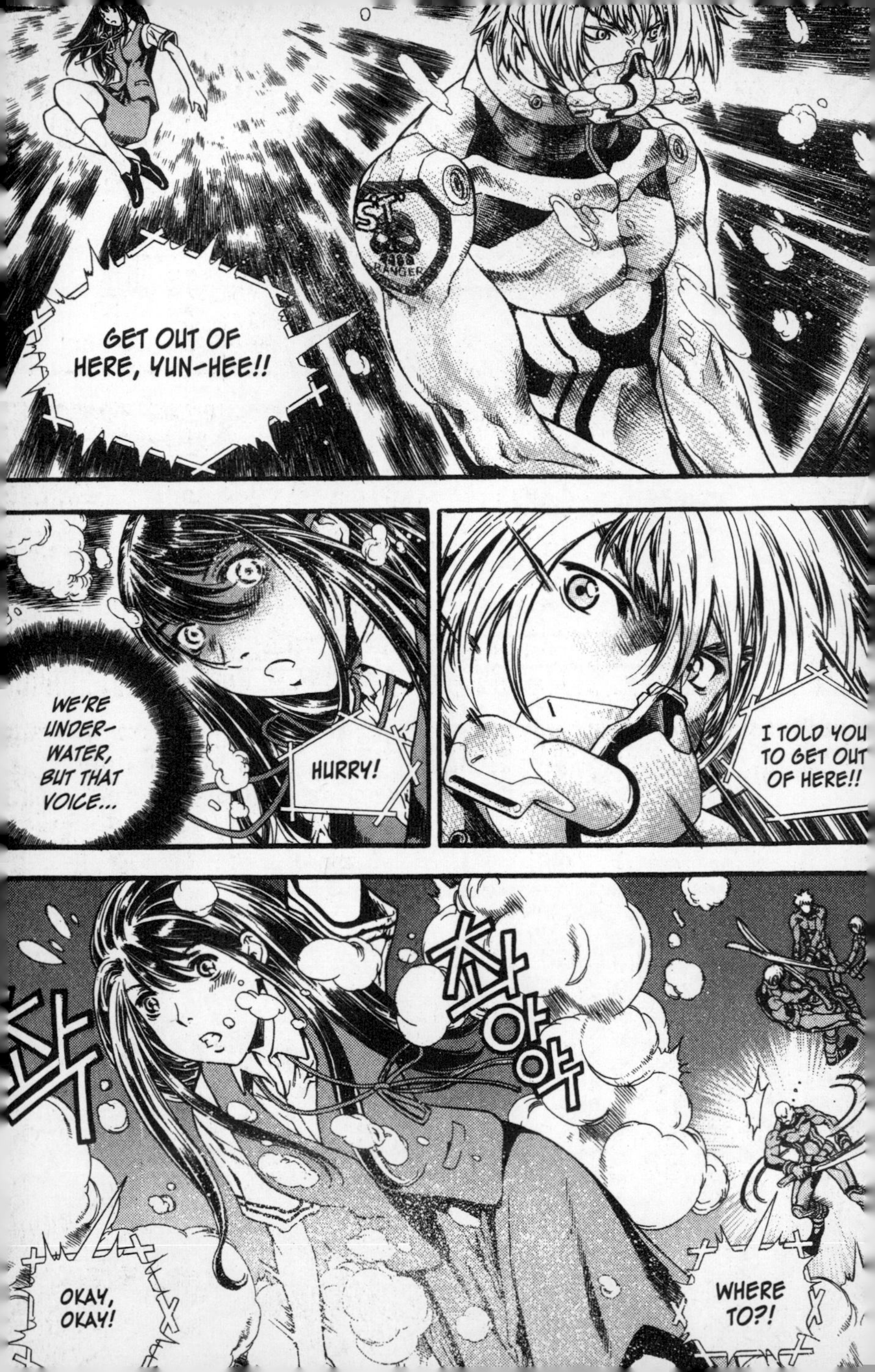
GET OUT OF HERE, YUN-HEE!!
WE'RE UNDER-WATER, BUT THAT VOICE...
HURRY!
I TOLD YOU TO GET OUT OF HERE!!
OKAY, OKAY!
WHERE TO?!

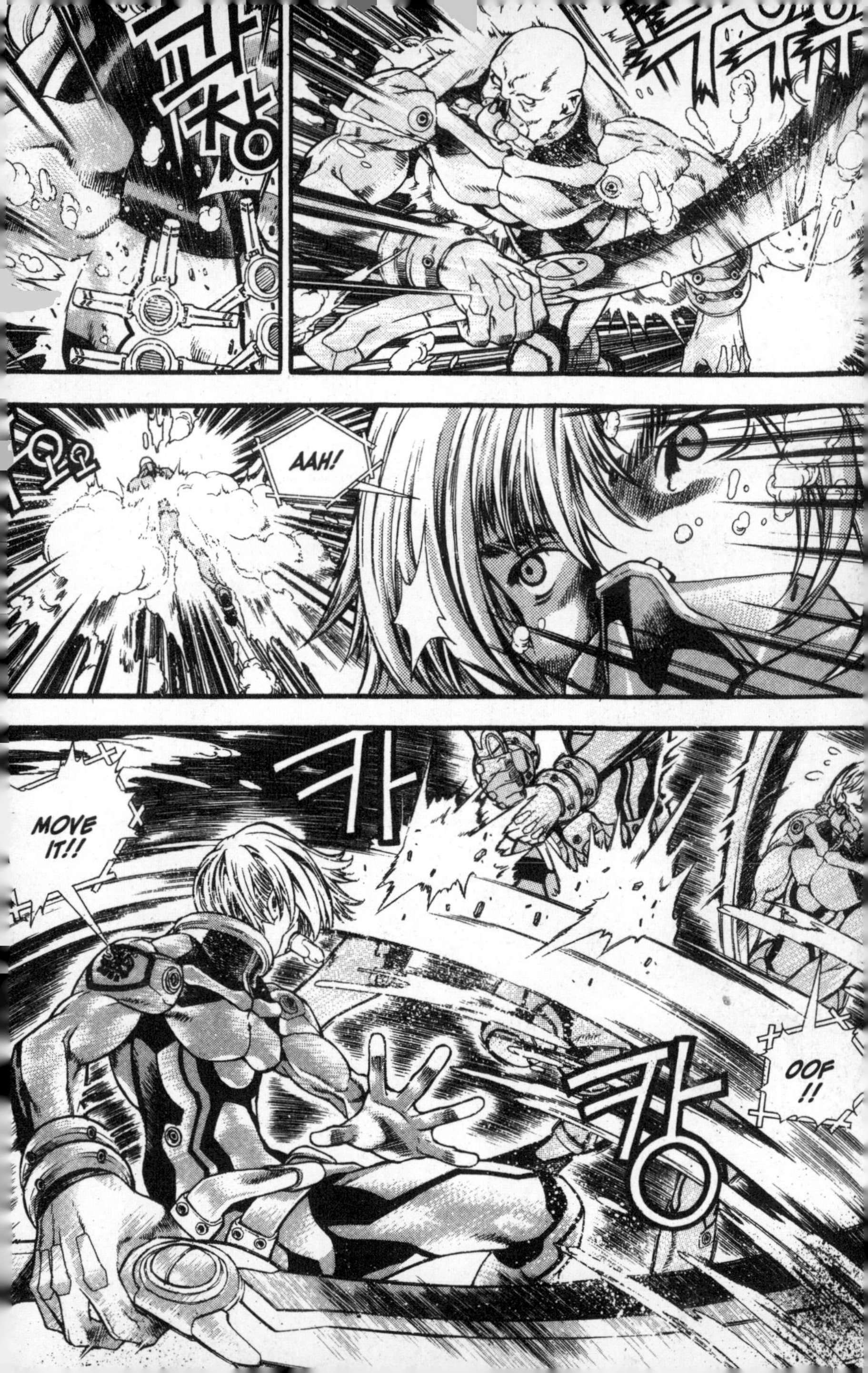
AAH!
MOVE IT!!
OOF !!

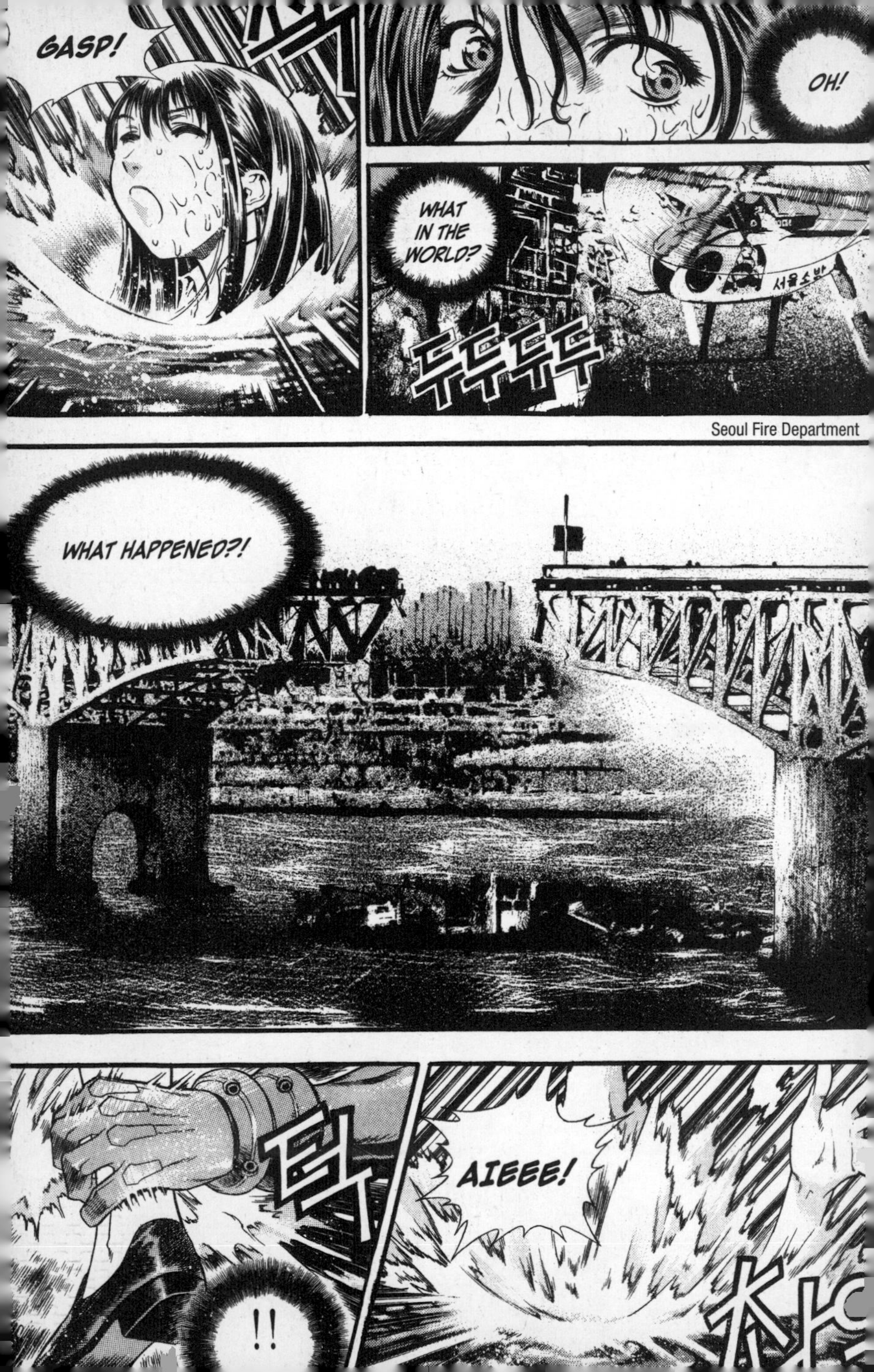
GASP!
OH!
WHAT IN THE WORLD?
두두두두
서울소방
Seoul Fire Department
WHAT HAPPENED?!
!!
AIEEE!

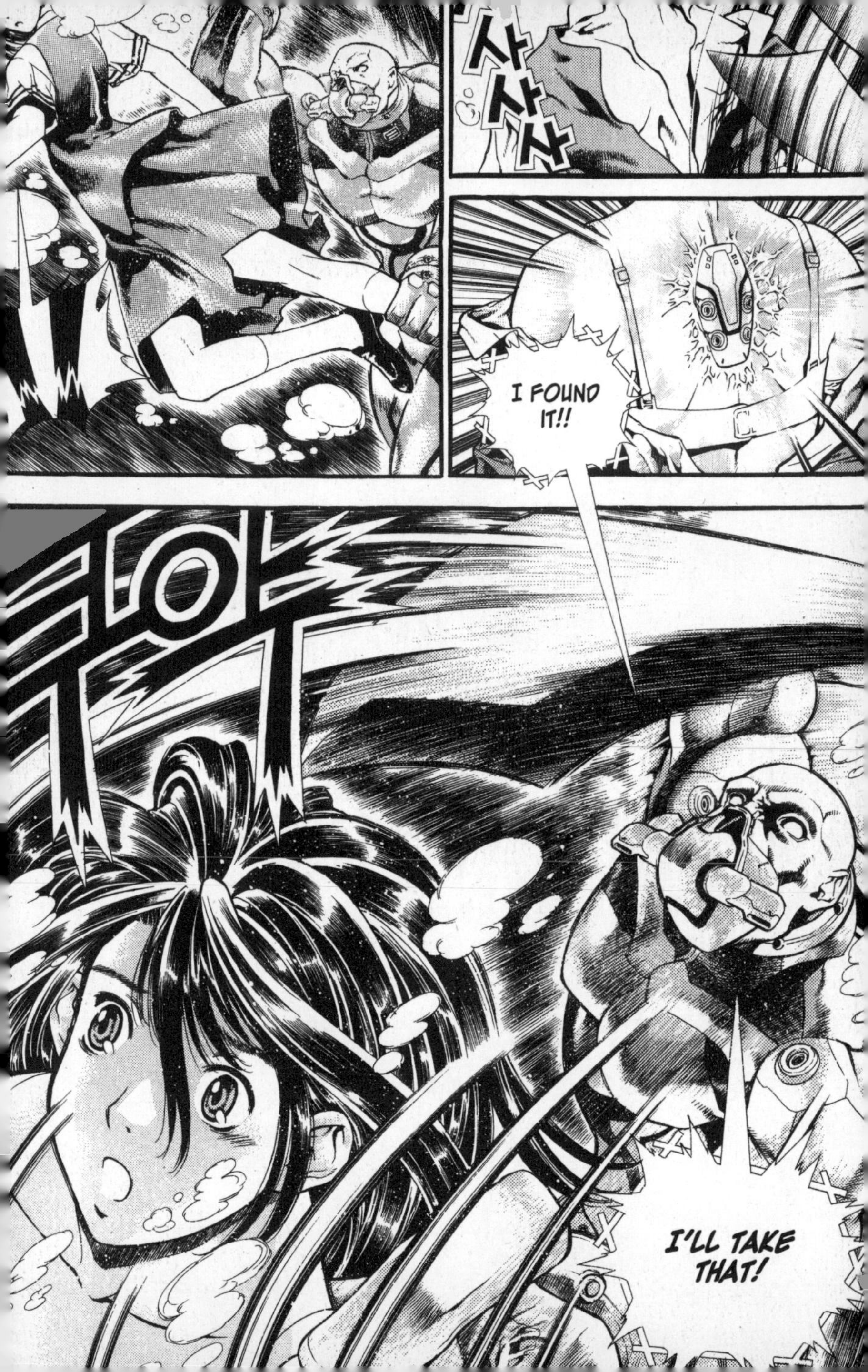

사사사
I FOUND IT!!
I'LL TAKE THAT!

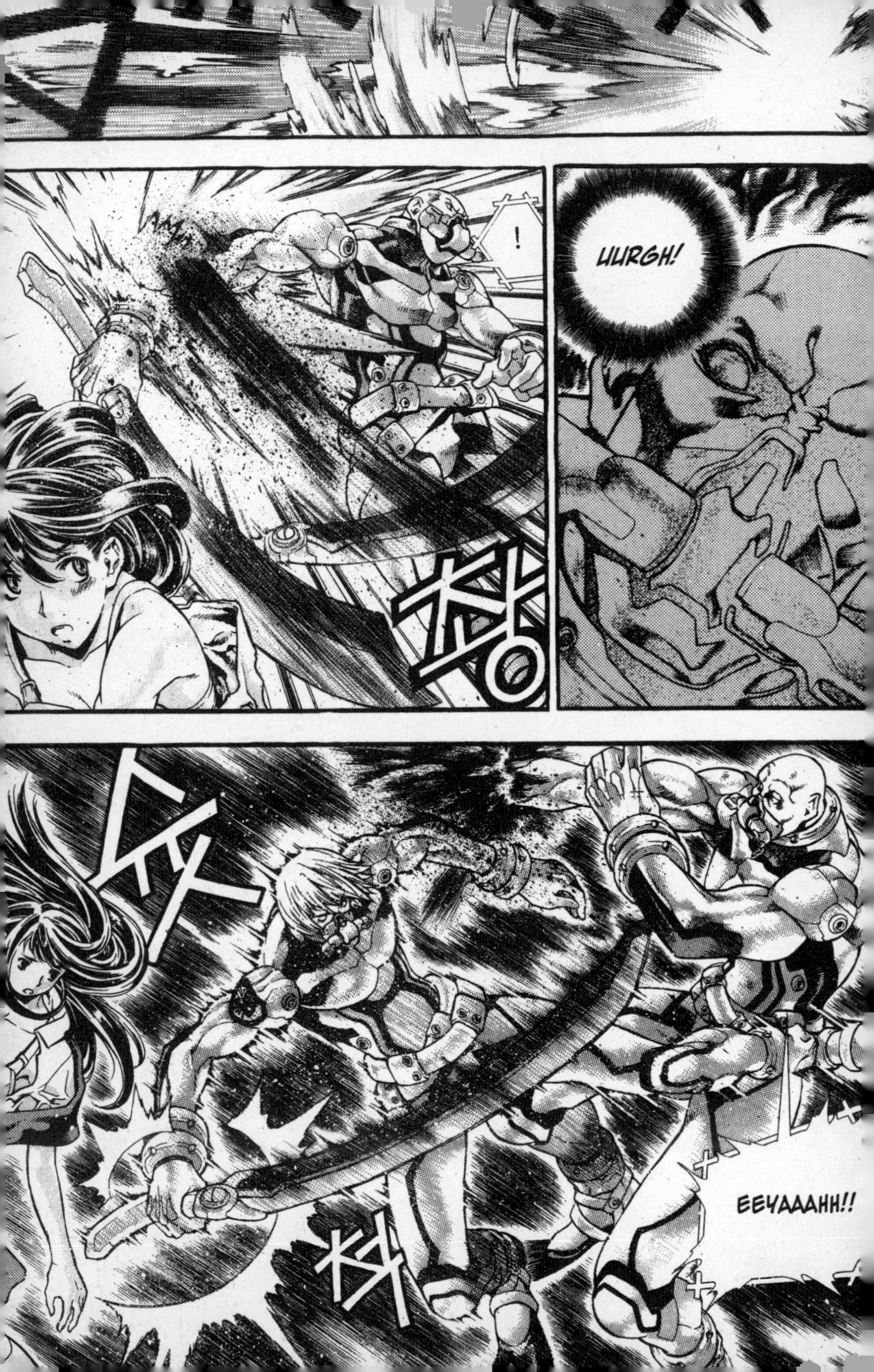
!
UURGH!
EEYAAAHH!!

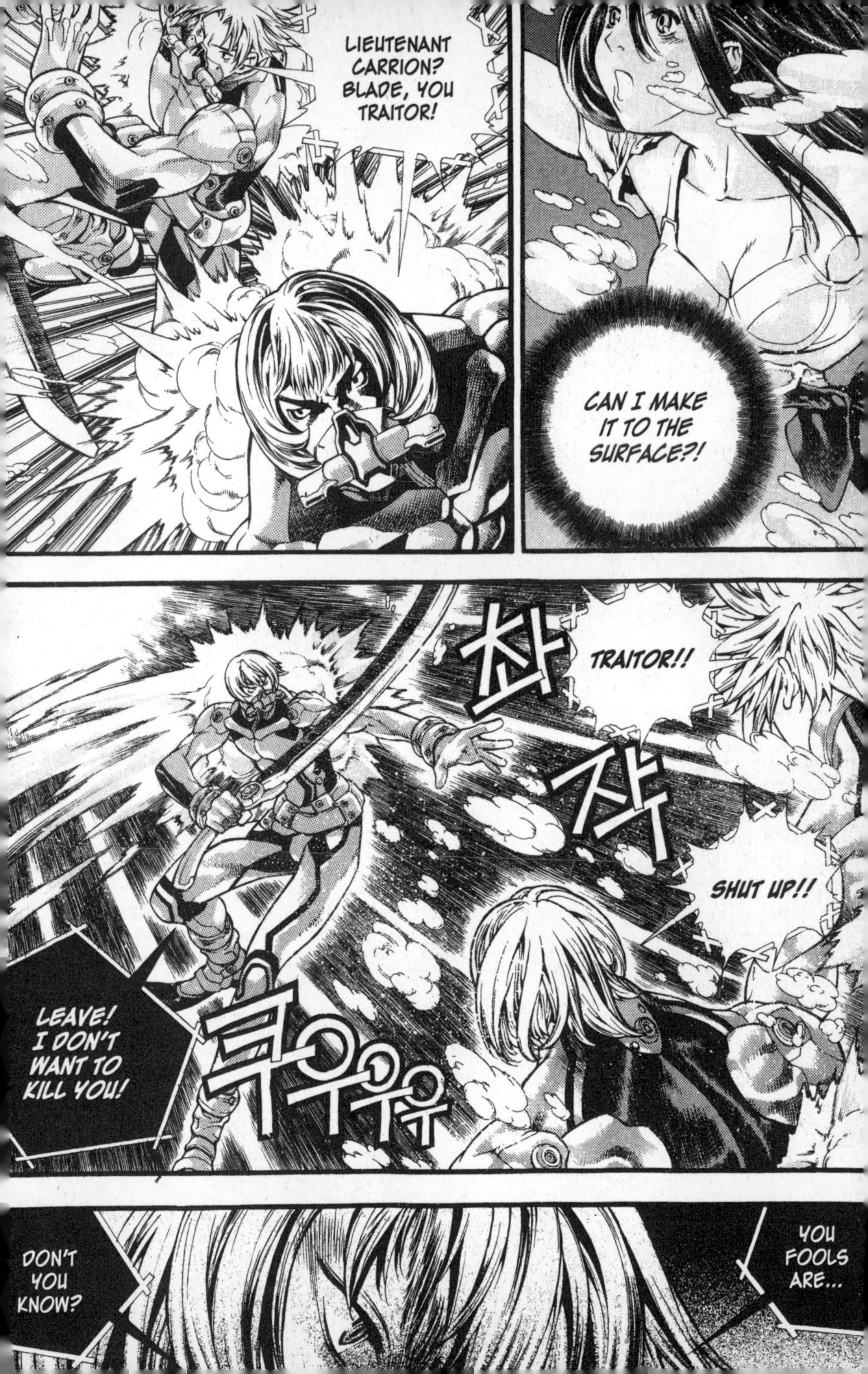
LIEUTENANT CARRION? BLADE, YOU TRAITOR!
CAN I MAKE IT TO THE SURFACE?!
LEAVE! I DON'T WANT TO KILL YOU!
TRAITOR!!
SHUT UP!!
DON'T YOU KNOW?
YOU FOOLS ARE...

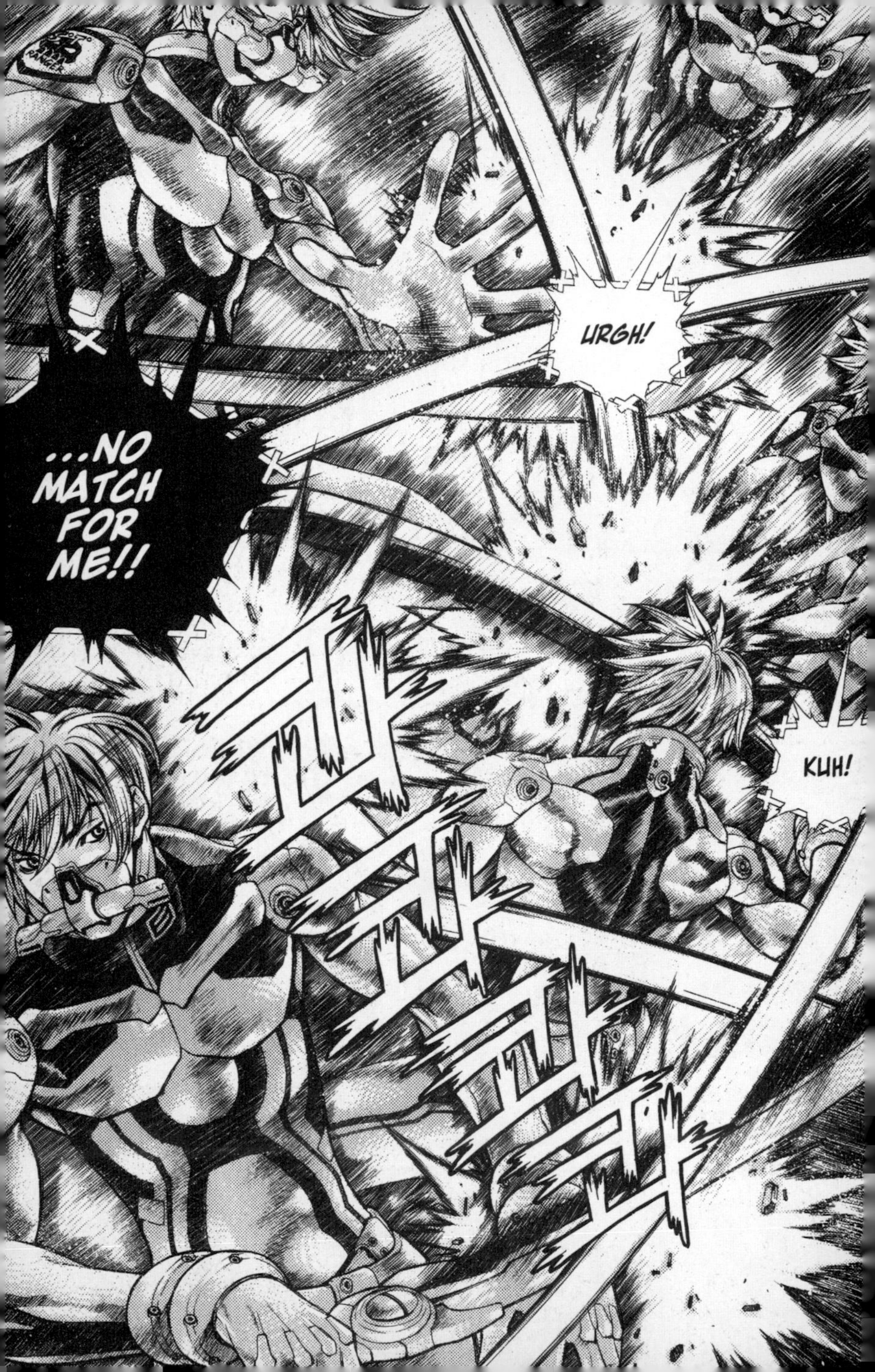
...NO MATCH FOR ME!!
URGH!
KUH!

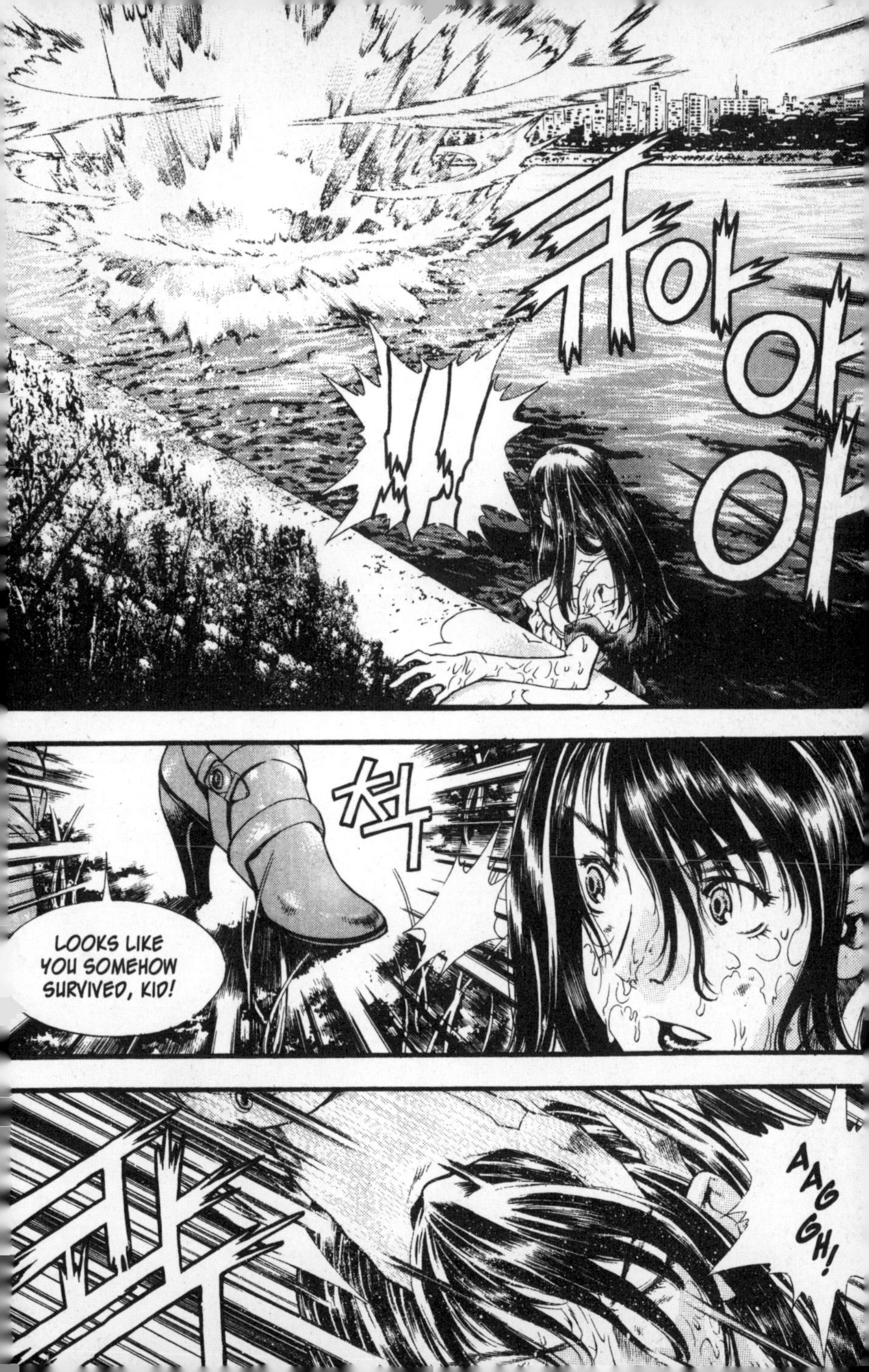
!!
착
LOOKS LIKE YOU SOMEHOW SURVIVED, KID!
AAGGH!

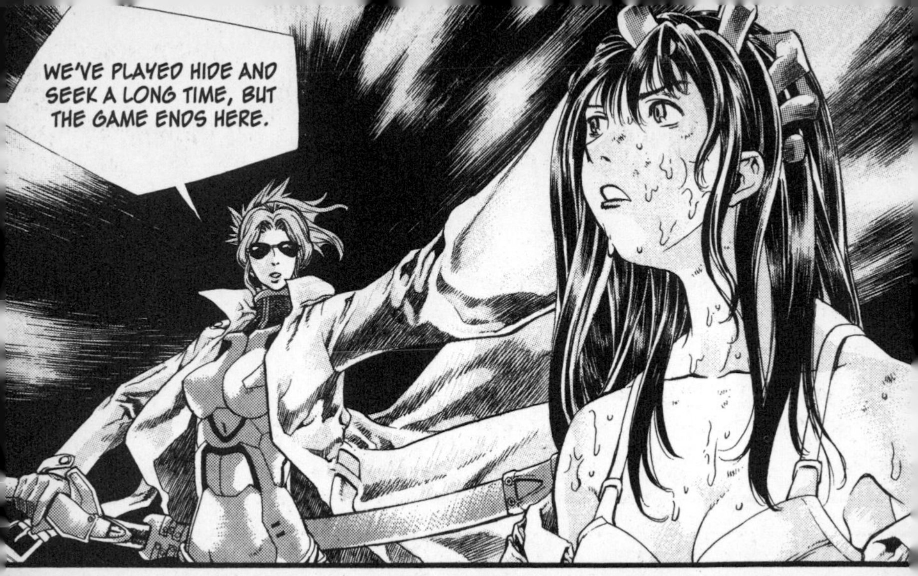
WE'VE PLAYED HIDE AND SEEK A LONG TIME, BUT THE GAME ENDS HERE.
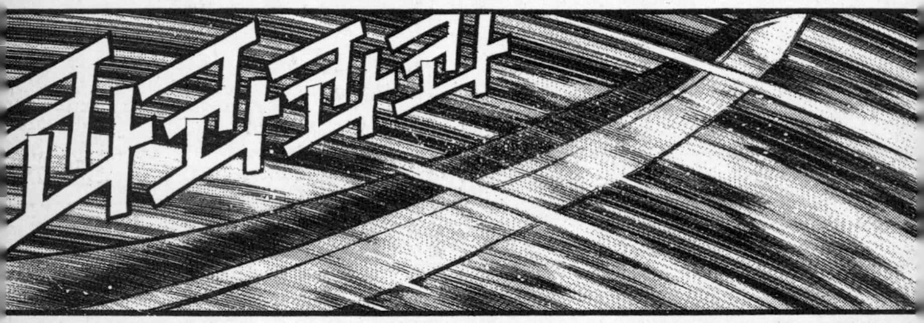
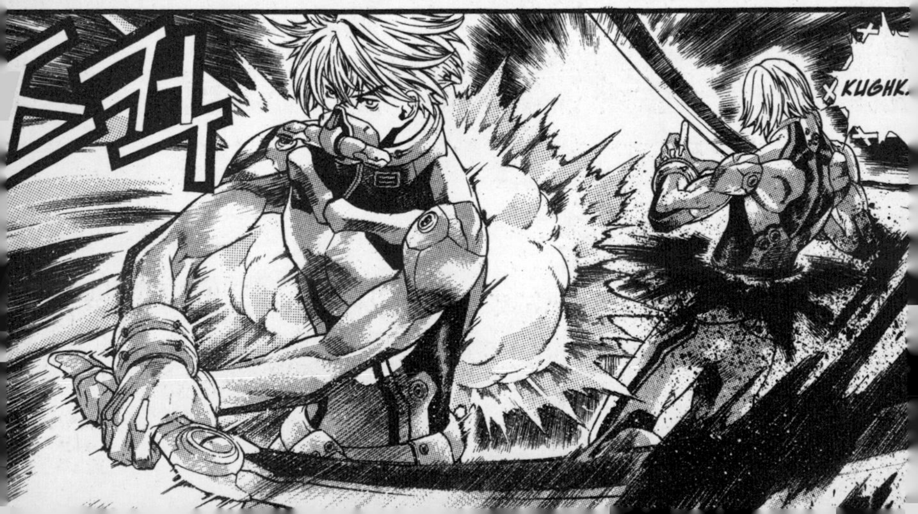
KUGHK.

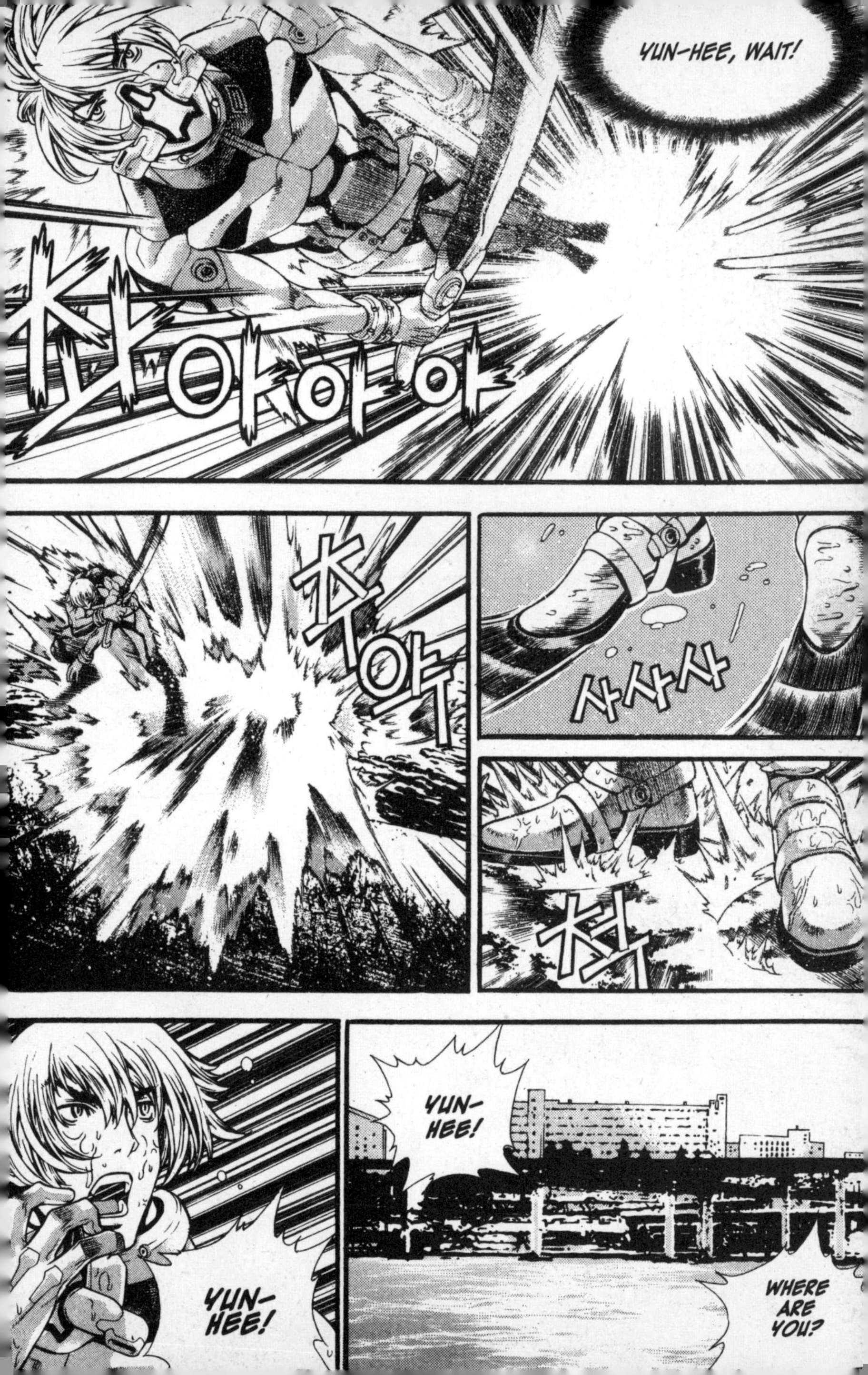
YUN-HEE, WAIT!
챠아아아
촤악
샤샤샤
척
YUN-HEE!
YUN-HEE!
WHERE ARE YOU?

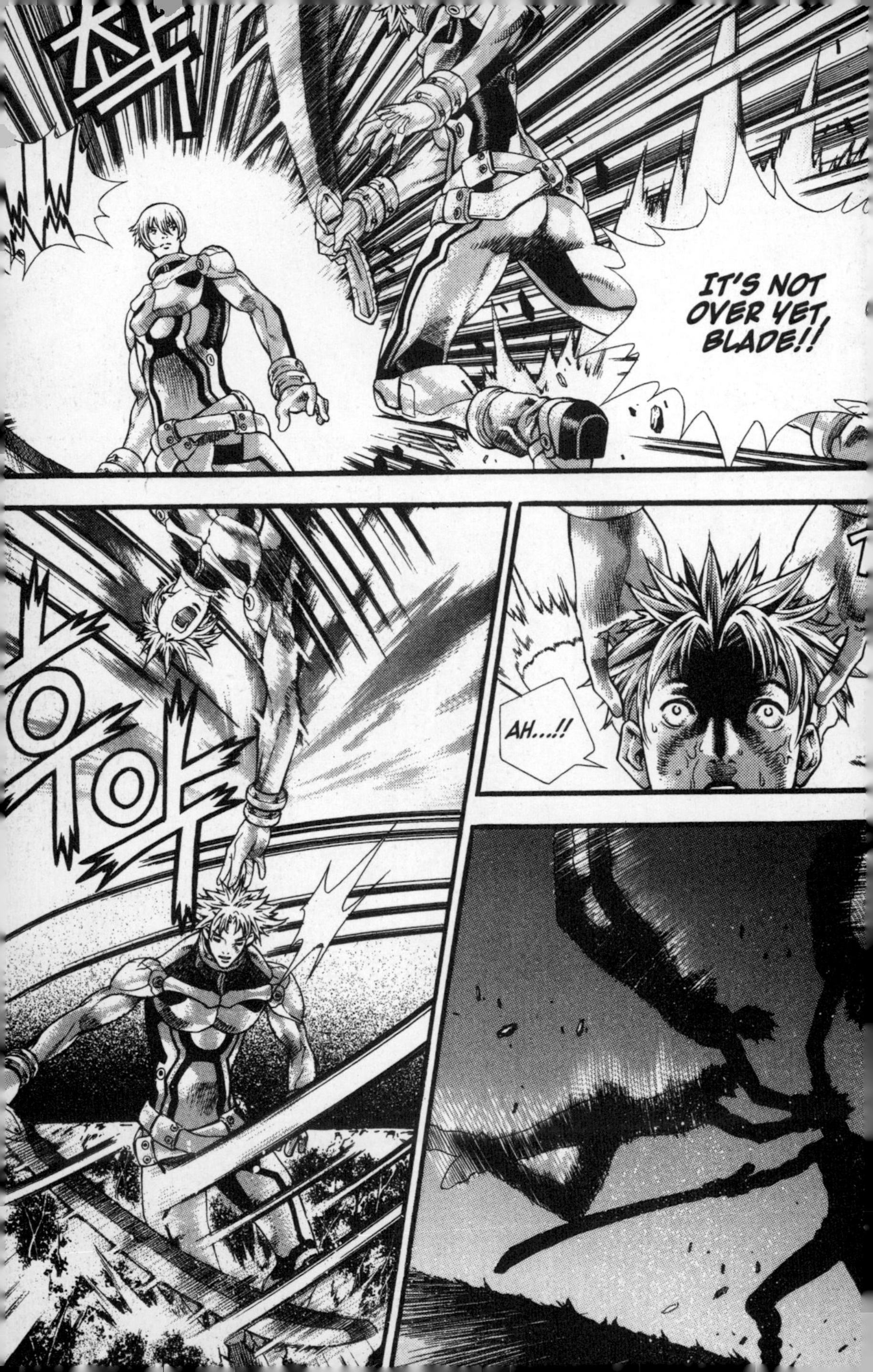
IT'S NOT OVER YET BLADE!!
AH...!!

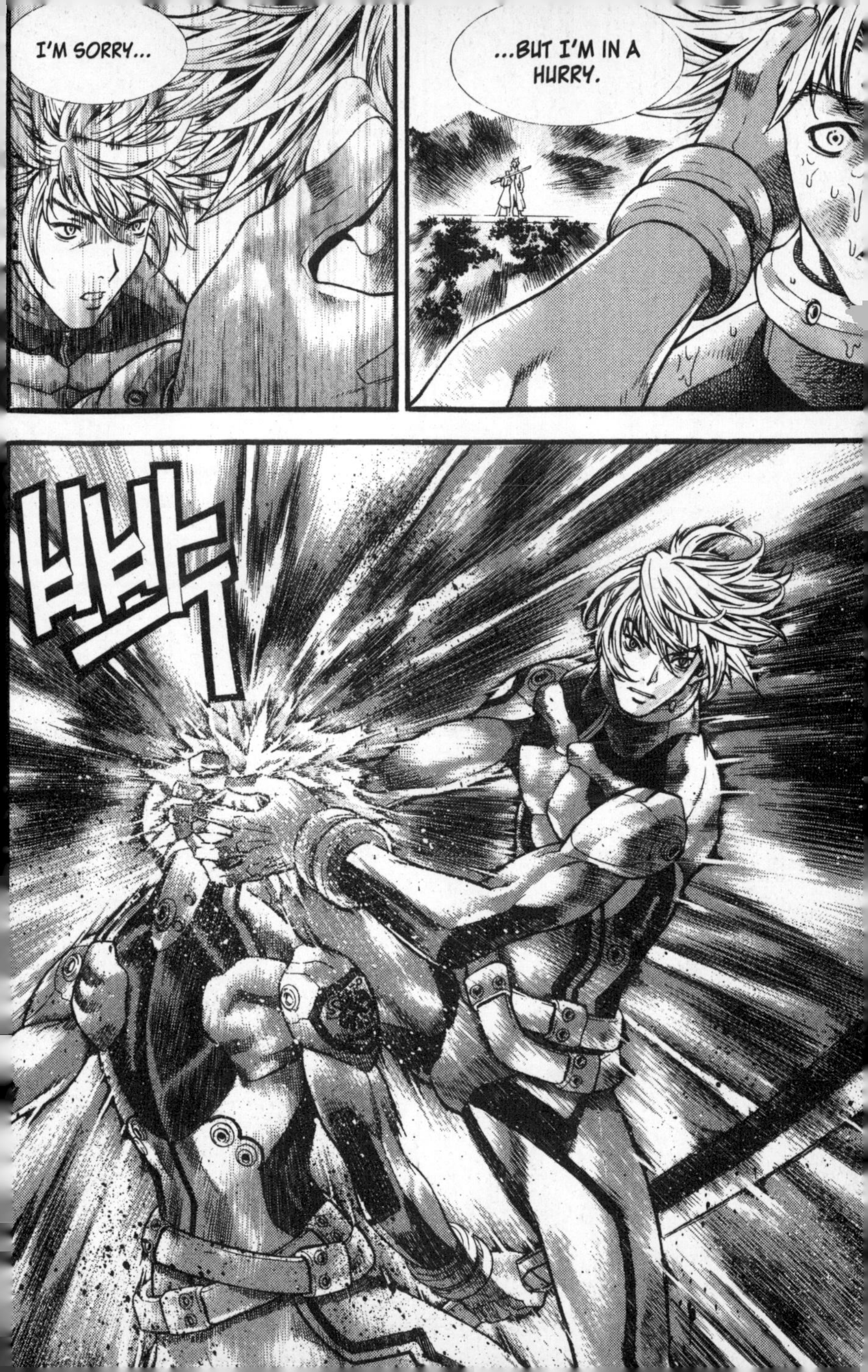
I'M SORRY...
...BUT I'M IN A HURRY.

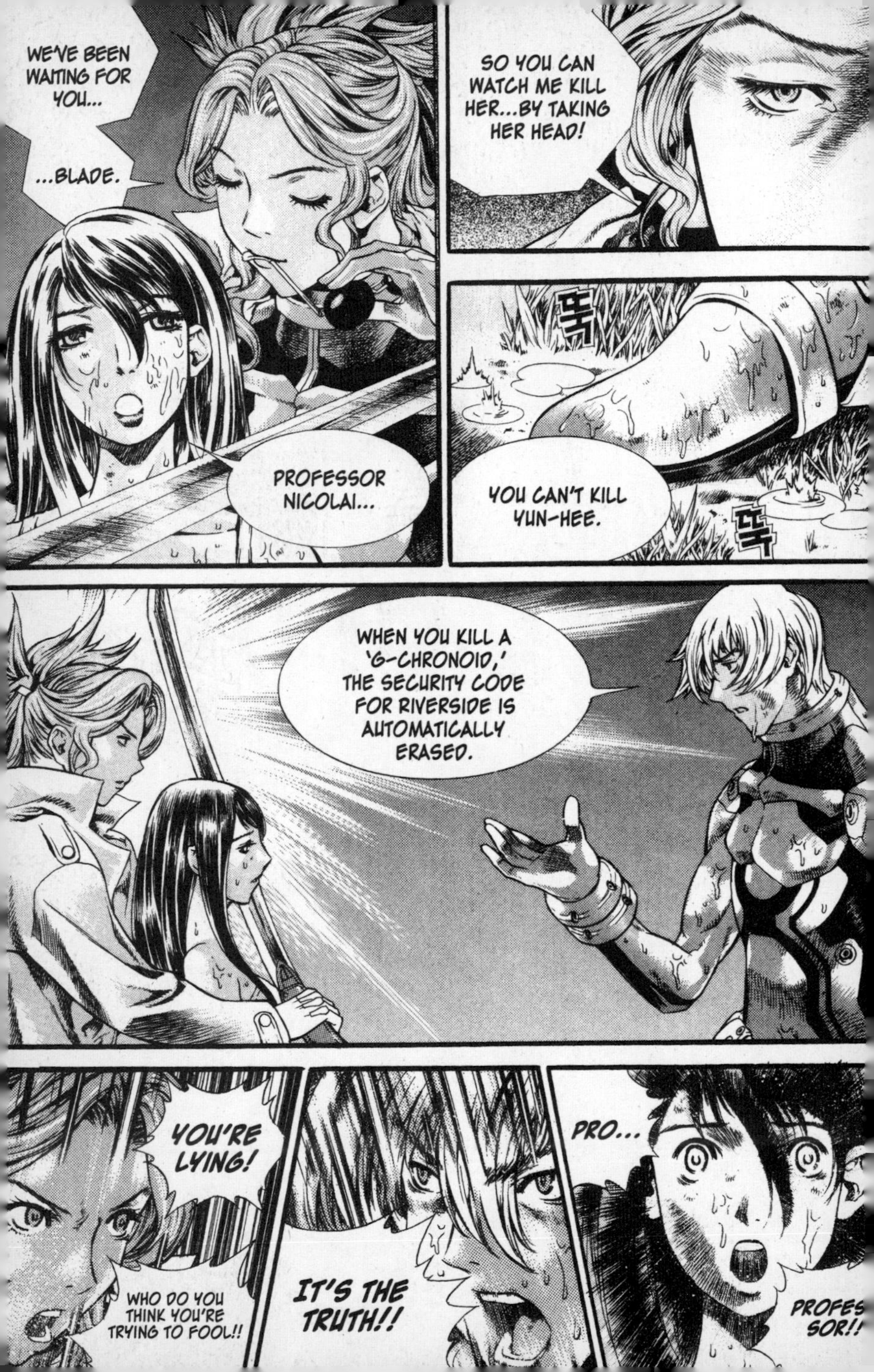
WE'VE BEEN WAITING FOR YOU...
...BLADE.
PROFESSOR NICOLAI...
SO YOU CAN WATCH ME KILL HER...BY TAKING HER HEAD!
똑
YOU CAN'T KILL YUN-HEE.
똑
WHEN YOU KILL A 'G-CHRONOID,' THE SECURITY CODE FOR RIVERSIDE IS AUTOMATICALLY ERASED.
YOU'RE LYING!
WHO DO YOU THINK YOU'RE TRYING TO FOOL!!
IT'S THE TRUTH!!
PRO...
PROFES SOR!!

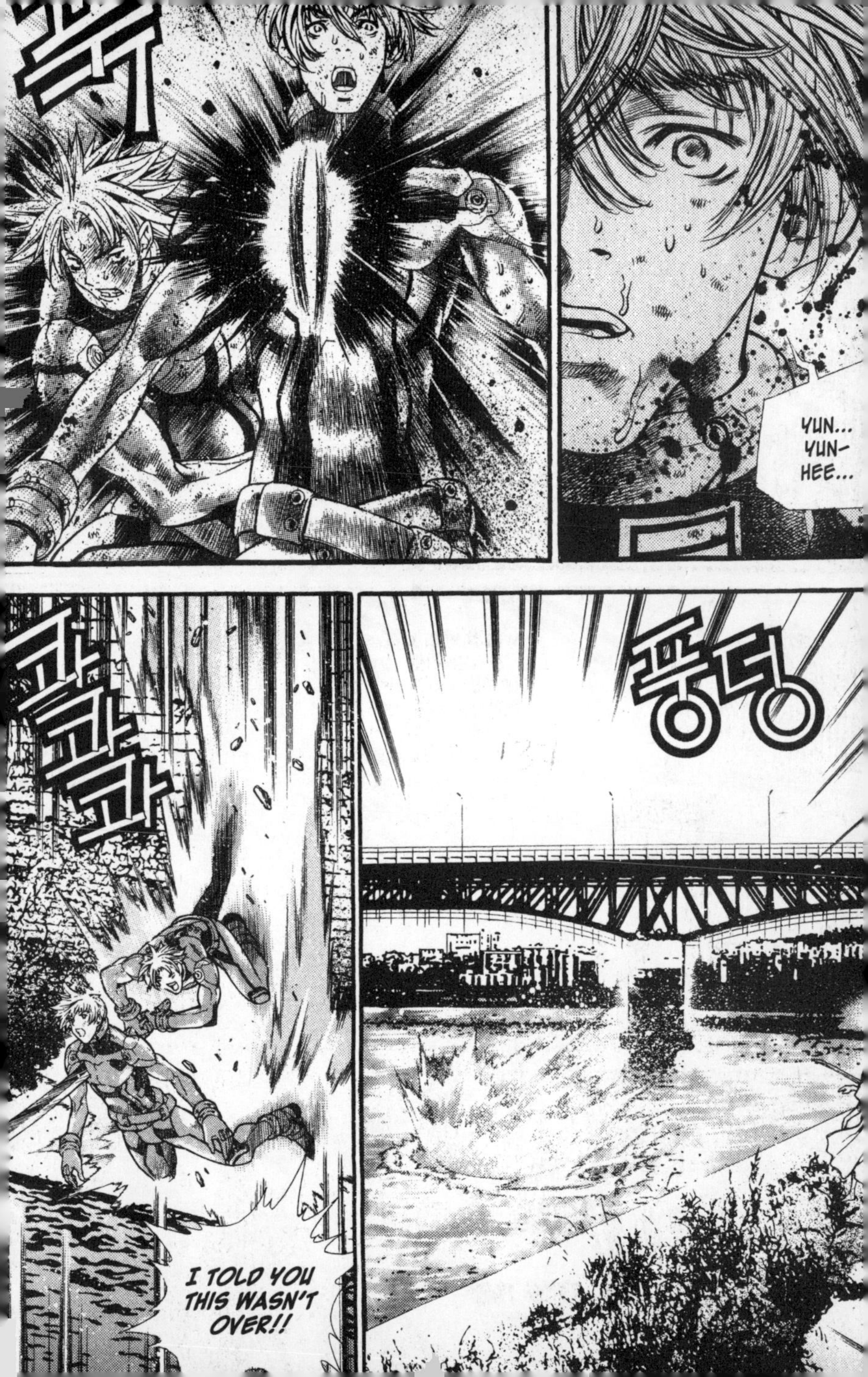
YUN... YUN-HEE...
I TOLD YOU THIS WASN'T OVER!!
풍덩

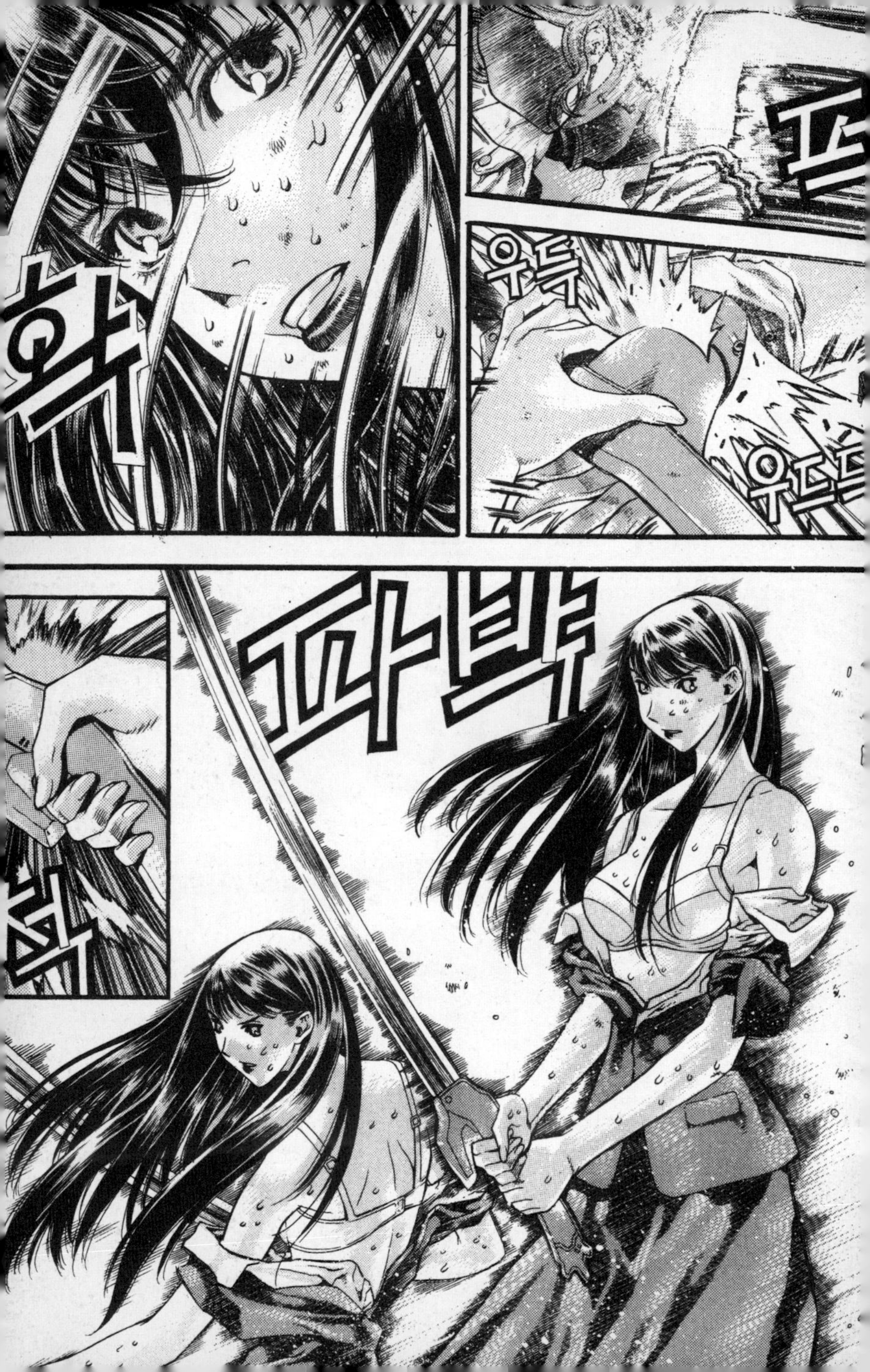
우득
파박

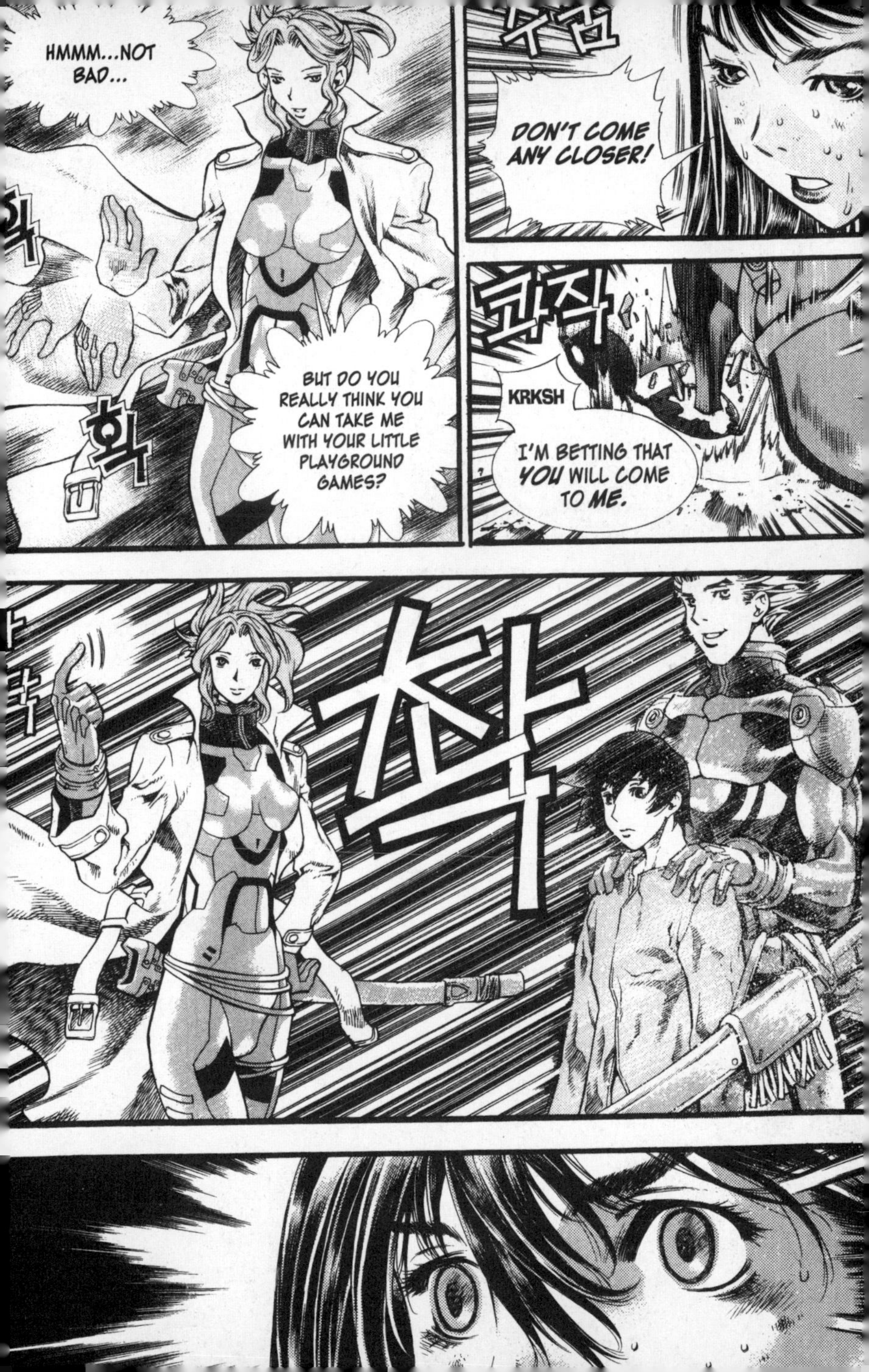
HMMM...NOT BAD...
BUT DO YOU REALLY THINK YOU CAN TAKE ME WITH YOUR LITTLE PLAYGROUND GAMES?
DON'T COME ANY CLOSER!
KRKSH
I'M BETTING THAT *YOU* WILL COME TO *ME*.

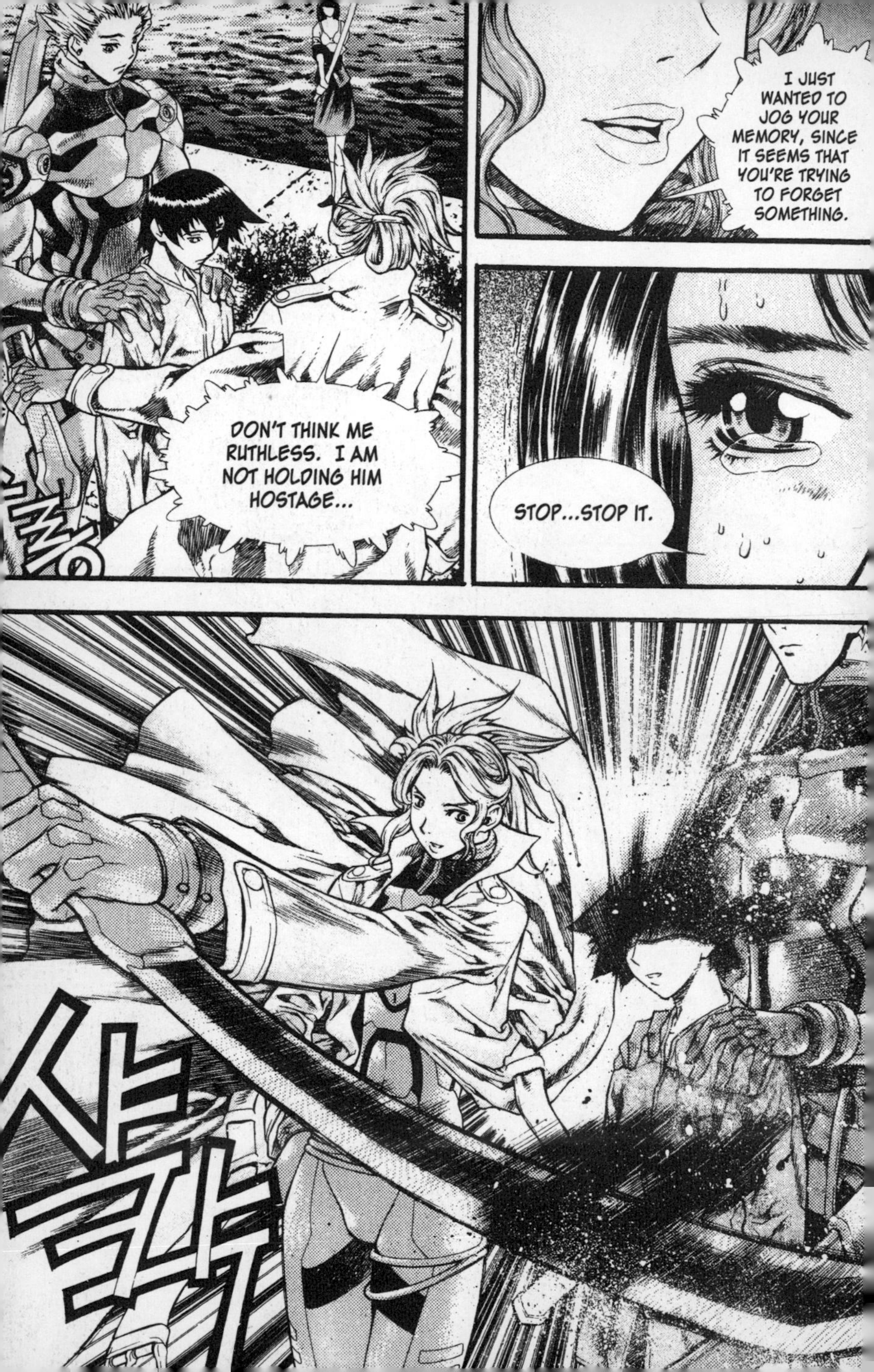
DON'T THINK ME RUTHLESS. I AM NOT HOLDING HIM HOSTAGE...
I JUST WANTED TO JOG YOUR MEMORY, SINCE IT SEEMS THAT YOU'RE TRYING TO FORGET SOMETHING.
STOP...STOP IT.

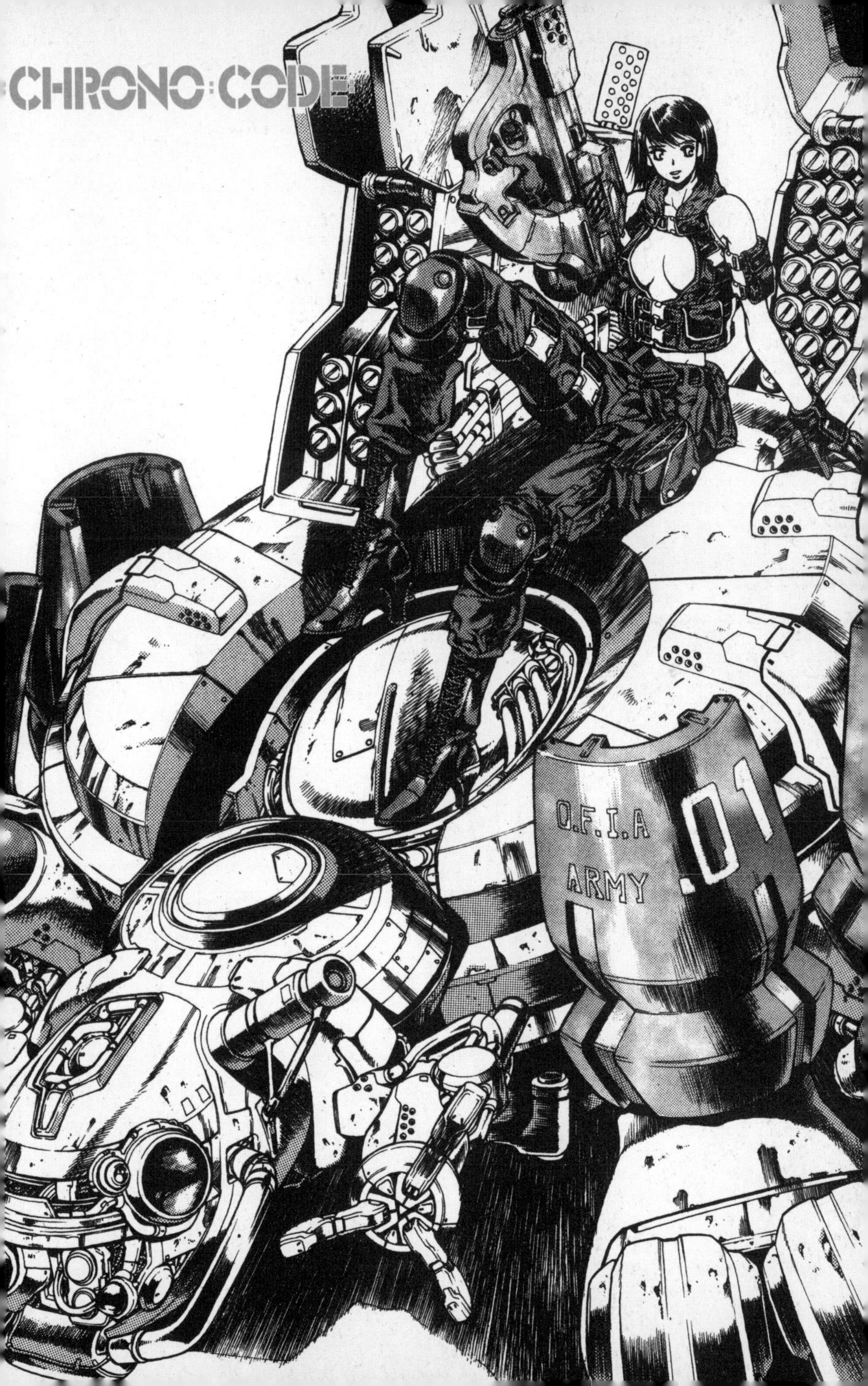
CHRONO CODE
O.F.I.A
ARMY
01

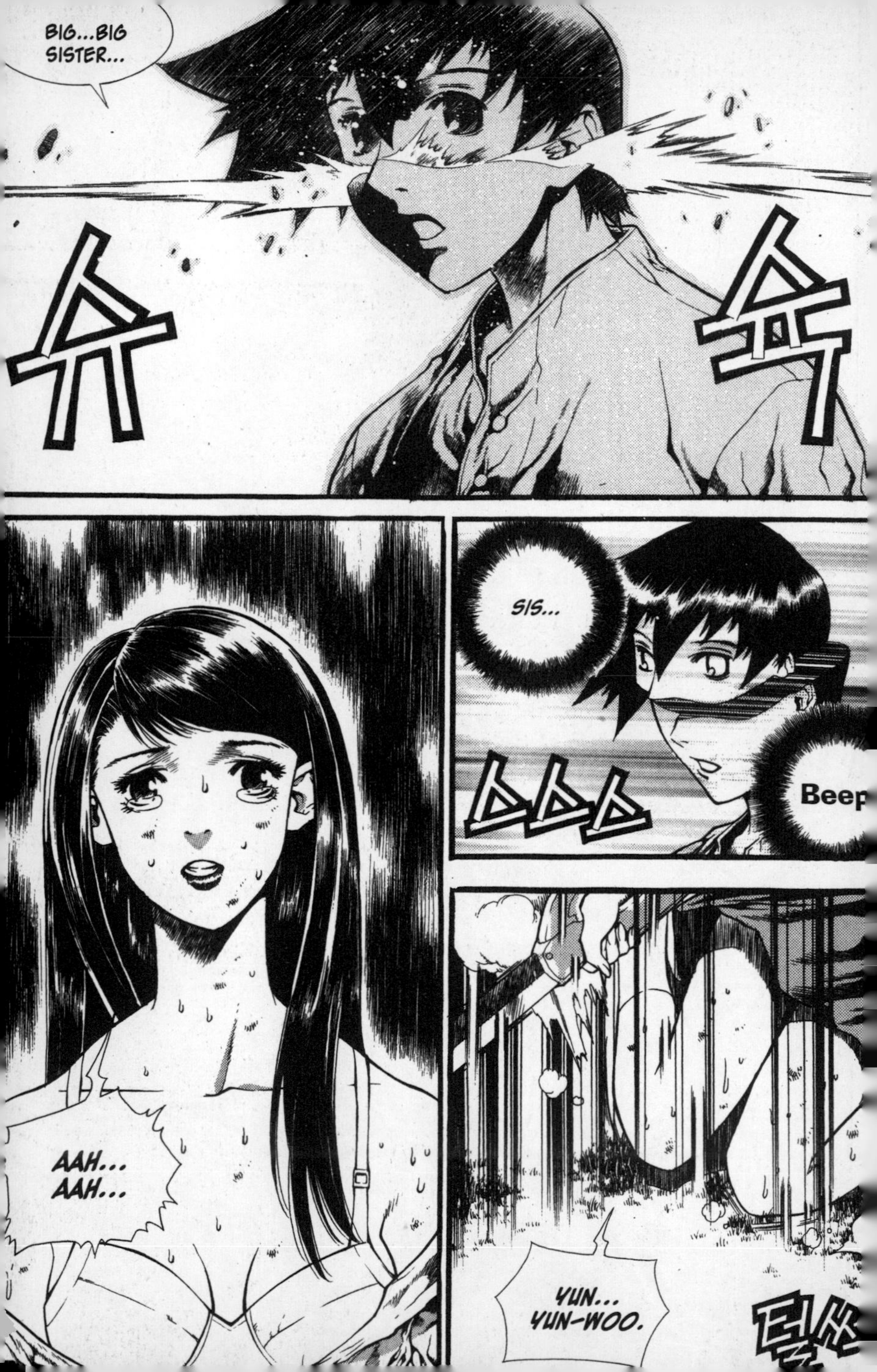
BIG...BIG SISTER...
스
윽
AAH... AAH...
SIS...
Beep
YUN... YUN-WOO.

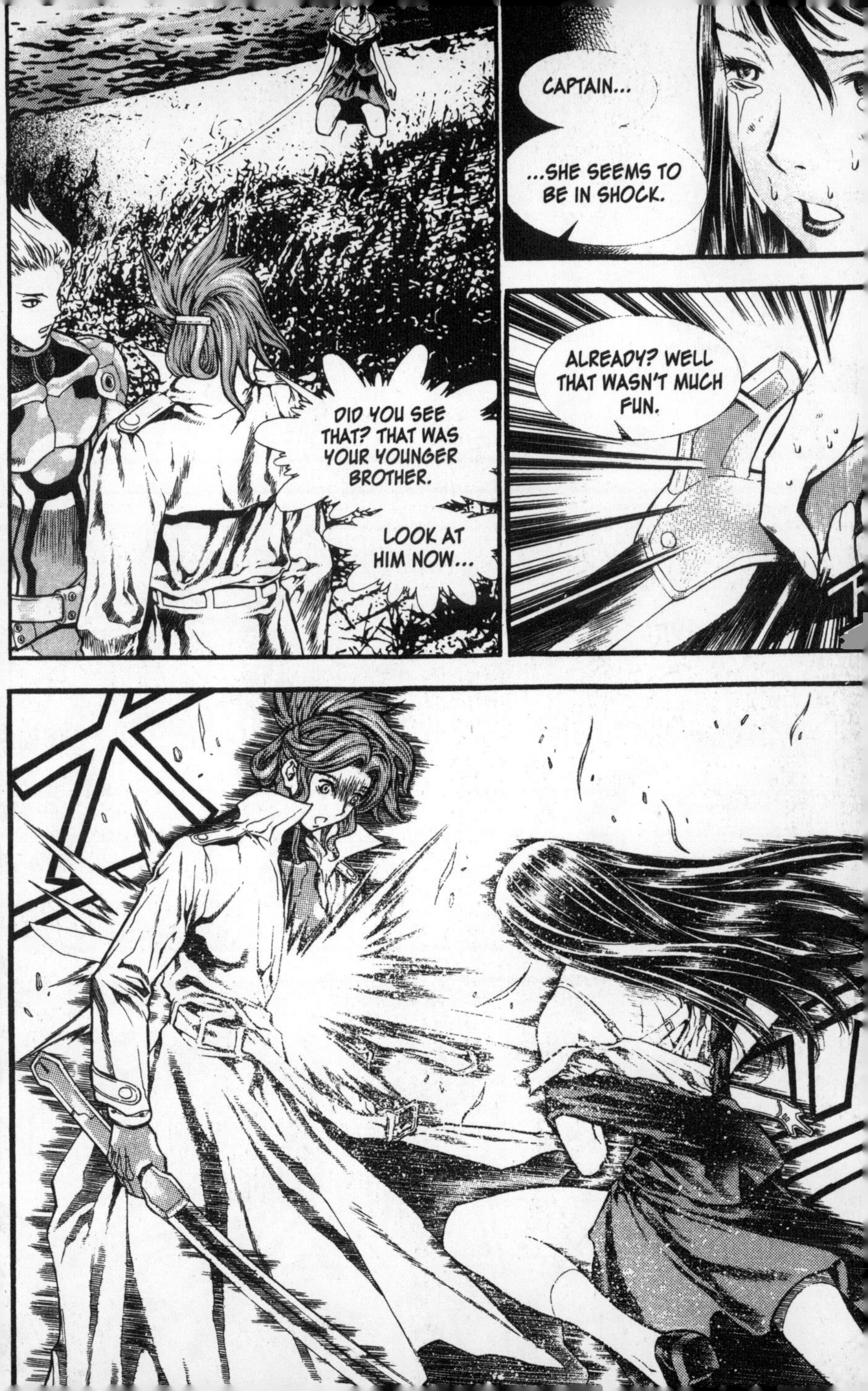
DID YOU SEE THAT? THAT WAS YOUR YOUNGER BROTHER.
LOOK AT HIM NOW...
CAPTAIN...
...SHE SEEMS TO BE IN SHOCK.
ALREADY? WELL THAT WASN'T MUCH FUN.

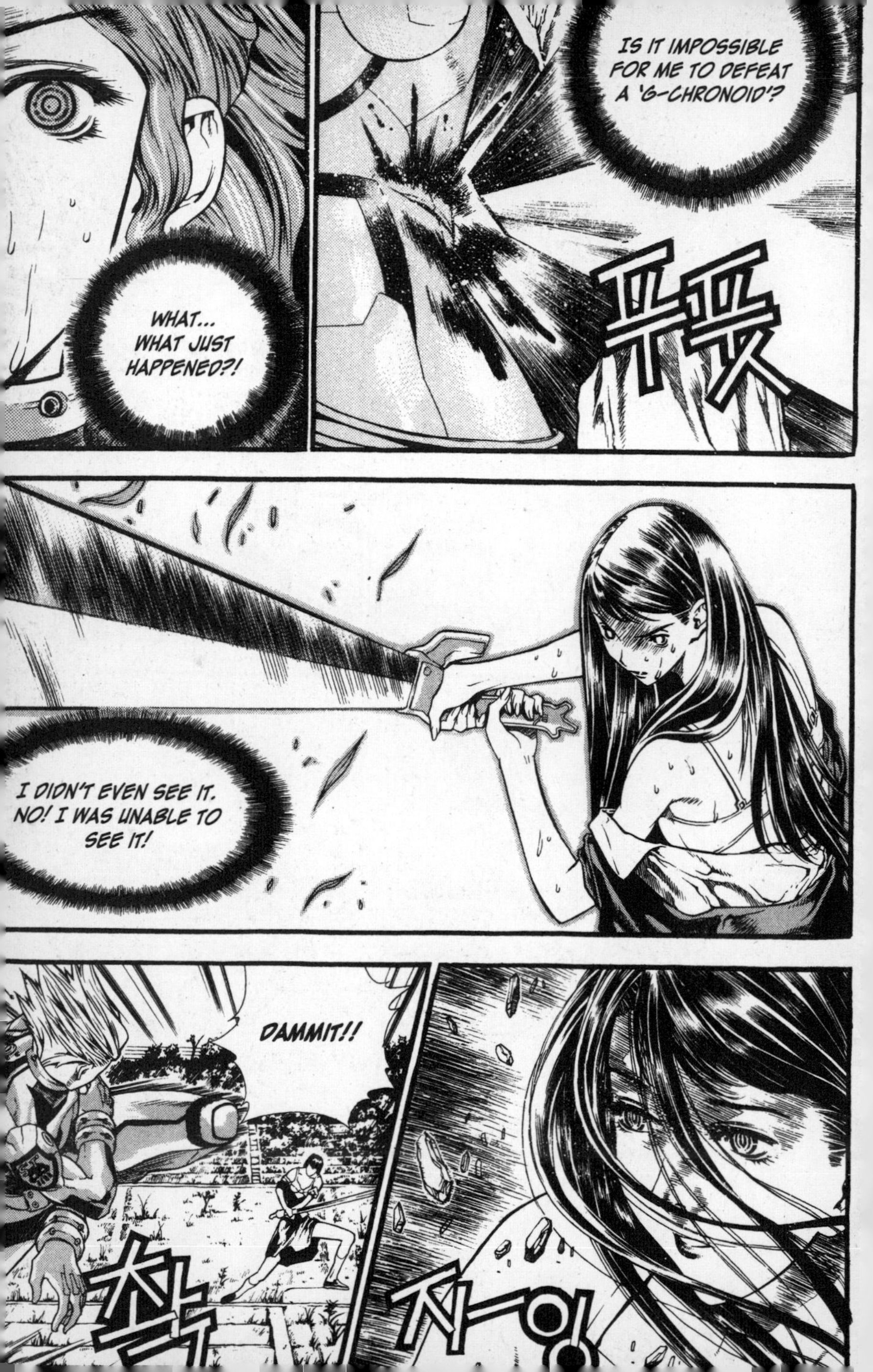
WHAT... WHAT JUST HAPPENED?!
IS IT IMPOSSIBLE FOR ME TO DEFEAT A 'G-CHRONOID'?
I DIDN'T EVEN SEE IT. NO! I WAS UNABLE TO SEE IT!
DAMMIT!!

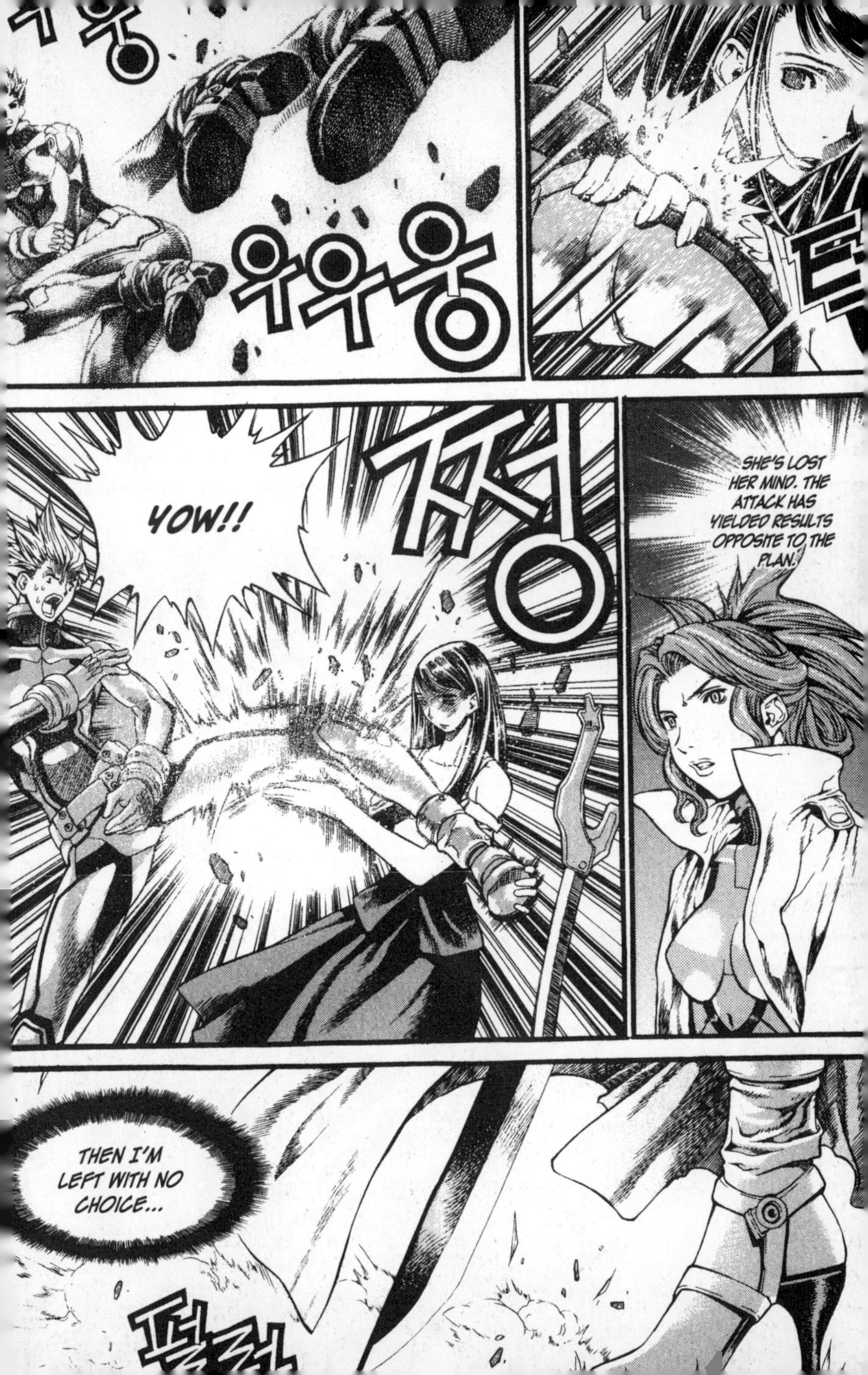

우우웅
YOW!!
SHE'S LOST HER MIND. THE ATTACK HAS YIELDED RESULTS OPPOSITE TO THE PLAN.
THEN I'M LEFT WITH NO CHOICE...

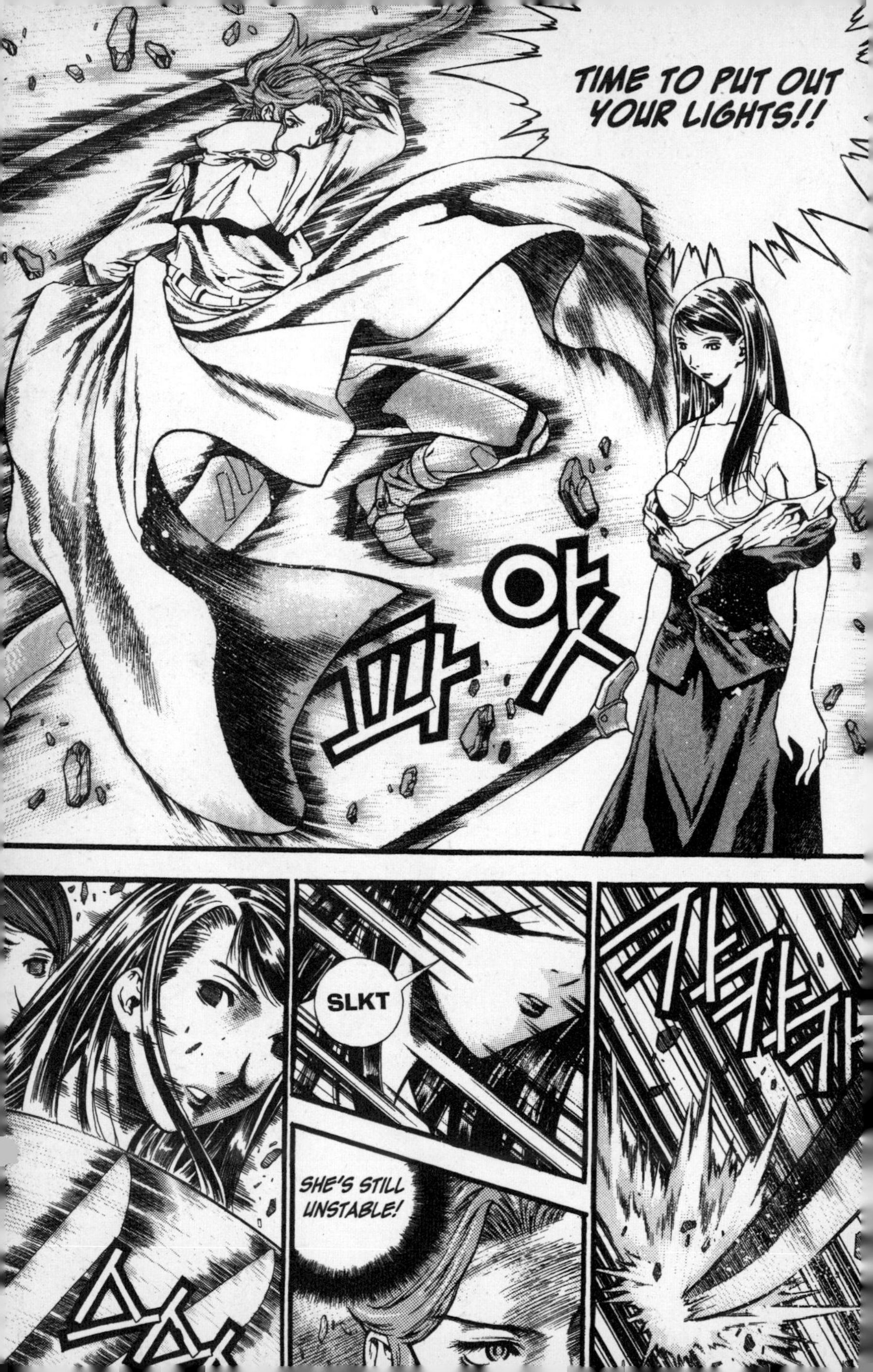
TIME TO PUT OUT YOUR LIGHTS!!
SLKT
SHE'S STILL UNSTABLE!

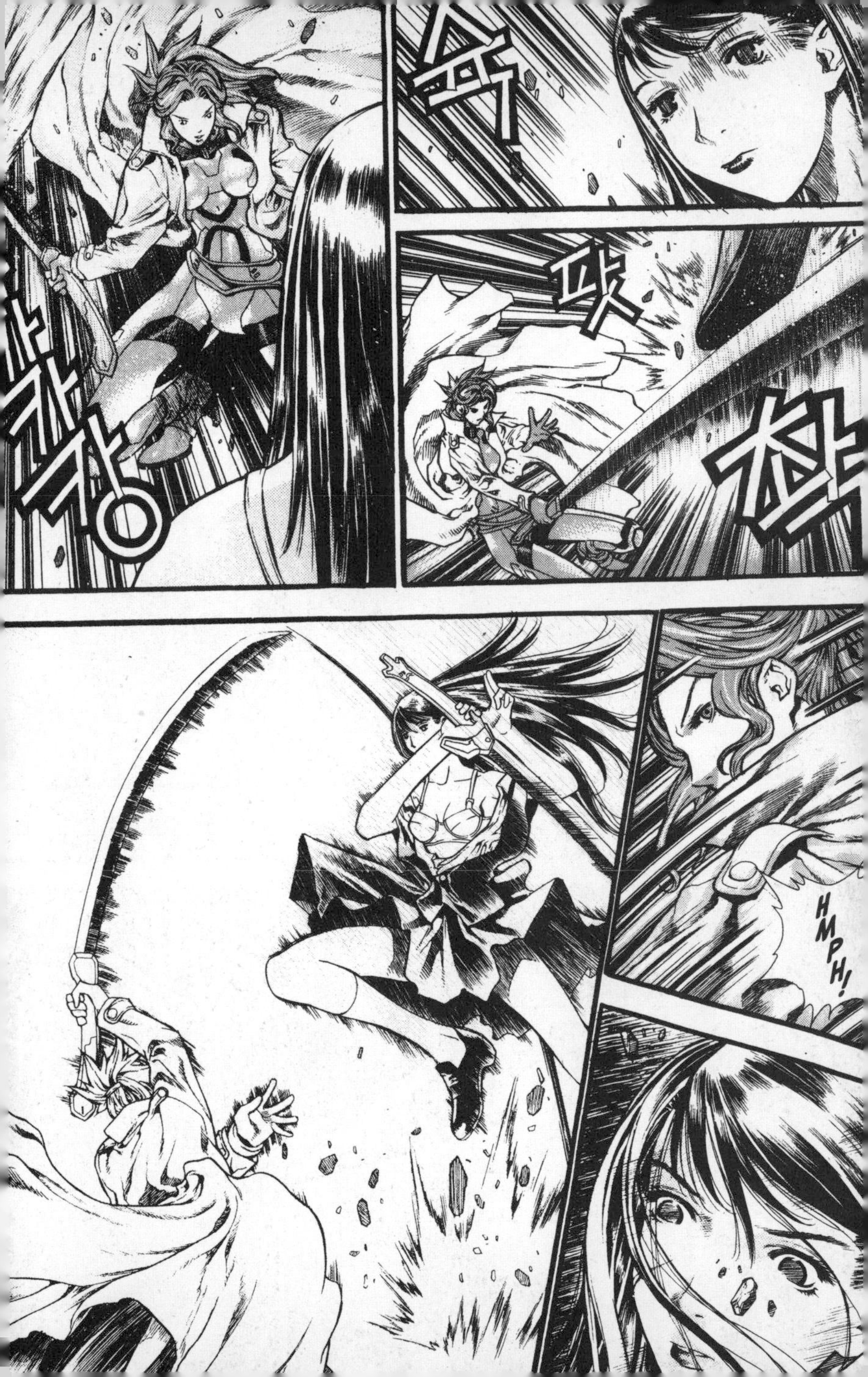
HMPH!

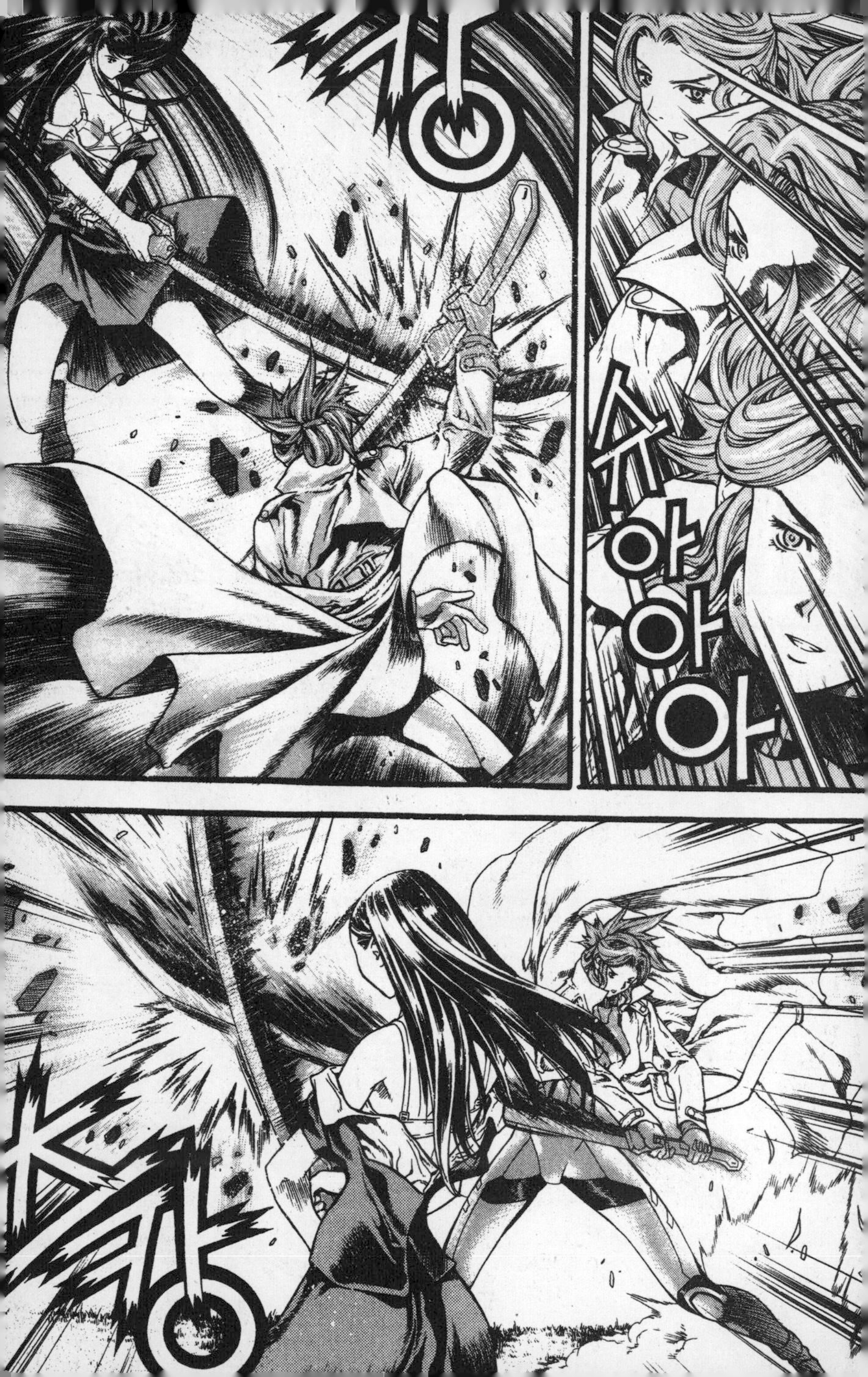
챙
샤아아아
카강

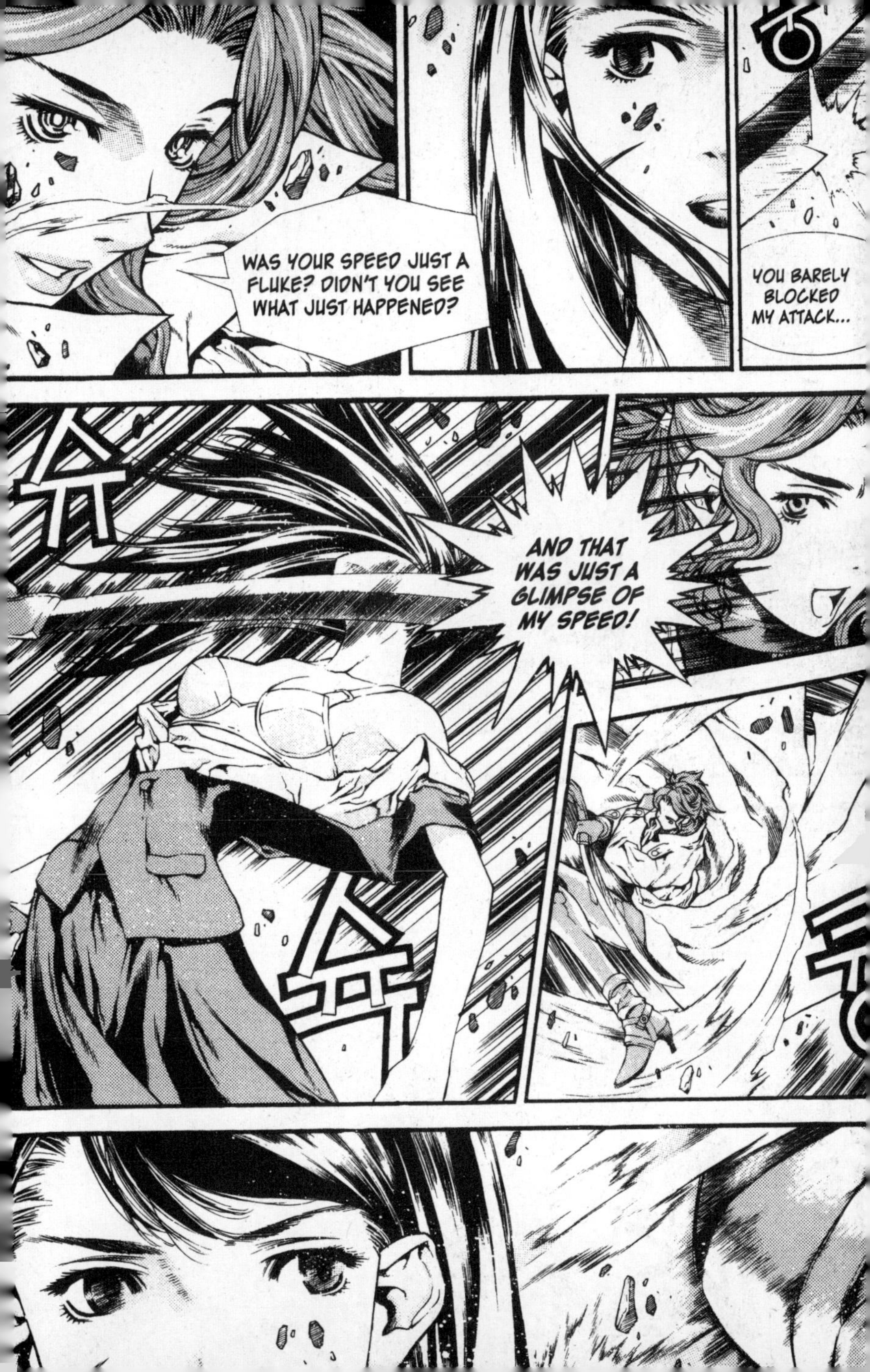
WAS YOUR SPEED JUST A FLUKE? DIDN'T YOU SEE WHAT JUST HAPPENED?
YOU BARELY BLOCKED MY ATTACK...
AND THAT WAS JUST A GLIMPSE OF MY SPEED!

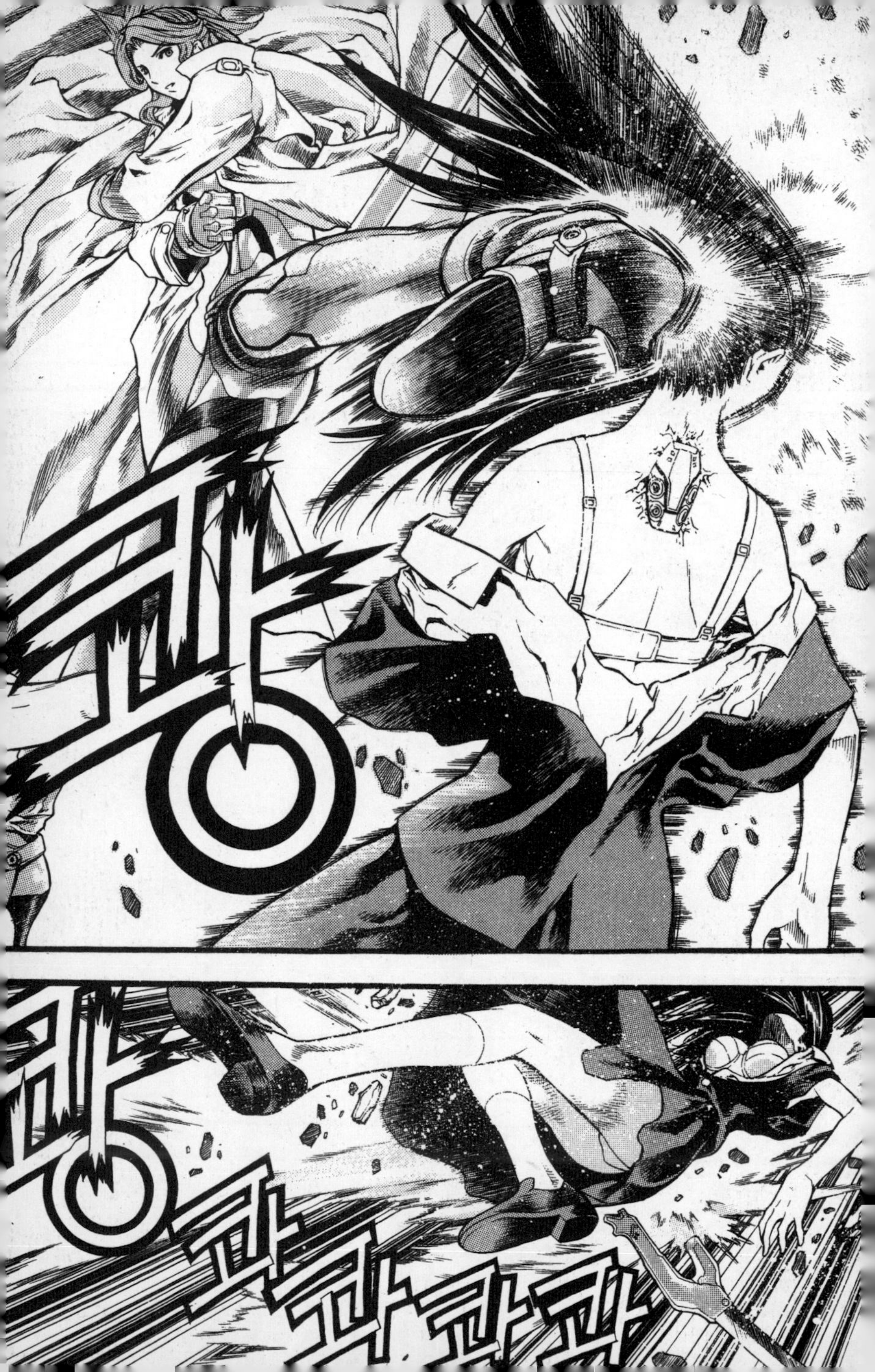
콰앙
콰앙
콰콰콰콰

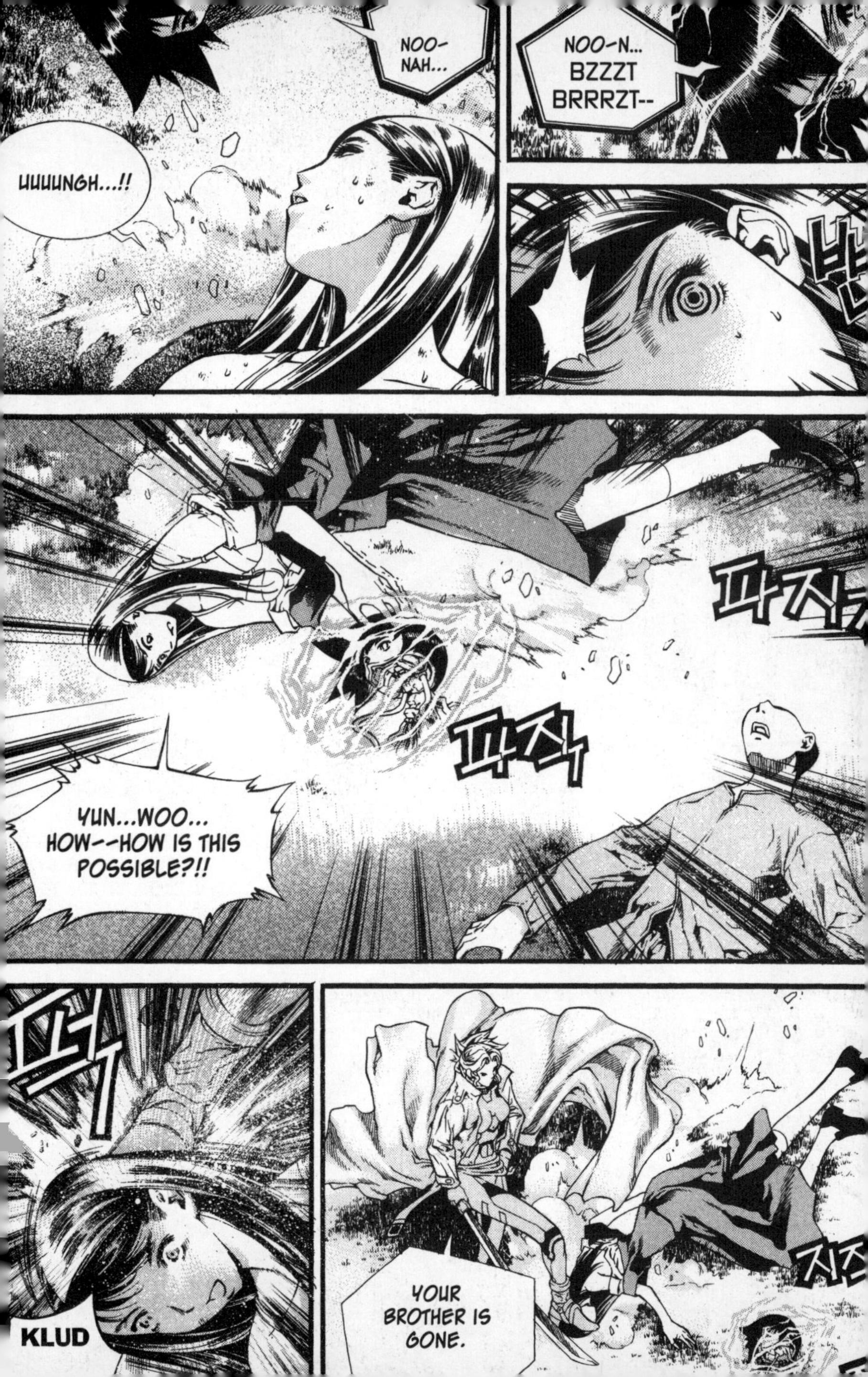
NOO-NAH...
UUUUNGH...!!
NOO-N... BZZZT BRRRZT--
파직
YUN...WOO... HOW--HOW IS THIS POSSIBLE?!!
KLUD
YOUR BROTHER IS GONE.

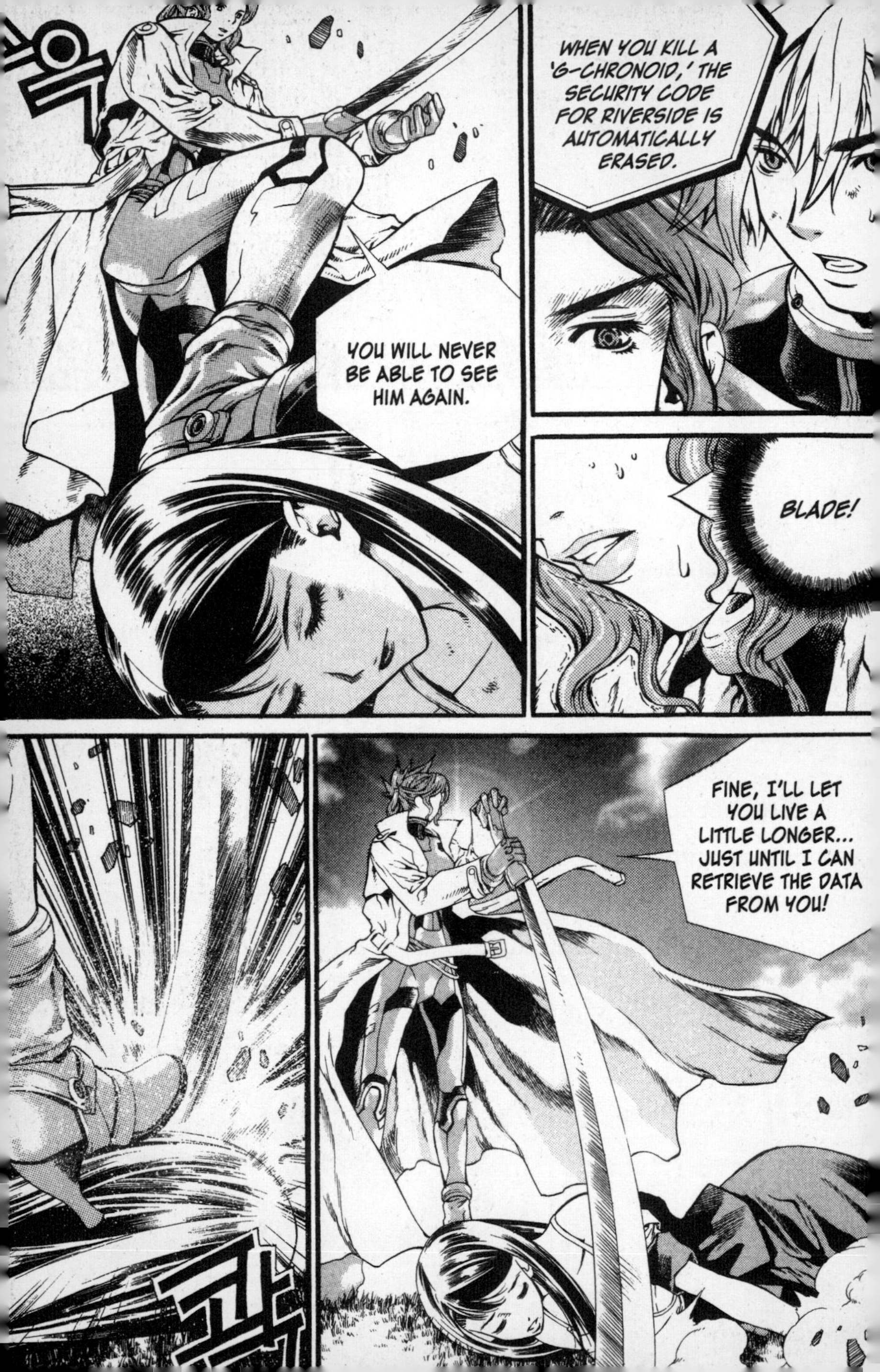
WHEN YOU KILL A 'G-CHRONOID,' THE SECURITY CODE FOR RIVERSIDE IS AUTOMATICALLY ERASED.
BLADE!
YOU WILL NEVER BE ABLE TO SEE HIM AGAIN.
FINE, I'LL LET YOU LIVE A LITTLE LONGER... JUST UNTIL I CAN RETRIEVE THE DATA FROM YOU!

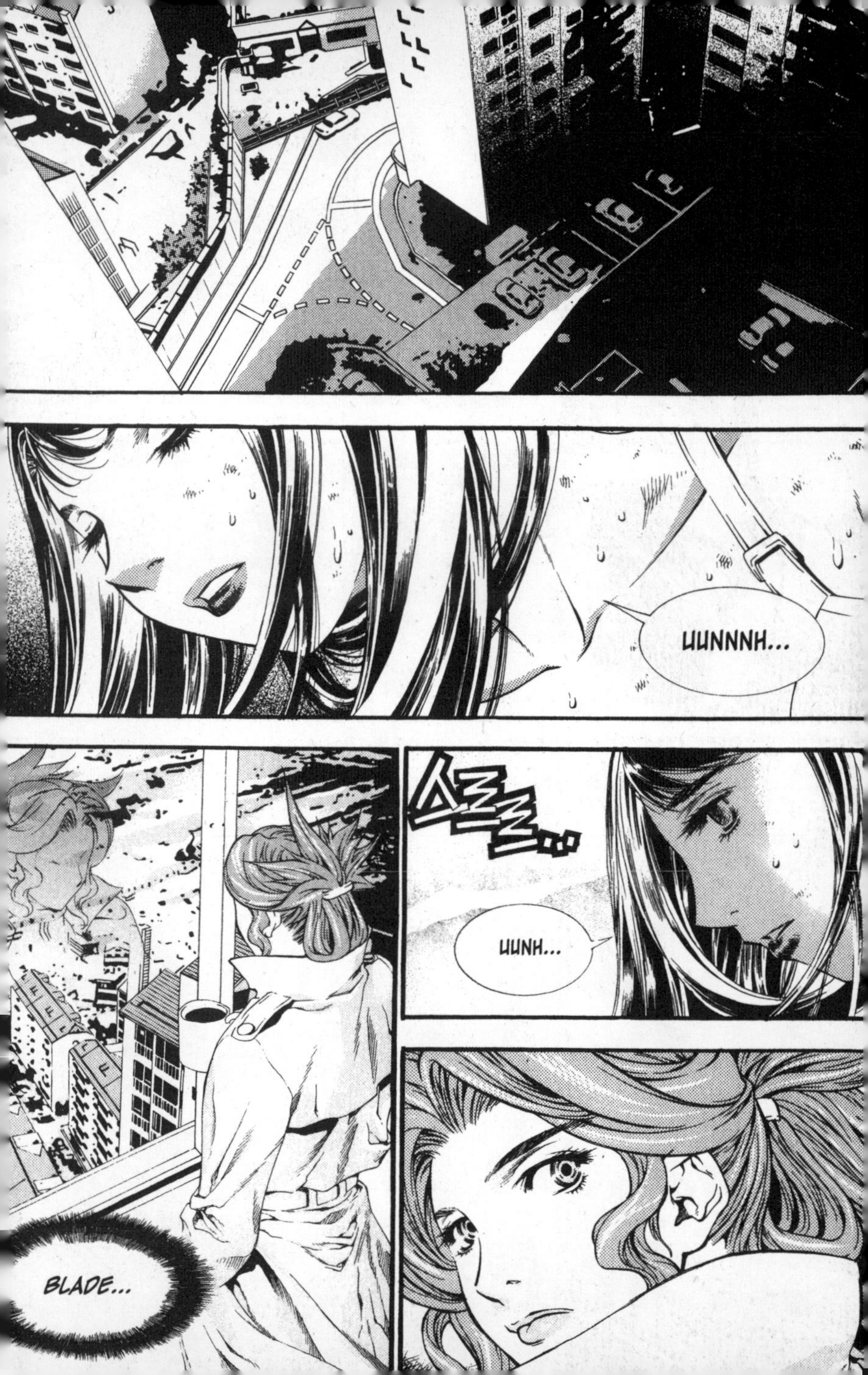
UUNNNH...
BLADE...
UUNH...

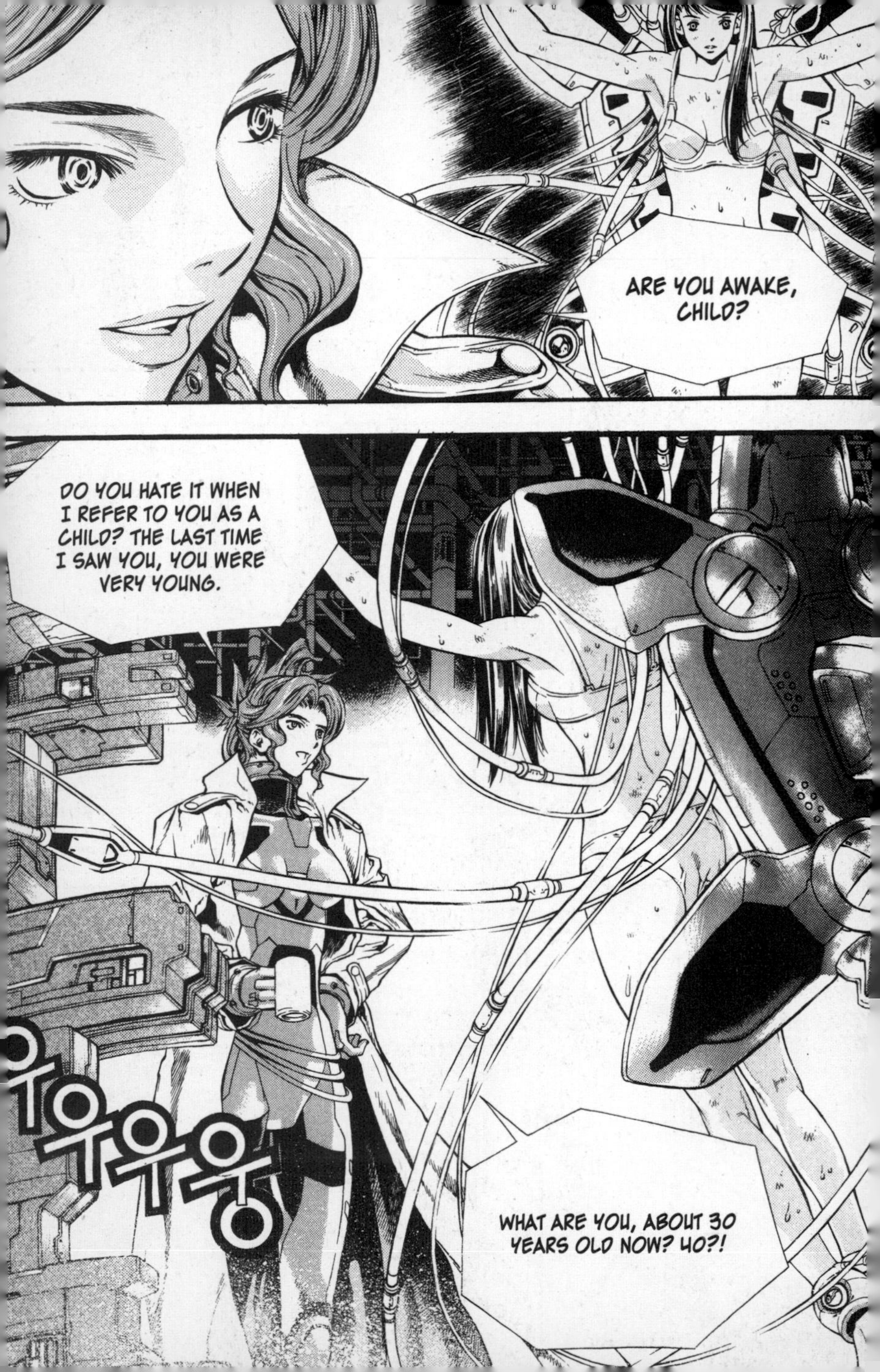
ARE YOU AWAKE, CHILD?
DO YOU HATE IT WHEN I REFER TO YOU AS A CHILD? THE LAST TIME I SAW YOU, YOU WERE VERY YOUNG.
WHAT ARE YOU, ABOUT 30 YEARS OLD NOW? 40?!

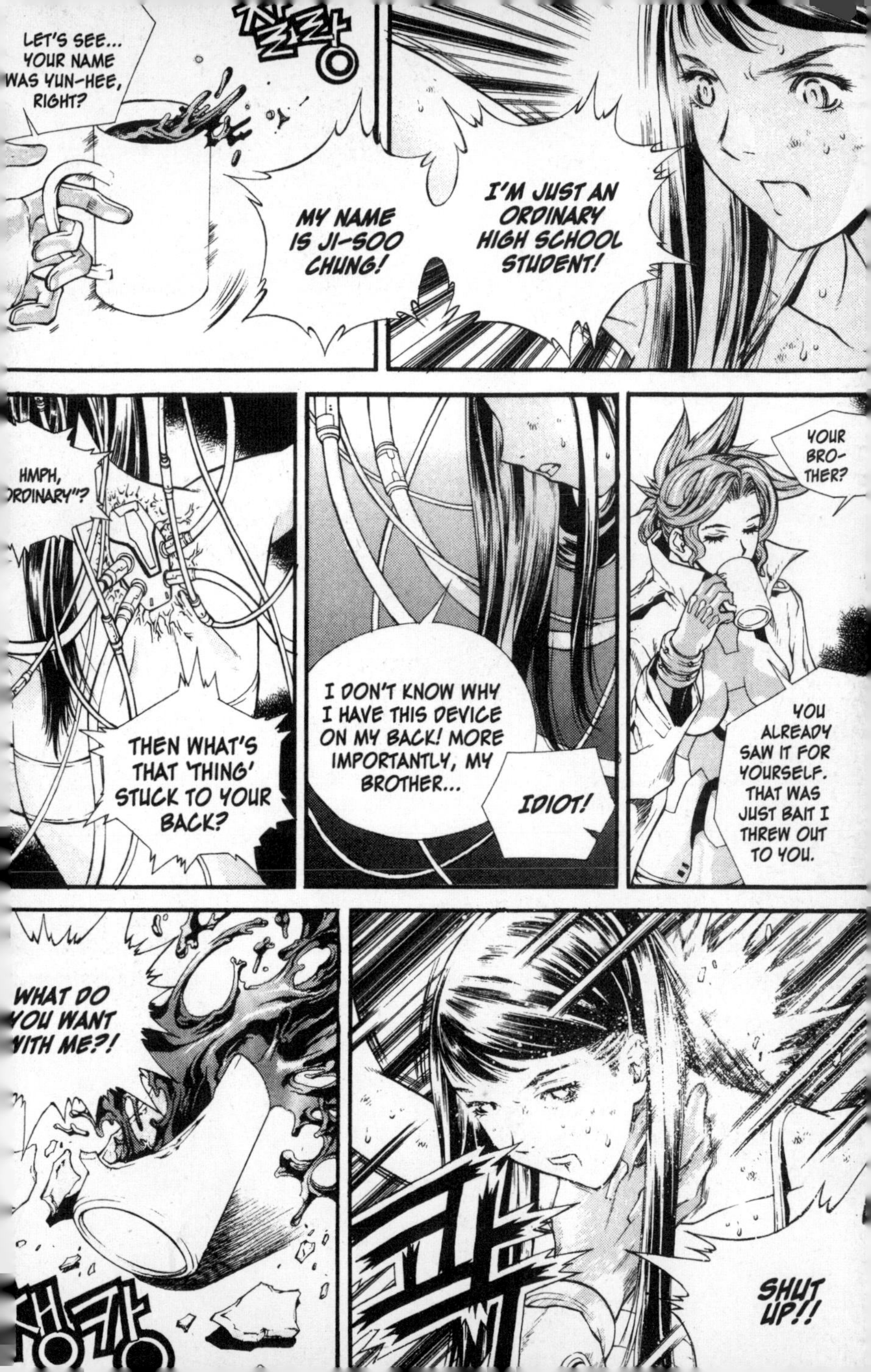
LET'S SEE... YOUR NAME WAS YUN-HEE, RIGHT?
MY NAME IS JI-SOO CHUNG!
I'M JUST AN ORDINARY HIGH SCHOOL STUDENT!
HMPH, "ORDINARY"?
THEN WHAT'S THAT 'THING' STUCK TO YOUR BACK?
I DON'T KNOW WHY I HAVE THIS DEVICE ON MY BACK! MORE IMPORTANTLY, MY BROTHER...
IDIOT!
YOUR BRO-THER?
YOU ALREADY SAW IT FOR YOURSELF. THAT WAS JUST BAIT I THREW OUT TO YOU.
WHAT DO YOU WANT WITH ME?!
SHUT UP!!

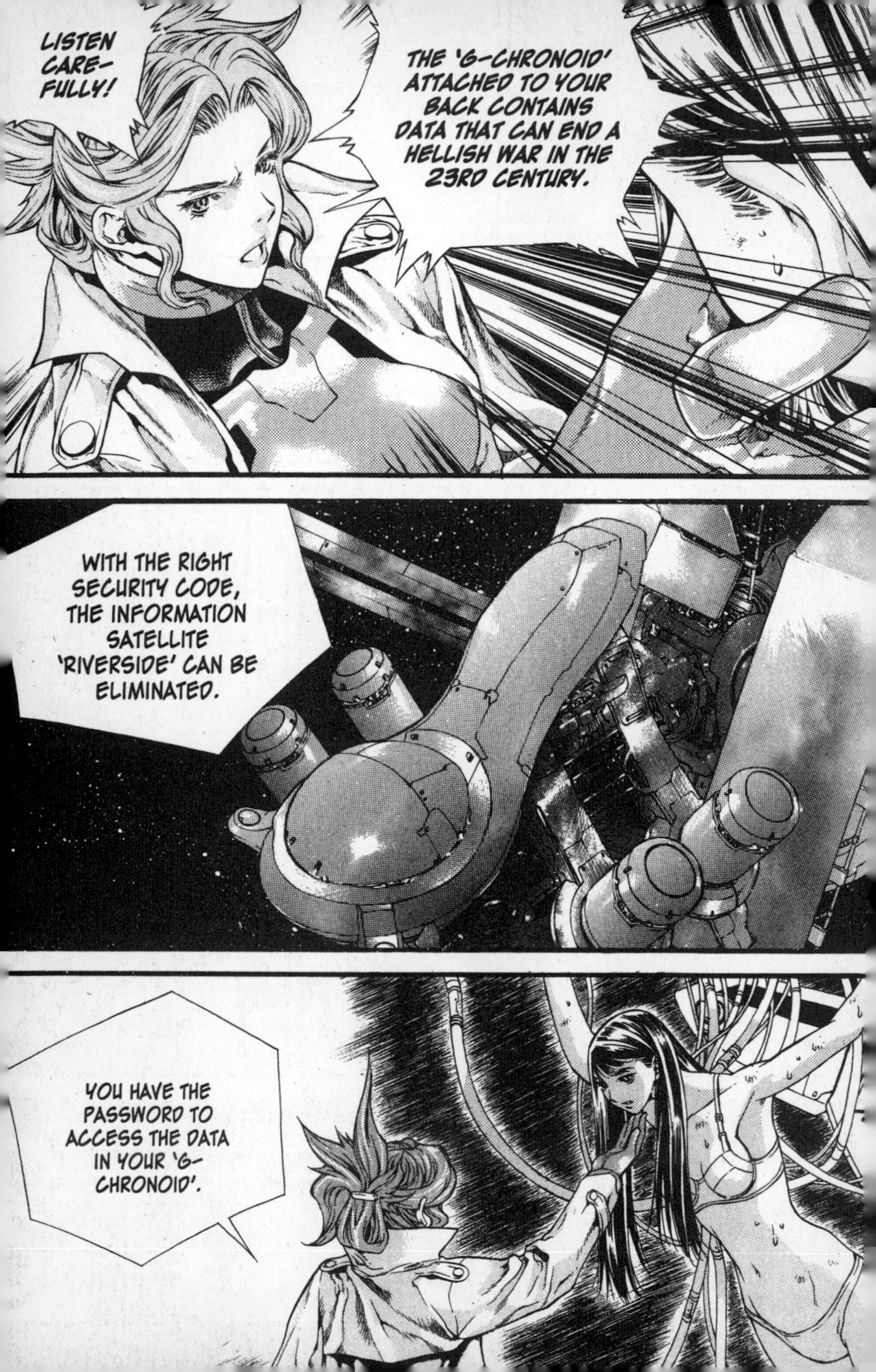
LISTEN CARE-FULLY!
THE 'G-CHRONOID' ATTACHED TO YOUR BACK CONTAINS DATA THAT CAN END A HELLISH WAR IN THE 23RD CENTURY.
WITH THE RIGHT SECURITY CODE, THE INFORMATION SATELLITE 'RIVERSIDE' CAN BE ELIMINATED.
YOU HAVE THE PASSWORD TO ACCESS THE DATA IN YOUR 'G-CHRONOID'.

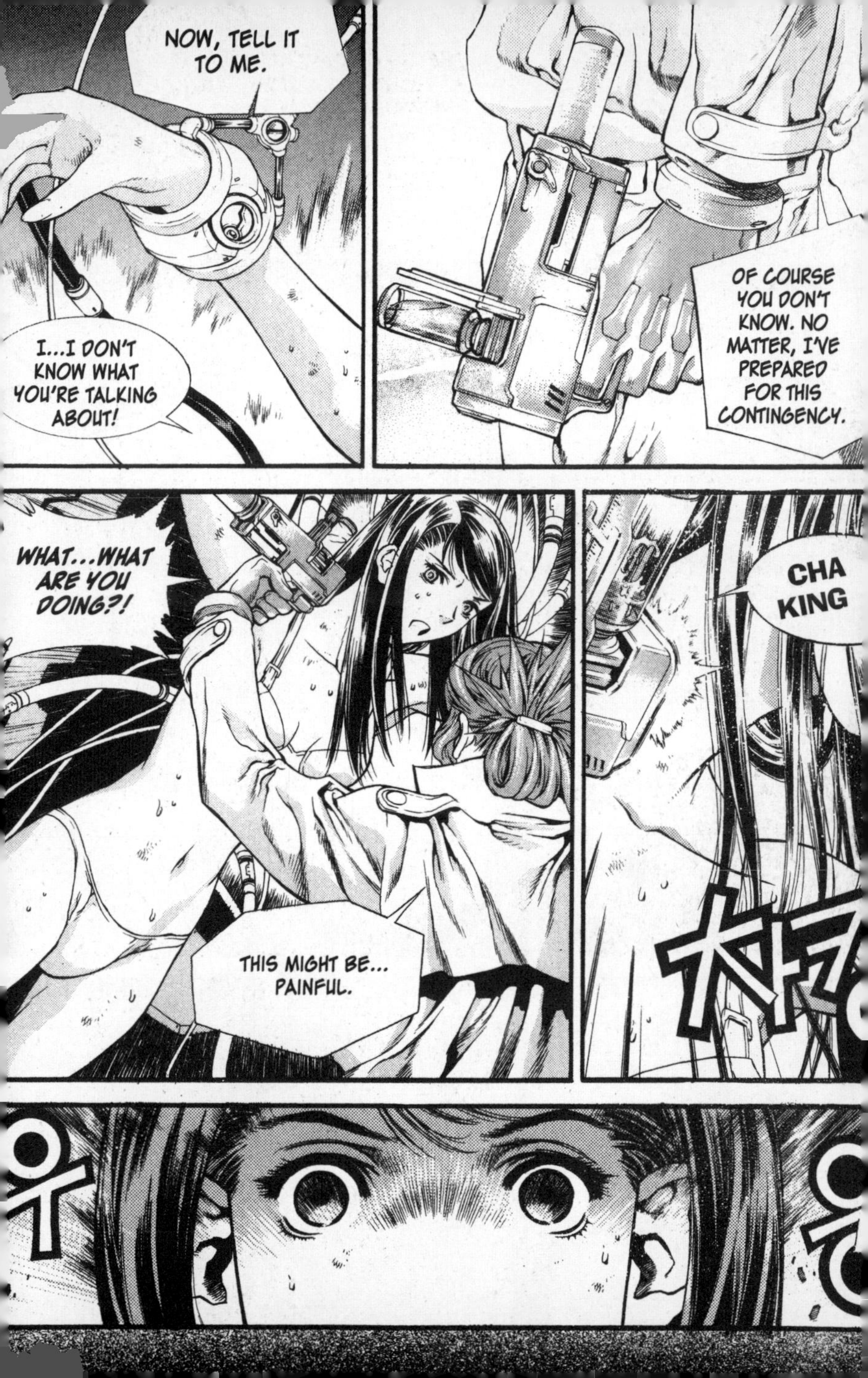
NOW, TELL IT TO ME.
I...I DON'T KNOW WHAT YOU'RE TALKING ABOUT!
OF COURSE YOU DON'T KNOW. NO MATTER, I'VE PREPARED FOR THIS CONTINGENCY.
WHAT...WHAT ARE YOU DOING?!
THIS MIGHT BE... PAINFUL.
CHA KING

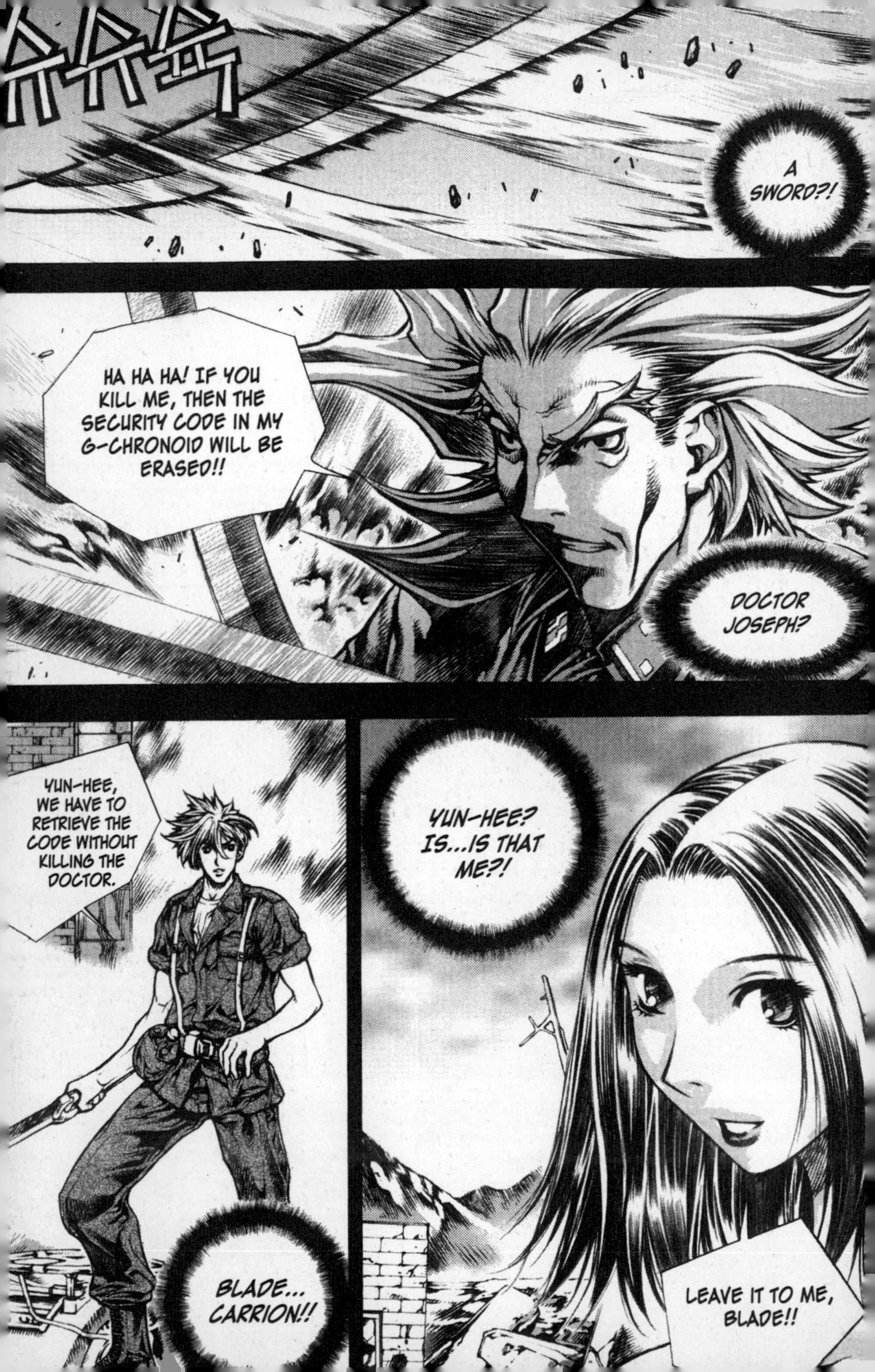
A SWORD?!
HA HA HA! IF YOU KILL ME, THEN THE SECURITY CODE IN MY G-CHRONOID WILL BE ERASED!!
DOCTOR JOSEPH?
YUN-HEE, WE HAVE TO RETRIEVE THE CODE WITHOUT KILLING THE DOCTOR.
BLADE... CARRION!!
YUN-HEE? IS...IS THAT ME?!
LEAVE IT TO ME, BLADE!!

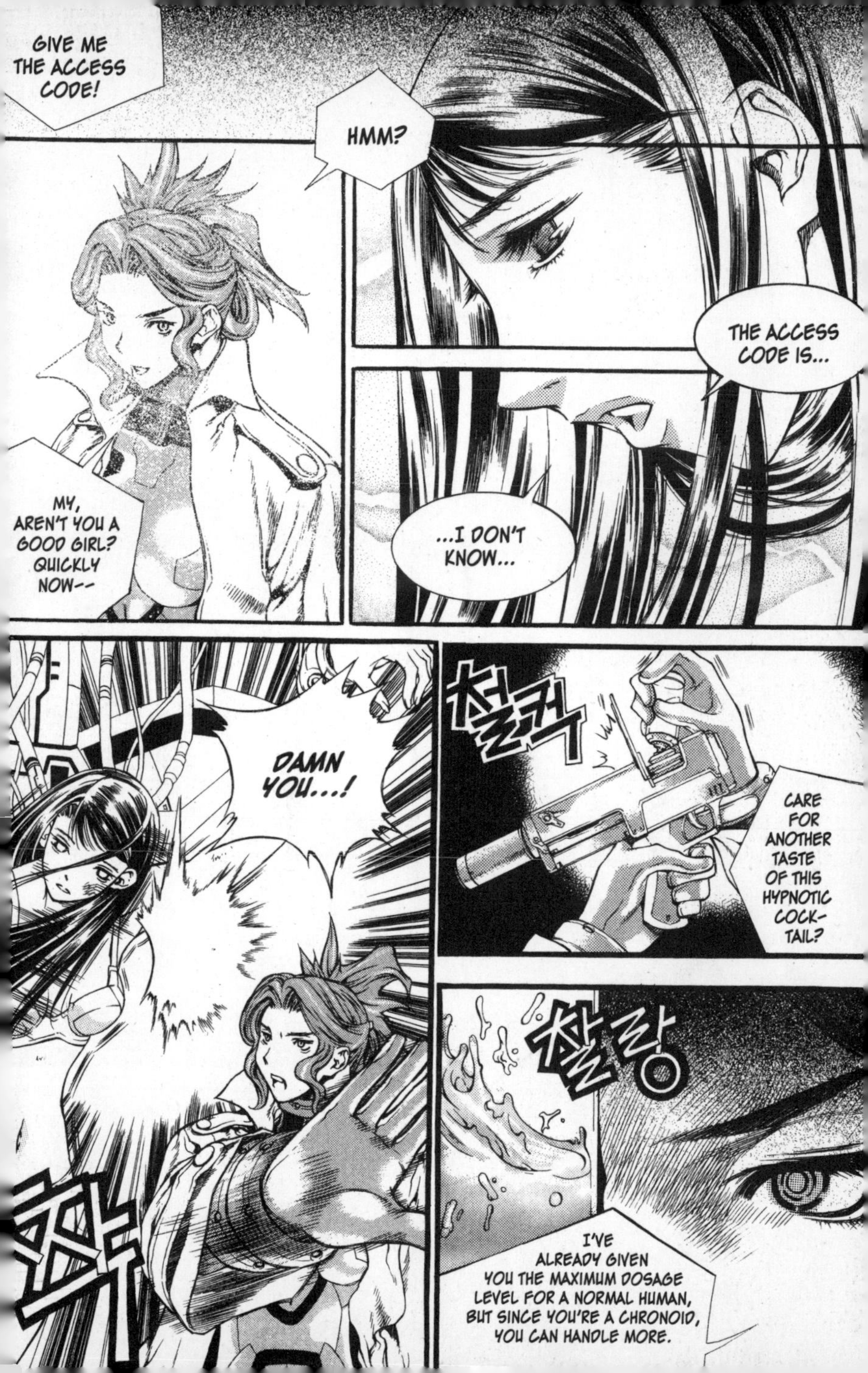
GIVE ME THE ACCESS CODE!
HMM?
MY, AREN'T YOU A GOOD GIRL? QUICKLY NOW--
THE ACCESS CODE IS...
...I DON'T KNOW...
DAMN YOU...!
철컥
CARE FOR ANOTHER TASTE OF THIS HYPNOTIC COCK-TAIL?
찰랑
I'VE ALREADY GIVEN YOU THE MAXIMUM DOSAGE LEVEL FOR A NORMAL HUMAN, BUT SINCE YOU'RE A CHRONOID, YOU CAN HANDLE MORE.

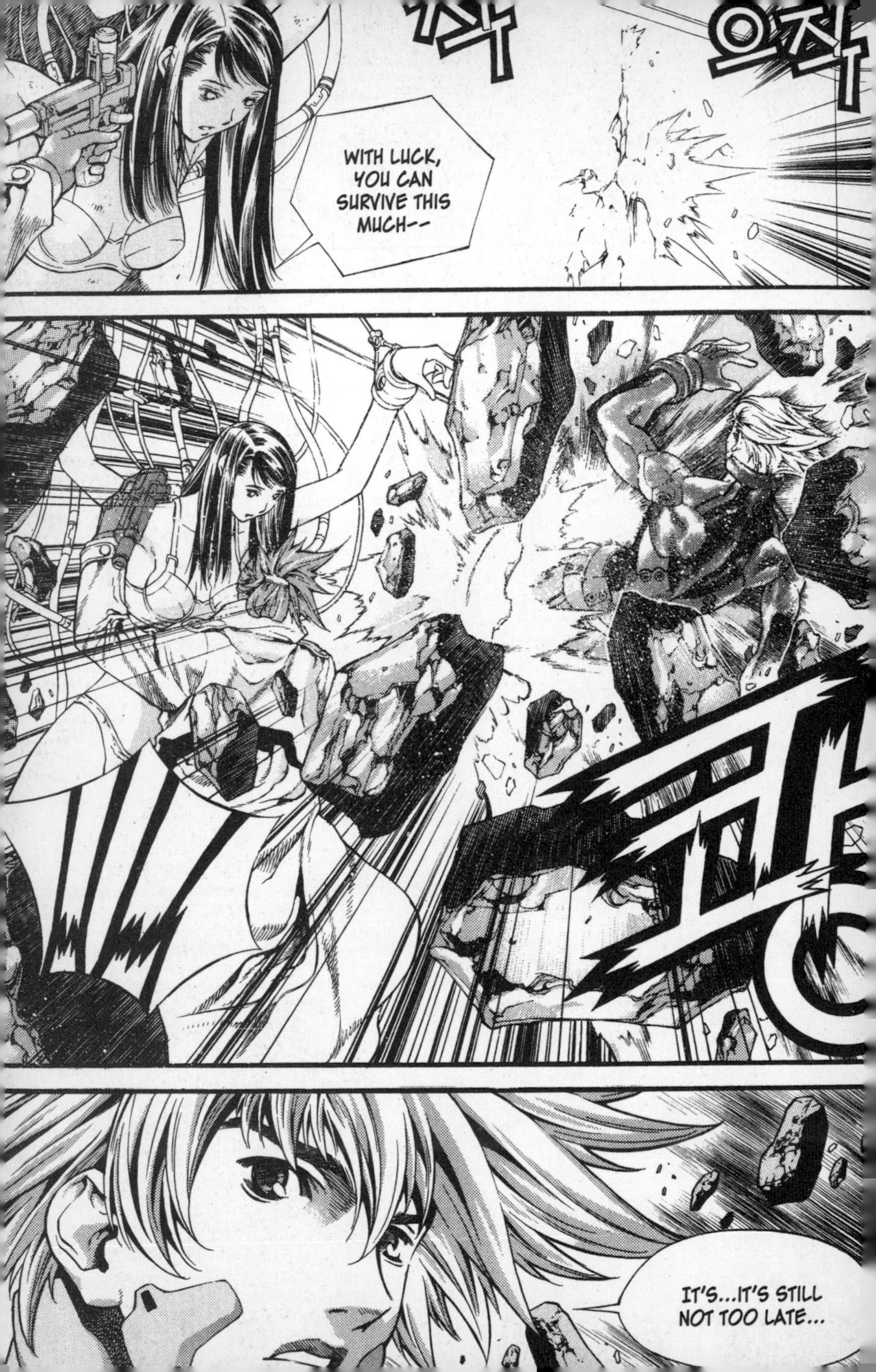
WITH LUCK, YOU CAN SURVIVE THIS MUCH--
으직
IT'S...IT'S STILL NOT TOO LATE...

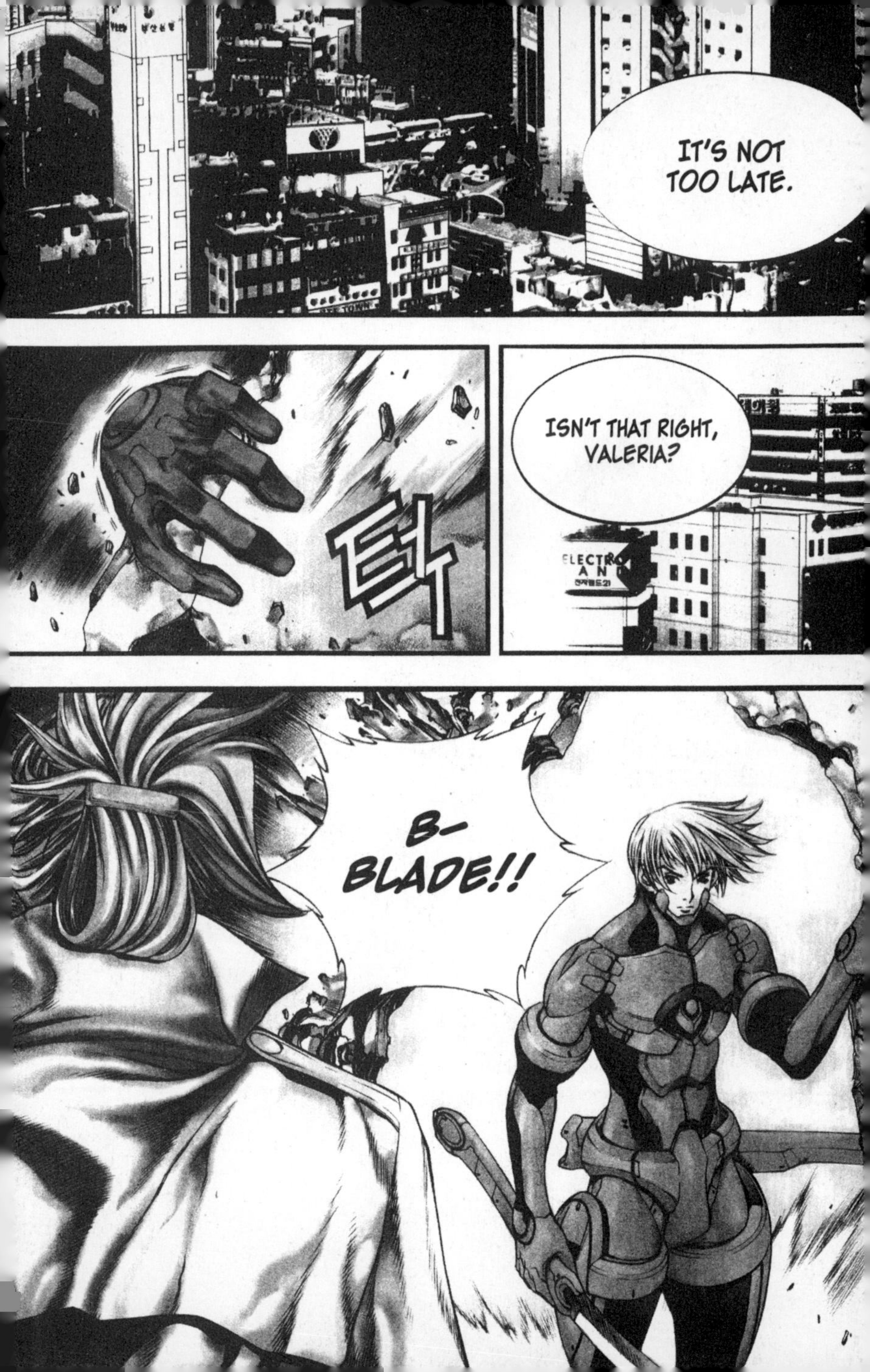
IT'S NOT TOO LATE.
ISN'T THAT RIGHT, VALERIA?
B- BLADE!!

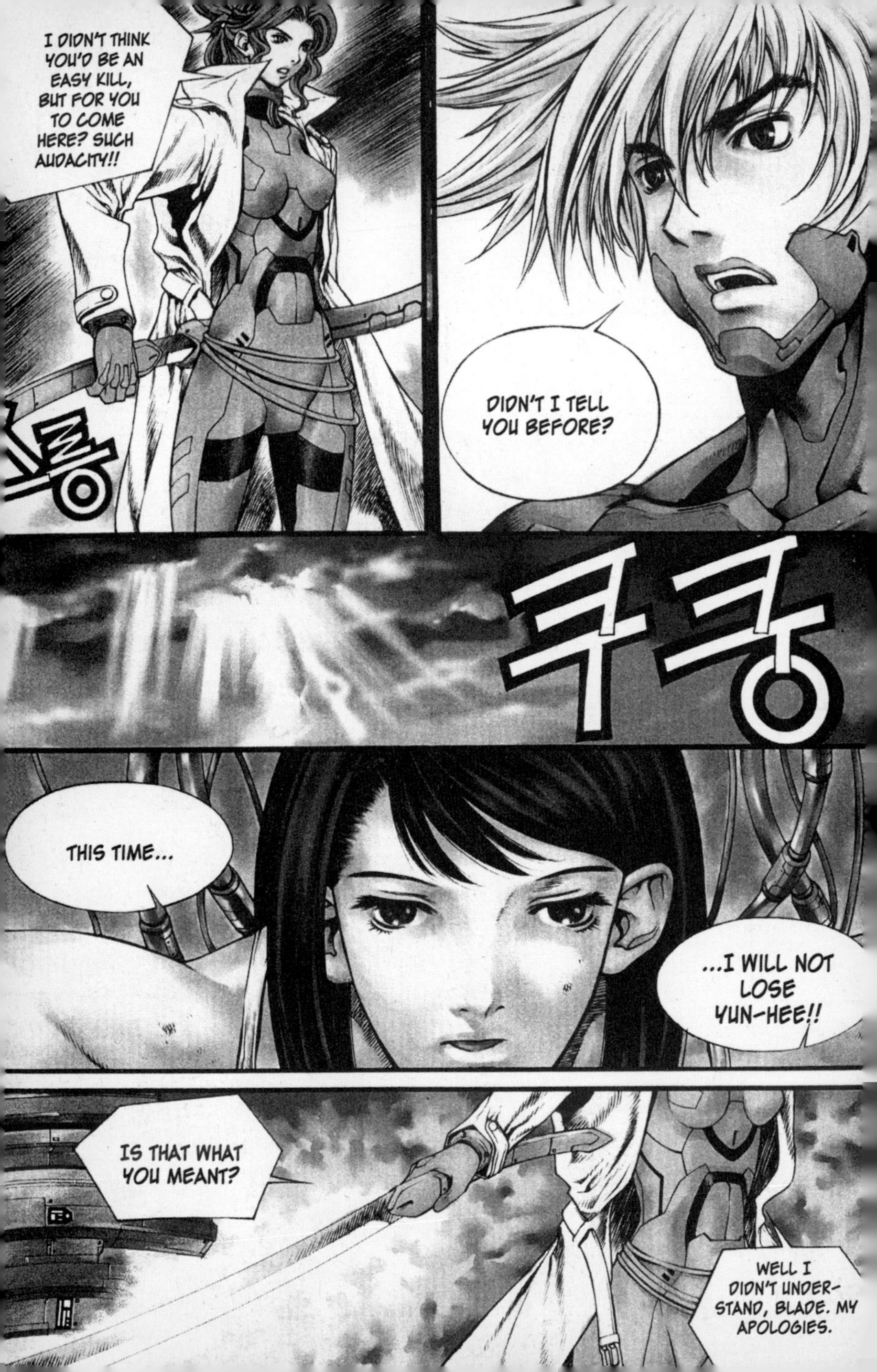
I DIDN'T THINK YOU'D BE AN EASY KILL, BUT FOR YOU TO COME HERE? SUCH AUDACITY!!
DIDN'T I TELL YOU BEFORE?
쿠쿵
THIS TIME...
...I WILL NOT LOSE YUN-HEE!!
IS THAT WHAT YOU MEANT?
WELL I DIDN'T UNDER-STAND, BLADE. MY APOLOGIES.

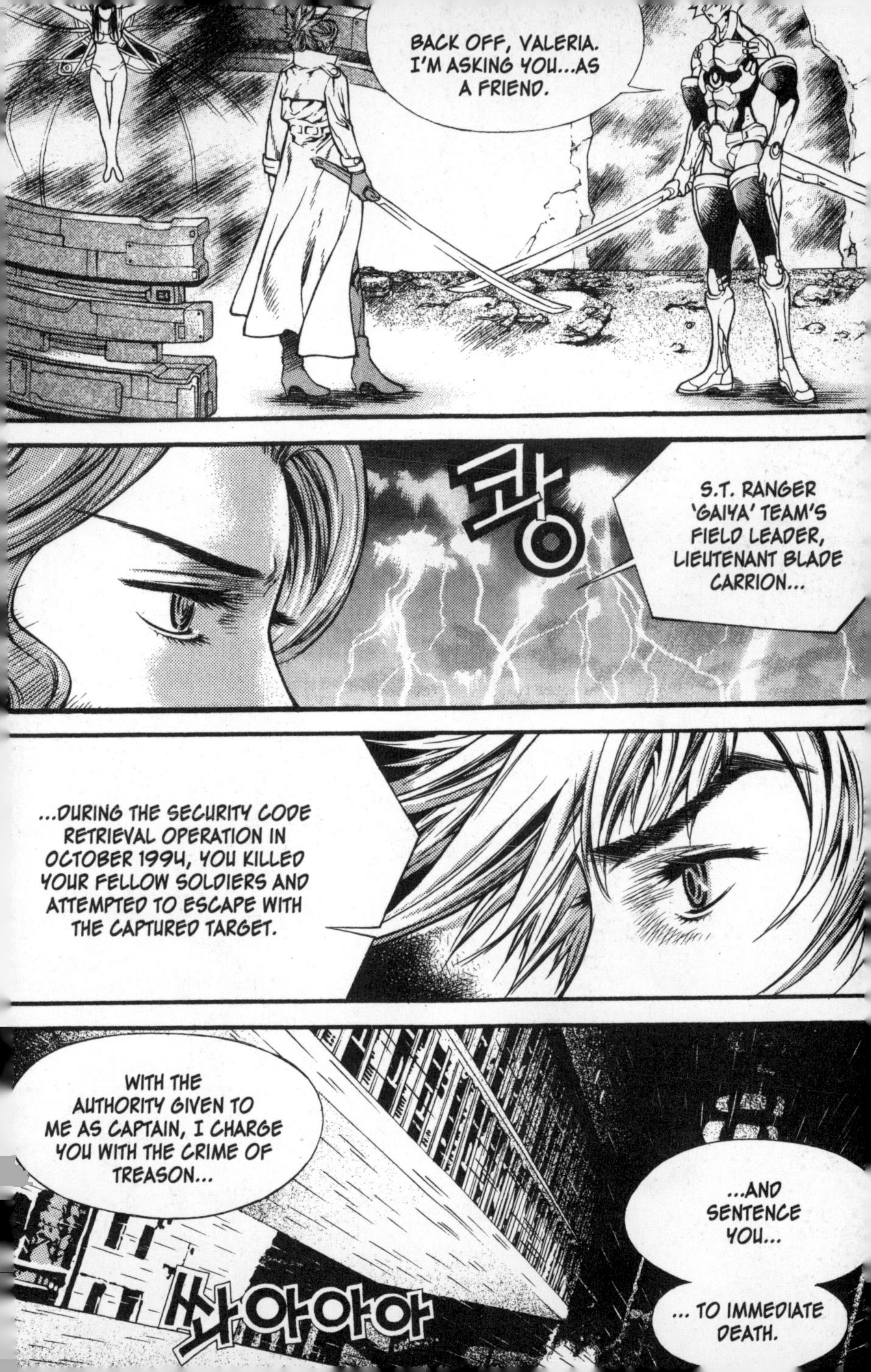
BACK OFF, VALERIA. I'M ASKING YOU...AS A FRIEND.
콰
S.T. RANGER 'GAIYA' TEAM'S FIELD LEADER, LIEUTENANT BLADE CARRION...
...DURING THE SECURITY CODE RETRIEVAL OPERATION IN OCTOBER 1994, YOU KILLED YOUR FELLOW SOLDIERS AND ATTEMPTED TO ESCAPE WITH THE CAPTURED TARGET.
WITH THE AUTHORITY GIVEN TO ME AS CAPTAIN, I CHARGE YOU WITH THE CRIME OF TREASON...
쏴아아아
...AND SENTENCE YOU...
... TO IMMEDIATE DEATH.

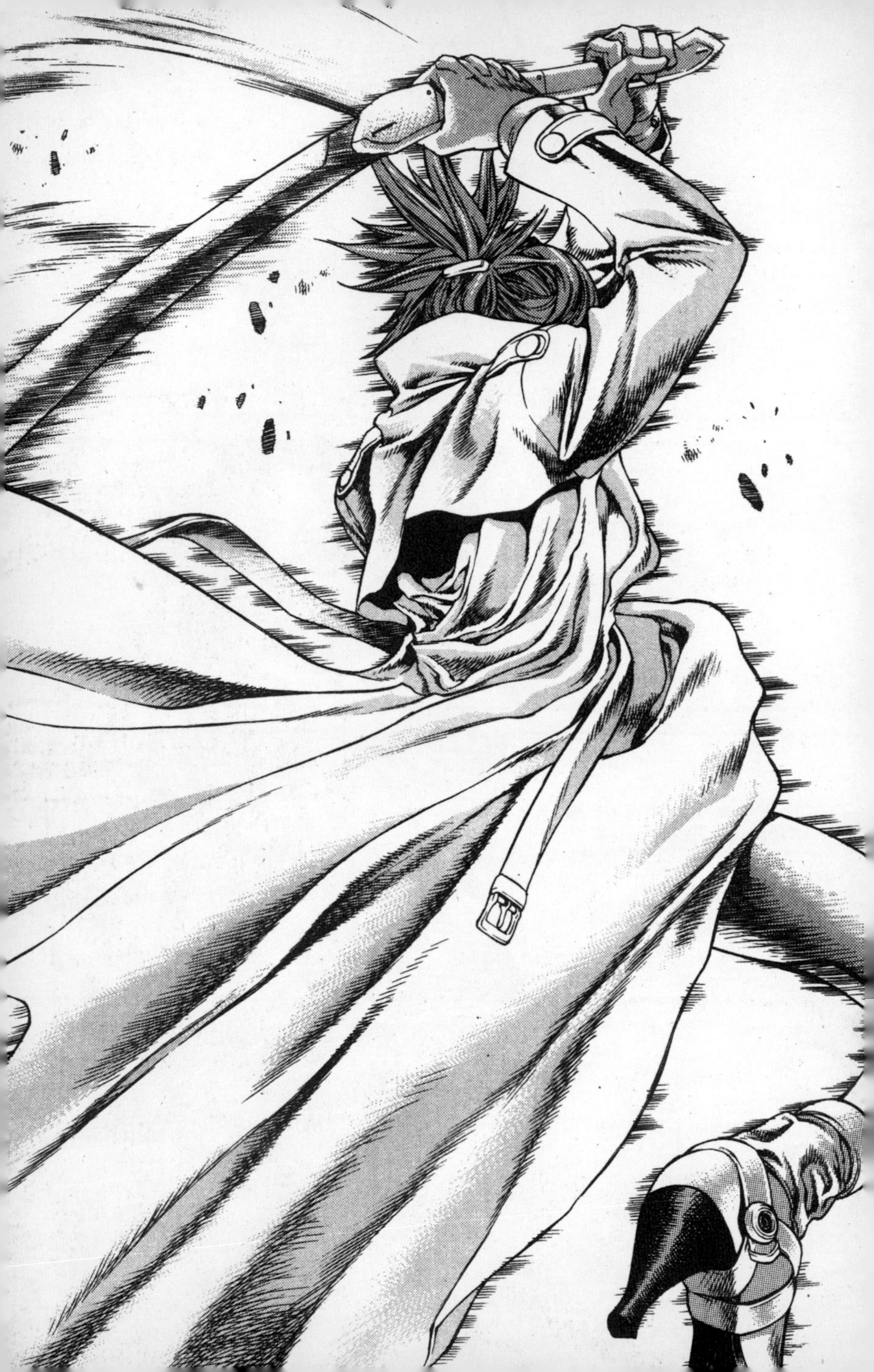

CHRONO CODE

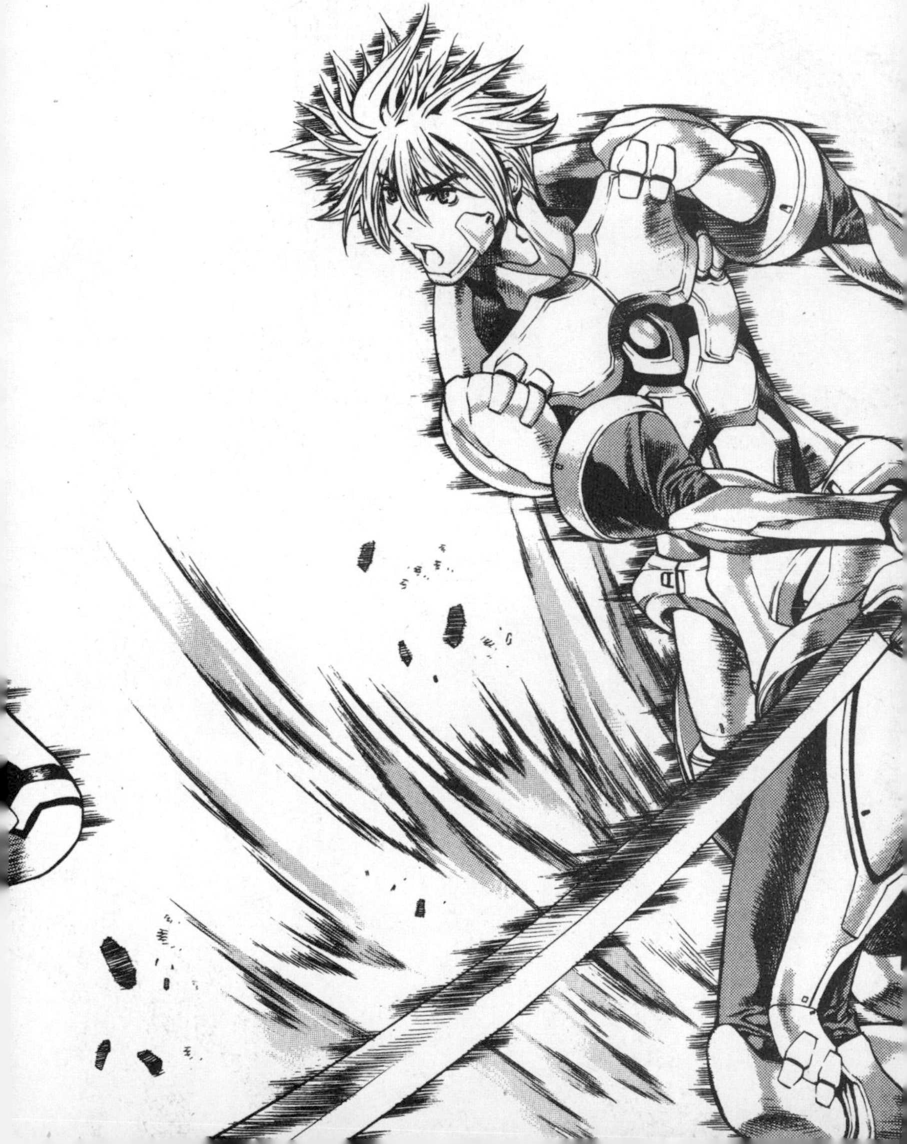

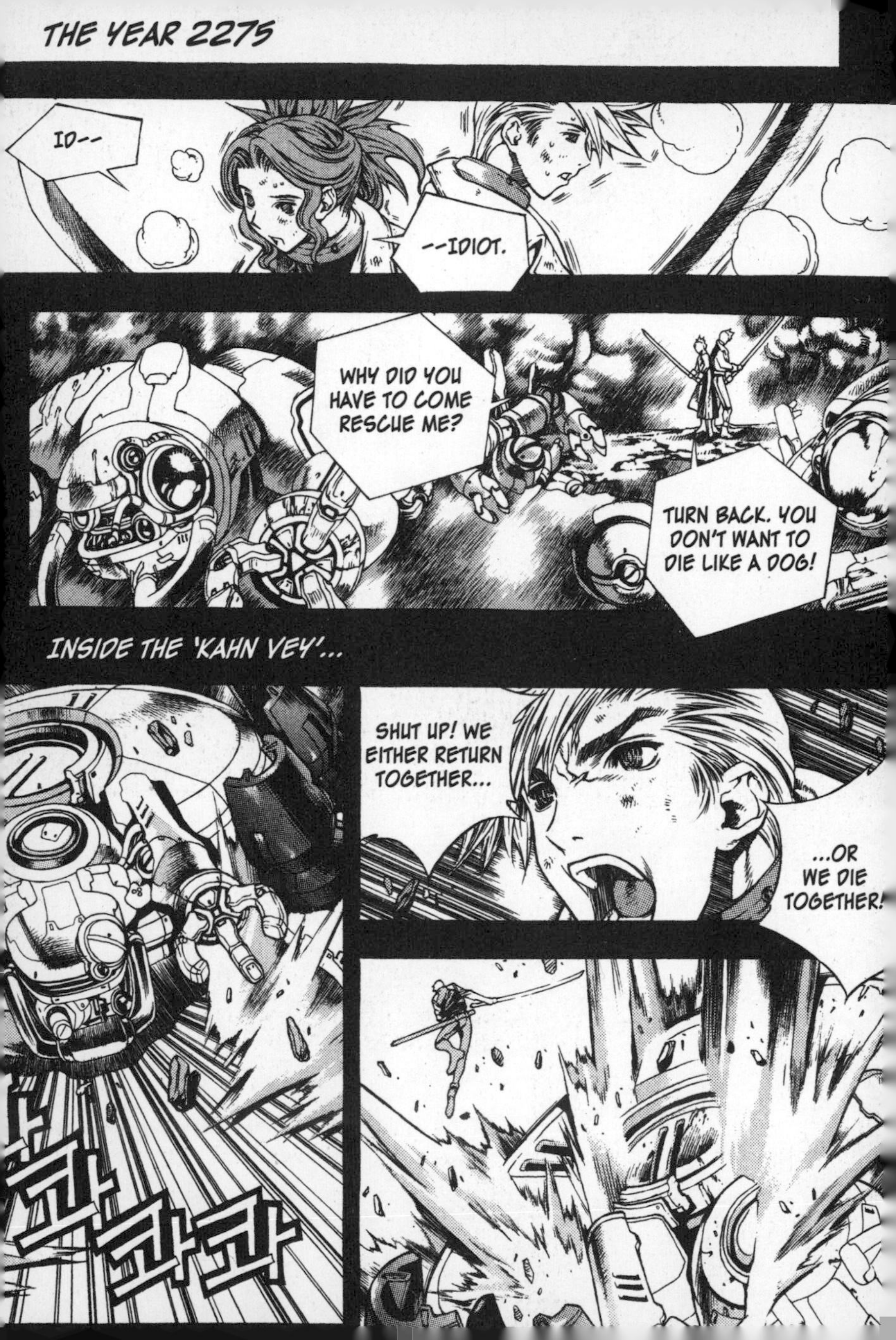
THE YEAR 2275
ID--
--IDIOT.
WHY DID YOU HAVE TO COME RESCUE ME?
TURN BACK. YOU DON'T WANT TO DIE LIKE A DOG!
INSIDE THE 'KAHN VEY'...
SHUT UP! WE EITHER RETURN TOGETHER...
...OR WE DIE TOGETHER!

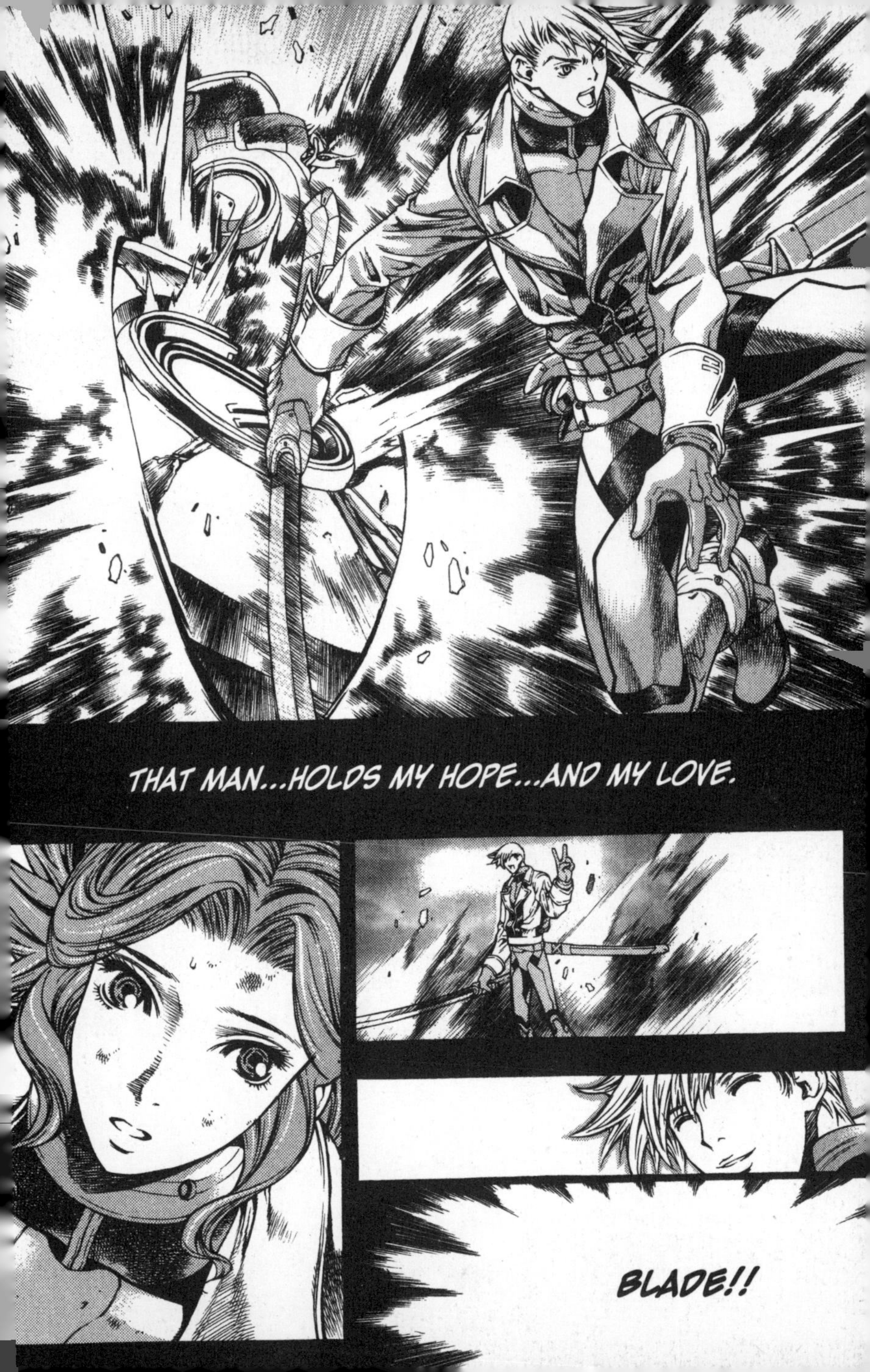
THAT MAN...HOLDS MY HOPE...AND MY LOVE.
BLADE!!

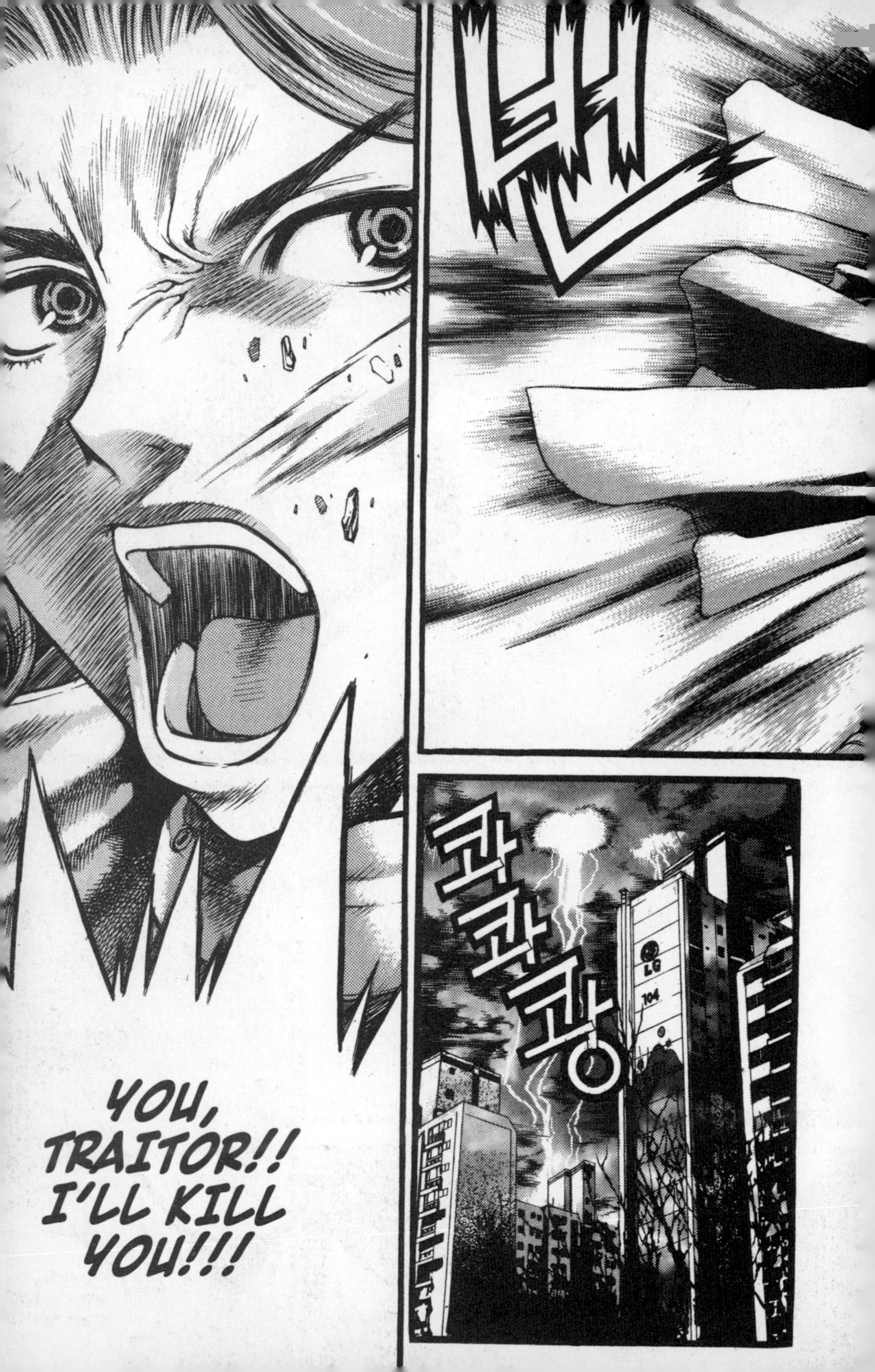
YOU, TRAITOR!! I'LL KILL YOU!!!
낸
콰콰광
LG
104

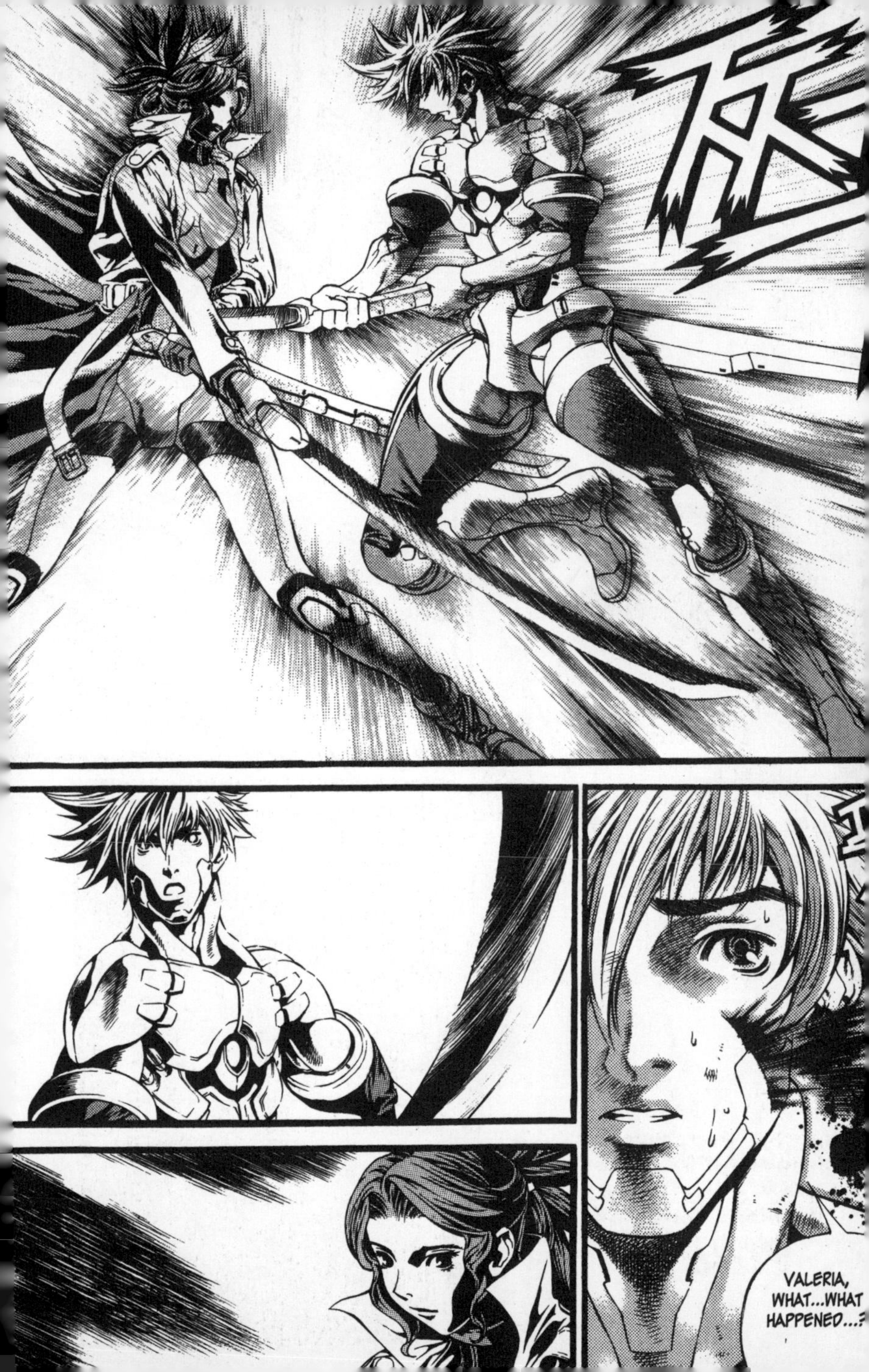

VALERIA, WHAT...WHAT HAPPENED...?

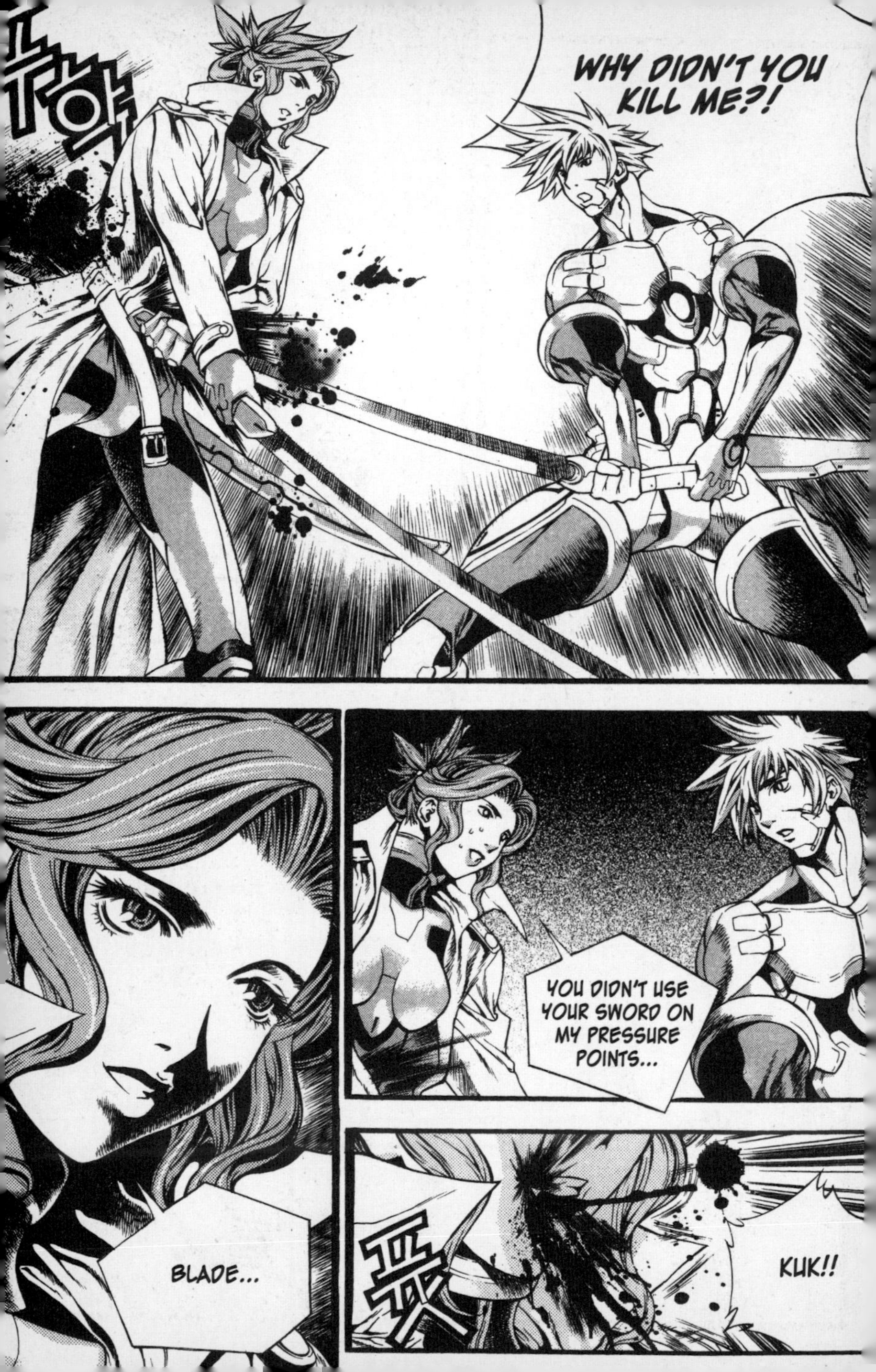
WHY DIDN'T YOU KILL ME?!
BLADE...
YOU DIDN'T USE YOUR SWORD ON MY PRESSURE POINTS...
KUK!!

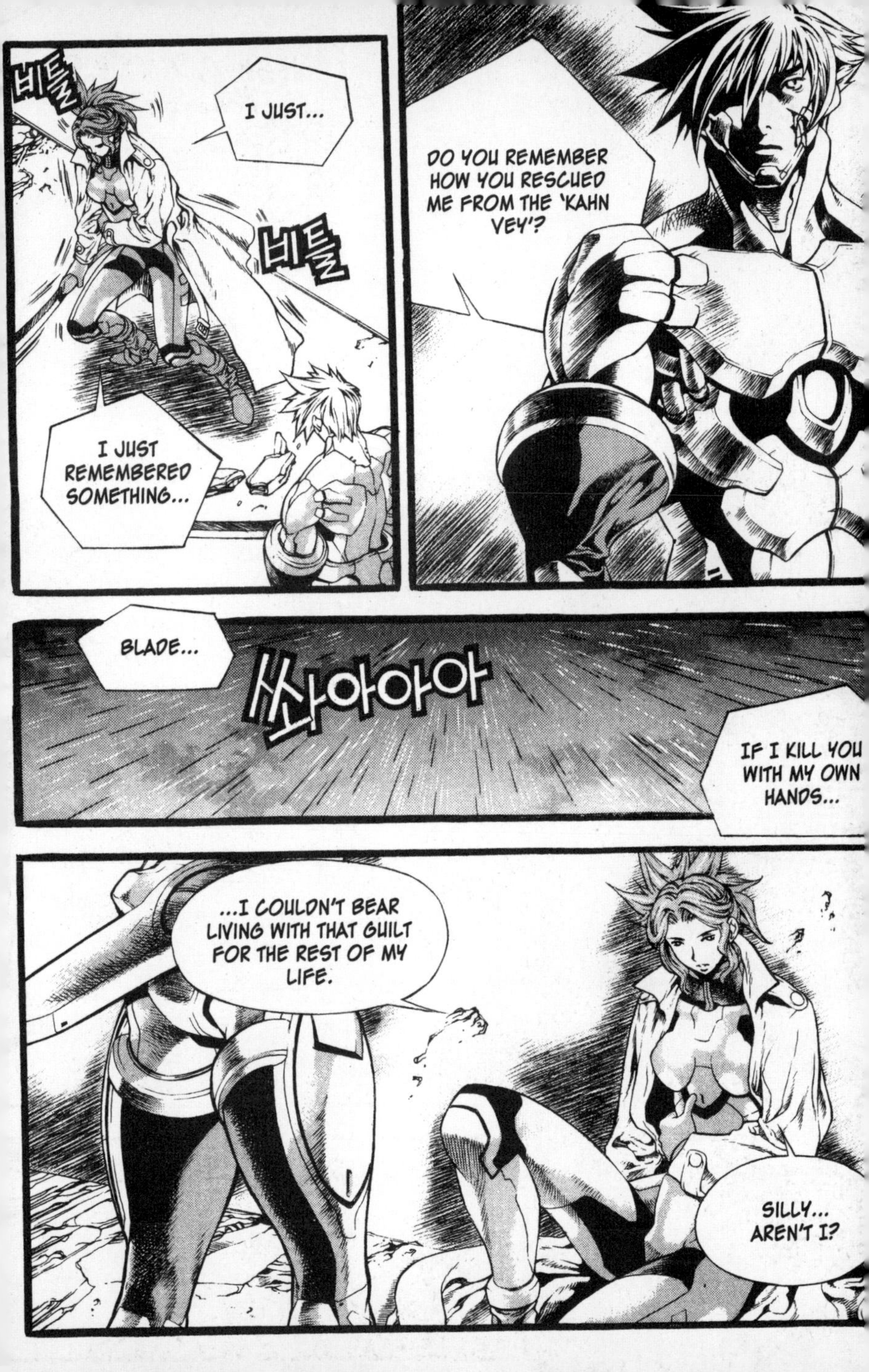

비틀
I JUST...
비틀
I JUST REMEMBERED SOMETHING...
DO YOU REMEMBER HOW YOU RESCUED ME FROM THE 'KAHN VEY'?
BLADE...
쏴아아아
IF I KILL YOU WITH MY OWN HANDS...
...I COULDN'T BEAR LIVING WITH THAT GUILT FOR THE REST OF MY LIFE.
SILLY... AREN'T I?

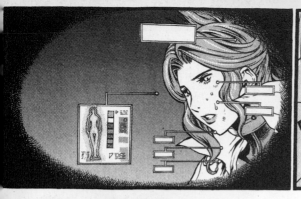

SO...

...THIS IS HOW IT UNFOLDS.

THE RIVER OF TIME...

YOU CAN SWIM AGAINST THE RIVER'S CURRENT BUT YOU CAN'T CHANGE ITS COURSE?

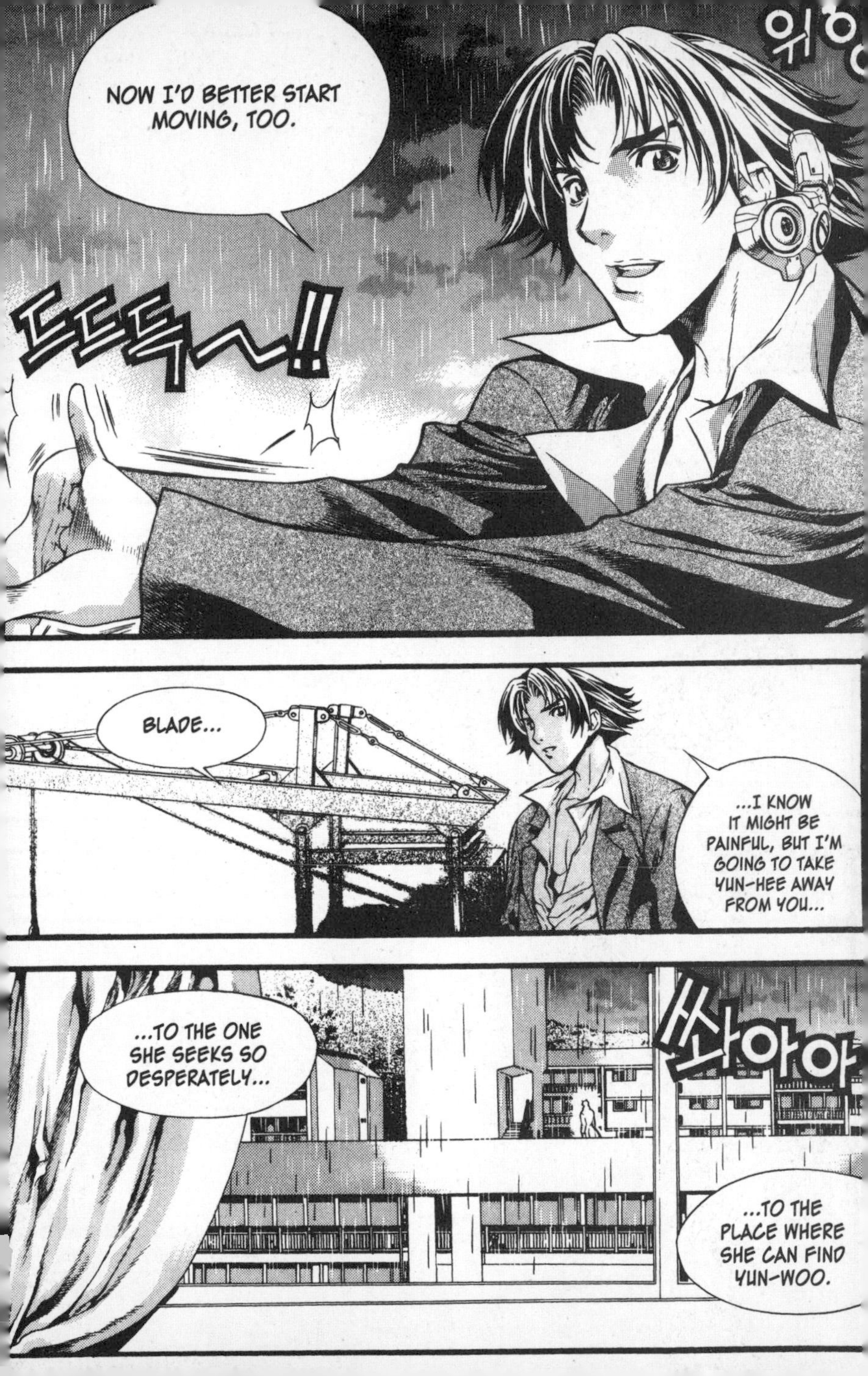
NOW I'D BETTER START MOVING, TOO.
드드득~!!
BLADE...
...I KNOW IT MIGHT BE PAINFUL, BUT I'M GOING TO TAKE YUN-HEE AWAY FROM YOU...
...TO THE ONE SHE SEEKS SO DESPERATELY...
쏴아아
...TO THE PLACE WHERE SHE CAN FIND YUN-WOO.

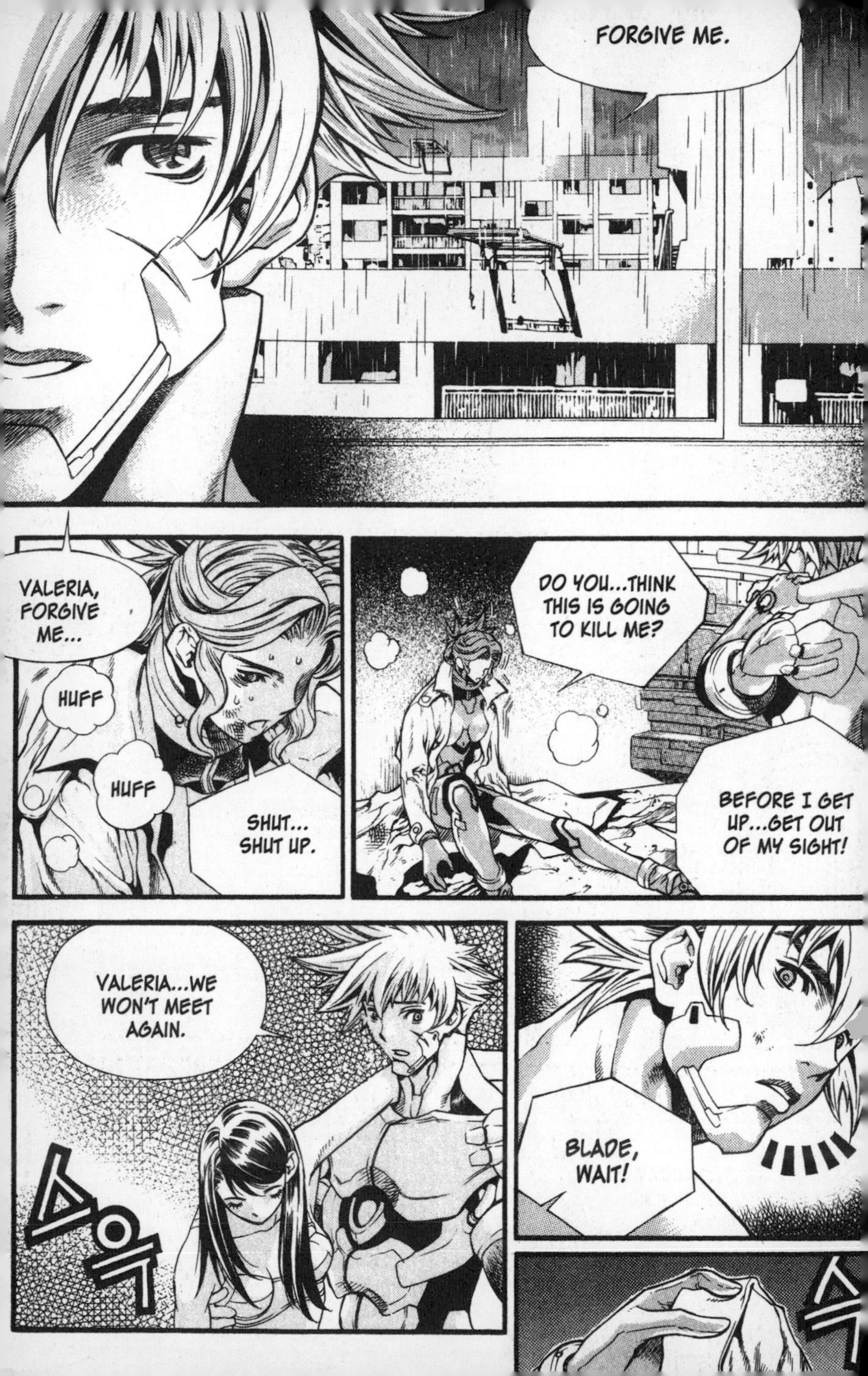
FORGIVE ME.
VALERIA, FORGIVE ME...
HUFF
HUFF
SHUT... SHUT UP.
DO YOU...THINK THIS IS GOING TO KILL ME?
BEFORE I GET UP...GET OUT OF MY SIGHT!
VALERIA...WE WON'T MEET AGAIN.
BLADE, WAIT!

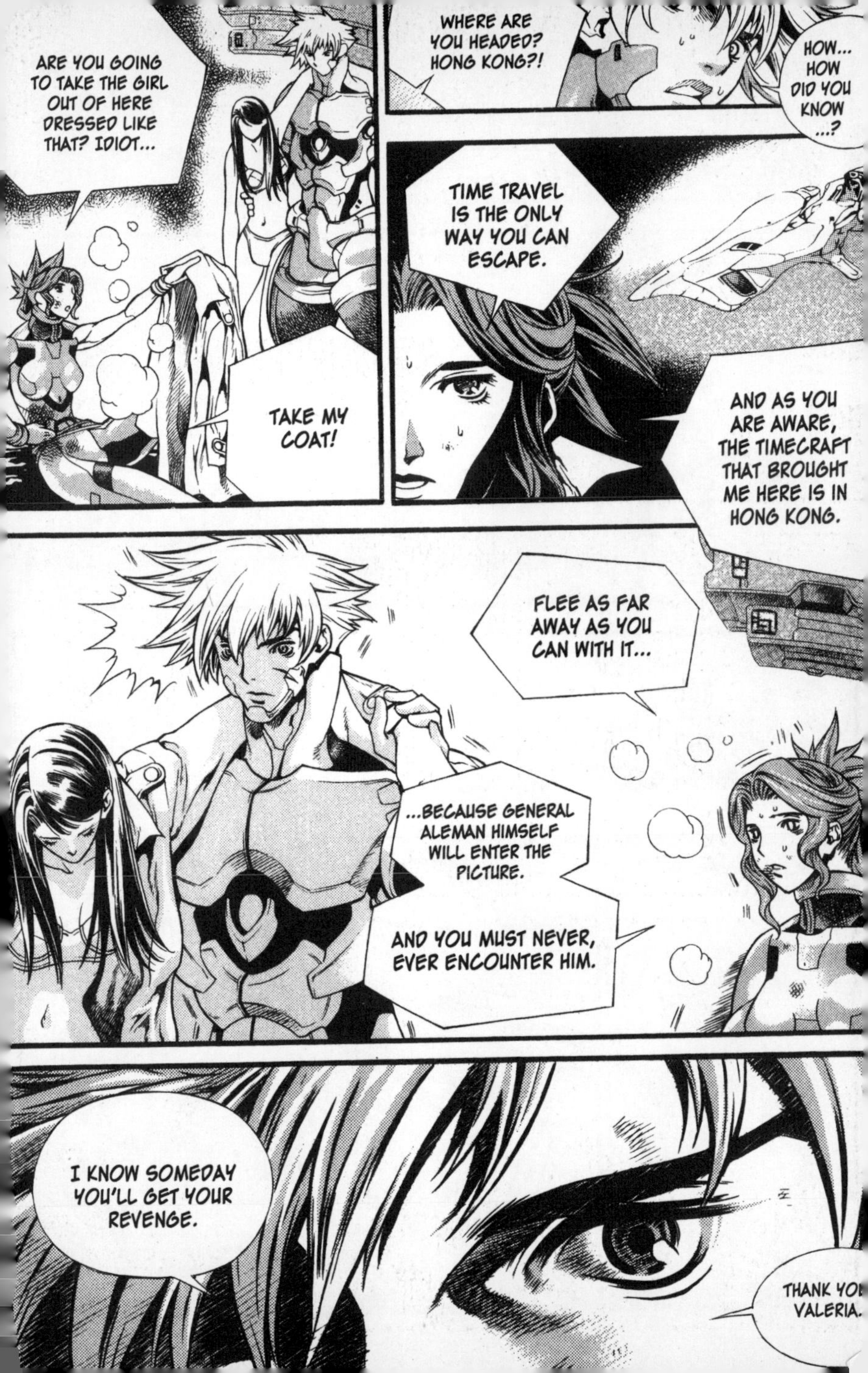
ARE YOU GOING TO TAKE THE GIRL OUT OF HERE DRESSED LIKE THAT? IDIOT...
TAKE MY COAT!
WHERE ARE YOU HEADED? HONG KONG?!
HOW... HOW DID YOU KNOW ...?
TIME TRAVEL IS THE ONLY WAY YOU CAN ESCAPE.
AND AS YOU ARE AWARE, THE TIMECRAFT THAT BROUGHT ME HERE IS IN HONG KONG.
FLEE AS FAR AWAY AS YOU CAN WITH IT...
...BECAUSE GENERAL ALEMAN HIMSELF WILL ENTER THE PICTURE.
AND YOU MUST NEVER, EVER ENCOUNTER HIM.
I KNOW SOMEDAY YOU'LL GET YOUR REVENGE.
THANK YO VALERIA.

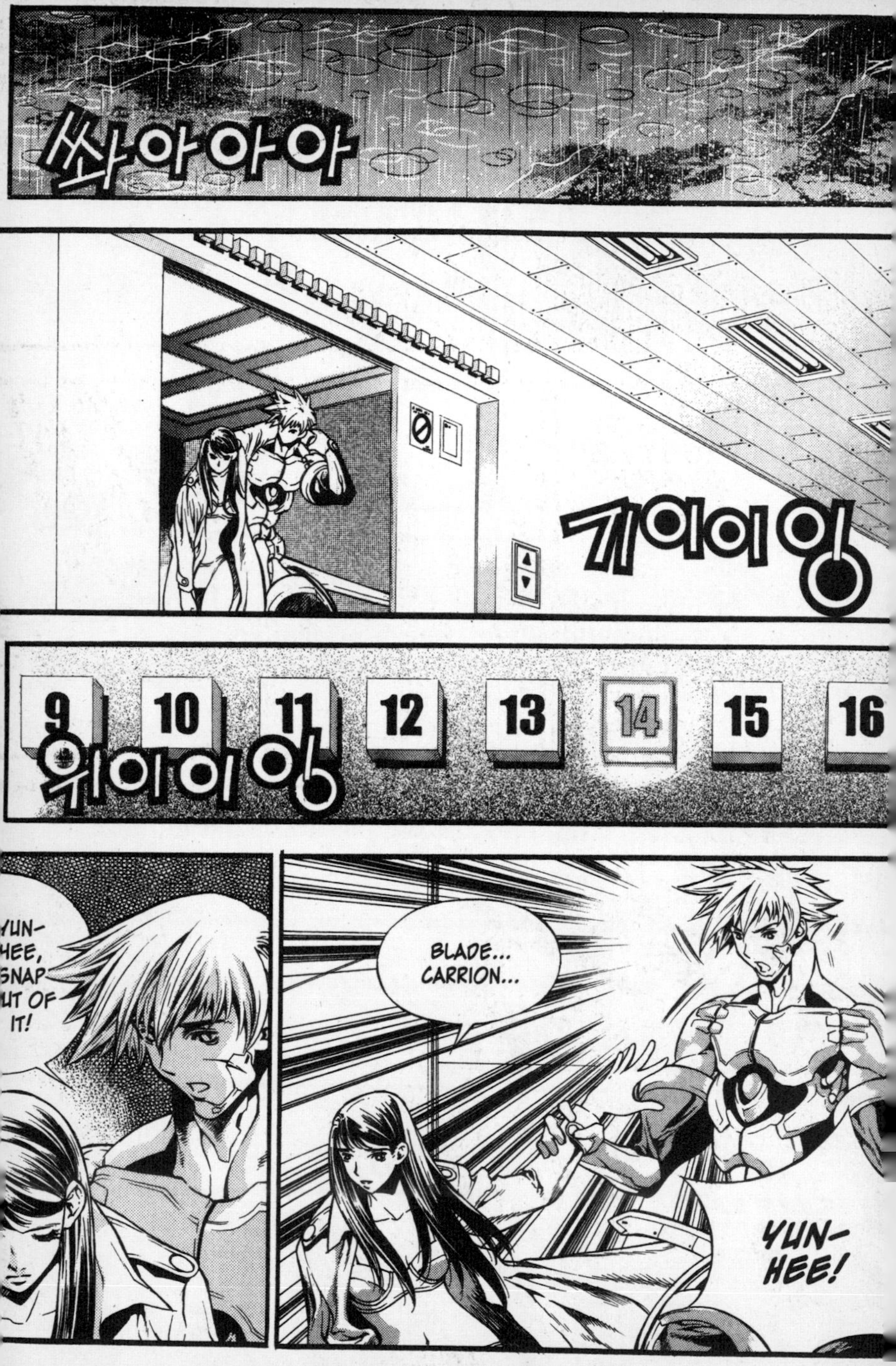
쏴아아아
기이이잉
9 10 11 12 13 14 15 16
위이이잉
YUN-HEE, SNAP UT OF IT!
BLADE... CARRION...
YUN-HEE!

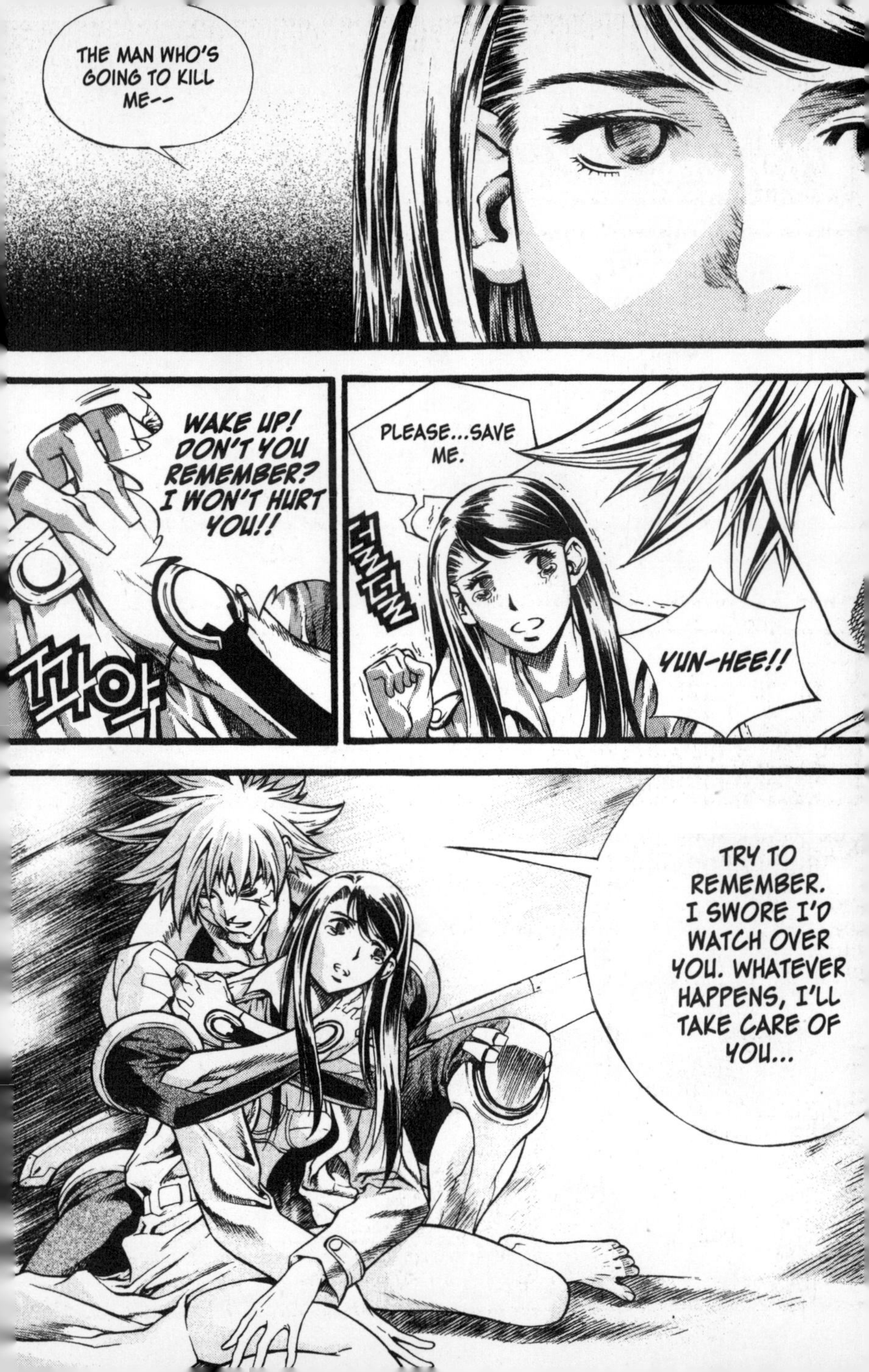
THE MAN WHO'S GOING TO KILL ME--
WAKE UP! DON'T YOU REMEMBER? I WON'T HURT YOU!!
꽈악
PLEASE...SAVE ME.
YUN-HEE!!
TRY TO REMEMBER. I SWORE I'D WATCH OVER YOU. WHATEVER HAPPENS, I'LL TAKE CARE OF YOU...

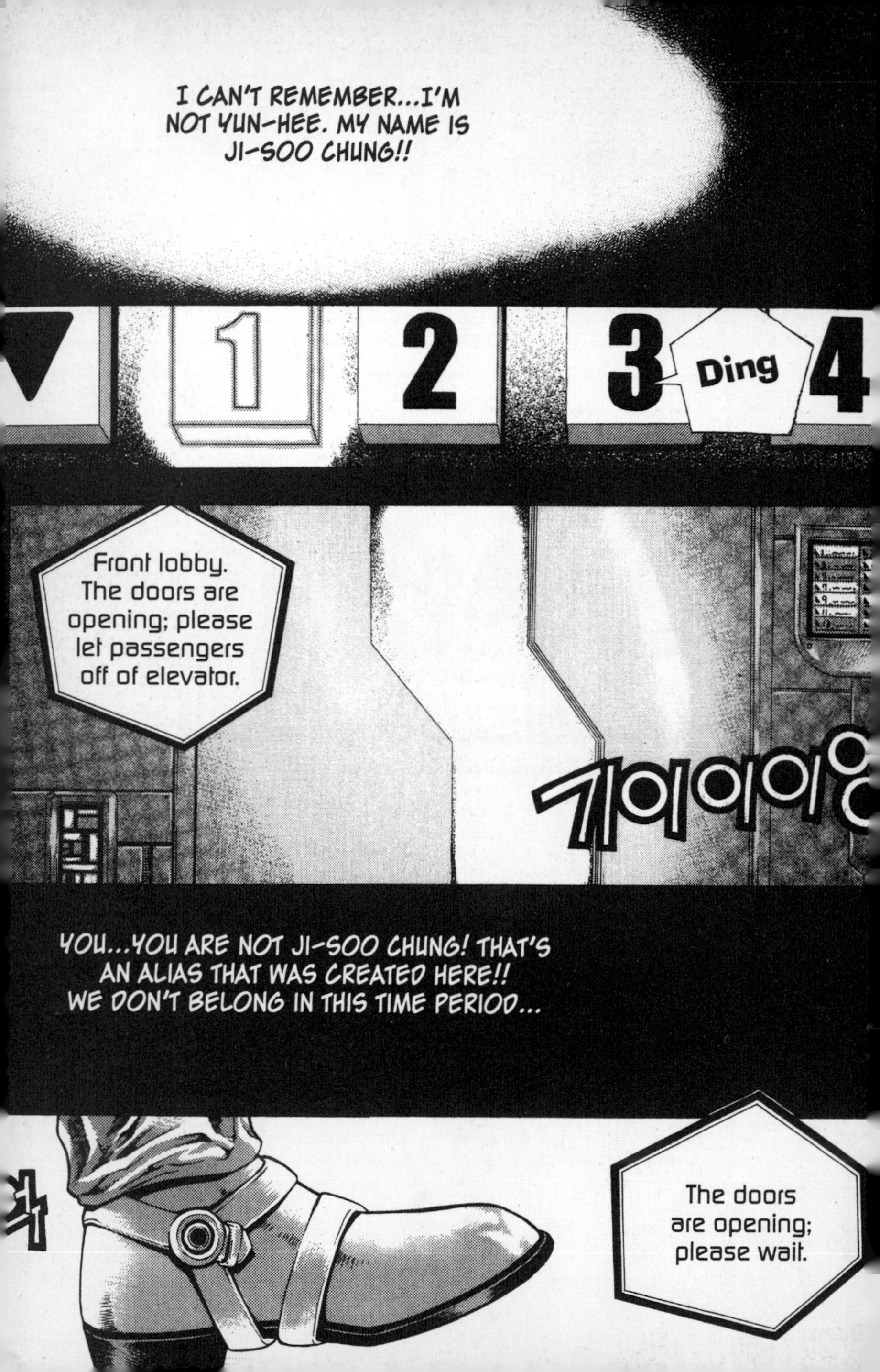
I CAN'T REMEMBER...I'M NOT YUN-HEE. MY NAME IS JI-SOO CHUNG!!
1 2 3 4
Ding
Front lobby. The doors are opening; please let passengers off of elevator.
YOU...YOU ARE NOT JI-SOO CHUNG! THAT'S AN ALIAS THAT WAS CREATED HERE!! WE DON'T BELONG IN THIS TIME PERIOD...
The doors are opening; please wait.

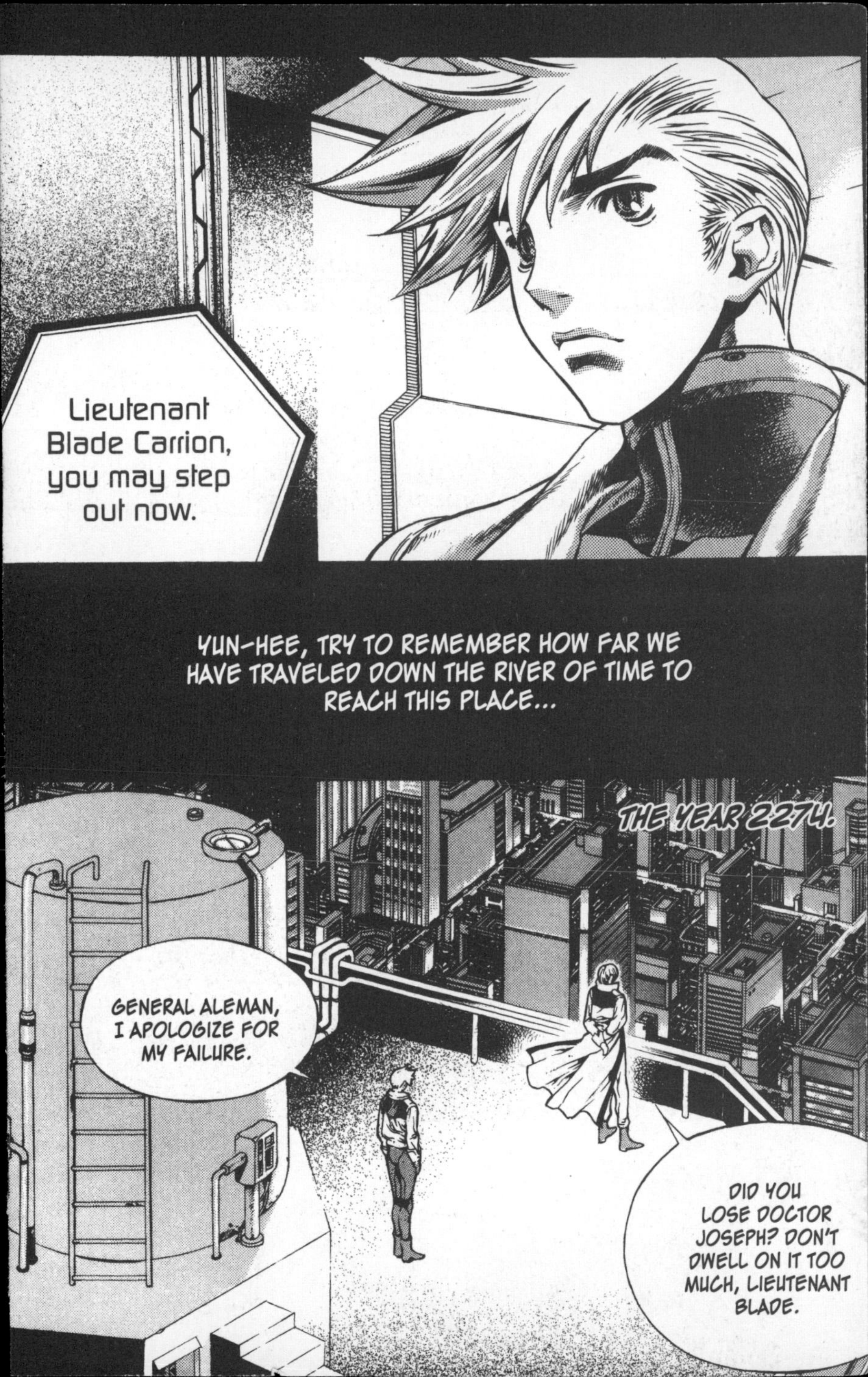
Lieutenant Blade Carrion, you may step out now.
YUN-HEE, TRY TO REMEMBER HOW FAR WE HAVE TRAVELED DOWN THE RIVER OF TIME TO REACH THIS PLACE...
THE YEAR 2274.
GENERAL ALEMAN, I APOLOGIZE FOR MY FAILURE.
DID YOU LOSE DOCTOR JOSEPH? DON'T DWELL ON IT TOO MUCH, LIEUTENANT BLADE.

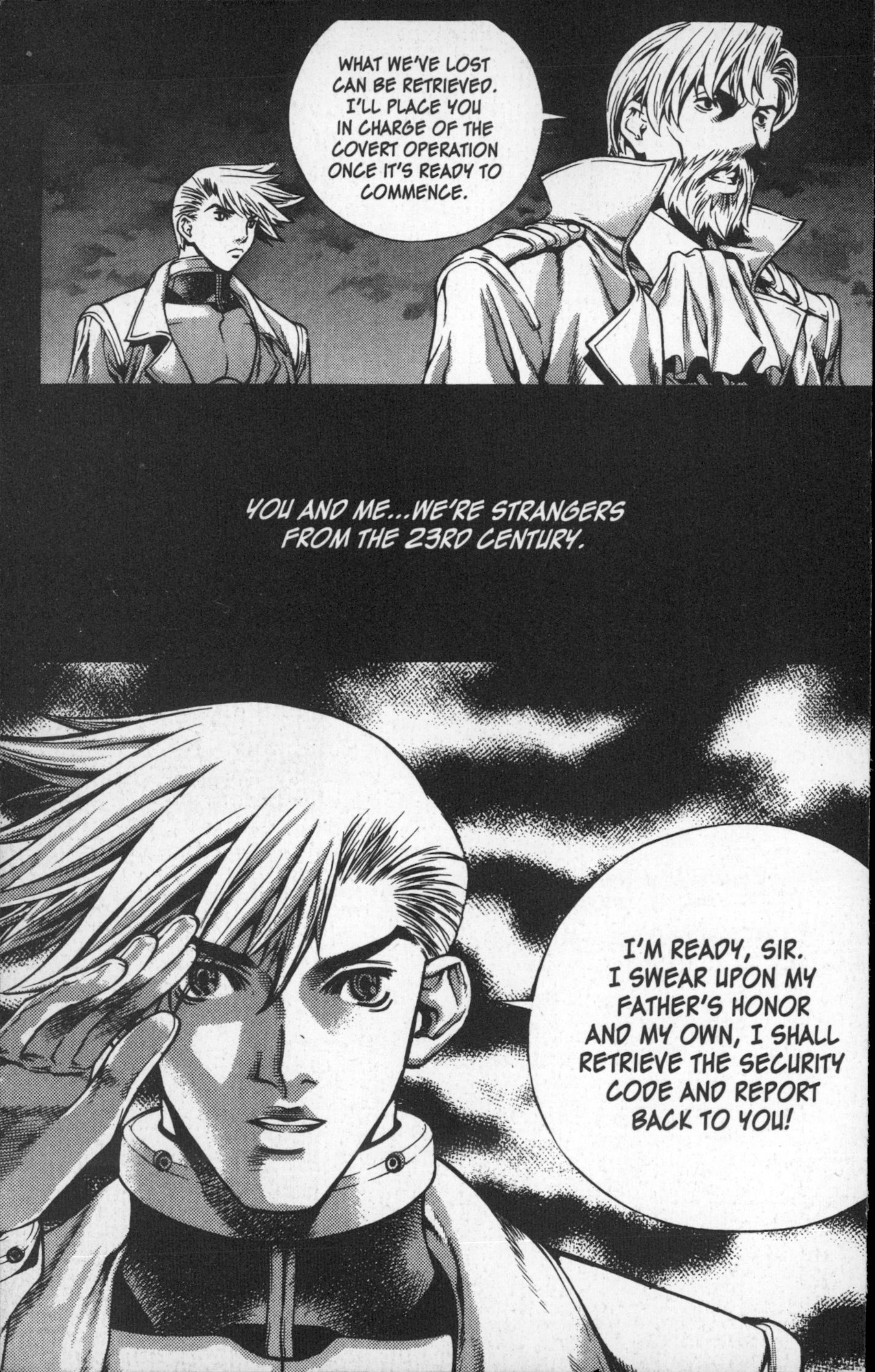
WHAT WE'VE LOST CAN BE RETRIEVED. I'LL PLACE YOU IN CHARGE OF THE COVERT OPERATION ONCE IT'S READY TO COMMENCE.
YOU AND ME...WE'RE STRANGERS FROM THE 23RD CENTURY.
I'M READY, SIR. I SWEAR UPON MY FATHER'S HONOR AND MY OWN, I SHALL RETRIEVE THE SECURITY CODE AND REPORT BACK TO YOU!

To be continued...

In the next volume of

:CHRONO:CODE:

Wondering just what the heck is going on? Then volume 2 is the book for you! In this prequel to volume 1, you'll learn about the great Armageddon war that left most of the world destroyed and led to the rise of the four federations: the African Federation, the American Federation, European/Russian Federation, and the Australian/Asian Federation.

The origin of the Chronoids is revealed and the complex relationship between Yun-Hee, Yun-Woo, Blade, Valeria, and Han-Young is explained. When it comes to getting answers, there's really no time like the past!

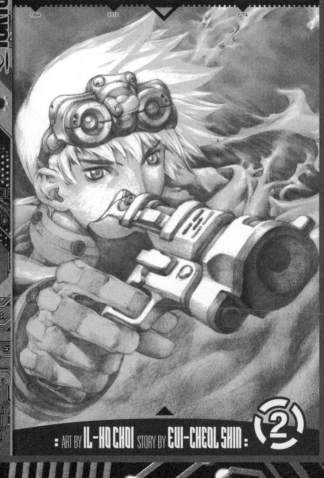

:CHRONO·CODE:

1994   2010   2274

: ART BY IL-HO CHOI STORY BY EUI-CHEOL SHIN : ②

TOKYOPOP SHOP

WWW.TOKYOPOP.COM/SHOP

HOT NEWS!
Check out the TOKYOPOP SHOP! The world's best collection of manga in English is now available online in one place!

SAKURA TAISEN

BECK: MONGOLIAN CHOP SQUAD

Princess Ai and other hot titles are available at the store that never closes!

PRINCESS AI VOL. 2: LUMINATION

- LOOK FOR SPECIAL OFFERS
- PRE-ORDER UPCOMING RELEASES
- COMPLETE YOUR COLLECTIONS

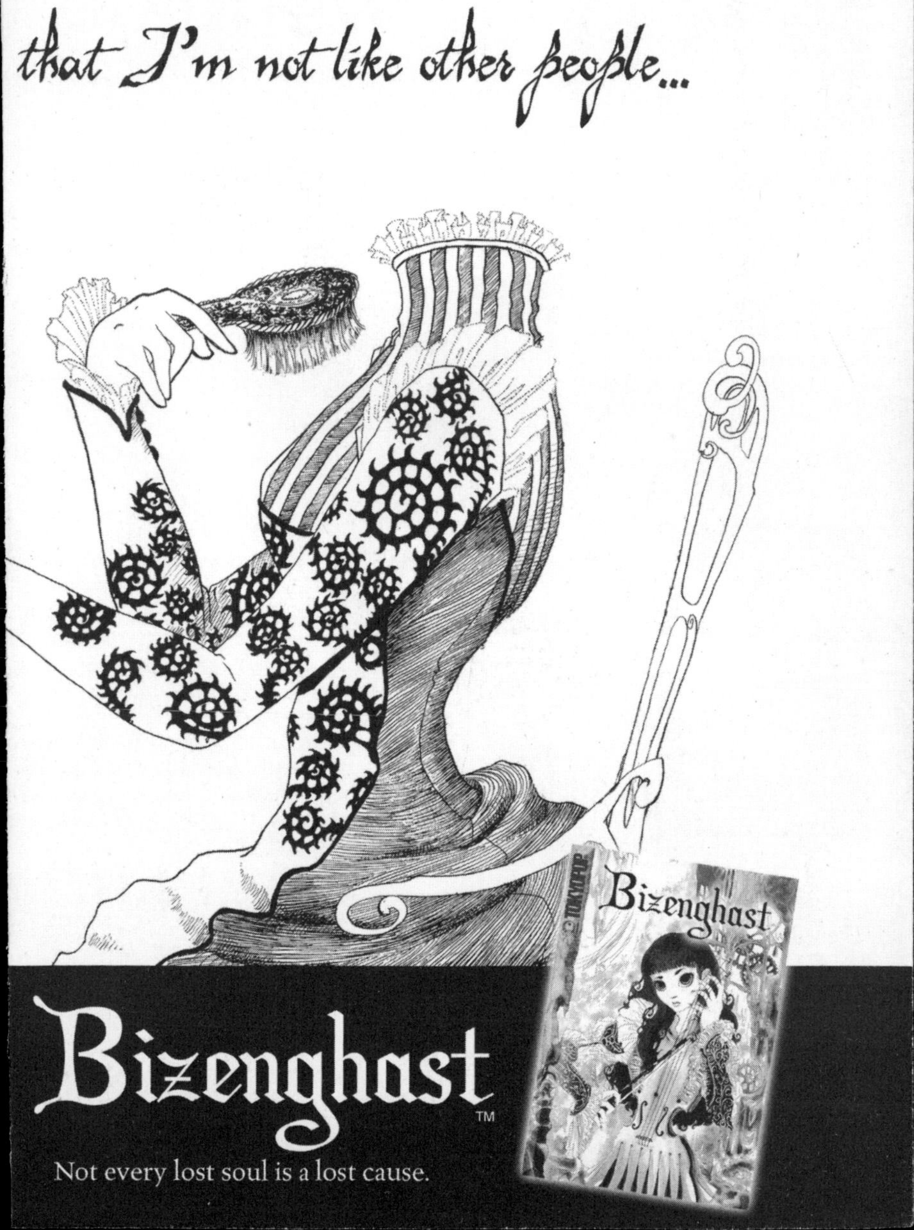
that I'm not like other people...
Bizenghast
TOKYOPOP
Bizenghast™
Not every lost soul is a lost cause.

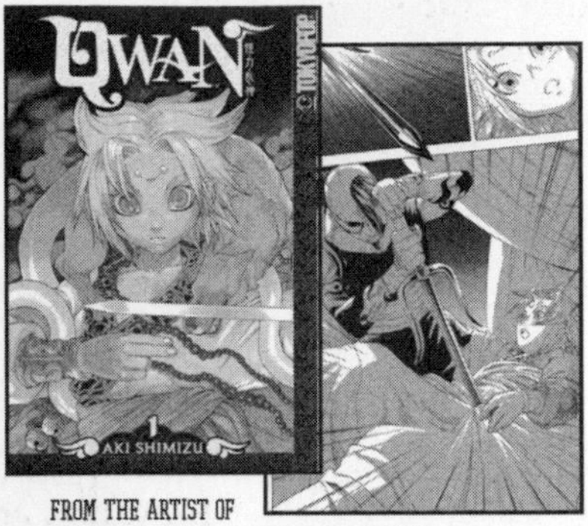
QWAN
TOKYOPOP
1
AKI SHIMIZU

FROM THE ARTIST OF SUIKODEN III

BY AKI SHIMIZU

QWAN

Qwan is a series that refuses to be pigeonholed. Aki Shimizu combines Chinese history, mythology, fantasy and humor to create a world that is familiar yet truly unique. Her creature designs are particularly brilliant—from mascots to monsters. And Qwan himself is great—fallen to Earth, he's like a little kid, complete with the loud questions, yet he eats demons for breakfast. In short, *Qwan* is a solid story with great character dynamics, amazing art and some kick-ass battle scenes. What's not to like?

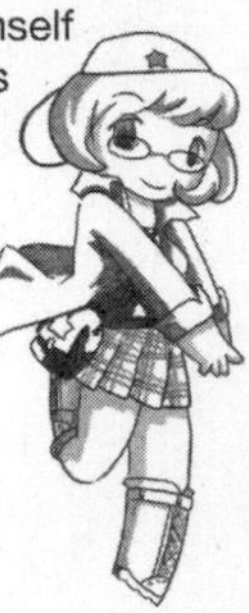

~Carol Fox, Editor

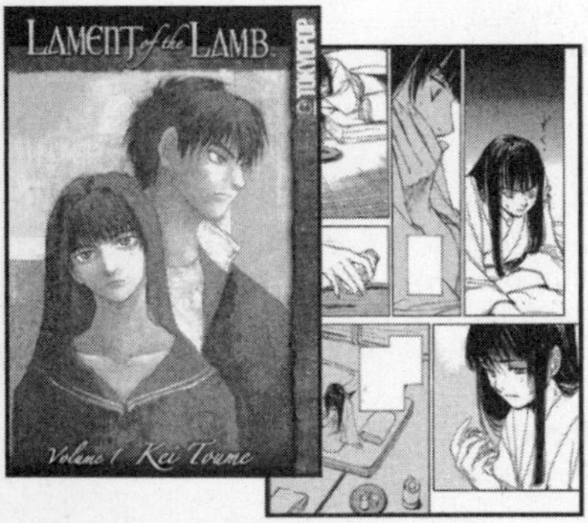
LAMENT of the LAMB
TOKYOPOP
Volume 1 Kei Toume

BY KEI TOUME

LAMENT OF THE LAMB

Kei Toume's *Lament of the Lamb* follows the physical and mental torment of Kazuna Takashiro, who discovers that he's cursed with a hereditary disease that makes him crave blood. *Lament* is psychological horror at its best—it's gloomy, foreboding and emotionally wrenching. Toume brilliantly treats the story's vampirism in a realistic, subdued way, and it becomes a metaphor for teenage alienation, twisted sexual desire and insanity. While reading each volume, I get goose bumps, I feel uneasy, and I become increasingly depressed. Quite a compliment for a horror series!

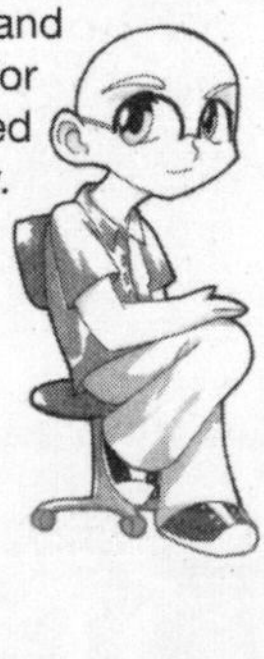

~Paul Morrissey, Editor

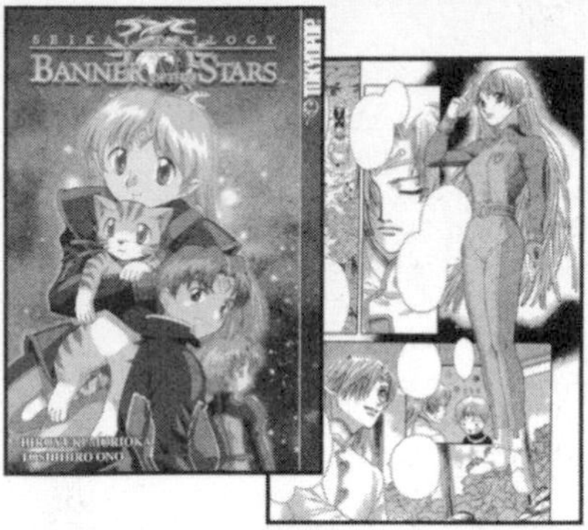

BY AYA YOSHINAGA, HIROYUKI MORIOKA, TOSHIHIRO ONO, AND WASOH MIYAKOSHI

THE SEIKAI TRILOGY

The Seikai Trilogy is one of TOKYOPOP's most underrated series. Although the trilogy gained popularity through the release of the anime, the manga brings a vitality to the characters that I feel the anime never did. The story is a heart-warming, exciting sci-fi adventure epic, the likes of which we haven't seen since *Star Wars*. *Banner of the Stars II*, the series' finale, is a real page-turner—a prison colony's security is compromised due to violent intergalactic politics. Each manga corresponds to the story from the novel...however, unless you read Japanese, the only way to enjoy the story thus far is through these faithful comic adaptations.

~Luis Reyes, Editor

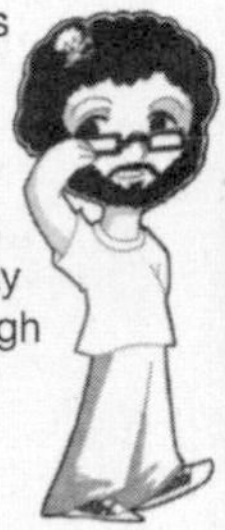

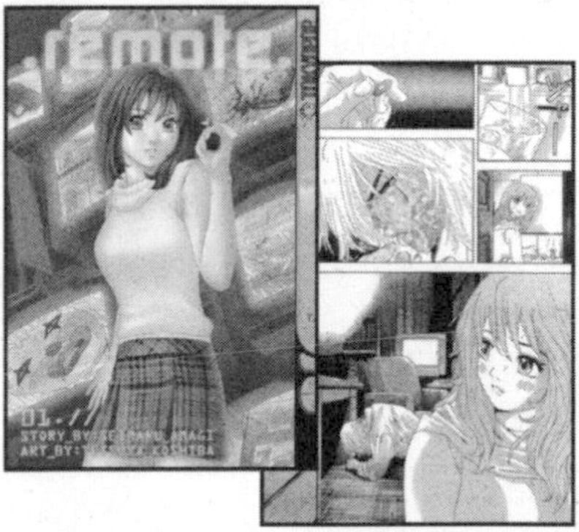
remote.

BY SEIMARU AMAGI AND TETSUYA KOSHIBA

REMOTE

Imagine Pam Anderson starring in *The Silence of the Lambs* and you've got a hint of what to expect from Seimaru Amagi and Tetsuya Koshiba's *Remote*. Completely out of her element, Officer Kurumi Ayaki brings down murderers, mad bombers and would-be assassins, all under the guidance of the reclusive Inspector Himuro. There's no shortage of fan-service and ultraviolence as Kurumi stumbles through her cases, but it's nicely balanced by the forensic police work of the brilliant Himuro, a man haunted by his past and struggling with suppressed emotions awakened by the adorable Kurumi.

~Bryce P. Coleman, Editor

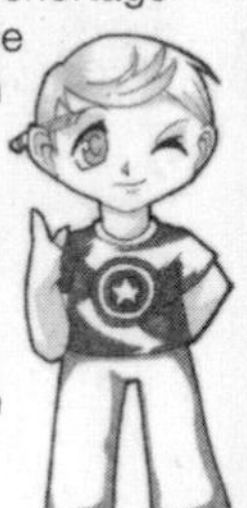

SHOWCASE

.HACK//AI BUSTER - NOVEL
BY TATSUYA HAMAZAKI

In the epic prequel to .hack, the avatar Albireo is a solo adventurer in The World, the most advanced online fantasy game ever created. When he comes across Lycoris, a strange little girl in a dungeon, he soon comes to realize that she may hold a very deadly secret—a secret that could unhinge everything in cyberspace... and beyond!

Discover the untold origins of the phenomenon known as .hack!

© Tatsuya Hamazaki © Rei Izumi

CHRONO CODE
BY EUI-CHEOL SHIN & IL-HO CHOI

Time flows like a river, without changing its course. This is an escape from the river's flow...

Three people must cross time and space to find each other and change their destinies. However, a powerful satellite, a secret code and the future police impede their progress, and their success hinges on an amnesiac who must first uncover the true nature of her past in order to discover who her friends are in the future.

T
TEEN
AGE 13+

© IL-HO CHOI & EUI-CHEOL SHIN, DAIWON C.I. Inc.

SAIYUKI RELOAD
BY KAZUYA MINEKURA

Join Sanzo, Gojyo, Hakkai, Goku and their updated wardrobe as they continue their journey west toward Shangri-La, encountering new challenges and new adventures along the way. But don't be fooled by their change in costume: The fearsome foursome is just as ferocious and focused as before...if not more so.

The hit manga that inspired the anime, and the sequel to TOKYOPOP's hugely popular *Saiyuki*!

OT
OLDER TEEN
AGE 16+

© Kazuya Minekura